CORRECTION SYMBOLS IN ALPHABETICAL ORDER

Boldface numbers refer to chapters or sections of the book.

W9-BRH-360

ab	Faulty abbreviation, **28**
ad	Misuse of adjective or adverb, **9**
agr	Error in agreement, **8**
appr	Inappropriate diction, **31a**
awk	Awkward construction
bib	Error in bibliographical form, **35c**
ca	Error in case form, **6**
cap	Use capital letter, **26**
con	Be concise, **31c**
coord	Faulty coordination, **16a**
cs	Comma splice, **11a–b**
d	Error in diction, **31**
dev	Inadequate essay development, **1**
div	Incorrect word division, **30**
dm	Dangling modifier, **14g**
emph	Emphasis lacking or faulty, **18**
exact	Inexact word, **31b**
fn	Error in footnote form, **35h**
frag	Sentence fragment, **10**
fs	Fused (run-on) sentence, **11c**
gl/gr	See glossary of grammatical terms
gl/us	See glossary of usage
gr	Error in grammar, **5–9**
hyph	Error in use of hyphen, **34d**
inc	Incomplete construction, **15c–d**
ital	Italicize (underline), **27**
k	Awkward construction
lc	Use lowercase letter, **26f**
log	Faulty logic, **4**
mixed	Mixed construction, **15a–b**
mm	Misplaced modifier, **14a–f**
mng	Meaning unclear
ms	Incorrect manuscript form, **App. B**

no cap	Unnecessary capital letter, **26f**
no ⋏	Comma not needed, **21j**
no ¶	No new paragraph needed, **3**
num	Error in use of numbers, **29**
p	Error in punctuation, **20–25**
. ? !	Period, question mark, exclamation point, **20**
⋏	Comma, **21**
;	Semicolon, **22**
'	Apostrophe, **23**
" "	Quotation marks, **24**
: — ( ) [ ] ... /	Colon, dash, parentheses, brackets, ellipsis mark, slash, **25**
par, ¶	Start new paragraph, **3**
¶ *coh*	Paragraph not coherent, **3b**
¶ *dev*	Paragraph not developed, **3c**
¶ *un*	Paragraph not unified, **3a**
pass	Ineffective passive voice, **18d**
ref	Error in pronoun reference, **12**
rep	Unnecessary repetition, **31c–2**
rev	Proofread or revise, **2**
run-on	Run-on sentence, **11c**
shift	Inconsistency, **13**
sp	Misspelled word, **34**
sub	Faulty subordination, **16b–c**
t	Error in verb tense, **7**, *pp. 155–58*
var	Vary sentence structure, **19**
vb	Error in verb form, **7**, *pp. 149–54*
w	Wordy, **31c**
ww	Wrong word, **31b**
/ /	Faulty parallelism, **17**
x	Obvious error
∧	Something missing

THE
LITTLE, BROWN
HANDBOOK

THE
LITTLE, BROWN
HANDBOOK

H. Ramsey Fowler
MEMPHIS STATE UNIVERSITY

With the Editors of Little, Brown

Little, Brown and Company
BOSTON   TORONTO

Sponsoring Editor Charles Christensen
Developmental Editor Jane E. Aaron
Book Editor Janet B. Welch
Cover and Text Designer Anna Post

Manuscript Editors Dale Anderson, Carol Beal,
Thomas P. Mancuso, Carol J. Verburg
Editorial Assistants Patrice I. Boyer, Carol L. McIntyre,
Elizabeth Philipps, Lesley V. Ripley, Susan W. Warne
Permissions Editor Carolyn Woznick
Art and Design Assistant Susan Creelman-Carr

Library of Congress Catalog Card No. 79–6869

ISBN 0–316–289612

10 9 8 7 6

MU

Published simultaneously in Canada
by Little, Brown & Company (Canada) Limited

Printed in the United States of America

(Credits *continued on page 531*)

Preface

The Little, Brown Handbook for English composition responds to what I and its editors see as important changes in how composition handbooks are used and in the students who use them. Instructors increasingly call on handbooks to fill roles once performed by two texts—a handbook *and* a rhetoric. Thus a modern handbook should be designed for use as both a reference guide and a classroom text. In addition, many of today's students are entering college with less familiarity or comfort with the fundamentals of writing than their predecessors possessed. Thus a handbook should take care to teach those fundamentals without assuming students' previous knowledge of them.

This handbook was conceived from the outset as both a reference guide and a classroom text. The organization facilitates reference by, for instance, grouping all chapters on sentences together and placing the glossary of usage at the back of the book. At the same time, however, the book begins where most composition courses begin—with writing and revising essays and paragraphs. The editors and I have worked to devise a complete and clear system of reference that will be equally useful to instructors marking papers and to students seeking information on their own (see "Using This Book"). But we have also made the book readable and provided enough explanations, examples, and exercises to promote class discussion.

The book responds to students' needs by providing clear definitions of terms, concise explanations of how to apply the conventions, and unambiguous examples of the conventions at work. We have assumed that students will rely on the basic grammar chapter (5) as much to teach them as to refresh their existing knowledge. We have also provided self-teaching chapters in areas such as the dictionary, vocabulary, and spelling where students' needs vary widely. Appendixes on avoiding plagiarism, preparing a manuscript, and improving study skills should be useful to students throughout college.

An English handbook is necessarily normative. As explained in the introduction to students, this handbook is also somewhat conservative in its usage recommendations. However, we have confined the use of prescriptions to matters in which the careful writer has little choice (grammar, punctuation, mechanics) and have opted for a more relaxed approach to composing and style.

The handbook is the core of an educational package designed to assist students and instructors alike. Its components include a workbook whose organization exactly parallels the handbook's; a diagnostic test; a correction chart; and two separate booklets containing answers to the handbook's and workbook's exercises. (The booklets may be made available to students at the instructor's option.) An instructor's manual offers suggestions for using the handbook with its supplements and includes the complete contents of the two answer booklets as well as sample pages from the other supplements. The manual also discusses the ideas behind each handbook section and includes a bibliography on teaching composition.

Acknowledgments

Literally hundreds of instructors have contributed to *The Little, Brown Handbook*. Most of them answered the early questionnaires from which the book's goals were derived. The editors and I thank them all. We also thank the following people who reviewed parts of the manuscript in various stages and offered valuable advice: Maurice Baudin, Jr., New York University; Richard Dodge, Santa Monica College; Patrick J. Ireland, College of the Holy Cross; Russell R. Larson, Eastern Michigan University; Patricia Licklider, John Jay College; Peter Lindblom, Miami-Dade Community College; Richard Marius, Harvard University; David Skwire, Cuyahoga Community College; Joseph F. Trimmer, Ball State University; and Harvey S. Wiener, LaGuardia Community College.

We are especially grateful to several people who bore with us and shared their huge store of knowledge throughout the development of the book: Sylvan Barnet, Tufts University; Richard S. Beal, Boston University; C. Michael Curtis, Associate Editor, *The Atlantic Monthly;* Melinda G. Kramer, Purdue University; and Richard L. Larson, Lehman College. Barbara Carson of the University of Georgia, Quentin L. Gehle, and Lyda E. LaPalombara of Southern Connecticut State College not only read the manuscript but also prepared the answers to the handbook's exercises, the workbook and its answers, and the diagnostic test, respectively.

This project was conceived as a collaboration between author and publisher, and so it has proved to be. I am extraordinarily indebted to all the people listed on page iv, and I am pleased to share the title page with them.   H.R.F.

Using This Book

A handbook is more than a textbook. It is a comprehensive reference guide to the essential information in a field or discipline, whether it be stamp collecting, home maintenance, or chemistry. *The Little, Brown Handbook* is no exception. A basic resource for English grammar, usage, and composition, it can serve you as a basic text and reference for writing not only in a composition course but also in other courses and outside college.

How you use this book in your composition course, the order in which you read or refer to chapters, the extent to which you complete exercises, even the sections of the book you consult—these will depend on your instructor's expectations and requirements. No matter what use you make of the handbook, however, you will surely benefit from a few minutes spent familiarizing yourself with it. This introduction attempts to orient you by describing briefly the handbook's organization and store of information, the ways to locate that information, and the standard of usage recommended.

The handbook's organization and coverage

An overview of the handbook's contents appears inside the back cover. The first four chapters discuss problems such as discovering a purpose, generating and organizing ideas, composing paragraphs, being convincing, and revising that are common to all writing you do. These chapters you may want to read and digest even if they aren't assigned by your instructor.

You may also want to read Chapter 5, which presents the system of English grammar. Though much of the material will be familiar to you, the chapter will repay your attention because it helps make clear that the grammar of English is more than just a hodgepodge of rules. Understanding the basic structure of the English sentence will also give you a background for understanding and using the fourteen chapters that follow. Each of them deals with a single convention or principle of grammatical correctness (Chapters

6 to 9), clarity (Chapters 10 to 15), or effectiveness (Chapters 16 to 19). Your instructor may work through some or all of these chapters or may only suggest that you refer to the chapters dealing with problems in your writing.

Chapters 20 to 30 of the handbook describe the current conventions of punctuation and the closely related conventions of mechanics—capitalization, the use of abbreviations, and the like. Although your instructor may ask you to study particular chapters or sections of them, you should think of all eleven chapters as resources to consult continually for advice on specific questions.

Chapters 31 to 34 of the handbook deal with words—from their effective use to their correct spelling. Chapter 31, which discusses the principles guiding effective word choice, is intended to help you express your meaning exactly and concisely. Chapter 32 introduces the features of any desk dictionary and the ways to use it. The usefulness to you of Chapters 33 and 34 on building a vocabulary and spelling will depend on your needs, but familiarity with the principles of English spelling and vocabulary will always help your writing.

The last chapters of the handbook deal with specific writing tasks. Chapter 35 traces the process of writing and documenting a so-called research or library paper for which you consult books and periodicals on some issue or question. Chapter 36 provides specific advice on writing essay examinations for courses in all areas and on writing letters to make complaints or requests or to apply for a job.

The handbook includes three appendixes, each one addressing a specific practical problem. Appendix A explains your responsibility for acknowledging the ideas and information that you draw from other writers. Appendix B describes a widely accepted standard, which your instructor may add to, for preparing a manuscript. And Appendix C offers specific suggestions on studying effectively for any course.

Two glossaries conclude the handbook. The first, a glossary of usage, provides brief notes on words and expressions that often cause problems for writers at all levels of experience. When you are in doubt about the appropriateness of a word or phrase you want to use, check this glossary or a dictionary. The second glossary gives definitions of all the grammatical terms used in the handbook as well as a few others. All terms are defined in the handbook where they first appear and are redefined when necessary or useful, but you may find the glossary a convenient reference when you encounter a term in another context.

Finding information in the handbook

The Little, Brown Handbook provides a wealth of specific information—what form of a verb to use, how to express an idea concisely, whether to punctuate with a comma or a semicolon, whether to capitalize a word, how to arrange the title page of a paper, and so on. The handbook also provides many ways of quickly locating such information. When you seek information on your own, you can check the guide to useful lists inside the front cover; you can refer to the table of contents inside the back cover or immediately after this introduction; or you can refer to the index that occupies the book's last pages. The table of contents shows all the book's parts, chapters (with page numbers), and main sections within chapters. The sections are preceded by letters (*a, b*, and so on). These letters and the corresponding chapter numbers (for instance, 9d or 12a) also appear before the appropriate convention or guideline in the text itself, and they are printed in colored boxes on the sides of the pages. Thus you can find a section heading in the contents and thumb the book until you arrive at its number and letter on the side of the page. If you aren't sure of what you're looking for and need a more detailed guide to the book's contents, consult the index. It includes every term used in the book and every form the term can take as well as many specific words and phrases that may give you trouble.

Your instructor may mark your papers using heading numbers and letters, symbols, or written comments. Pages 38 to 41 show samples of student work marked each way. If your instructor marks your paper with, say, 21a, you can refer to the contents to learn that you have made an error involving a comma. If you need further information to correct the error, you can then refer to the text by finding the appropriate page number or by locating 21a in a box on the side of the page, as described above. If your instructor uses symbols to mark your paper, you can find out how to correct the error by referring to the contents at the back of the book, where the symbols are listed by chapter, or to the alphabetical list of symbols inside the front cover. Using the latter guide, you would be directed by the symbol *frag* to Chapter 10, which discusses sentence fragments. The symbols are also contained in the colored boxes on the sides of the pages. The best way to find specific handbook sections from your instructor's written comments is to consult the index. Look up the term used by your instructor—for instance, *agreement*—and scan the subentries under it until you find one that seems to describe the error you have made. Then turn to the page number given.

The handbook's recommended usage

The conventions of grammar, usage, punctuation, mechanics, and other matters that *The Little, Brown Handbook* describes and advises you to use are those of standard, written English—the written language commonly used in business and the professions. Written English is more conservative than spoken English, and a great many words, phrases, and constructions that are widely used by all speakers remain unaccepted in careful writing.

When clear distinctions exist between the language of conversation and that of careful writing, the handbook provides examples of each and labels them *spoken* and *written*. When usage in writing itself varies with the level of formality expected, examples are labeled *formal* and *informal*. When usage is mixed or currently changing, the handbook generally recommends that you choose the more conservative usage because it will be acceptable to all readers.

If you follow the guidelines discussed in this handbook, your writing will be clearer and more demanding of serious attention than it might otherwise have been. However, the real challenges and rewards of writing come not from adhering to established conventions but from using them to communicate your own message effectively.

Contents

I

The Whole Paper and Paragraphs

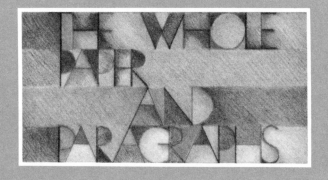

1
Developing an Essay

Most of the papers you write in college are essays or special forms of essays such as reports or research papers. Whether you argue against the use of pesticides, describe a physics experiment, analyze a business case, criticize a novel, examine the causes of a historical event, or tell of a personal experience, you are exploring your relation to the world and presenting ideas for serious consideration. You are writing **essays,** nonfiction compositions that analyze and interpret a topic, offering your personal view of it.

Essays take a variety of forms. They may be (and very often are) **argumentative.** That is, they state an opinion and defend it logically with supporting ideas and evidence. Their purpose is to convince readers to appreciate—if not accept—the opinion. An essay urging tighter (or looser) controls on drug use is argumentative. So is one maintaining that health care is an obligation of the government (or none of the government's business), or one calling for the abolition of college examinations.

Other essays are narrative, descriptive, or expository: they do not so much state opinion as they embody it in the organization of ideas, selection of details, and tone. **Narrative essays** relate a sequence of events, whether factual or not. You might tell of your first experience with white-water canoeing or with using public transportation, or you might outline the steps involved in making a clay pot. You might also use narration in one part of an otherwise non-narrative essay—say, by telling what it's like to take an exam when arguing for the abolition of exams.

Descriptive essays evoke a scene, person, object, emotion, or event, usually by drawing on words that are concrete, that appeal to the senses. We use description, like narration, in many other kinds of writing, including poetry and letters to friends as well as essays. In a descriptive essay you might paint a picture of an imposing person or try to convey the sensation of eating an apple.

Finally, **expository essays** explain. They may explain how a baseball team broke a losing streak, why the 1960s were a time of social upheaval, or why you are majoring in business. They may use aspects of argumentation, narration, and description, but their primary purpose is to expose information, not to convince or narrate or describe. It is the expository form that you use most often in college writing.

These essay forms are one way of looking at writing. We may choose among them in deciding how to approach a topic, and we can use them to evaluate the effectiveness of an essay. But another way of understanding writing focuses on it as a process through which we clarify, develop, and shape ideas and feelings that may once have been undefined.

Writing is a process of synthesis. As you write, you use words and information to express your viewpoint in a coherent whole, an essay. But writing draws on intuition as well as reasoning, on sensation and emotion as well as fact and memory. Thus it is not always, or even most often, an orderly procedure. You and every other writer may find that the process of writing is smooth and sequential one day, disjointed or disorderly the next. No two writers approach writing the same way, and no individual approaches it the same way from one experience to the next. Because writing is as personal as thinking and communicating, it is also as varied.

Nonetheless, the process of writing can be described in a general, orderly way that enables inexperienced writers to master its steps and be surer of their results. In writing, your thoughts move over and over again from the general to the specific and from the specific to the general. You start with a broad subject and limit it to a single topic. You come up with ideas on your topic by directing your thoughts from the abstract to the concrete and from the vague to the definite. You group your ideas around a particular point of view, and then you select from among them, turning generalizations into explicit, precise statements. You appeal to your audience and make your writing understandable by selecting the ideas, details, and tone that will work best. You organize all the ideas and details so that relations among them will be clear. And as you write and revise, you flesh out your general plan with specific words.

This chapter will trace this step-by-step process from the general to the specific. By practicing the steps, much as you would practice the moves of a dance or the notes of a piece of music, you will become a more accomplished and relaxed writer.

1a
Finding and limiting a subject

Many writers (including experienced ones) encounter their first stumbling block in trying to find a subject to write about. Your instructor may suggest a list of subjects for you to choose from or a kind of essay for you to write. But if not, you will have to come up with something on your own.

The best way to find an essay subject is to review your own experiences, interests, and curiosities. Look for a subject you already know something about or have been wondering about. Cast back over what you've discussed with others or read or seen in a movie or on television. Think about things that make you especially happy or angry. The purpose here is to think of a subject that interests you and that you can interest others in by providing details and examples that embellish your viewpoint.

The subject you get—whether by assignment or on your own—may be one like "the ill effects of pollution," "what I do to relax," "why college education is overrated," "how politics works," or "why baseball is popular." But an area as broad as any one of these is too broad to be covered interestingly or even intelligently in an essay of, say, 500 to 750 words (two or three double-spaced typewritten pages). You probably would not be able to provide enough specific information in so little space to be interesting, much less understandable. In most writing, treating a narrow subject thoroughly is more effective than treating a broad subject skimpily. These broad subjects need to be scaled down to manageable topics, subdivisions of the larger categories.

If you chose or were assigned the subject of "the ill effects of pollution," you would shortly find that too many different kinds of pollution produce too many different effects for you to cover them all in a brief essay. If you tried to deal with water pollution, air pollution, noise pollution, visual pollution, and all the rest, you'd spend 750 words just distinguishing among them. Because you could not devote much space or detail to any one kind of pollution, you would not easily convince a skeptical reader that pollution is seriously harmful. However, if you chose a subcategory such as noise pollution and devoted the entire essay to a specific example—what it's like to live one block from an airport runway—you'd be more likely to have an impact on your readers.

One student, Marcia Torres, considered these problems in narrowing the subject for an essay we will follow in this chapter and the next. Torres chose the topic "what I do to relax" from several assigned. Her nonschool activities, the ones that relax her, include photography, skating, and cooking. Should she write on them all? What should she say about them? Should she describe how she became interested in them? Should she explain what she likes best about each one? In a 750-word essay she wouldn't be able to do justice to them all, because she couldn't devote much more than a paragraph to each one. So she selects her favorite hobby, photography. But that still seems a very broad subject, full of different angles: the technical knowledge required to work a camera and develop pictures, working on the campus newspaper, the possibilities for a career, her experience of taking pictures, the fun of seeing pictures come out. At this point Torres is narrowing the assigned subject, and moving away from it slightly, to suit her own special interests. She is thinking of topics, each suitable for an essay because it is specific enough to be treated thoroughly in only a few pages. In the end she decides to write about her experience of taking pictures. Since her feelings about it are vague, she sees in the topic an opportunity to learn something about herself while completing an assignment.

Here are some other examples of narrowing a subject to a manageable topic.

BROAD	MORE SPECIFIC
The differences between high school and college. [Too many dimensions to discuss adequately. Choose a single dimension.]	Learning to live without a guidance counselor. The differences between high school and college chemistry.
Politics is a dirty business. [A judgment that needs extensive support. Perhaps choose a single example of dirty politics and explore it carefully.]	How one student government president changed for the worse during her one-year term. Why it took a month to repair the sewer in front of my house.
Relations between parents and children. [Too many possible dimensions. Perhaps choose a specific kind of relation.]	Some ways a child learned to cope with his parents' divorce. The differences in the ways parents treat the oldest and the youngest of their six children.

When choosing and then limiting your subject, try not to lose track of its meaning to you, the personal perspective you started with. Select a comfortable topic and then define it carefully. Your essay will be easier for you to write and more original and interesting for your readers.

(For information on narrowing the subject for a paper requiring library research, see 35a and 35b.)

EXERCISE 1

Review your own experiences and interests and think of three or four general subjects for an essay. What are you curious about? What activity have you been involved in lately? What interesting discussions have you participated in? What makes you angry?

EXERCISE 2

Narrow each of the broad subjects from Exercise 1 to a specific topic suitable for a brief essay (500 to 750 words). What aspect of the subject interests you most? What aspect can you discuss most effectively, using enough specific information to convey your perspective on it?

EXERCISE 3

By applying your own perspective, narrow each of the following general subjects to a topic suitable for a brief essay.

1. Saturday nights
2. working
3. magazines
4. child abuse
5. science course requirements

1b
Getting ideas

Once you have a topic, you need to think of the specific ideas and details that will illustrate or support it. You may find that the ideas tumble forth, especially if your topic is a very personal one. Or you may use a strategy like one of the following to come up with and remember ideas.

1
Making a list

Ideas rarely occur in fully developed form. Instead, they straggle to the surface, often half complete, sometimes silly, usually in random order. A thought begun at dinner may not be completed until the next day, and dozens of others will intervene. To keep track of all your ideas, write them down as they occur to you. You may allow your mind to roam over your topic for a day or two. Or you may prefer to brainstorm, allowing only 30 minutes, say, in which to write down every thought that occurs to you. Don't edit your ideas because they seem irrelevant or dumb or repetitious. Doing so will probably slow up the flow of ideas and may cause you to delete something that could help you later.

Marcia Torres made a list to generate and collect her thoughts on the experience of taking pictures. Here is part of the list she had compiled after a couple of days.

> my own decision about what and how to shoot
> camera as companion
> have to go out alone, on my own—no courses
> self-teaching the technical side—shutter speeds, etc.
> redoing the world, in a way
> recreating scenes in a way they never existed—black and white, rectangular, stopped
> color or black and white—the world simplified
> the world highlighted?
> spooky darkroom—mystery, magic
> learning physics and chemistry
> good career opportunities—money, hours, freedom
> being in the world—framing the world—seeing it differently
> seeing a picture develop is like seeing the world for the first time
> freedom to come and go, do it my way
> you steal a person's soul when you take his picture
> that frightened look on the kid I took the picture of last week

This partial list is quite informal. Some items are sketchy, others are fuller. Some—like "career opportunities"—don't seem related to the rest. And Torres has not made connections between thoughts that are clearly similar—for instance, between redoing the world and seeing it for the first time. But the list does suggest an essay on the creativity Torres feels when she takes pictures, and that idea is a manageable refinement of her topic. Having discovered it, she will be able to expand on and further refine it until it becomes her thesis (see 1d).

| 2
| Filling one page

Another way to discover ideas is to begin with a blank page, focus on your topic, and write without stopping until you have filled at least one sheet. As in making a list, you shouldn't stop to edit but simply force yourself to keep writing. Don't be concerned if the thoughts are not organized. Don't worry about the grammar of your sentences or the correct use of words. The point is to record as many different ideas on your topic as you can, as fast as you can. The result will not be an essay, but it will very likely lead you to specific ideas that you hadn't considered.

3
Talking to someone

Sometimes you may find that neither making a list nor filling a page provides you with the ideas you seek. In that case, chat with a friend. For instance, you've decided to write on the tapping of telephone lines by the police, but you haven't been able to get beyond your opinion that they should be able to tap the lines of known criminals. You decide to try the idea on a friend. If it is a good one, he will probably tell you so and offer some supporting reasons. However, if he thinks your idea is inadequate, he will probably tell you why. Perhaps he will ask you what the United States Constitution says about the right of privacy (and you make a mental note to check the Constitution). Perhaps he will want to know what a "known criminal" is (someone with a prison record, or just someone suspected of crime?). Or perhaps he will want to know whether you mean that the police should tap the telephones of known criminals whenever they want to or only when they can show a compelling reason (so you make a note to think about that, too). Your friend may ask you questions that will force you to think of more ideas and thus broaden the base of your inquiry.

EXERCISE 4

Make a list, fill a page, or talk with a friend to come up with ideas for one of the narrowed topics from Exercise 2 or 3 (p. 6).

EXERCISE 5

Fill a page on one of the following topics. This exercise will give you practice both in getting ideas and in writing.
1. who you are
2. the appearance (or taste) of an apple
3. borrowing (or lending) money
4. prejudice in my hometown
5. news on television versus news in newspapers

1c
Grouping ideas

After thinking about a subject, narrowing it, and developing some ideas, you still may not see what you really have to say or how you can best say it. The next step is to group the ideas into broad patterns. Organizing ideas brings them into order, weeds out the irrelevant ones, shows which ones need more thought, and gives you more control. In grouping your ideas, you will discover your central theme and begin to understand how specific ideas are related to it.

After generating ideas with a list, Marcia Torres begins grouping them. Her topic has already shifted from "the experience of taking pictures" to the more specific "how photographs make me feel creative." The new topic helps Torres toss out unrelated ideas, such as those on photography as a career, learning about science, or using the camera as a companion (see p. 7). Sorting through the remaining ideas, arranging them and changing some, Torres ends up with these groups of related ideas:

> Ways photography makes me feel creative
> > my own decision about what and how to shoot
> > self-teaching the technical side
> > doing it on my own, alone
> > redoing the world
>
> What happens when I take a picture and develop it
> > being in the world—framing it—simplifying it
> > putting frames around scenes
> > highlighting scenes
> > using black and white to simplify
> > stealing a person's soul?
> > darkroom mystery and magic—developing image, eerie darkness
>
> How my pictures show what I never saw when I took them
> > took a picture of a cute kid playing, but in the photo his face is so frightened
> > black and white—not the real world
> > seeing a picture develop is like seeing the world for the first time
> > the frame makes a picture artificial but more real

When she finishes editing and arranging her ideas, Torres has fewer than she started with, but she is much further along. Her thoughts divide into three main ideas, each relating to how photography makes her feel creative, but each exploring a different aspect of that topic. Some repetition still occurs (in ideas about framing or redoing the world, for instance), and the main ideas are not necessarily developed completely nor are they final. But Torres is ready to move on to a crucial step, forming a central thesis for her essay.

EXERCISE 6

Group each set of ideas you generated in Exercises 4 and 5 (p. 8) into general categories. Delete, add, or modify ideas if necessary to reflect your thinking at this new stage.

1d

Developing the thesis

Finding and limiting a subject, getting ideas, and grouping those ideas are steps on the way to determining the main idea of your writing. The parts in a piece of writing must be focused on, controlled by, and related to that one main idea. If they aren't, the parts will probably fail to cohere, and the writing will almost certainly fail to interest or convince a reader. The central idea is called the **thesis.** It contains your own approach to your topic, your reason for writing, your goal. Your thesis not only names the topic but also asserts something about it.

If your topic were noise pollution as experienced by someone living near an airport, your thesis might be an assertion like this one: "To discover how damaging noise pollution can be, you only need to live a block from an airport runway." For the topic of why television soap operas are so popular, your thesis might be "Soap operas are thought to offer escape, but their real attraction may be in convincing viewers that their own lives aren't so bad." These sentences both describe the essay topic specifically and assert an opinion about it.

1

Writing the thesis sentence

As the two examples above illustrate, an essay's thesis is often expressed in a single sentence, called the **thesis sentence.** It generally falls near the beginning of the essay. As an expression of the thesis, the thesis sentence serves three crucial functions:

1. It narrows your topic to a single idea.
2. In asserting something about the topic, it conveys your own outlook—the special perspective you are taking.
3. It may provide a specific, concise preview of your ideas and suggest how you will arrange them in the essay.

Here are several examples of topics and corresponding thesis sentences that fulfill these three functions.

TOPIC	THESIS SENTENCE
Tapping of telephone lines by police	Though abuses have occurred and probably always will, the police should be permitted to tap a telephone line when they can demonstrate potential danger to public safety.

Topic	Thesis sentence
Living without a guidance counselor in college	Without a guidance counselor I have mistakenly ended up in courses that aren't related to my major or career, and I have had trouble using my time effectively.
Some ways a child learned to cope with his parents' divorce	Seeing himself at first as an agent carrying love back and forth between his divorced parents, a child eventually learns to love each one as an individual.
The effects of strip-mining	From the raw cuts defacing a once-beautiful mountain, to the clouded and dangerous streams flowing from it, to the troubled lives of the people living below it, the effects of strip-mining can be devastating.
How one student government president changed for the worse during her one-year term	As student government president, I found myself being a yes-man to the principal, failing to take students' sides against teachers, and getting more from the power of the job than from its responsibilities and potential for reform.
Why the freshman English requirement should be abolished	Freshman English does no one any good: it frustrates those who simply aren't interested in the subject, and it holds back those who are interested in more advanced courses.
How to buy a stereo	Since a good stereo is an expensive investment, it pays to read up, shop around, ask questions, be skeptical, and trust your own ears.
Why it took a month to repair the sewer in front of my house	If you want to wait a month for your sewer line to be repaired, have an argument with a neighbor on the Public Works Commission before asking the commission to do the repair.

In moving from groups of ideas to thesis sentence, the most important step is to discover just what you want to say about the collections of thoughts. What main theme arises from the ideas? What impression do you want a reader to take away? How can you summarize your topic in one specific, pointed sentence that is broad enough to encompass all your ideas yet narrow enough to form the core of your essay?

2
Revising the thesis sentence

When Marcia Torres finished grouping her ideas (p. 9), she had taken a large step toward a thesis sentence. She had rejected irrelevant ideas, added new ones, combined some, and separated others. In the end she had moved from a vague topic ("the experience of taking pictures") to a more definite one ("how photography makes me feel creative"). Yet she still lacked a thesis sentence, an assertion about her topic.

Working again with her ideas and the groups they had fallen into, Torres tries turning her topic into an assertion:

Photography makes me feel creative.

But the result tells less than the topic suggests about her intended subject—how photography makes her feel creative. So she tries again, limiting her topic by explaining how:

Photography is a way of creating something real for me.

This time, Torres asserts something about how she feels creative. But after some thought, Torres sees how little the word *real* actually says, how little it would guide and control her writing of the essay. Thus for her next effort Torres concentrates on conveying specific ideas:

Photography makes me feel creative because I do it on my own and it changes the way the world looks.

This sentence is much more specific: it conveys Torres's special perspective on photography, and it suggests a course for her essay.

Although Torres could proceed with her newest thesis sentence, she might still encounter trouble. This sentence is specific and definite, but its two parts are not closely related or equally complex. If Torres were to begin writing from this thesis, devoting equal space to both parts, she might discover that she has nothing much to say about doing photography on her own and too much to say about how photography changes the way the world looks. She might see that a sense of independence has little to do with her feeling of creativity. So after examining her thesis sentence once more, asking if all its parts relate to each other and to her central idea, Torres revises it again:

> Photography makes me feel creative because it lets me present the world in my special way and because it shows me things I never knew I saw.

In this last revision Torres has grasped what she meant by "creating something real" and "changes the way the world looks." Her thesis sentence is *limited* and *specific*. It is also *unified*, because both parts support the central idea and complement each other. It tells a reader what to expect, and it promises to guide Torres and control her later work. Although she may want to modify the thesis further as she writes (see 2b), she can be satisfied with it now.

Here are other examples of thesis sentences revised to be limited, specific, and unified.

ORIGINAL	REVISED
Fad diets are dangerous. [A vague statement that needs limiting with specific information: Which diets? Dangerous when and for whom?]	Fad diets may be dangerous when they alter your body chemistry.
Inexpensive travel can be fun. [Too general, and an assertion that leads nowhere. So what?]	Traveling on a small budget teaches you more about a country and its people than traveling expensively does.
We all feel aggression, but since it usually means violence, perhaps injury and death, we should figure out how to use it constructively. [Not unified: emphasis on violence detracts from assertion at the end.]	By channeling our natural feelings of aggression, we can use them constructively rather than destructively.

EXERCISE 7

Evaluate the following thesis sentences, considering whether each one is sufficiently limited, specific, and unified. Rewrite the sentences as necessary to meet these goals.

1. Gun control is essential.
2. There will always be friction between the people who don't have money but want it and the people who have money and show it.

3. Good manners make our society work.
4. I learned about discipline and pride when I first took the responsibility of a job.
5. City people are different from country people.
6. Television is a useful baby-sitter and an escape for people who don't want to think about their own problems.
7. The best rock concerts are those in which the performers transform a passive crowd into a waving, stamping, screaming mob.
8. I liked American history in high school, but I don't like it in college.
9. Summer is an important time for everyone.
10. We're encouraged to choose a career in college, but people change jobs frequently.

EXERCISE 8

Write a thesis sentence for each of your sets of grouped ideas from Exercise 6 (p. 9).

EXERCISE 9

Write a thesis sentence on five of the following topics (or select topics of your own).
1. wearing blue jeans
2. how to conserve energy
3. what one can learn from travel
4. why old houses are better than new ones (or vice versa)
5. how to survive in the city
6. why no one should marry before thirty
7. how to care for a plant
8. why students attend college
9. deciding whom to vote for in an election
10. the opportunities for women

1e
Considering an audience

The purpose of an essay—or, for that matter, of almost any writing—is to *communicate to a reader*. Readers are your audience. If they don't understand what they read or don't react the way you want, then you may be at fault. The chances are good that you have not considered carefully enough what the audience must be told in order to understand and react appropriately.

Considering your audience begins when you select your subject—when, for an obvious example, you decide not to write on macroeconomic theory for your English literature instructor. You continue to consider your audience as you collect ideas and devise a thesis sentence—for an article on jobs for students, say, focusing on entry-level positions with flexible hours, not on full-time management positions. But considering your audience becomes crucial when you think about what to *say* about your thesis and how to say it. Both the statements you make and the facts, details, and examples you use to support them may vary depending on whom you're writing for. The attitude you adopt toward your material—the tone of your writing—depends on the impression you want to give the reader.

1
Using specific information

You use specific information to inform your readers and to convince them. (See 4c.) In both cases the facts, details, and examples you choose should take into account your audience's background—its familiarity with your topic, its biases and special interests.

Consider the student who needs money. He writes two letters—one to his parents and another to his school's Office of Student Aid. First he writes to his parents:

> Well, I did it again. Only two weeks into the new semester, and I'm broke already. But you know I needed a sweater, and besides, book prices have just skyrocketed and I've got this Constitutional History course that almost broke the bank all by itself ($60.00 for books!). Oh, and I've met this really great girl (more later). So anyway, I'm pretty low on cash right now and am going to need another $50.00 to make it through the rest of the month. This should be the last time I have to ask you for money, though. Starting next week I'm going to work part-time at a restaurant—doing some short-order cooking and general kinds of work—so if you want your money back . . .

Then he writes to the Office of Student Aid:

> I am writing to request a short-term loan of $50.00 for bill consolidation and for other personal reasons. Starting in ten days, I will be employed for 30 hours per week, as a cook, at Better-Burgers, 315 North Main Street, so I will be able to repay the loan easily within the three-month limit you provide. I understand that if I fail to make any payment . . .

The two letters make the same request, but their approaches are very different. The first letter is informal and personal; the second, formal and impersonal. The first letter is quite specific about the need for money, including details of purchases. The second letter avoids saying too much about why the money is needed but is quite direct on the certainty of repayment. In the first letter the student presents himself as a still scatterbrained but always lovable and almost responsible son. In the second he seems a mature citizen, aware of his responsibility to his creditors. If, by accident, the student mailed the second letter to his parents, they might be hurt by its impersonality. And if he mailed the first letter to the Office of Student Aid, they'd most likely deny his request.

In preparing to write you should ask yourself how much your readers already know about what you're saying. You don't want to provide so little information that they're confused, nor do you want to provide so much information that they're bored. In preparing her essay on photography Marcia Torres asks herself how much information she needs to supply about photographers and photographic technique in order to make her feelings about photography understandable to her readers. If she is writing to fellow students, she might assume they have no special technical knowledge and explain everything, without loading her essay with unnecessary information. However, if she is writing for the campus photography journal, she makes different assumptions. If it serves her purposes, she might mention specific lenses, filters, or papers, without bothering to explain their significance. (Indeed, an audience of photographers might be offended if she explained too much.) She might de-emphasize her feeling of creativity (which all photographers may share) and emphasize instead the specific technique she uses to transform a scene into a picture.

2
Adopting a suitable tone

Your use of ideas, words, and sentence structures produces the **tone** of your writing. Tone may be informal or formal—two approaches shown clearly in the student's requests for money. (Compare, for example, *so if you want your money back* with *so I will be able to repay the loan*.) It may also be sincere or flippant, impersonal or personal, eager or indifferent, and many qualities between and in addition to these. Because tone reflects your attitude toward both your subject and your readers, it strongly influences how your audience reacts. Look at this opening paragraph.

> All over the country people are swimming, jogging, dancing, playing tennis—anything to keep fit. Newspapers and national magazines claim we may be on the verge of a health revolution.

But you'd never know it here. This college has consistently refused to provide money or land for athletic facilities and programs that would benefit all students, not just varsity athletes. The administrators rejected a petition for a track around the football field, on the grounds that students using the track might interfere with football practice. They turned down a donor's offer to build a swimming pool because the only available space might someday be needed for a dormitory. They even refused to begin a noncredit course in dance because, they said, "It would serve no academic purpose." Because of these and other decisions, students have no place except their own rooms and the dangerous highways to participate in the fitness revolution. It's past the time for the college's administrators to deal positively with the problem.

This student's tone is forceful. His sentences almost march to his thesis. He demonstrates how out of step his college is by bringing in people *all over the country* and citing major periodicals. His words are strong and uncompromising: *revolution, never, consistently, confront.* Though clearly angry, the student hasn't allowed his anger to muddle his thesis, nor has he failed to support it. If the rest of the essay is equally effective, the writer will very likely convince his readers—including nonathletic students and even, perhaps, college administrators—that his main point is valid. He has used tone effectively.

If her essay on photography is directed at fellow students, Marcia Torres might adopt an informal, personal tone to win her readers' confidence and to complement the consideration she gives them by providing extra information. For the campus photography journal, however, she might use a more distant, professional tone to complement the technical information she uses and to convince her readers that she should be taken seriously.

(For more on the tone of writing, see 4a.)

3
Writing to a general audience

What do you do when you don't know much about your audience—when you can't pinpoint it as your parents or the Office of Student Aid or the readers of a photography journal? Unless you are taking courses in advertising or the communications media, most of the writing you do in college will be directed to a general college-level audience. This group of teachers and students is diverse, to be sure, but its members have many characteristics in common. College-level readers are serious and thoughtful, and they will look for similar qualities in the tone of your writing. Though they may not share all your interests, they can understand and appreciate anything you write, so long as it is specific, fresh, honest, and clear. They will want you to support the assertions you make and the conclusions you draw.

Of course, much of your college writing will have only one reader besides yourself—the instructor of the course you're writing for. Suppose you are taking an American history course and have been asked to write an essay on the economic background of the War of 1812. You certainly may assume that your instructor is familiar with your subject and expects an essay that shows careful reading of available information and your own interpretation of the facts. Your instructor will judge your essay on the clarity of your prose, the adequacy of your research, and the ability of your examples to support your conclusions.

EXERCISE 10

Choose one of the following topics and list the different kinds of specific information you would use in two papers directed at the audiences specified.

1. the effects of smoking: for elementary school students and for adult smokers
2. your opinion of your English course: for your instructor and for a friend
3. the advantages of a summer camp: for a prospective camper and for his or her parents
4. why your neighbors should remove the wrecked truck from their front yard: for your neighbors and for your town zoning board
5. the dangers of overpopulation: for a city audience and for a rural audience

EXERCISE 11

Evaluate the tone in the following paragraphs. What do the writers' selection of information and use of words and sentence structures convey about their attitudes toward their subjects and toward their readers?

1. It is Friday night at any of ten thousand watering holes of the small towns and crossroads hamlets of the South. The room is a cacophony of the ping-pong-dingdingding of the pinball machine, the pop-fizz of another round of Pabst, the refrain of *Red Necks, White Socks and Blue Ribbon Beer* on the juke box, the insolent roar of a souped-up engine outside and, above it all, the sound of easy laughter. The good ole boys

have gathered for their fraternal ritual—the aimless diversion that they have elevated into a life-style.

—Bonnie Angelo, "Those Good Ole Boys"

2.   These days it seems that everyone belongs to the cult of candor, that everything must be spoken and that everyone speaks the same dialect. Are you relating? Good. Are you getting in touch with yourself? Fine. Exactly how heavy are those changes you're going through? Doing your own thing? Is your head screwed on straight? Are your going to get your act together? Are you a whole person or only a fraction thereof?

—R. D. Rosen, *Psychobabble*

3.   The tarpaulin is down, and a midafternoon rain is falling steadily. Play has been halted. The lights are on, and the wet, pale-green tarp throws off wiggly, reptilian gleams. The players are back in their locker rooms, and both dugouts are empty. A few fans have stayed in their seats, huddling under big, brightly colored golf umbrellas, but almost everybody else has moved back under the shelter of the upper decks, standing there quietly, watching the rain. The huge park, the countless rows of shiny-blue wet seats, the long emerald outfield lawns—all stand silent and waiting. By the look of it, this shower may hold things up for a good half-hour or more. Time for a few baseball stories.

—Roger Angell, *Five Seasons*

EXERCISE 12

Choose one topic from Exercise 10. Write a paragraph for each audience, making clear the two different tones.

1f
Organizing an essay

If your essay is disorganized, if its ideas don't come in a clear order, or if they aren't clearly related to each other and to the thesis sentence, then much of your effort to produce a good thesis sentence and select appropriate details and tone will be wasted. You can't communicate to a reader unless the reader can distinguish among ideas and determine their relative importance and their connections.

Writers can sometimes organize their ideas effectively while they write, once they have their thesis firmly in mind and know roughly what they want to say. But putting your ideas in clear order and tying them together will be easier if you organize your thoughts before you begin writing.

1
Arranging and outlining the parts of an essay

Organizing

A carefully written thesis sentence will do a great deal to help you organize the parts of your essay, for it is likely to contain your main supporting ideas and point the way toward their eventual arrangement. Each of the thesis sentences on pages 10–11 suggests an overall organization for an essay. And in each case the suggested pattern corresponds to a common way of organizing ideas: spatial, chronological, general to specific, specific to general, and less important to more important. (These are also discussed in relation to paragraphs in 3b-1.)

A **spatial organization** is useful when you are describing a geographical area, an object, or a person. Following the pattern in which people normally survey something, you move through space in an orderly way from a chosen starting point to other aspects of the scene or object or person. Describing a friend, you might begin with his shoes and move upward, or begin with his face and move downward. Unless you had an obvious reason for doing so, your arrangement would probably lose some effectiveness if you started with his hands, moved to his face, then went to his shoes and back up to his arms. The thesis sentence below (repeated from p. 11) lends itself to a spatial organization, though the purpose is more than mere description of a scene.

> From the raw cuts defacing a once-beautiful mountain, to the clouded and dangerous streams flowing from it, to the troubled lives of the people living below it, the effects of strip-mining can be devastating.

A **chronological organization** reports events as they occurred in time, usually from first to last. This pattern, too, corresponds to readers' own experiences and expectations. Thus in writing an essay from the following thesis sentence (repeated from p. 11), the author's most effective approach would be to proceed chronologically, from the breaking of the sewer line, to the argument, to the appeal to the commission, to the results.

> If you want to wait a month for your sewer line to be repaired, have an argument with a neighbor on the Public Works Commission before asking the commission to do the repair.

Organizing from the **general to the specific** or from the **specific to the general** depends on your material, of course. If you find it most effective to present your main points first and then back them up with specifics—for instance, when you make initial strong and general statements to gain the reader's attention—you will want to follow the general-to-specific pattern. If you wish to relate the specifics first, letting them build to more general ideas, then you will want to follow the specific-to-general pattern. Specific-to-general is the approach of the writer of the following thesis sentence (repeated from p. 11).

> As student government president, I found myself being a yes-man to the principal, failing to take students' sides against teachers, and getting more from the power of the job than from its responsibilities and potential for reform.

In her essay, the writer will discuss how she dealt with the principal and others before moving on to the larger point: how those events led her to compromise her principles. This thesis sentence can also be seen as moving from the less important (or dramatic) to the more important (or dramatic).

These patterns are like the spatial and chronological organization in that they correspond to readers' expectations of what they will encounter next. Whatever pattern you select you should stick to that pattern or risk confusing or frustrating your readers. In the essay about athletic facilities, whose opening paragraph we saw on pages 16–17, the author would weaken his case if he were to arrange his ideas like this:

> the college will lose students [secondary reason]
>
> the college's responsibility is fitness of mind *and* body [main reason]
>
> faculty as well as students would benefit [another secondary reason]

Instead, he should save the second reason for last, so that he leaves the reader with the strongest of his arguments.

Outlining

Most essays are made up of an introduction, a body, and a conclusion. The introduction draws your readers into the world of your essay, stating your topic and sometimes your thesis sentence. The conclusion may state what you hope readers will take away from your essay or may summarize your essay's main points. (Both introductory and concluding paragraphs are discussed with other special paragraphs in 3d.) The body of your essay is its center, the part in which you offer specific details, examples, or reasons to support your thesis. In an essay of 500 to 750 words the body may be three to five substantial paragraphs, each one presenting a major piece of supporting evidence for your thesis. If you decide before you write what you will cover in each paragraph, the actual writing will be easier, better organized, and less in need of major revision.

The best method for planning an essay is to devise an outline that shows major points as well as supporting information. For long and complicated projects such as a research paper, you may want to (or be required to) construct a formal outline (see 35f). But for brief essays, an informal working outline is probably enough. It differs from the preliminary groups of ideas (1c) because it occurs further along in the writing process. Now you are no longer discovering your main idea. Instead, you have your main idea (your thesis sentence) and a sense of what you want to say, what information and tone will suit your audience, and what overall organization might be most appropriate. All that's left before starting to write is arranging the parts of your essay in some sensible order that will guide your writing.

Your thesis sentence will usually suggest the skeleton of your working outline, in the same way that it suggests an overall pattern of organization. As we saw on page 20, the essay on strip-mining will have a spatial organization dictated by its thesis sentence. In devising a working outline the writer adds a definition of strip-mining and fills in the specific details and examples that support his main points.

THESIS SENTENCE

From the raw cuts defacing a once-beautiful mountain, to the clouded and dangerous streams flowing from it, to the troubled lives of the people living below it, the effects of strip-mining can be devastating.

WORKING OUTLINE

1. Definition of strip-mining: removing earth's crust to get at mineral resources underneath
2. The mountain
   200 cubic yards removed each minute
   once sloping surface—now a series of deep, jagged steps
   erosion—deep gulleys—mud slides
   once green, now brown and gray
   no wildlife
3. The streams
   once clear—now muddy or cloudy
   once full of fish—now lifeless
   once drinkable—now poisoned with acids from mining
4. The people
   lose the beauty of their surroundings

lose supplies of fish and wildlife—no fishing and hunting
lose their drinking water
lose their meager farmland and sometimes their homes to erosion, mud slides, increased acidity of the soil
not compensated by the mining companies
not employed by the mining companies (only skilled technicians and machines needed)
gain little, lose much

This outline shows a lot of thought: the details and examples are present for a brief yet convincing essay on the disadvantages of strip-mining; and the specific information is organized effectively (for increasing drama) under each main point. The writer should have little difficulty moving from the outline to a good first draft.

Marcia Torres also produces a working outline for her essay on photography. Since she's had trouble being specific about her feelings and narrowing her focus to one central idea, this planning and outlining stage is essential if her first draft is to be more than a collection of vague, jumbled thoughts.

THESIS SENTENCE

Photography makes me feel creative because it lets me present the world in my special way and because it shows me things I never knew I saw.

WORKING OUTLINE

1. Presenting the world my own way—selectivity

    Using the difference between a photograph and the "real" world

    > photograph 2-dimensional, framed, black and white
    > even color not "real"

    My own interests—what fascinates me

    > people's hands
    > leaves in late fall
    > living things in winter snow

2. Surprising me with unexpected things

    Photographs form their own worlds

    > like looking through panes of glass in a window
    > can't always anticipate the effects of a frame or black and white
    > same scene framed differently looks different—people in park

    Photographs show unseen aspects of scenes and people

    > focusing on one thing and overlooking others
    > an instant is made permanent
    > my mother's hands in a photo of a leaf
    > the cute kid with the terrified expression

2

Maintaining unity and coherence

In devising and checking your outline, and in writing your essay, you should be aware of two qualities of good writing that are related to organization: unity and coherence. An essay has **unity** if all its parts relate to the thesis sentence and to each other. It has **coherence** if readers can see the relations and move easily with the writer from one thought to the next. Unity and coherence underlie successful paragraphs, and so we deal with them in detail in Chapter 3 (see 3a and 3b). But they are also important when you are planning the elements in the whole essay.

When your working outline is nearly completed, examine it for unity. Is each main point relevant to the thesis sentence? Within major sections of the outline, does each example and detail support the main point of that section? You may become sidetracked by ideas that don't really fit, so you are wise to weed them out fairly ruthlessly at the outline stage. If, later, you find a way to get some of them in, you can always retrieve them.

In the working outline for an essay on strip-mining (pp. 22–23), the writer might have included a section on the mine owners' defenses of the damage their strip mines do, or one on government's responses to the conditions created by the mining. Although such topics might be made to fit into the essay, they don't relate directly to the thesis sentence, which focuses only on the devastating results of strip-mining, and they might even dilute the effectiveness of the writer's argument. In the brief outline below the writer loses control of unity at point 3.

THESIS SENTENCE

Whether or not teachers are successful seems to depend not on how hard they work but on how much they care and how well they communicate what they know.

WORKING OUTLINE

1. Caring and communicating

   caring is knowing students' names—showing interest in their work and problems—treating them like adults and individuals

   communicating is changing approach to match students' needs—saying only what needs to be said—getting across the interesting things about a subject

2. Unsuccessful teachers

   need to be asked for help—don't offer

   treat each student the same way

either talk over students' heads or talk down to them
have an unchanging approach to class activities

3. Effects on students

unsuccessful teachers make learning a chore
students treated like children will act like children
need to bring attention to unsuccessful teachers—force them
to change

4. Successful teachers

know when students are in trouble
give ample time to each student
don't talk down to students
vary class environment to keep interest alive

In an essay, point 3 would muddy the writer's focus and detract from the main argument. Although bad teachers' effects on students' performance and behavior and what should be done about them are both valid topics, they don't relate to the writer's chosen topic of the difference between teachers.

Coherence is achieved by an easy movement from one idea to another, a movement that corresponds to readers' expectations of logical order. In looking over your working outline, be sure your overall organization is sensible, whether it's spatial, chronological, specific to general, or vice versa. Review the main points and details to ensure that you know how you will get from one to another. In writing, you will use transitional expressions like *although, then, for example,* and *in addition* to move from one sentence or paragraph to another. (Transitional expressions are discussed fully in 3b-6.) However, you can't rely on them to make your connections clear to readers. The progression of your ideas must be clear enough so that it alone helps readers follow the relations you intend.

The paragraph below is incoherent. The writer has not provided enough clues in her ideas or between her sentences for us to understand exactly where she's going.

Men say women drivers are a highway menace. I don't think it's women who are the problem. Confidence in both sexes is important. Lack of confidence or too much confidence makes a bad driver. Lack of confidence shows in slowness to make decisions and frequent mind changing. A driver who acts as if he or she owns the road—going too fast, weaving in and out of traffic, taking illegal turns—is overconfident. Hesitant drivers and cocky drivers are both a menace. Women aren't the only drivers with a confidence problem.

This paragraph is unified: all the ideas are related to the main idea that amount of confidence is more important than gender in producing bad drivers. But the sentences are difficult to follow because they jump around. The paragraph would have been much more effective had the writer tied her ideas together to produce a unified *and* coherent paragraph like this one:

> Men say women drivers are a highway menace, but confidence seems to be more of a problem than gender in producing bad drivers. Some bad drivers lack confidence. They are slow to make decisions, and they change their minds a lot. Other bad drivers are overconfident. They act as if they own the road—going too fast, weaving in and out of traffic, and making illegal turns. Hesitance and cockiness are the highway menace, not women.

EXERCISE 13

List four to six main points for each topic below, arranging them in the pattern specified in parentheses.

1. why dogs should not be allowed to foul the streets (less dramatic to more dramatic)
2. a day on a mountaintop (chronological)
3. the street I live on (spatial)
4. how students release frustration (specific to general)
5. how to make a great dessert (chronological)

EXERCISE 14

Evaluate the following outline for unity. What points or specific details don't support the thesis sentence?

THESIS SENTENCE

If I had a million dollars, I'd treat myself to luxuries I've never had: good food in fine restaurants, a great car, and plenty of travel.

WORKING OUTLINE

Food

> no McDonald's or Burger King
> good French restaurants with black-coated waiters
> elegant desserts (puff pastry, chocolate mousse)
> no dishes to wash, no pots to scrub

Car

> no buses or subways
> a 5-speed Mercedes with air conditioning
> unlimited gas—no restrictions on travel
> danger of theft

Travel

> first Paris, then Egypt, then China
> a trip a year, all over the world
> learn to appreciate the benefits of the U.S.

Problems
   getting used to luxuries
   what to do when the money runs out?
   readjusting to the "before" life-style

EXERCISE 15

Make a list of the ideas in the following paragraph. You will see that it is incoherent because the relations among its ideas are not clear. Rearrange the ideas so their connections are clear and they correspond to an expected organization.

> Being left-handed has no benefits. At dinner parties, you have to eat with your elbow tucked into your ribs, or you have to make a fuss about the seating arrangements. As a child, you are constantly told to use your right hand. It's a condition with no pluses, unless you like being disadvantaged. In school there are few left-handed desk chairs. You can't even make scissors work properly. And when you write, you look to others as if you're writing upside down. It's as if you have leprosy or a social disease.

EXERCISE 16

Using your set of grouped ideas from Exercise 6 (p. 9) and the corresponding thesis sentence from Exercise 8 (p. 14), devise a working outline that reflects basic patterns of organization, contains the main points necessary to support the thesis sentence, and, under each main point, includes specific details and examples that are themselves logically arranged.

2

Writing and Revising the Essay

In the previous chapter we dealt with the planning steps in the writing process: choosing and limiting the subject, getting ideas and grouping them, writing a thesis sentence, considering an audience, and organizing ideas effectively. This chapter will complete the process with writing and revising the essay. Throughout we'll continue to follow Marcia Torres's essay on photography, which we saw in its initial stages throughout Chapter 1.

2a
Writing the first draft

Marcia Torres begins the first draft of her essay by reviewing her working outline (p. 23). She writes in longhand, not attempting to achieve perfection but instead trying to proceed steadily without halting too often to reread. Even so, she does stop, rethink, and correct as she goes along, taking the equivalent of one step backward for every two or three steps forward. Along the way she tries to achieve a serious and thoughtful tone suitable for a general audience. Although her outline serves her well, some points seem almost to rearrange themselves, whereas others do not seem to fit and must be wedged in. Torres's method of writing is as individual as her way of thinking. However, almost all writers experience the same stop-and-go progress and find that the best-laid plans in an outline don't always work out in actual writing.

Torres's first draft, which she typed over so she could work on it, took her a couple of hours to complete. Read it carefully and critically. Look especially for disunity (where Torres allows irrelevant ideas to creep in), for incoherence (where she has failed to link her ideas clearly), for faulty paragraphing, for errors in grammar and usage, and for words that may be poorly chosen.

Title (?)

There are many reasons for taking up a hobby, but one of the best in my opinion is so that you can do something that will make you feel creative. Photography makes me feel creative because it lets me present the world in my special way and because it shows me things I never knew were there.

A lot of people still think that cameras take pictures by gobbling up little pieces of the world, and then spit them back. On the contrary photographers take pictures, and a photograph does not show the real world. To be sure photographs seem more like the real thing than lets say drawings or paintings are, but like drawings or a painting, photographs isolate a part of a scene in a frame, they are only two dimensional, and besides, they are usually black-and-white. And even when they are in color, those colors are never exactly those of the real world. Some color films are strong in the blue range, others in brown range, and so on. And the print (the frame) comes in a standard size to match the paper you buy: 2-1/2" x 3-1/4", 4" x 5", 5" x 7", 8" x 10", etc.

Besides, I know that a camera lets me capture the things that interest me. I love to concentrate on hands, for example. I think I could photograph them all day long. I couldn't get away with just stareing at hands. People would think I was some kind of weirdo. But I can use a telephoto lense. They don't seem to notice just what you take a picture of, and I like hands. I also like leaves in late fall that refuse to drop from trees. And I like to take photographs of living things in snow--birds, plants. And I like patches of ice that refuse to melt in early spring, a flower that survives a spring frost, a puppy who sumoned the courage to stop into a stream, or a child who had gone up a pole for the first time. I've got pictures of all of these things. What photography does is let me select the things about life that I like and to concentrate on those. I know that my pictures aren't all there is to life, but then I wouldn't want them to be. They are my world. They are what I want to create.

There is another thing that I have noticed about photography too--photographs make their own worlds. A person can't always anticapate how a photo will come out. The best way I can think of explaining this is to think of how a scene looks through a window made up of many panes. Each pane looks out at the same scene, yet the scene looks different through each pane. A photograph is like a pane of glass. They have their own special angle that make them different from those of any other photograph. It is as if eight or ten photographers took pictures of the same scene, no two would see the same scene, no two would shoot from quite the same angle or direction, for no two would light or shadow be quite the same.

There is a final way in which photography is creative. Sometimes a photograph will show something that I didn't even know was there. For example that small child playing last week. I took a lot of pictures in a hurry because he seemed so happy. When I developed and printed them, I noticed the strangest thing. In two or three he looks

3

scared--even terrified. I don't know what he was thinking about while he was playing but my camera was quicker at seeing than I was and those pictures seem real independant of me. Yet I took them thus the camera is an extension of me. Another example is a picture of a leaf I took a few months ago. I was concentrating so much on the leaf itself that I didn't notice my mother's hands come into the back ground. She was picking flowers. It's a strange photograph.

In all of these ways, then, photography can make you feel creative.

Like almost all first drafts, this one is rough. It has problems in grammar, usage, spelling, and diction. The whole essay and its individual paragraphs suffer from disunity. The relations among ideas are not always clear, and some paragraphs are not coherent. Some ideas don't seem to further the assertion in the thesis sentence; in fact, Torres seems to discuss not just two but several ways in which photography makes her feel creative. Nonetheless, Torres has produced a draft that can be revised effectively.

2b
Revising the first draft

Before you begin to revise your first draft, take a break for at least a few hours to clear your mind. Then you will return to your essay refreshed, ready to tackle one of the most crucial stages in any writing.

Revision is proofreading: hunting for errors in grammar, spelling, punctuation, and mechanics. But revision is also much more than simple correction of errors. It is a true rethinking. Your first draft is the testing ground for your thesis sentence, your ideas, and your arrangement of ideas. It is the stage at which you make ideas work for your thesis or see that the thesis needs changing to encompass your ideas. In the first draft you discover how your thoughts work when spelled out in complete sentences and how those sentences combine in paragraphs. You find out what you really have to say and how to say it.

More than a few writers, including many experienced ones, have reached the end of the first draft only to reject the whole thing because they weren't comfortable with their thesis or even with their topic. If you work through the planning steps outlined in Chapter 1 and stick to your outline, your first draft will probably be workable, as Torres's is. But it will always need revision.

You should set aside almost as much time for revising your first draft as you took to write it. In writing you were pushing to record your ideas in sentences and paragraphs; in revising you will be looking at your materials as your readers will, critically, hunting for lapses in sense and for errors. Count on going through the essay several times to examine its structure and several more times just to catch careless mistakes. Read through the essay for each of the items in the following revision guide. (The chapter and heading numbers in parentheses refer you to the appropriate sections of this handbook.)

Revision checklist

1. Does everything in your essay support or develop your thesis sentence? Are the relationships clear? (1d and 1f.)
2. Are your choice of information and your tone appropriate for your audience? (1e.)
3. Is your essay organized sensibly? Is it unified and coherent? (1f.)
4. Are your paragraphs unified (3a), coherent (3b), and well developed (3c)?
5. Are your assertions believable and well supported? (4b and 4c.) Have you avoided faulty reasoning? (4d.)
6. Are your sentences grammatical? Have you avoided errors in case (Chapter 6), verbs (Chapter 7), agreement (Chapter 8), and adjectives and adverbs (Chapter 9)?
7. Are your sentences clear? Have you avoided sentence fragments (Chapter 10), comma splices and run-on sentences (Chapter 11), errors in pronoun reference (Chapter 12), shifts (Chapter 13), misplaced or dangling modifiers (Chapter 14), and mixed or incomplete constructions (Chapter 15)?
8. Are your sentences effective? Have you used subordination and coordination (Chapter 16) and parallelism (Chapter 17) appropriately? Are your sentences emphatic (Chapter 18) and varied (Chapter 19)?
9. Is your use of commas, semicolons, colons, periods, and other punctuation correct? (Chapters 20–25.)
10. Are your sentences mechanically correct in use of capitals, italics, abbreviations, numbers, and hyphens? (Chapters 26–30.)
11. Have you relied on standard diction? (31a.) Do your words denote and connote what you intend? Have you avoided triteness? (31b.) Is your writing concise? (31c.)
12. Are your words spelled correctly? (Chapter 34.)

If you need particular help in any one of these areas, study the appropriate section of the handbook before you begin your revision.

Marcia Torres begins to revise her first draft, focusing especially on the items in the checklist. After proofreading and rethinking her essay, trying to read it as if she were seeing it for the first time, she ends up with the following revised draft.

Creating by Re-creating
Title (?)

There are many reasons for taking up a hobby, but one

of the best in my opinion is so that you can do something

is just such a hobby for me. It

that will make you feel creative. Photography~ makes me feel

re-create

creative because it lets me present the world in my special

way and because it shows me things I never knew were there.

A lot of people still think that cameras take pictures

by gobbling up little pieces of the world, and then spit

out bits of the real world.

them back. On the contrary photographers take pictures, and

a photograph does not show the real world. To be sure

photographs seem more like the real thing than, lets say,

do. B photographs are

drawings or paintings are, but like drawings or a painting,

in that they   and

photographs isolate a part of a scene in a frame, they are

Unlike most paintings and many

only two dimensional, and besides, they are usually black-

drawings, a photo is also often black-and-white, which

and-white. And even when they are in color, those colors

certainly does not reflect the real world. Even when it is

are never exactly those of the real world. Some color films

in color, those colors are never exactly those of the real

are strong in the blue range, others in brown range, and so

world. The choice of frame and the use of black-and-white or

on. And the print (the frame) comes in a standard size to

color film are up to the photographer, and they are

match the paper you buy: 2-1/2" x 3-1/4", 4" x 5", 5" x 7",

where many aspects of creativity comes in.

8" x 10", etc.

A Photography is also creative because

Besides, I know that a camera lets me capture the

especially things that show a struggle to exist.

things that interest me, I ~love~ to concentrate on hands,

for example. I think I could photograph them all day long.

I couldn't get away with just stareing at hands, People

b

would think I was some kind of weirdo. But I can use a

to photograph them so no one

telephoto lense, They don't seem to notice just what you

have photographed

take a picture of, and I like hands. I also like leaves, in

late fall (that refuse to drop from trees) And I like to

1

2

3

2

take photographs of living things in snow--birds, plants.

~~And I like patches of ice that refuse to melt in early~~
　　　　and　　　　　　　　　　*And I have photographed*
~~spring,~~ a~~,~~ flower*s* that survive*s* a spring frost. ~~a puppy who~~
　　m *ing*　　　　　　　*e*　　　　　*and*
sum~~o~~ned the courage to st~~o~~p into a stream~~,~~ ~~or~~ a child who
climbed
~~had gone up~~ a pole for the first time. ~~I've got pictures of~~
　　　　　　　　　　　　　　P
~~all of these things.~~ ~~What~~ photography ~~does is~~ let*s* me select
the things about life that I like and to concentrate on
those. I know that my pictures aren't all there is to life,
but then I wouldn't want them to be. They are my world.
They are what I want to create.

　　~~There is another thing that I have noticed about~~
　　　¶ P　　*also create*　　　　　　*because a*
~~photography too--~~photographs make their own worlds, ~~A~~ per-
　　　　　　　　　　　　　　　　　　i
son can't always antic~~a~~pate how a photo~~,~~ will come out. ~~The~~
　　　　best　　　　　　*by mentioning*
~~best~~ way I can ~~think of~~ explaining this ~~is to think of~~ how a
　　　　different　*each pane of a many-paned window.*
scene looks~~,~~ through ~~a window made up of many panes. Each~~
~~pane looks out at the same scene, yet the scene looks dif-~~
~~ferent through each pane.~~ A photograph is like a pane of
　　　It has its　　　　　　　　　　　　　　　*it*
glass. ~~They have their~~ own special angle that make*s* ~~them~~
　　　　　　　　　　　　　　　　　　　　　　　　I
different from ~~those of~~ any other photograph. ~~It is as~~ if
eight or ten photographers took pictures of the same scene,
no two would see the same scene, no two would shoot from
quite the same angle~~,~~ or ~~direction,~~ for no two would light or
shadow be quite the same.
　　¶ Photographs also make their own worlds by showing
　¶ ~~There is a final way in which photography is creative.~~
me things I never knew I saw when I took them.
Sometimes a photograph ~~will show~~ something that ~~I didn't~~
~~even know was there.~~ For example that small child playing
last week. I took a lot of pictures in a hurry because he
seemed so happy. When I developed and printed them, I
noticed the strangest thing. In two or three he looks

4

5

3

scared--even terrified. I don't know what he was thinking
about while he was playing but my camera was quicker at
seeing than I was.and those pictures seem real independant
of me. Yet I took them; thus the camera is an extension of
me. Another example is a picture of a leaf I took a few
months ago. I was concentrating so much on the leaf itself
that I didn't notice my mother's hands come into the background. She was picking flowers. ~~It's a strange photograph.~~

    In all of these ways, then, photography ~~can make you~~
is not only an
~~feel creative.~~ *enjoyable hobby but is a creative art. It requires choices*
and imagination and it returns the investment with
surprises of its own.

6

In revising her essay, Torres supplies a title and echoes it in her thesis sentence (paragraph 1). She corrects several errors in spelling, grammar, and word choice (for instance, cutting the slang *weirdo* in paragraph 3). She weeds out some repetition and wordiness (for instance, in the first half of paragraph 3 and in paragraph 4), and she eliminates a technical digression (end of paragraph 2). But Torres also concentrates on supplying a central idea for each paragraph (end of paragraph 2; beginning of paragraph 3) and on relating each paragraph to her thesis sentence (paragraphs 4 and 5). These changes help sharpen her ideas about creation and re-creation while they increase the coherence of her essay. Finally, Torres adds to her conclusion (paragraph 6) so that it ties her thoughts together more tightly and states the main point she wants readers to take away from her essay.

rev
2c

| 2c
| Preparing the final draft

Reading over Torres's revision, we can see its improvement as well as its remaining flaws. They range from minor errors in grammar and punctuation to more serious problems in paragraph coherence and unity. Although Torres has made some headway in relating her paragraphs to her thesis sentence, she has perhaps paid less attention to rethinking her essay than she has to correcting specific problems in grammar, punctuation, and spelling. She still has not succeeded in clarifying and illustrating her main points most effectively.

These are the criticisms that Torres's instructor will make, for Torres herself sees her revision as complete—the best she can do. She types it over in correct manuscript form (see Appendix B) and corrects her own typing errors, but otherwise she makes no further changes.

When you hand in your paper, your instructor will act as counselor and editor, helping you see your essay's errors and weaknesses and suggesting ways you can improve not only the essay you have submitted but your future writing as well. Repeated practice in working from ideas to essay and in responding to a critical reader's comments will help you become a more efficient and capable writer.

As her instructor reads Marcia Torres's essay, he directs her to consult appropriate sections of the handbook by using the correction code inside the back cover. And at the end of the essay he comments on the general weaknesses that Torres should attend to in revising this essay or in writing future essays.

rev
2c

Creating by Re-Creating

There are many reasons for taking up a hobby, but one
of the best in my opinion is so that you can do something
that will make you feel creative. Photography is just such
a hobby for me. It makes me feel creative because it lets
me re-create the world in my special way and because it
shows me things I never knew were there.

A lot of people still think that cameras take pictures
and spit out bits of the real world. On the contrary
photographers take pictures, and a photograph does not show
the real world. To be sure photographs seem more like the
real thing than, say, drawings or paintings do. But photographs are like drawings or paintings in that they isolate
a part of a scene in a frame and they are only two dimensional. Unlike most paintings and many drawings, a photo
is also often black-and-white, which certainly does not reflect the real world. Even when it is in color, those
colors are never exactly those of the real world. The
choice of frame and the use of black-and-white or color film
are up to the photographer, and they are where many aspects
of creativity comes in.

Photography is also creative because a camera lets me
capture the things that interest me, especially things that
show a struggle to exist. I concentrate on hands, for example. I couldn't just stare at hands, but I can use a
telephoto lens to photograph them so no one notices. I have
also photographed leaves that refuse to drop from trees in

31c

3d

1d

21b

21b

34d

12a

8a

31b

2

late fall and flowers that survive a spring frost. And I
have photographed (a puppy summoning) the courage to step into 〔17a〕
a stream and (a child who climbed) a pole for the first time.
〔17a〕 Photography lets me (select) the things about life that I like
and (to concentrate) on those. I know that my pictures aren't
all there is to life, but then I wouldn't want them to be.
They are my world. They are what I want to create.

　　Photographs also create their own worlds, because a
person can't always anticipate how a photograph will come
out. 〔3/c〕 I can best explain this by mentioning how a scene
looks different through each pane of a many-paned window. A
photograph is like a pane of glass. It has its own special
angle that makes it different from any other photograph. If
eight or ten photographers took pictures of the same scene,
no two would see the same scene, no two would shoot from
quite the same angle, for no two would light or shadow be 〔17b〕
quite the same.

　　Photographs also make their own worlds by showing me
things I never knew I saw when I took them. For example 〔10〕
that small child playing last week. I took a lot of pictures in a hurry because he seemed so happy. When I developed and printed them, I noticed the strangest thing. In
two or three he looks scared--even terrified. I don't know 〔2/a〕
〔3b〕 what he was thinking about while he was playing but my camera was quicker at seeing than I was. Those pictures seem
〔9a〕 (real) independent of me. Yet I took them; thus the camera is 〔18〕
an extension of me. Another example is a picture of a leaf 〔3/c〕
I took a few months ago. I was concentrating so much on the

rev
2c

3

leaf itself that I didn't notice my mother's hands come into ⎤ ③lc
the background. She was picking flowers.

  In all of these ways, then, photography is not only an
enjoyable hobby <u>but is</u> a creative art. It requires choices ⟨17a⟩
⟨2/a⟩ and imagination and it returns the investment with surprises
of its own.

Your essay is thoughtful and well organized.
Most ideas are well supported. With some
exceptions, paragraphs are well developed, unified and
coherent. Sentences are often nicely varied and
appropriately emphatic. In correcting errors in
grammar, punctuation, and sentence structure,
consult especially Chs. 21 (comma) and 17 (parallelism).

Your introduction is weak: it doesn't catch the
reader, and it doesn't really introduce your essay.
Compare thesis sentence with conclusion: which is
creative — you or photography? Your essay wavers.
Notice how you shift among "I," "photography,"
and "photographers" from one paragraph to the next.
Topic sentences do not relate as clearly as they
might to the thesis sentence.

Torres's instructor might also have commented verbally on her paper and used symbols instead of a code. The sample below shows the next to last paragraph of Torres's paper corrected in this manner. (The symbols appear inside the front cover of the handbook.)

> Photographs also make their own worlds by showing me things I never knew I saw when I took them. For example *frag* that small child playing last week. I took a lot of pictures in a hurry because he seemed so happy. When I developed and printed them, I noticed the strangest thing. In two or three he looks scared--even terrified. I don't know *¶* *coh* *p* what he was thinking about while he was playing, but my camera was quicker at seeing than I was. Those pictures seem *(try reversing order of examples) ad* real independent of me. Yet I took them; thus the camera is *emph* an extension of me. Another example is a picture of a leaf *w* I took a few months ago. I was concentrating so much on the leaf itself that I didn't notice my mother's hands come into the background. She was picking flowers.

The instructor's comments should be helpful to Torres. She had struggled through her draft to provide topic sentences and relate them to her thesis. The comments give her another point of view. If she were required to revise her paper and resubmit it, she would start by rethinking what she wants to write about. Being consistent in discussing herself or photographers or photography will strengthen the overall coherence of her paper. She also needs to locate and sharpen her topic sentences (see 3a), relating each one directly to her new thesis. She must be sure the details and examples in each paragraph relate clearly to the topic sentence and help to further her thesis. If necessary, she must revise her conclusion to correspond to the new thrust of her paper. If she were to do these things and correct the other, smaller problems, she would have a very competent essay.

EXERCISE 1

To become familiar with using the handbook's code, revise Marcia Torres's paper to correct errors and improve style as suggested by her instructor. Using her instructor's written comments and referring to the revision checklist (p. 33), how would you sharpen Torres's thesis sentence and supporting ideas to make the essay more effective?

EXERCISE 2

Write an essay of 500 to 750 words from one of the outlines you developed in Chapter 1, Exercise 16 (p. 27). Revise your essay carefully, using the revision checklist on page 33.

EXERCISE 3

Read the following essays carefully, evaluating them against the revision checklist on page 33. Correct sentences for punctuation, grammar, and spelling as necessary, and rewrite sentences you think could be phrased more effectively. Concentrate on each writer's development of the idea expressed in the thesis sentence. How well does each paragraph support the essay's central point? Are the writer's ideas and details arranged coherently and effectively? Is the essay unified? Is the tone appropriate and consistent? Within each paragraph, does the writer identify a main idea and stick to it? Which essay is more effective in making you see and accept the writer's perspective?

The Gentle Manatee

Part of the controversy over saving endangered species of animals and plants seems to center on the uselessness of these species to humans. Why save them if they don't serve us? The answer may lie mainly in understanding more about how every form of life serves us at least indirectly. But there is also virtue in saving living things just because they are different from us. Of all the endangered species, none could be more useless or more worth saving than the manatee.

The manatee is a huge water-dwelling mamal. It lives mostly in rivers and shallow coastal waters in North and South America and western Africa. It cannot survive in cold waters, and the largest number in our part of the world live in southern Florida. It is a vegetarian that eats only water plants.

Manatees once served a useful purpose for humans—food. Indians harpooned them from canoes, ate their meat, and used the oil from their fat. The Spaniards who came after the Indians used them the same way. And up until recent times when they weren't killed for food they were killed for sport. Natural laws now protect manatees, along with other endangered species. But their numbers are still small because people break the laws and their motorboats run over the animals in shallow waters when they come up to breathe.

Another reason manatees are few in number is because they are slow breeding animals. Each female manatee only gives birth to one calf, the gestation period is over a year. A calf after it is born nurses for up to a year and a half. A full-grown manatee may be up to twelve feet long and weigh 2000 pounds.

Besides their size, the most remarkable thing about a manatee is the way it looks. It is shaped and colored like a torpedo with a thicker middle than ends. Its body is rough, like an elephant's, but not as wrinkled. It has a small flat tail, like a whale's, that it uses to move. And it has small flippers on each side of its body, near the front. Most striking is its face. Tiny, clouded eyes peer out of a wrinkled, bristly face that can only be called ugly. Huge, fleshy lips are strong and movable enough to grasp plants and push them back into the mouth.

Manatees are harmless, and this is their most interesting characteristic. They don't have any natural predators, nor do they prey on anything but plants. They swim away from danger, because they have no way to defend themselves. They are somewhat social animals that communicate by making noises and rubbing each other. They will even rub against humans who are swimming under water, and may seem to hug with their flippers.

Manatees live an ideal existence. Most of their time is spent browsing along the bottom for food or in rest. When resting, they push themselves up for air every so often and then sink to the bottom. When not eating or resting, they seem to play games like tag or follow-the-leader or riding currents in a kind of body surfing.

Now that we no longer eat manatees or use their oil, they may seem useless to us and not worth protecting. However their friendliness and gentleness and their relaxed and harmless way could teach us humans something about living our lives.

The Fine Art of Flunking

Sometimes the things that would seem to be the simplest, most effortless tasks require cleverness. This includes flunking. The dedicated failure is really less concerned with failing itself than with the effectiveness of his ventures. Three of the most effective many ways to flunk a class are: completely ignoring the subject matter, having a rotten attitude, and sleeping in class.

The failure usually has a rotten attitude. At one time or another everyone has a rotten attitude about something, but the failure is proud of the fact that he has a rotten attitude about everything. Facial expression should be of concern. The failure should strive to revive the look of nausea he had after eating four plates of his brother's sloppy joes. If this effort, however, is not satisfactory, a sneer may be even better. If, by some remote possibility, the failure finds himself feeling sympathy for his subject or instructor, he reminds himself of the injustices he has suffered. He should never forget that instructor who chain smokes in class and aggravates his asthma, or the teacher who doesn't know he exists.

Ignoring the subject matter is not as simple as it may sound. We have been conditioned to pretend we're paying attention from the beginning of our student careers. The truly adept failure is a master of inattention. His fondest memory is the day he answered an unexpected question from a geography instructor that "arthropod" was the name of the peninsula formed by Spain and Portugal. The aspiring failure should also avoid homework assignments and term papers, no matter how relevant or interesting they may seem. In spite of the fact that he can never go to sleep before two A.M., the good failure resists the temptation to read that chapter on "insomnia" in his Psychology textbook.

Assuming a rotten attitude, experienced failures know yet a more affective way of making anyone aware of their existence: sleeping in class. Most failures share this basic characteristic, but the expert failure makes the most of a catnap. Instead of struggling to sit upright with his eyes politely closed, he makes a spectacle of himself. The most popular position for sleeping in class is undoubtedly the "head-on-desk" position, however, the great failure lets his head hang over the back of his chair with his mouth open. The significance of proper snoring can hardly be overemphasized. Unless the sleeping person is irritating about it, he might be mistaken for a knock in the heating system. An expert varies the tone and quality of his snore. One technique used by experienced failures (who just happen to be musical prodigies) is snoring in pitch while sleeping in a desk near the instructor's podium. This type of snoring makes any lecture hall sound system roar. The snorer's objective is always distraction, and imagination is of great importance.

Flunking, then, involves much more than most success-oriented students can understand, yet the methods involved are not difficult to master. With a minimum of practice, a student may become a success as a failure.

3

Composing
Good Paragraphs

Prose writing may take almost any form, and the ideas may be simple or complex. But no matter what form or subject we choose, we will probably write in **paragraphs,** self-contained units of thought that contribute to the whole. Paragraphs enable us to break down complex ideas into manageable parts, to deal with each separately and completely, and then to relate the parts back to the central idea.

A paragraph is like a mini-essay. It is unified, it is coherent, and it is developed. (See 1e and 1f.) A paragraph can be perceived as residing in a frame—freestanding; understandable by itself; having a beginning, a middle, and an end.

> Regarded from the receiving end, it seems that the principal failing of latter-day scientists is inaccuracy of aim rather than insufficiency of endeavor. Researchers still insist on applying all their best efforts—and most of our money—to providing us with new things that we don't want. They give us the Concorde when we'd much prefer a cure for the common cold. They provide us with intimate pictures of Mars, although we'd sooner have an everlasting shoelace. They present us with transistor radios when all we really want is a little public peace and quiet.

1
2
3
4
5

—Patrick Ryan, "It Ticks and It Talks"

Though we would like to know what else this writer has to say, we have no doubt about this paragraph's central idea (sentences 1 and 2), how the author supports that idea (sentences 3, 4, and 5), how all the thoughts are related to each other (for example, by the parallel sentence structures of sentences 3 to 5), and what the author's attitude is toward us, his readers (we are his allies). The paragraph is about one idea: it has unity. All its parts relate clearly to each other: it is coherent. And its assertions are well supported by details and examples: it is well developed. These are the goals of paragraph writing and the topics of this chapter.

3a
Maintaining paragraph unity

Paragraph **unity**—like the unity of an essay—depends, first, on identifying a clear topic and an approach to it, and then on sticking to that topic to the end. In an essay the thesis sentence contains the main idea (see 1d). In a paragraph the **topic sentence** alerts readers to the main point of the paragraph by stating the central idea and expressing the writer's attitude toward it. In the framed paragraph on page 45, the topic sentence is sentence 1. The author makes a general statement about scientists. The next sentence in the paragraph clarifies that statement and makes it more specific. And the three sentences following give specific examples of the author's point.

In an essay of 500 to 750 words, each paragraph is likely to be about one aspect of the thesis sentence. In that case the topic sentences may be restatements and elaborations of parts of the thesis. A topic sentence will not, of course, guarantee a unified paragraph—any more than a thesis sentence guarantees a unified essay. The next several sections deal with how to write unified paragraphs around strong topic sentences.

1
Focusing on the central idea

The framed paragraph on page 45 works because it remains attentive to its topic sentence. The sentences that follow the first do not stray off to other subjects, such as the methods or cost of scientific research. The details in the paragraph do not introduce new ideas, except to illustrate the paragraph's central point.

The following paragraph, in contrast, begins to lose its way at sentence 6.

> One of the best-run races was the relay. The four teams' 1, 2
> runners were evenly matched for the first two laps. They 3
> were never more than a foot or two apart. Then, just after 4
> the third runner on each team took the baton, the runner in
> lane 2 took a ten-foot lead. The people in the stadium be- 5
> came hushed for a moment and then began cheering wildly.
> Some spectators almost hurt others in their efforts to get a 6
> clear view of the track. All afternoon, the people in the 7

crowd alternated between quiet watching and noisy, active cheering. Their behavior matched the varied pace of the 8 track meet itself.

¶ un

3a

By the end of this paragraph the author seems to have forgotten that her purpose (stated in sentence 1) was to describe a well-run race. In sentence 6 she becomes distracted herself by the excitement in the stands, and she never returns to the runners.

This writer might have avoided such disunity if she had thought out beforehand what she wanted the paragraph to accomplish and had used a **sentence of clarification** after her topic sentence, explaining exactly what she meant by *best-run*. For instance: *One of the best-run races was the relay. It showed teams of athletes working together as well as one especially great individual performance.* This sentence focuses the topic more narrowly, for reader and writer alike. When her thoughts come to the excitement in the stands, the writer is less likely to let that excitement distract her from her main purpose.

Experienced writers use sentences of clarification often to amplify their main topic before going on to support it. Sentence 2 in the framed paragraph on page 45 is a sentence of clarification. It explains further what the author means, in sentence 1, by *inaccuracy of aim rather than insufficiency of endeavor.*

Writers also pair topic sentences with **sentences of limitation**, so their topic will not be too unwieldy or the opportunities for wandering too many. Sentences of limitation draw tight borders around a topic, making it more specific. In the next example the author has used his second sentence to limit the broad topic that he stated in the first.

> Children also attend closely to what surprises them, to a 1
> novel image or event that violates their expectations about
> the order of their world. Since adults often spend consid- 2
> erable time in the effort to convince children of adult in-
> fallibility, one of the most remarkable and pleasing novelties
> for children is to observe adults making errors that children
> easily identify as such. One series of segments on *Sesame* 3
> *Street* was designed to exploit the interest for children of
> adults making obvious mistakes while trying to solve a
> simple problem. "Buddy and Jim" are two adults who con- 4
> front a series of such simple problems, but can never seem
> to get the obvious solutions quite right. They attempt to
> place a picture on a wall by hammering the blunt end of the
> nail into the wall, fail to observe that the nail should be
> turned around, and then conclude that they must walk to 5
> the wall on the opposite side of the room in order to point
> the nailhead into the wall.
> —Gerald S. Lesser, "Growing Up on Sesame Street"

2
Choosing a paragraph "shape"

Within its imaginary frame a paragraph's central idea and details may be arranged differently to correspond to different ways of developing the central idea. In the most common format—the one used in the paragraphs examined so far—a topic sentence comes first, then sometimes a clarifying or limiting sentence, then illustrations and details that support the topic sentence. But this is only one paragraph format. Thinking of the topic sentence as the point of a paragraph and the supporting sentences as its body, we can imagine several paragraph "shapes" that are useful for different writing purposes.

Central idea at the beginning

The paragraph in which the central idea comes first is the model we have been studying so far: topic sentence, optional sentence of limitation or clarification, and supporting sentences.

This model is the most useful for inexperienced writers, because announcing the topic clearly at the outset helps to direct the writer's thoughts to the choice of appropriate details.

The following two-sentence paragraph shows how this model works.

> We have come to expect incompetence as a necessary 1
> feature of civilization. We may be irked, but we are no 2
> longer amazed, when our bosses make idiotic decisions,
> when automobile makers take back thousands of new cars
> for repairs, when store clerks are insolent, when law reforms
> fail to check crime, when moon rockets can't get off the
> ground, when widely used medicines are found to be poisons, when universities must teach freshmen to read, or
> when a hundred-ton airliner is brought down by a duck.
> —Raymond Hull, "The Peter Principle," *Esquire*

In a common variation of this model, the first sentence is a transition from the preceding paragraph and the second sentence is the topic sentence. The following paragraph was preceded by a description of older brothers.

> The tactics of the younger brother are governed by dif- 1
> ferent considerations. Not having had disciplinary authority 2

delegated to him, he doesn't develop the authoritarian approach. His smaller physical size leaves him free to harrass ₃ his older brother, since the parents caution the older brother not to hurt him, and also because the younger son may not feel obliged to observe adult standards. His smaller size, ₄ which puts him at a disadvantage in physical combat with the older brother, leads him to adopt indirect methods of aggression. He waits for a weakness in the older brother, and ₅ then, with deception and surprise, he ambushes him. Be- ₆ cause his parents' expectations have left him less ambitious than his older brother to win the hard way, he may feel it is enough merely to win—and forget the rules. For all these ₇ reasons, the indirect, devious style of aggression is more common among later sons than among first.

—Irving Harns, "Who Would Kill a President?"

Central idea at the end

In some paragraphs the central idea (and the topic sentence) may come at the end, after supporting sentences have made a case for the general statement. The paragraph ends with a point.

This shape is useful for leading the reader to an idea by presenting all the evidence before drawing a conclusion. And because the paragraph's point is withheld until the end, this shape can be dramatic. For example:

He inspired scores of imitators, sold millions of records. ₁ He got drafted in the Army, got his infamous D.A. and ₂ 'burns clipped, served a tour of duty in Germany, sold millions of records. He went to Hollywood, appeared in 33 mov- ₃ ies, sold millions of records. He played Vegas, got married, ₄ filled amphitheaters, got divorced, lived a gaudy life so high and wide that it seemed like a parody of an American success story. And he kept selling records, well over 500 million ₅ in all. The music got slicker and often sillier, turned from ₆ rock toward rhinestone country and spangled gospel. Only ₇ the pace remained the same. Elvis Aron Presley always lived ₈ fast, and last week at the age of 42, that was the way he died.

—*Time*

Central idea in the middle

In another kind of paragraph, details and examples come first and are summed up in a topic sentence, which is then supported

¶ *un*
3a

further with more details and examples. The point of the paragraph comes in the middle.

This paragraph form is useful when the central idea benefits from support both before it is stated (to make it more acceptable) and after (to drive the point home). After posing a question, Anne Roiphe uses this shape to illustrate the difficult idea of sentence 4:

> Why are there laws insisting on alimony and child sup- 1
> port? Well, everyone knows that men don't have an instinct 2
> to protect their young and, given half a chance, with the
> moon in the right phase, they will run off and disappear.
> Everyone assumes a mother will not let her child starve, yet 3
> it is necessary to legislate that a father must not do so. We 4
> are taught to accept the idea that men are less than decent;
> their charms may be manifold but their characters are rid-
> dled with faults. To this day I never blink if I hear that a 5
> man has gone to find his fortune in South America, having
> left his pregnant wife, his blind mother, and taken the family
> car. I still gasp in horror when I hear of a woman leaving her 6
> asthmatic infant for a rock group in Taos because I can't
> seem to avoid the assumption that men are naturally heels
> and women the ordained carriers of what little is moral in
> our dubious civilization.
> —Anne Roiphe, "Confessions of a Female Chauvinist Sow"

Central idea at the beginning and the end

You may want to state the topic sentence at the beginning and then restate it at the end to provide a new twist supported by the intervening sentences. This shape has a point at top and bottom.

In the following paragraph Jerzy Kosinski provides a topic sentence (sentence 1) and then restates it on the basis of new information (sentence 6).

> In the little world of television, all is solved within its 1
> magic 30 minutes. In spite of the commercials, the wounded 2
> hero either rises or quickly dies, lovers marry or divorce, vil-
> lains kill or are killed, addicts are cured, justice usually wins,
> and war ends. All problems are solved again this week, as 3
> they were last, and will be next week. Life on TV must be 4

visual. This means single-faceted, revealed in a simple 5
speech and through the obvious gesture. No matter how 6
deep the mystery or ambiguity, the TV camera claims it has
penetrated it.

—Jerzy Kosinski, "TV as Baby Sitter"

Writers sometimes restate their topic sentence in a last-ditch
effort to rescue a paragraph whose middle part has gone astray. But
trying to achieve unity by forcing it will not work. To be most effective, a restated topic sentence must gain from all the sentences preceding it.

Central idea at the beginning and in the middle

In another paragraph shape the central idea is stated, developed briefly, then restated and perhaps added to, and developed
some more. The point appears twice, in beginning and middle.

This form gives a writer flexibility, because the topic can be examined a bit at a time. In the following paragraph about his childhood
friend Wallace, the author states his topic in sentence 1, restates
part of it in sentence 2, and restates the remainder in sentence 6.

The two most expressive things about him were his 1
mouth and the pockets of his jacket. By looking at his 2
mouth, one could tell whether he was plotting evil or had recently accomplished. If he was bent upon malevolence, 3
his lips were all puckered up, like those of a billiard player
about to make a difficult shot. After the deed was done, the 4
pucker was replaced by a delicate, unearthly smile. How a 5
teacher who knew anything about boys could miss the fact
that both expressions were masks of Satan I'm sure I don't
know. Wallace's pockets were less interesting than his 6
mouth, perhaps, but more spectacular in a way. The side 7
pockets of his jacket bulged out over his pudgy haunches
like burro hampers. They were filled with tools—screw- 8
drivers, pliers, files, wrenches, wire cutters, nail sets, and I
don't know what else. In addition to all this, one pocket al- 9
ways contained a rolled-up copy of *Popular Mechanics*,
while from the top of the other protruded *Scientific American* or some other such magazine. His breast pocket con- 10
tained, besides a large collection of fountain pens and mechanical pencils, a picket fence of drill bits, gimlets, kitchen
knives, and other pointed instruments. When he walked, he 11
clinked and jangled and pealed.

—Richard Rovere, "Wallace," *The New Yorker*

¶ *un*

3a

This paragraph model has several hazards, because its effective use requires making and following a plan. As in the diamond-shaped model, the restated or enlarged topic must be closely related to the first topic, or the paragraph will go awry. And the second statement should not attempt to cover up a lack of unity.

Central idea not stated

Sometimes a paragraph's topic sentence will be contained in the previous paragraph or will be so obvious that it need not be stated explicitly. The following paragraph, from an essay on the actor Humphrey Bogart, has no explicit topic sentence.

> Usually he wore the trench coat unbuttoned, just tied with the belt, and a slouch hat, rarely tilted. Sometimes it was a captain's cap and a yachting jacket. Almost always his trousers were held up by a cowboy belt. You know the kind: one an Easterner waiting for a plane out of Phoenix buys just as a joke and then takes a liking to. Occasionally, he'd hitch up his slacks with it, and he often jabbed his thumbs behind it, his hands ready for a fight or a dame.
>
> —Peter Bogdanovich, "Bogie in Excelsis"

The effectiveness of this paragraph rests on the power of details to describe Bogart. Thus a stated topic sentence—such as "Bogart's character could be seen in the details of his clothing"—not only would weaken the paragraph but would contradict its intention.

Producing a paragraph without a topic sentence does not release the writer from the need to unify. The topic must be firmly in the writer's mind and supported by well-chosen details, so the reader does not have to struggle to understand.

EXERCISE 1

Identify the central idea in each paragraph below and describe the paragraph's "shape."

1.   You can make computers that are almost human. In some respects they are superhuman; they can beat most of us at chess, memorize whole telephone books at a glance, compose music of a certain kind and write obscure poetry, diagnose heart ailments, send personal invitations to vast parties, even go transiently crazy. No one has yet programmed a computer to be of two minds

about a hard problem, or to burst out laughing, but that may come. Sooner or later, there will be real human hardware, great whirring, clicking cabinets intelligent enough to read magazines and vote, able to think rings around the rest of us.

—Lewis Thomas, *The Lives of a Cell*

2.　At each step, with every graduation from one level of education to the next, the refrain from bystanders was strangely the same: "Your parents must be so proud of you." I suppose that my parents were proud, although I suspect, too, that they felt more than pride alone as they watched me advance through my education. They seemed to know that my education was separating us from one another, making it difficult to resume familiar intimacies. Mixed with the instincts of parental pride, a certain hurt also communicated itself— too private ever to be adequately expressed in words, but real nonetheless.

—Richard Rodriguez, "Going Home Again"

3.　Calvin Coolidge was a champion of order in a time of disorder. He opposed progressivism when it was attracting thousands. He weeded out corruption when corruption was the order of the day. He urged thrift when everyone was spending like mad. He never smiled when most people seemed to smile day and night. The 1920s thus saw a bizarre mismatch of presidential character and popular feeling, yet President Coolidge was enormously popular. His "I do not choose to run" in 1927 was a blow to the nation.

—A student

4.　But, in a larger sense, we cannot dedicate—we cannot consecrate—we cannot hallow—this ground. The brave men, living and dead, who struggled here have consecrated it, far above our poor power to add or detract. The world will little note, nor long remember, what we say here, but it can never forget what they did here. It is for us the living, rather, to be dedicated here to the unfinished work which they who fought here have thus far so nobly advanced. It is rather for us to be here dedicated to the great task remaining before us— that from these honored dead we take increased devotion to that cause for which they gave the last full measure of devotion; that we here highly resolve that these dead shall not have died in vain; that this nation, under God, shall have a new birth of freedom; and that government of the people, by the people, for the people, shall not perish from the earth.

—Abraham Lincoln, "The Gettysburg Address"

¶ *un*
3a

EXERCISE 2

The paragraphs below contain ideas or details that do not support their central idea. Identify the topic sentence in each paragraph and delete the unrelated material.

1.   In the southern part of the state, some people still 1 live much as they did a century ago. They use coal- or 2 wood-burning stoves for heating and cooking. Their 3 homes do not have electricity or indoor bathrooms or running water. The towns can't afford to put in sewers 4 or power lines, because they don't receive adequate funding from the state and federal governments. Beside 5 most homes there is a garden where fresh vegetables are gathered for canning. Small pastures nearby sup- 6 port livestock, including cattle, pigs, horses, and chickens. Most of the people have cars or trucks, but the ve- 7 hicles are old and beat-up from traveling on unpaved roads.

2.   Most people don't realize how difficult it is to work 1 and go to school at the same time. If you want to make 2 good grades but need to pay your own way, the burdens are tremendous. I work in an office sixteen hours a 3 week. Each term I have to work out a tight schedule 4 that will let me take the courses I want and still be at work when I'm needed. I like the job. The people there 5,6 are pleasant, and they are eager to help me learn. In the 7 end my job will be good training for the kind of managerial position I hope to have some day, because I'm gaining useful experience in office procedures and working with people. It's hard for me to have a job and 8 go to school, but when I graduate both will make me more employable.

EXERCISE 3

Select the details below that relate to the topic sentence provided. Then use the relevant details to write a unified paragraph. (If you prefer, select your own topic for a unified paragraph.)

Topic sentence

The characters in F. Scott Fitzgerald's novels can be seen as re-creations of himself and his wife Zelda.

Characters

people of the Jazz Age
handsome and beautiful
rich and famous
often couldn't find one person to settle with
lived high lives in fancy American and European hotels
sometimes faulted by critics as unreal people

FITZGERALDS
named the Jazz Age
glamorous, wealthy, and adored by the public
both died young and broken
lived at the best hotels in Europe and U.S.
talented—Zelda as a dancer, Scott as a writer
partied constantly
danced in the fountain at the Plaza Hotel

¶ *coh*
3b

3b
Achieving paragraph coherence

A paragraph is unified if it holds together—if its details and examples support the central idea. A paragraph is **coherent** if readers can see *how* the paragraph holds together without having to puzzle out the writer's reasons for adding each new sentence.

The paragraph with which this chapter started (p. 45) is coherent. As the writer moves from one sentence to the next, we move with him, easily. The following paragraph is not coherent, because the relations among the thoughts are blurred.

> No matter how often you talk about it or do it, sailing is 1
> always interesting. The wind is the reason. I never knew 2,3
> from one moment to the next what it would do. The element 4
> of surprise adds tension and also excitement. It will be mad- 5
> deningly calm for an hour and then suddenly blow out the
> sail and tilt the boat. A person could be hurt by a swinging 6
> boom and dumped into the water when the boat tips. Of 7
> course, the potential in these surprises is what makes me an
> avid sailor.

This paragraph is unified. The writer first asserts his interest in sailing and then sticks to the reasons why it interests him. But the paragraph is still hard to read. Sentences do not follow each other smoothly. Verb tense changes in almost every line (*talk, is, knew, adds, will be, blow, could be hurt, is*), and so does person (*you, I, it, a person, me*). *It* in sentence 5 seems at first to refer to *the element* or *excitement* in sentence 4 but turns out to mean *the wind*. And sentence 6, though its content contributes to the whole paragraph, shifts the main subject abruptly from the wind's action to the boat's action. Each time we confront a tense or person change, a word with unclear meaning like *it,* or an abrupt shift in subject, we must stop, even briefly, to figure out the writer's meaning. And every stop we make breaks our concentration and reduces the chances that we will respond appreciatively to what the author is trying to say.

Achieving paragraph coherence consists primarily of thinking through what you want to say—your main topic and the supporting points you want to make. Your sentences then are likely to fall in with each other, the relations staying clear, the transitions from sentence to sentence occurring smoothly. But there are several ways to make relations clear. These include organizing the paragraph according to a plan; using parallel sentence structure, repetition, and pronouns; being consistent in such matters as person, tense, and voice; and using transitional expressions.

1
Organizing the paragraph

Like patterns of essay organization (see 1f), patterns of paragraph organization correspond to readers' expectations of how thoughts should be arranged. When your readers can accurately anticipate the next sentence—or when each sentence, even if not predictable, seems natural and inevitable when read—then you've done much of the work of achieving coherence. However, when you violate an expected pattern, you frustrate your readers and risk losing their attention altogether. In the following paragraph George Orwell arranges details so we focus more and more clearly on the men in the cells.

> It was in Burma, a sodden morning of the rains. A sickly [1,2] light, like yellow tinfoil, was slanting over the high walls into the jail yard. We were waiting outside the condemned cells, [3] a row of sheds fronted with double bars, like small animal cages. Each cell measured about ten feet by ten and was [4] quite bare within except for a plank bed and a pot for drinking water. In some of them brown, silent men were squat- [5] ting at the inner bars, with their blankets draped round them. These were the condemned men, due to be hanged [6] within the next week or two.
> —George Orwell, "A Hanging"

Simply moving sentence 2 to follow sentence 4 shows how a careless arrangement of details can weaken a paragraph.

> It was in Burma, a sodden morning of the rains. We [1,3] were waiting outside the condemned cells, a row of sheds fronted with double bars, like small cages. Each cell meas- [4] ured about ten feet by ten and was quite bare within except for a plank bed and a pot for drinking water. A sickly light, [2] like yellow tinfoil, was slanting over the high walls into the jail yard. In some of the cells brown, silent men were squat- [5] ting at the inner bars, with their blankets draped round them. These were the condemned men, due to be hanged [6] within the next week or two.

Spatial pattern

George Orwell's paragraph is organized in a **spatial pattern.** A spatial paragraph locates the reader in one place and scans a scene from there, looking outward or (as in Orwell's paragraph) moving inward from a farther point to a closer one. A spatial organization parallels the way we actually look at a place for the first time, and thus conforms to readers' expectations. It is especially useful in writing descriptions of places or people, whether in descriptive or expository essays or in fiction.

¶ *coh*

3b

Chronological pattern

Another familiar way of organizing the elements of a paragraph is **chronologically**—that is, in order of their occurrence through time. In a chronological paragraph, as in experience, the earliest events come first, followed by more recent ones.

> There is no warning at all—only a steady rising intensity 1
> of the sun's light. Within minutes the change is noticeable; 2
> within an hour, the nearer worlds are burning. The star is ex- 3
> panding like a balloon, blasting off shells of gas at a million
> miles an hour as it blows its outer layers into space. Within a 4
> day, it is shining with such supernal brilliance that it gives
> off more light than *all the other suns in the Universe com-*
> *bined.* If it had planets, they are now no more than flecks of 5
> flame in the still-expanding shells of fire. The conflagration 6
> will burn for weeks before the dying star collapses back into
> quiescence.
> —Arthur C. Clarke, "The Star of the Magi"

Because the events in this paragraph are related in clear sequence, we receive a clear picture of the death of a distant star. The author has also provided signals (such as *within minutes* in sentence 2) that let us know how much time separates events. These transitional devices (see 3b-6) alert us to each new event and clarify relations between events.

Like spatial paragraphs, chronological paragraphs can be almost automatically coherent because readers expect the progression of events. Chronological paragraphs appear most often in narrative essays, though they are useful in almost any kind of essay.

General-to-specific and specific-to-general patterns

When a paragraph's subject dictates that neither a spatial nor a chronological pattern is appropriate, your arrangement of details must be based solely on common ways of thinking. One arrangement is to order details from the **general to the specific,** as in the following paragraph.

> Perhaps the simplest fact about sleep is that individual 1
> needs for it vary widely. Most adults sleep between seven 2
> and nine hours, but occasionally people turn up who need
> twelve hours or so, while some rare types can get by on
> three or four. Rarest of all are those legendary types who re- 3
> quire almost no sleep at all; respected researchers have re-
> cently studied three such people. One of them—a healthy, 4
> happy woman in her seventies—sleeps about an hour every
> two or three days. The other two are men in early middle 5
> age, who get by on a few minutes a night. One of them com- 6
> plains about the daily fifteen minutes or so he's forced to
> "waste" in sleeping.
>
> —Lawrence A. Mayer, "The Confounding Enemy of Sleep"

In moving from the general statement of the first sentence, to the broad examples of sentences 2 and 3, to the very specific examples of sentences 4, 5, and 6, this paragraph parallels the triangular shape—topic sentence first—that we discussed on page 48.

The other expected arrangement of details in a paragraph is from the **specific to the general.** Often this pattern corresponds to the inverted triangle shape, because the topic sentence comes at the end. The paragraph about Elvis Presley (p. 49) is an excellent example of the specific-to-general organization.

Less dramatic–to–more dramatic pattern

Details may be arranged in order of increasing drama or importance, saving the punch for the end. Increasing drama is the basis for organizing this paragraph:

> B. F. Skinner has never responded fully to any of his 1
> critics, despite their number and stature. Often he has failed 2
> to understand them. Sometimes he has even branded them 3
> as neurotic or even psychotic. Occasionally he has seemed 4
> to imply that he himself is beyond criticism. "When I met 5
> him, he was convinced he was a genius," Yvonne Skinner
> remembers.   *—Time*

2
Using parallel structures

Another way to achieve coherence, although not necessarily in every paragraph, is to use **parallelism**—similar structures for similar elements within a sentence or between sentences. Parallel structure appears in sentences 3 to 5 of our first paragraph (p. 45), where the writer reuses the sentence pattern set by *They give us . . . when we'd much prefer. . . .* In the paragraph below Joan Didion uses parallel structure with equal effectiveness.

> Joan Baez was a personality before she was entirely a person, and, like anyone to whom that happens, she is in a sense the hapless victim of what others have seen in her, written about her, wanted her to be and not to be. The roles assigned to her are various, but variations on a single theme. She is the Madonna of the disaffected. She is the pawn of the protest movement. She is the unhappy analysand. She is the singer who would not train her voice, the rebel who drives the Jaguar too fast, the Rima who hides with the birds and the deer. Above all, she is the girl who "feels" things, who has hung on to the freshness and pain of adolescence, the girl ever wounded, ever young.
> —Joan Didion, "Where the Kissing Never Stops"

(sentence numbers in margin: 1, 2, 3,4, 5,6, 7)

In this paragraph Didion uses parallel structure both between and within sentences. Sentences 3 through 7 have the same basic structure: *She is the Madonna. . . . She is the pawn. . . . She is the unhappy analysand. . . . She is the singer. . . . Above all, she is the girl. . . .* Within sentence 6 parallel structures echo each other (*the singer who . . . the rebel who . . . the Rima who*) and are echoed in sentence 7. (*the girl who*). The similarity in structures ties the paragraph neatly together. (See Chapter 17 for more discussion of using parallel structures within sentences. And see Chapter 15 for advice on avoiding faulty parallelism.)

3

Repeating or restating words and word groups

You can repeat words or word groups to link sentences and ideas and make paragraphs coherent. In the following paragraph the repetition of *mother* and *face* not only focuses our attention on the two important elements of the paragraph but also holds the paragraph together.

> I look at photographs of my mother when she was a young and a very beautiful bride. It is odd to think that when they were taken, my mother was 20 years younger than I am now. The stranger in the photograph—fragile, shy, with a look of dewy vulnerability—bears no resemblance to the self-contained, armored, aloof woman I call Mother now. I search the face in the photographs compulsively; my feelings are opaque and obscure, but I sense that if I can

(sentence numbers in margin: 1, 2, 3, 4)

"read" that lovely face, I will understand not only my own fate but that of my daughter.
—Barbara G. Harrison, "Finding the Way to Be Friends"

In the paragraph below the repetition is just as effective but more difficult to see because the writer rewords rather than repeats the similar ideas. The paragraph is about the marriage between an American divorcée and a man who was the king of England.

> When the sweet, not-all-that-young prince with the melancholy eye met the fascinating lady from Baltimore in 1931, he asked her if she missed central heating, being far away from home. The subject, of course, was of absolutely no interest to either one of them, and they were thus able to go right ahead and start up a romance that only came to an end on May 28 when the Duke of Windsor died in Paris at the age of 77. Their love affair, as old folks with good memories will tell you somewhat incorrectly, rocked the very foundations of an empire. Actually it did cause a frightful row in 1936 when David, who had been Prince of Wales but was just then the still-to-be-crowned King Edward VIII, decided he wanted to marry Wallis Simpson, who was getting her second divorce. Such an astounding idea, if carried out, would have dreadfully embarrassed the Tory government. So Edward Albert Christian George Andrew Patrick David, who's always been happiest away from the palace, anyway, renounced his throne.
>
> —*Life*

(The sentence numbers 1–6 appear in the right margin of the above paragraph.)

Line by line, the writer of this paragraph adds information to the story by changing the characters' names and otherwise rewording key phrases. The prince of sentence 1 becomes a person with seven names by sentence 6, while the fascinating lady becomes a woman who was getting her second divorce. The romance of sentence 2 turns into a love affair by sentence 3. And the prince's decision to marry Wallis Simpson in sentence 4 becomes the "astounding idea" of sentence 5. The rewording not only emphasizes the paragraph's important ideas—the personalities involved, their romance, and its effect on the government of England—but links sentences into a coherent paragraph.

4
Using pronouns

The previous example illustrates yet another device for achieving paragraph coherence—the use of pronouns. Pronouns refer to and function as nouns (see 5a-3), and they can help relate sentences to each other. In the paragraph below the pronouns *he*, *him*, and *his* make it clear that the patient is still the subject while enabling the writer to avoid repeated use of *the patient* or *the patient's*.

> The experience is a familiar one to many emergency-room medics. A patient who has been pronounced dead and unexpectedly recovers later describes what happened to him during those moments—sometimes hours—when his body exhibited no signs of life. According to one repeated account, the patient feels himself rushing through a long-dark tunnel while noise rings in his ears. Suddenly, he finds himself outside his own body looking down with curious detachment at a medical team's efforts to resuscitate him. He hears what is said, notes what is happening but cannot communicate with anyone. Soon, his attention is drawn to other presences in the room—spirits of dead relatives or friends—who communicate with him nonverbally. Gradually he is drawn to a vague "being of light." This being invites him to evaluate his life and shows him highlights of his past in panoramic vision. The patient longs to stay with the being of light but is reluctantly drawn back into his physical body and recovers.
> —Kenneth L. Woodward, "Life After Death?"

The pronouns in this paragraph give it coherence, in part because it's clear what noun the pronouns refer to. The opposite effect will occur if the reader can't tell exactly what noun a pronoun is meant to refer to. (For a discussion of the problems associated with pronoun reference, see Chapter 12.)

5
Being consistent

Being consistent is the most subtle way to achieve paragraph coherence, because readers are aware of consistency only when it is absent. Consistency (or the lack of it) occurs primarily in the person and number of nouns and pronouns and the tense of verbs (see Chapter 13). Although some shifts will be necessary because of meaning, unnecessary shifts will prevent a reader from easily following the development of ideas. The following paragraphs shift person, number, and tense, respectively, destroying coherence.

> An enjoyable form of exercise is modern dance. If *one* wants to stay in shape, *you* will find that dance tones and strengthens most muscles. The leaping and stretching *you* do also improves *a person's* balance and poise. And *I* found that *my* posture improved after only a few months of dancing.

> Politics is not the activity for everyone. It requires

quickness and patience at the same time. *A politician* must 3
like speaking to large groups of people and fielding questions without having time to think of the answers. *Politicians* 4
must also be willing to compromise with the people *they*
represent. And no matter how good *a politician* is, *they* must 5
give up on becoming popular with all constituents. It isn't 6
possible.

I *am developing* an interest in filmmaking. I *tried* to take 1,2
courses that relate to camera work or theater, and I *have
read* books about the technical and artistic sides of movies.
Though I *would have liked* to get a job on a movie set right 3
away, I *will* probably *continue* my formal education and
training in filmmaking after college. There simply *aren't* 4
enough jobs available for all those who *wanted* to be in
films but *have* no direct experience.

6
Using transitional expressions

The methods for achieving coherence discussed above give
readers the sense that sentences are related without actually stating
the relations. But writers also use specific words and word groups to
draw clear connections between ideas. Sometimes the omission of
these words or word groups will make an otherwise coherent paragraph choppy and hard to follow, as this student paragraph shows.

The drivers in this town have to be the worst in the 1
world. They drive in the left lane at 20 mph. They pass on 2,3
the right. They back out of driveways without looking. I saw 4,5
a man turn right from the left lane of the expressway. He 6
didn't look to see if there was any traffic in the right lane. A 7
car stopped on a steep hill. The driver got out to check his 8
turn signals. Several cars behind his were stalled. 9

This paragraph is unified and fundamentally coherent because the
sentences do seem related to each other. However, we can only
guess that the writer might have intended the precise relationships
indicated by the italic words in this revision:

The drivers in this town have to be the worst in the 1
world. They drive in the left lane at 20 mph, pass on the 2
right, *and* back out of driveways without looking. *Yesterday* I 3
saw a man turn right from the left lane of the expressway,
without looking to see if there was any traffic in the right
lane. *Then* a car stopped on a steep hill, *and* the driver got 4
out to check his turn signals. *As a result,* several cars behind 5
his were stalled.

The italicized words and word groups are called **transitional**

expressions. They help to state relationships clearly and thus enhance paragraph coherence. The following is a partial list of transitional expressions, arranged by the functions they perform.

To ADD OR SHOW SEQUENCE

again, also, and, and then, besides, equally important, finally, first, further, furthermore, in addition, in the first place, last, moreover, next, second, too

To COMPARE

in the same way, likewise, similarly

To CONTRAST

although, and yet, but, but at the same time, despite, even so, even though, for all that, however, in contrast, in spite of, nevertheless, notwithstanding, on the contrary, on the other hand, regardless, still, though, yet

To GIVE EXAMPLES OR INTENSIFY

after all, an illustration of, for example, for instance, indeed, in fact, it is true, of course, specifically, that is, to illustrate, truly

To INDICATE PLACE

above, adjacent to, below, elsewhere, farther on, here, near, nearby, on the other side, opposite to, there, to the east, to the left

To INDICATE TIME

after a while, afterward, as long as, as soon as, at last, at length, at that time, before, earlier, formerly, immediately, in the meantime, in the past, lately, later, meanwhile, now, presently, shortly, simultaneously, since, so far, soon, subsequently, then, thereafter, until, until now, when

To REPEAT, SUMMARIZE, OR CONCLUDE

all in all, altogether, as has been said, in brief, in conclusion, in other words, in particular, in short, in simpler terms, in summary, on the whole, that is, to put it differently, to summarize

To SHOW CAUSE OR EFFECT

accordingly, as a result, because, consequently, for this purpose, hence, otherwise, since, then, therefore, thereupon, thus, to this end, with this object

The following paragraph by René Dubos illustrates how transitional expressions like these can link ideas and smooth the way between sentences. (The transitional expressions are italicized.)

    The losing animal in a struggle saves itself from destruc- 1
tion by an act of submission, an act usually recognized and

accepted by the winner. *In some cases, for instance,* the loser   2
presents to its rival a vulnerable part of its body *such as* the
top of the head or the fleshy part of the neck. The central   3
nervous system of the winner recognizes the "meaning" of
the presentation, *and* the instinct to kill is inhibited. *Typical*   4
of this natural pattern is the behavior of two wolves in combat. *As soon as* one of the animals realizes it cannot win, it   5
offers its vulnerable throat to the stronger wolf; *instead of*
taking advantage of the opportunity, the victor relents, *even*
though an instant earlier it had appeared frantic to reach the
now proffered jugular vein.

—René Dubos, "Territoriality and Dominance"

(For a discussion of transitional paragraphs, see 3d-3.)

7
Combining devices to achieve coherence

The devices we have examined for achieving coherence rarely
appear one at a time in effective paragraphs. Writers must often use
a combination of sensible organization, parallelism, repetition, pronouns, consistency, and transitional expressions in any single paragraph or group of paragraphs to carry the full weight of paragraph—
or essay—coherence.

EXERCISE 4

Analyze the organizing principle of each paragraph below. How
does the paragraph's organization lend it coherence?

1.   I wrote wildly pornographic books when I was in   1
junior high and fantasized about a love affair with my
math teacher, but when I went—alone—to dances my
partner (if I danced at all) would be some wise guy with
a hand buzzer and a cowlick. It seems to me now a
fairly poignant picture: two 13- or 14-year-olds sitting
stiffly on folding chairs across the room from one another, the boy crossing to the girl, grunting something
that indicates he'd consent to dance with her, and then
jerking frantically—eyes never meeting, bodies never
touching—under a crepe paper tulip for three minutes
while the Rolling Stones sing "Let's spend the night together, Now I need you more than ever. . . ." And then,   3
when the song is over, the two stop abruptly and go
back to their chairs without a word.

—Joyce Maynard, "My Secret Life
with the Rolling Stones"

2.   A single knoll rises out of the plain in Oklahoma,   1
north and west of the Wichita Range. For my people,   2

¶ *coh*

3b

the Kiowas, it is an old landmark, and they gave it the ₃
name Rainy Mountain. The hardest weather in the
world is there. Winter brings blizzards, hot tornadic ₄
winds arise in the spring, and in summer the prairie is
an anvil's edge. The grass turns brittle and brown, and it ₅
cracks beneath your feet. There are green belts along ₆
the rivers and creeks, linear groves of hickory and pe-
can, willow and witch hazel. At a distance in July or Au- ₇
gust the steaming foliage seems almost to writhe in fire.
Great green and yellow grasshoppers are everywhere in ₈
the tall grass, popping up like corn to sting the flesh,
and tortoises crawl about on the red earth, going nowhere in the plenty of time. Loneliness is an aspect of ₉
the land. All things in the plain are isolate; there is no ₁₀
confusion of objects in the eye, but one hill or one tree
or one man. To look upon that landscape in the early ₁₁
morning, with the sun at your back, is to lose the sense
of proportion. Your imagination comes to life, and this, ₁₂
you think, is where Creation was begun.
                    —N. Scott Momaday, "The Way to Rainy Mountain"

3.   One must descend to the basement and move along ₁
a confusing mazelike hall to reach it. Twice the passage ₂
seems to lead against a blank wall; then at last one en-
ters the brightly lighted auditorium. And here, finally, ₃
are the social workers at the reception desks; and there,
waiting upon the benches rowed beneath the pipes carrying warmth and water to the floors above, are the
patients. One sees white-jacketed psychiatrists carrying ₄
charts appear and vanish behind screens that form the
improvised interviewing cubicles. All is an atmosphere ₅
of hurried efficiency; and the concerned faces of the
patients are brightened by the friendly smiles and low-
pitched voices of the expert workers. One has entered ₆
the Lafargue Psychiatric Clinic.
                    —Ralph Ellison, *Shadow and Act*

EXERCISE 5

Identify the central idea in each group of sentences below; then
rearrange the sentences to form a well-organized and coherent
paragraph.

1.   We hear the negative side too often—probably be- ₁
cause so much of it is true. But we should not forget ₂
what the Postal Service does *right*. The total volume of ₃
mail delivered by the Postal Service each year makes up
more than half the total delivered in all the world. Its ₄
70,000 employees handle 90,000,000,000 pieces of mail
each year. In fact, on any given day the Postal Service ₅
delivers almost as much mail as the rest of the world

combined. That means over 1,250,000 pieces per em-   6
ployee and over 400 pieces per man, woman, and child
in the country. And when was the last time they failed   7
to deliver something of yours?

2.   A single visit to New York City will tell you why the   1
city is both loved and hated by so many people.
Whether you arrive by car, bus, train, plane, or boat, the   2
skyline will take your breath away. Your view will only   3
be strengthened when you walk down the canyons
formed by skyscrapers, look in the shop windows, go to
the theater or a museum, stroll in the neighborhoods
where no one speaks English. And the streets seem so   4
dirty: cans and bags and newspapers lie in the gutters
and on the sidewalks or sometimes fly across your path.
You'll know right off that this has to be the greatest city   5
on earth. But all is not perfect—far from it. You start to   6,7
notice the noise of traffic and get annoyed at the
crowds. Even the people who do speak English won't   8
smile or say "Excuse me" or give you good directions.
After a few days, when your reactions balance out, you   9
have the same love-hate feelings as everyone else.

EXERCISE 6

Study the paragraphs in Exercise 1 (pp. 52–53) for the authors' use
of various devices to achieve paragraph coherence. Look especially for parallel structures and ideas, repetition, use of pronouns,
and transitional expressions.

EXERCISE 7

The paragraph below is made incoherent by inconsistencies in person, number, or tense. Identify the inconsistencies and revise the
paragraph to give it coherence.

I rebel against the idea of males always being the   1
sole family provider. For me to be happy, I needed to   2
feel useful, and so I work to support myself and my
daughter. I did not feel that it is wrong for one to be a   3
housewife while a man supports your household—but
that way is not for me. I enjoy the business world, and I   4
have been pleased with my job. Working, I make   5
enough now to support the two of us, and I know that
when I graduate, I will be able to earn even more. I can   6
do very well as my own provider.

EXERCISE 8

Write one coherent paragraph using all the facts below, combining
and rewriting the sentences as necessary to introduce parallelism,

repetition, pronouns, consistency, and transitional expressions. Or, if you prefer, choose your own topic and write a paragraph that uses these devices.

> The potential of hypnosis lies in its power to relax people. Hypnosis can relax us without drugs. Hypnosis is unlike drugs. Hypnosis is not addictive. Hypnosis has no dangerous side effects for you. Hypnosis is inexpensive, even if people haven't learned self-hypnosis. Hypnosis can be as effective as any drug in relieving tension. Tension is one of the major contributors to people's psychological problems. With hypnosis, you can reduce pain. People can achieve sleep at night. One can stay alert during the day. Your self-confidence may increase. You can use your time more effectively. All these things are possible with hypnosis alone. No drugs are necessary.

3c
Developing the paragraph

A paragraph may be both unified and coherent but still be skimpy, unconvincing, or otherwise inadequate. The paragraph below is unified: it sticks to the topic of bad television commercials. And it is also coherent, in that the relations between sentences are apparent. But it is not a good paragraph.

> Despite complaints from viewers, television com- 1
> mercials aren't getting any more realistic. Their makers still 2
> present idealized people in unreal situations. And the ad- 3
> vertisers also persist in showing a version of male-female
> relationships that can't exist in more than two households.
> What do the advertisers know about us, or about how we 4
> see ourselves, that makes them continue to plunge millions
> of dollars into these kinds of commercials?

This paragraph is all bones, no flesh. We know the writer's main ideas, but we know nothing about the specific commercials that prompted the ideas. The paragraph lacks **development,** completeness. It does not convince us that we know everything both possible and necessary to evaluate the writer's central point in sentence 1.

Paragraph development—the adequate support of main ideas so that readers stay interested and come away convinced—always involves being specific by supplying details, examples, or reasons for your assertions. Very often it also involves a specific method of development that is determined by your topic and what you want to say about it.

1
Using details, examples, and reasons

Details, examples (or illustrations), and reasons are the heart of paragraph development. In paragraphs they enter into the whole essay (see 1e-1), and through paragraphs they convince your readers (see 4c). They are usually the basis of the general statements you make in any writing that involves explanation or description, as most writing does. To appreciate those statements, your readers need to know what you base them on. Here is the actual version of the bare-bones paragraph we just discussed. Notice how the writer's descriptions of commercials make a skeleton paragraph into an interesting piece of writing.

> Despite complaints from veiwers, television com- 1
> mercials aren't getting any more realistic. Their makers still 2
> present idealized people in unreal situations. Friendly shop- 3
> keepers stock only their favorite brand of toothpaste or cof-
> fee or soup. A mother cleans and buffs her kitchen floor to a 4
> mirror finish so her baby can play on it. A rosy-cheeked 5
> pregnant woman uses two babies, two packaged diapers
> neatly dissected, and two ink blotters, to demonstrate the
> diaper's superior absorbancy to her equally rosy-cheeked
> and pregnant friend. The advertisers also persist in showing 6
> a version of male-female relationships that can't exist in
> more than two households. The wife panics because a med- 7
> dlesome neighbor points out that her husband's shirt is
> dirty. Or she fears for her marriage because her finicky hus- 8
> band doesn't like her coffee. What do the advertisers know 9
> about us, or about how we see ourselves, that makes them
> continue to plunge millions of dollars into these kinds of
> commercials?

This paragraph is developed by examples—specific, concrete illustrations of more general, abstract statements. The examples use details—words like *rosy-cheeked, meddlesome,* and *finicky*—that not only set the scene for us but also tell us exactly what the author's attitude is.

In the following paragraph Edward T. Hall uses a single extended example to support his point (sentence 1) about cultural differences in the ways people communicate.

One of my earliest discoveries in the field of inter- 1
cultural communication was that the position of the bodies
of people in conversation varies with the culture. Even so, it 2
used to puzzle me that a special Arab friend seemed unable
to walk and talk at the same time. After years in the United 3
States, he could not bring himself to stroll along, facing forward while talking. Our progress would be arrested while he 4
edged ahead, cutting slightly in front of me and turning side-
ways so we could see each other. Once in this position, he 5
would stop. His behavior was explained when I learned that 6
for the Arabs to view the other person peripherally is regarded as impolite, and to sit or stand back-to-back is considered very rude. You must be involved when interacting 7
with Arabs who are friends.
                              —Edward T. Hall, *The Hidden Dimension*

¶ *dev*

3c

2
Choosing a method of development

Sometimes you may have difficulty thinking of details, examples, or reasons, or you may have them in mind but not see a way to
use them effectively. Then you can draw on the various methods of
paragraph development. Experienced writers use these methods all
the time, though usually not consciously. Inexperienced writers can
ask themselves questions that will suggest not only a method of development but also the supporting details.

What is it? (Definition)

Definition involves naming the class of things to which something belongs and the characteristics that distinguish it from the
other members of the class. You can define concrete, noncontrover-
sial terms in a single sentence: *A knife is a cutting instrument* (its
class) *with a sharp blade set in a handle* (the characteristics that set
it off from, say, scissors or a razor blade). But defining a complicated, abstract, or controversial topic requires extended explanation (see 4b-2), and you may need to devote a whole paragraph to it.
Such a definition uses details and perhaps one or more examples to
identify the subject's characteristics. It may also involve other methods of paragraph development discussed below, such as division
(separating things into different parts), classification (combining
things into groups), or comparison and contrast.

The following paragraphs are both developed by definition,
though their subjects could not be more different.

A soap opera deals with the plights and problems 1
brought about in the lives of its permanent principal charac-

ters by the advent and interference of one group of individuals after another. Thus, a soap opera is an endless sequence of narratives whose only cohesive element is the eternal presence of its bedevilled and beleaguered principal characters. A narrative, or story sequence, may run from eight weeks to several months. The ending of one plot is always hooked up with the beginning of the next, but the connection is unimportant and soon forgotten. Almost all the villains in the small-town daytime serials are émigrés from the cities—gangsters, white-collar criminals, designing women, unnatural mothers, cold wives, and selfish, ruthless, and just plain cussed rich men. They always come up against a shrewdness that outwits them or destroys them, or a kindness that wins them over to the good way of life.

—James Thurber, "Ivorytown, Rinsoville, Anacinburg, and Crisco Corner"

I would define science as the systematic attempt to understand and comprehend the natural world. It is a determination to enter deeply into the natural world, not just superficially, but to achieve a rational expression in language and mathematical symbolism of the order and beauty of operation that lies behind all natural phenomena. This is what the aim of science is. Its scope is not just the external world. The scope of science includes ourselves. By that I mean that all aspects of our own experiences of ourselves—our perceptions, imaginings, emotions, and actions—everything properly comes into the purview of science.

—John C. Eccles, "The Discipline of Science"

What are its parts? (Division) Or what groups does it belong to? (Classification)

Division or **analysis** involves scrutinizing a larger subject by separating it into manageable parts or detailing its components, as we might examine a family by dividing it into its individual members—mother, father, daughter, son. **Classification** involves combining something with other, similar things or sorting individual elements into related groups or classes. Using classification to study families, we might examine different family structures in various cultures—matriarchal, patriarchal, nuclear, extended, and so on. Division and classification are so closely related that we often use them together in developing an idea, a paragraph, or an essay. Thus in analyzing the family we might first classify the types and then divide each type into the separate roles of the individual family members.

In the paragraph below Albert Einstein uses division to analyze human rights.

> In talking about human rights today, we are referring 1 primarily to the following demands: protection of the individual against arbitrary infringement by other individuals or by the government; the right to work and to adequate earnings from work; freedom of discussion and teaching; adequate participation of the individual in the formation of his government. *These* human rights are nowadays recognized 2 theoretically, although, by abundant use of formalistic, legal maneuvers, they are being violated to a much greater extent than even a generation ago. There is, however, one other hu- 3 man right which is infrequently mentioned but which seems to be destined to become very important: this is the right, or the duty, of the individual to abstain from cooperating in activities which he considers wrong or pernicious. The first 4 place in this respect must be given to the refusal of military service. I have known instances where individuals of un- 5 usual moral strength and integrity have, for that reason, come into conflict with the organs of the state. The Nurem- 6 berg Trial of the German war criminals [after World War II] was tacitly based on the recognition of the principle: criminal actions cannot be excused if committed on government orders; conscience supersedes the authority of the law of the state.
>
> —Albert Einstein, "Human Rights"

The author of the following paragraph classifies the kinds of "internal tides" (sentence 1) and further classifies us as "larks" and "owls" (sentence 2).

> The person who listens to his internal tides will sense 1 that his attention ebbs and flows in periods of roughly an hour and a half (ultradian cycles) while his strength and vitality show daily (circadian) and monthly (infradian) peaks. Some of us are larks who rise swiftly from sleep with body 2 temperature high and ready for action; others are owls, whose circadian rhythms bring them to full activity late in the day. Larks and owls differ in the shape of their phys- 3 iological circadian rhythms—and our society punishes the inconvenient owl, who rarely appears in a morning class. Even as small children we are trained not to listen to our 4 bodies or trust our sensations. We are forced to attend 5 classes from eight to three or work an arbitrary shift. No 6 wonder we are out of touch with our bodies, and have many pathologies, by age 50.
>
> —Gay Gaer Luce, "Trust Your Body Rhythms"

How is it like, or different from, other things? (Comparison and contrast)

Contrast and **comparison** may be used separately or together to develop an idea or to relate two or more things. In the paragraph below Jacob Bronowski uses comparison to develop his view that scientific reasoning is the same as poetic imagining.

Many people believe that reasoning, and therefore sci- 1
ence, is a different activity from imagining. But this is a fal- 2
lacy, and you must root it out of your mind. The child that 3
discovers, sometimes before the age of ten, that he can
make images and move them around in his head has entered the same gateway to imagination and to reason. Rea- 4
soning is constructed with movable images just as certainly
as poetry is. You may have been told, you may still have the 5
feeling, that $E = mc^2$ is not an imaginative statement. If so, 6
you are mistaken. The symbols in that master-equation of 7
the twentieth century—the E for energy, and m for mass, and
c for the speed of light—are images for absent things or concepts, of exactly the same kind as the words "tree" or "love"
in a poem. The poet John Keats was not writing anything 8
which (for him at least) was fundamentally different from
an equation when he wrote,

"Beauty is truth, truth beauty,"—that is all
Ye know on earth, and all ye need to know.

There is no difference in the use of such words as "beauty" 9
and "truth" in the poem, and such symbols as "energy" and
"mass" in the equation.

—Jacob Bronowski, *Imagination and the University*

In the next paragraph E. B. White uses contrast to make us see the unusual beauty of most Florida days.

On many days, the dampness of the air pervades all life, 1
all living. Matches refuse to strike. The towel, hung to dry, 2,3
grows wetter by the hour. The newspaper, with its headlines 4
about integration, wilts in your hand and falls limply into
the coffee and the egg. Envelopes seal themselves. Postage 5,6
stamps mate with one another as shamelessly as grasshoppers. But most of the time the days are models of beauty 7
and wonder and comfort, with the kind sea stroking the
back of the warm sand. At evening there are great flights of 8
birds over the sea, where the light lingers; the gulls, the peli-
cans, the terns, the herons stay aloft for half an hour after
land birds have gone to roost. They hold their ancient for- 9
mations, wheel and fish over the Pass, enjoying the last of
day like children playing outdoors after suppertime.

—E. B. White, "The Ring of Time"

The most effective contrasts occur between ideas or things that are usually perceived as similar. White's days are like that. So are, say, two modern science fiction writers with different views of the future, or two photographic techniques using the Polaroid camera. Comparisons, on the other hand, are most effective when they show similarities between ideas or things usually perceived as different, such as reason and imagination in Bronowski's paragraph. And because we would expect differences in the writings of two authors a century apart, comparison could be effective in showing how they are alike.

Is it comparable to something unlike itself but more familiar to us? (Analogy)

Whereas we draw comparisons (and contrasts) between elements in the same general class (appearance and behavior, Florida days, styles of writing), we use the kind of comparison called **analogy** to link elements in different classes. Most often we use one familiar and concrete class of things to illuminate or explain another unfamiliar, complex, abstract class of things. In the paragraph below the author develops an analogy between clothing and life and uses it to contrast the attitudes of women and men toward life.

> A woman can always get some practical use from a   1
> torn-up life, Gabriel decided. She likes mending and patch-   2
> ing it, making sure the edges are straight. She spreads the   3
> last shred out and takes its measure: "What can I do with
> this remnant? How long does it need to last?" A man puts on   4
> his life ready-made. If it doesn't fit, he will try to exchange it   5
> for another. Only a fool of a man will try to adjust the   6
> sleeves or move the buttons; he doesn't know how.
> —Mavis Gallant, "Baum, Gabriel, 1935–(   )"
> *The New Yorker*

Sometimes an analogy will be offered as proof of an idea. But analogy never proves. For a discussion of false analogy, see 4d-3.

What are its causes or effects? (Cause-and-effect analysis)

When you want to analyze why something happened or what is likely to happen, then you want to determine causes and effects. **Cause-and-effect analysis** is especially useful in writing about social, economic, or political events or problems, as the following paragraphs illustrate. In the first, Barbara Tuchman examines how people in the fourteenth century explained the causes of the Black Death, the bubonic plague.

The nightmare of the plague was compounded for the ₁
fourteenth century by the awful mystery of its cause. The ₂
idea of disease carried by insect bite was undreamed of.
Fleas and rats, which were in fact the carriers, are not men- ₃
tioned in the plague writings. Contagion could be observed ₄
but not explained and thus seemed doubly sinister. The ₅
medical faculty of the University of Paris favored a theory of
poisonous air spread by a conjunction of the planets, but
the general and fundamental belief, made official by a papal
bull, was that the pestilence was divine punishment for
man's sins. Such horror could only be caused by the wrath ₆
of God. "In the year of our Lord, 1348," sadly wrote a profes- ₇
sor of law at the University of Pisa, "the hostility of God was
greater than the hostility of men."
—Barbara Tuchman, "History as Mirror"

In the next example George Wald first presents what he thinks is a
wrong link between effects and causes (sentences 1–3), then states
his analysis and supporting reasons (sentences 4–5), and finally suggests new effects that might result from a change in circumstances
(sentences 6–7). Thus Wald uses the methods of both contrast and
cause-and-effect analysis.

We are often told that the famine already in progress in ₁
increasing parts of the Third World, and hunger among the
poor in some developed countries, is somehow the fault of
the hungry. This is the familiar tactic of blaming the victim. ₂
It is frequently said that the poor should not have so many ₃
children, that they are poor because they have too many
children. All of us should realize by now that it's the other ₄
way around: People have too many children because they
are poor. Having many children is a strategy for survival ₅
among the very poor; they need to have many children so
that one or two may survive to feed them in their old age
and bury them when they die. The only way to get the poor ₆
to have fewer children is to give them some assurance that
the children they have will survive. Once that is achieved, ₇
they will be glad to have smaller families.
—George Wald, "There Isn't Much Time"

(For a discussion of the mistakes often made in analyzing
cause-and-effect relationships, see 4d.)

How does it work? (Process analysis)

When you describe how something works, you are describing
a **process,** the steps taken to get from one point to another. Paragraphs developed by analyzing a process are usually organized
chronologically or spatially, as the steps in the process occur or be-

come apparent. The following paragraph traces the process by which a rising air current known as a *thermal* is created.

The second type of rising current is heated air, known 1 as a thermal. A field warmed by the sun heats the air above 2 it, causing it to expand and rise. If the field is surrounded by 3 a cooler forest, the heated pocket of air may rise in the form of a great bubble or of a column. Everyone has seen birds 4 soaring in wide circles over land; usually they are coasting around the periphery of a rising air column. Over the ocean, 5 when the water warms colder air above it, the air rises in a whole group of columns, packed together like the cells of a honeycomb. If the wind then freshens, it may blow the col- 6 umns over until they lie horizontally on the water. The flat- 7 lying columns of air may rotate around their axes, each in the opposite direction from its neighbor. This has been dem- 8 onstrated in the laboratory by blowing smoke-filled air over a warmed surface at increasing speed, corresponding to an increase in the wind over the ocean. If you put your two fists 9 together and rotate them, the right clockwise and the left counter-clockwise, you will see that the two inner faces of the fists rise together. Just so two adjoining air cells rotating 10 in opposite directions will push up between them a ridge of rising air. Birds can glide in a straight line along such a 11 ridge.

—John H. Storer, "Bird Aerodynamics"

Combining methods of development

Whatever dominant method a paragraph uses for its development, other methods may also play some part. The same is even more true in a sequence of paragraphs within an essay.

In the student essay that follows, the author's central purpose is to explain attitudes toward hyperactivity by using the analogy of a collage, an assembly of diverse fragments. The author develops her paragraphs in several ways, including definition in sentences 11–16 and cause-and-effect analysis in sentences 17–24.

A hyperactive club woman is a good person to have 1 around; she will get the work done. A hyperactive salesman 2 is a valuable employee; he will make profits rise. But when a 3 child is hyperactive, people—even parents—may wish it had never been born. Hyperactivity in children is so great a 4 problem that it demands understanding. To achieve it, even 5 slightly, it is helpful to visualize a collage—not of colored paper, but of the thoughts, feelings, and attitudes of all who must deal with the problem—doctors, parents, even himself.

As the first part of our collage, let us consider the doc- 6 tors. In their terminology, the word "hyperactive" is likely to 7 mean "abnormally or excessively busy" or an H-LD, a hyperkinesis-learning disability syndrome. The problem, 8 though, is that doctors are uncertain of how to deal with it. For example, some may recommend special diet; others be- 9 havior modifying drugs; and still others, who do not consider hyperactivity to be a medical problem, a psychiatrist for the entire family. It can all become a merry-go-round of 10 tests, confusion, and frustration for the parents and the child.

As the parent of a hyperactive child, I think I can speak 11 for other parents as to what the word "hyperactive" means to all of us. It means a worry that is deep and enduring. It 12,13 means a despair that is a companion on dark and sleepless nights. It means a fear that is heart twisting and constant, 14 for the hyperactive child is most destructive toward himself. It means a mixture of frustration, guilt, and anger. And fi- 15,16 nally, since there are times when that anger goes out of control and the child is in danger from the parent, it means self-loathing.

The darkest pieces of our collage, however, are reserved 17 for the hyperactive child himself. From early childhood, he 18 is dragged from doctor to doctor, is attached to strange and frightening machines, and is tested or discussed by physicians, parents, neighbors, teachers, peers. His playmates dis- 19 like him because of his temper and his unwillingness to follow rules, and even his pets fear and mistrust him, for he treats them erratically, often hurting them without meaning to. He has seen his parents in tears and anger and has 20 known that it was because of him. Moreover, he is an under- 21 achiever. He is highly intelligent, but he does poorly in 22 school because of a short attention span. He is fond of 23 sports but never plays because he has an uncontrollable temper and poor coordination. And he has self-knowledge: 24 "Mama," my son asks me, "why do I have to be hyperactive?"

The collage is nearly finished; it is dark and somber. 25 "Hyperactive"—as applied to children—is a word that has 26 uncertain, unattractive, and bitter associations. But there is 27 one bright and final piece to be added. There is a saying: 28 "Inside of every fat person, there lives a thin person waiting to appear." I believe that inside of every hyperactive child 29 there is a loving, trustful person waiting to be recognized.

3
Checking length

In any essay of 500 to 750 words, the average paragraph may be between 100 and 150 words, or between four and eight sentences.

These numbers are averages, of course; the actual length of a paragraph will depend on its topic, its role in the development of the thesis sentence, and its position in the essay. Nevertheless, very short paragraphs are often inadequately developed. And very long paragraphs often contain irrelevant details or are so unfocused that following their main idea is difficult.

¶ *dev*

3c

When you are revising your essay, reread the paragraphs that seem very long or very short, checking them especially for unity and adequate development. If the paragraph wanders, cut everything from it that does not support your main idea. If it is undeveloped, supply the specific details, examples, or reasons needed, or try one of the methods of development we have discussed here.

EXERCISE 9

Identify the details, examples, and reasons that make each of the following paragraphs well developed. What central idea and general statements does the specific information support in each case?

1. Every American sport directs itself in a general way toward certain segments of American life. Baseball is basically a leisurely, pastoral experience, offering a tableau of athletes against a lush green background, providing moments of action amid longer periods allowed for contemplation of the spectacle. In its relaxed, unhurried way, it is exactly what it claims to be—the national "pastime" rather than an intense, sustained game crammed with action. Born in a rural age, it offers still the appeal of an untroubled island where, for a few hours, a pitcher tugging at his pants leg can seem to be the most important thing in a fan's life.
      —Pete Axthelm, *The City Game*

2. He had the emotional stability of a six-year-old child. When he felt out of sorts, he would rave and stamp, or sink into suicidal gloom and talk darkly of going to the East to end his days as a Buddhist monk. Ten minutes later, when something pleased him, he would rush out of doors and run around the garden, or jump up and down on the sofa, or stand on his head. He could be grief-stricken over the death of a pet dog, and he could be callous and heartless to a degree that would have made a Roman emperior shudder.
      —Deems Taylor (on Richard Wagner),
      Of Men and Music

EXERCISE 10

The paragraphs below are not well developed. Analyze them, looking especially for general statements that lack support or leave questions in your mind. Then rewrite one into a well-developed paragraph, using your own details.

1.   Gestures are one of our most important means of   1
     communication. We use them instead of speech. We   2,3
     use them to supplement the words we use in speech.
     And we use them to communicate some things that   4
     words could not possibly express.
2.   The tax laws also discriminate against married   1
     people. Contrary to the old saying, two people do *not*   2
     live more cheaply than one, especially when both wife
     and husband are working students. Instead, the reverse   3
     is more likely to be true. At the very least, single and   4
     married people should be treated equally.

EXERCISE 11

Write a paragraph that uses details, examples, and reasons to develop one of the following ideas or an idea of your own. Be sure your paragraph is unified and coherent as well as adequately developed.

1. how billboards blight (or decorate) the landscape
2. why you like (or don't like) poetry
3. a place where you feel comfortable
4. an unusual person you know
5. the consequences of not disciplining children (or of disciplining them too much)
6. an instance of unusual kindness or cruelty

EXERCISE 12

Identify the method or methods used to develop each of the following paragraphs. How does the author also use details, examples, or reasons to achieve development?

1.   In his lifelong quest to conquer fear, Dylan Bright   1
     first left his mother's skirts to become a daredevil quasi-
     delinquent. As a youth he got more cerebral concus-   2
     sions than anybody else in the Study. Then, with the   3
     passage of time, his mastery became more graceful. Af-   4
     ter eighteen, he learned to do what he called "responsi-
     bly adventurous things"; and there were no further in-
     juries. From an all-state football lineman in high school,   5
     he became a fiercely competitive wrestler. Playing ten-   6
     nis for blood, he shunned doubles for the joy of single
     combat. After college, his fierce devotion to tennis and   7

wrestling was replaced by an equally fierce devotion to poetry; but he was still out to win. Despite average intellectual equipment, he raced through Yale graduate school with absolutely top grades. He accepted an appointment at Princeton for the prestige and a few years later exulted in his early acquisition of academic tenure. 8 9
—George E. Vaillant, *Adaptation to Life*

2. The inner life of the White House is essentially the life of the barnyard, as set forth so graphically in the study of the pecking order among chickens which every freshman sociology student must read. It is a question of who has the right to peck whom and who must submit to being pecked. There are only two important differences. The first is that the pecking order is determined by the individual strength and forcefulness of each chicken, whereas in the White House it depends upon the relationship to the barnyard keeper. The second is that no one outside the barnyard glorifies the chickens and expects them to order the affairs of mankind. They are destined for the frying pan and that is that. 1 2 3 4 5 6
—George E. Reedy, *The Twilight of the Presidency*

3. A dying person may pass through five separate attitude stages, according to the psychiatrist Elizabeth Kübler-Ross. In the first stage, denial, the patient ignores symptoms of illness and refuses to accept diagnosis and sometimes even treatment. Then, in a stage of anger, the patient feels outraged at the injustice of dying. A stage of bargaining may follow, when the patient tries to make an exchange with the hospital staff or his or her family or God for a little more time. Then the patient may enter a period of depression that comes when he or she realizes that everything is soon to be finished, that life is almost over. And finally, that dying person may feel acceptance of death, a quiet resignation to the power of death. 1 2 3 4 5 6
—A student

4. We can thus say that while the average human being is a mixture, some people are mainly "digestion-minded," some "muscle-minded," and some "brain-minded," and correspondingly digestion-bodied, muscle-bodied, or brain-bodied. The digestion-bodied people look thick; the muscle-bodied people look wide; and the brain-bodied people look long. This does not mean the taller a man is the brainier he will be. It means that if a man, even a short man, looks long rather than wide or thick, he will often be more concerned about what goes on in his mind than about what he does or what he eats; but the key factor is slenderness and not 1 2 3 4

¶ *dev*

3c

height. On the other hand, a man who gives the impres- 5
sion of being thick rather than long or wide will usually
be more interested in a good steak than in a good idea
or a good long walk.

—Eric Berne, *A Layman's Guide To Psychiatry
and Psychoanalysis*

5.   In American society there exist people classified by 1
encyclopedia salesmen as "mooches." Mooches can be 2
generally defined as people who like to buy the product;
they see the encyclopedia salesman as the bearer of a
rare and desirable gift. Mooches are people whose in- 3
comes and occupational levels exceed their educational
attainments; persons whose income is in the middle-
middle range but whose education doesn't exceed high
school, or may not even attain that level. Without edu- 4
cation, mooches cannot have professional status, although they might make as much money as a professional; consequently, mooches try to assume pro-
fessionalism by accruing what they think are in-
dications of professional status. A conspicuously dis- 5
played set of encyclopedias tells the mooch's friends
that he can afford to consume conspicuously, that he
values a highly normative product over creature com-
forts, and that he provides for the long-range benefit of
his protectorate. The mooch associates all these charac- 6
teristics with professional persons. For him, then, en- 7
cyclopedias function as easily interpreted professional-
status indicators.

—Lynn M. Buller, "The Encyclopedia Game"

EXERCISE 13

Identify the appropriate method or methods for developing a paragraph on each of the following topics. (Choose from definition,
division and classification, comparison and contrast, analogy,
cause-and-effect analysis, and process analysis.)

1. the influences of a person's biorhythms or astrological sign on
   his or her behavior
2. the parts of an orange
3. tuning an engine
4. rock music and country music
5. what a disco is
6. making houseplants grow
7. the kinds of people involved in the tax revolt
8. the picture of aliens shown by recent science fiction movies
9. dancing as pure motion, like a kite in the wind
10. one consequence of the energy shortage

EXERCISE 14

Write a paragraph about a topic from Exercise 13, using the development method you chose in that exercise. Or, if you prefer, choose a topic of your own and develop it by using one of the six methods.

¶ dev

3C

EXERCISE 15

Write paragraphs using the method of development indicated below and one of the ideas provided here or in Exercise 13. Or choose your own topics.

1. definition
   a. fire
   b. a sphere
   c. an adult
   d. fear
   e. a football
2. division and classification
   a. kinds of greeting cards
   b. factions in a campus controversy
   c. styles of playing poker
   d. parts of a barn
   e. kinds of sports fans
3. comparison and contrast
   a. driving American and foreign compact cars
   b. AM and FM radio announcers
   c. high school and college football
   d. movies on TV and in a theater
4. analogy
   a. running and flying
   b. the U.S. Constitution and a building's foundation
   c. graduating from high school and being released from prison
5. cause-and-effect analysis
   a. connection between unemployment and college enrollments
   b. causes of thunder and lightning
   c. one way pollution affects you
   d. connection between credit cards and debt
   e. why go to college
6. process analysis
   a. preparing for a job interview
   b. drying fresh herbs
   c. making a cabinet
   d. peeling a banana
   e. making a jump shot

3d
Writing special kinds of paragraphs

Several kinds of paragraphs do not always follow our guidelines for unity, coherence, development, and length because they serve special functions. These are the essay introduction, the essay conclusion, the transitional paragraph, and the paragraph of spoken dialogue.

1
Opening an essay

Most essays open with a paragraph that draws readers from their world into the writer's world. An opening paragraph should arouse the reader's curiosity about what the writer has to say. The safest kind of introduction opens with a statement of the essay's general subject, clarifies or limits the subject in one or more sentences, and then, in the thesis sentence, asserts the topic of the essay. (See 1d.) This is the pattern in Donald Hall's introduction to an essay on reading habits.

> Everywhere one meets the idea that reading is an activity desirable in itself. It is understandable that publishers and librarians—and even writers—should promote this assumption, but it is strange that the idea should have general currency. People surround the idea of reading with piety, and do not take into account the purpose of reading, or the value of what is being read. Teachers and parents praise the child who reads, and praise themselves, whether the text be *The Reader's Digest* or *Moby-Dick*. The advent of TV has increased the false values ascribed to reading, since TV provides a vulgar alternative. But this piety is silly; and most reading is no more cultural nor intellectual nor imaginative than shooting pool or watching *What's My Line*.
> —Donald Hall, "Four Kinds of Reading"

Several other types of introduction can be equally effective, though they are sometimes harder to invent and control. One kind begins with a quotation that leads into the thesis sentence.

> "It is difficult to speak adequately or justly of London," wrote Henry James in 1881. "It is not a pleasant place; it is not agreeable, or cheerful, or easy, or exempt from reproach. It is only magnificent." Were he alive today, James, a connoisseur of cities, might easily say the same thing about New York or Paris or Tokyo, for the great city is one of the paradoxes of history. In countless different ways, it

has almost always been an unpleasant, disagreeable, cheerless, uneasy and reproachful place; in the end, it can only be described as magnificent.

—*Time*

Another kind of introduction opens by relating an incident that sets the stage for the thesis.

> Canada is pink. I knew that from the map I owned [1,2] when I was six. On it, New York was green and brown, [3] which was true as far as I could see, so there was no reason to distrust the map maker's portrayal of Canada. When my [4] parents took me across the border and we entered the immigration booth, I looked excitedly for the pink earth. Slowly it [5] dawned on me: This foreign, "different" place was not so different. I discovered that the world in my head and the [6] world at my feet were not the same.
>
> —Robert Ornstein, *Human Nature*

An introduction may also start with an opinion, preferably a startling one that will grab the reader's attention.

> Caesar was right. Thin people need watching. I've been [1,2,3] watching them for most of my adult life, and I don't like what I see. When these narrow fellows spring at me, I quiver [4] to my toes. Thin people come in all personalities, most of [5] them menacing. You've got your "together" thin person, [6] your mechanical thin person, your condescending thin person, your tsk-tsk thin person. All of them are dangerous. [7]
>
> —Suzanne Britt Jordan, "That Lean and Hungry Look"

A historical comparison or contrast may be an effective introduction when some background to the essay topic is useful.

> Throughout the first half of this century, the American [1] Medical Association, the largest and most powerful medical organization in the world, battled relentlessly to rid the country of quack potions and cure-alls; and it is the AMA that is generally credited with being the single most powerful force behind the enactment of the early pure food and drug laws. Today, however, medicine's guardian seems to [2] have done a complete about-face and become one of the pharmaceutical industry's staunchest allies—often at the public's peril and expense.
>
> —Mac Jeffery, "Does Rx Spell Rip-off?"

All these examples show basic attributes of good introductions. They are concise. They are direct because they tell us specifically what the author will discuss and what his or her viewpoint is. They are sincere, so we believe the author will talk to us honestly. And they are interesting without being misleading about the content

3d

of the essay that follows. To achieve these attributes, an introductory paragraph need not be long, as this opener shows.

> I've often wondered what goes into a hot dog. Now I [1,2] know and I wish I didn't.
>
> —William Zinsser, *The Lunacy Boom*

2

Closing an essay

Most essays end with a closing statement of some kind—a signal to readers that the writer has not simply stopped writing but has actually finished. The closing statement—usually set off in its own paragraph—may be a single sentence or a group of sentences. It may summarize the evidence presented in the essay, restate the thesis with a fresh emphasis, suggest a course of action, ask a question, strike a note of hope or despair, introduce a startling fact, quote an authority, or tell an anecdote.

The two concluding paragraphs below illustrate different uses of such paragraphs. In the first Ada Louise Huxtable sums up, with a final shot, her highly critical essay on the Rayburn House Office Building in Washington, D.C. In the second Peter F. Drucker finishes an essay on environmental protection with a summary and a call for action.

> An old architectural saying has it that there's no point in [1] crying over spilled marble. Several million pounds of it have [2] been poured onto Capital Hill in this latest Congressional building venture, and there is nothing quite as invulnerable as a really monumental mistake. The Rayburn Building's ul- [3] timate claim to fame may well be that it is the biggest star-spangled architectural blunder of our time.
>
> —Ada Louise Huxtable, "The Rayburn Building"

> Until we get the answers, I think we had better keep on [1] building power plants and growing food with the help of fertilizers and such insect-controlling chemicals as we now have. The risks are well known, thanks to the environmen- [2] talists. If they had not created a widespread public aware- [3] ness of the ecological crisis, we wouldn't stand a chance. But such awareness by itself is not enough. Flaming mani- [4,5] festos and prophecies of doom are no longer much help, and a search for scapegoats can only make matters worse. The time for sensations and manifestos is about over. Now [6,7] we need rigorous analysis, united effort and very hard work.
>
> —Peter F. Drucker, "How Best to Protect the Environment"

These two paragraphs also illustrate how to avoid several conclusion don'ts. First, don't simply restate your introduction—statement of subject, thesis sentence, and all. Presumably the paragraphs in the body of your essay have contributed something to the opening statements, and it's that something you want to capture in your conclusion. Second, don't start off in a new direction, with a subject different from or broader than the one your essay has been about. For instance, Huxtable might have violated this principle (and weakened her conclusion) had she veered off to the quality of Washington architecture in general. Third, don't conclude more than you reasonably can from the evidence you have presented. If your essay is about your frustrating experience trying to clear a parking ticket, you cannot reasonably conclude that *all* local police forces are too tied up in red tape to be of service to the people. And fourth, don't use your conclusion to apologize for your essay or otherwise cast doubt on it. Don't say, "Even though I'm no expert," or "This may not be convincing, but I believe it's true," or anything similar. Rather, to win your readers' confidence, display confidence.

¶ 3d

3
Using transitional paragraphs

Short transitional paragraphs, usually a sentence or two, direct a reader's attention to a turn in an essay or emphasize an idea to follow. Because they are separate paragraphs and longer than words or phrases, transitional paragraphs move a discussion from one place to another more slowly or more completely than any single expression can. Here are some examples.

These, then, are the reasons for keeping the drinking age at twenty-one. Now let's look at some of the reasons for lowering it to eighteen.

The conclusion would seem to be obvious. To be sure, however, we must look at a few other facts.

So the debates were noisy and emotion-packed. But what did they accomplish? Historians agree on at least three direct results.

Transitional paragraphs should not be overused. When they *are* used, they should mark a major turn in the movement of the essay. A paragraph like the one below, which simply stops the flow rather than redirecting it, makes writing seem labored.

Now that we have examined these facts, we can look at some others that are equally important to an examination of this issue.

4
Writing dialogue

When recording a conversation between two or more people, start a new paragraph for each person's speech. This establishes for the reader the point at which one speaker stops talking and another begins. For example:

> "Are you saying that you are going to go now and not come back?"
> "Oh, God. Yes, I'm saying that."
> Jessica began to scream.
>
> —Iris Murdoch, *The Nice and the Good*

Though bits of dialogue may sometimes give freshness and vitality to expository prose, extended dialogue appears more often in fictional writing. (For help in using quotation marks and other punctuation in dialogue, see 24c.)

EXERCISE 16

Write introductory and concluding paragraphs for an essay on one of the following topics (or a topic of your own).

1. how organized crime takes over or controls a business or neighborhood
2. the influence of weather on mood or personality
3. how good and evil are depicted in a movie like *Star Wars* (or any other movie)
4. the advantages (or disadvantages) of dogs (or cats) as pets
5. the importance of psychology (or any field of study) in our daily lives

---

EXERCISE 17

Analyze each of the paragraphs below for unity, coherence, and development. Identify the paragraph's central idea and shape, its organizing principle, the devices used to achieve coherence, its use of specific information, and its method of development (if any).

1.   There is in this country no place that could even be ¹ suggested as being anywhere near the Massachusetts State House for bone politics. Throughout the nation, ² the complaint with state legislatures is that they are part-time bodies. Not even that in many places. New ³,⁴ York, supposedly so efficient, has a state legislature which meets in January and averages three days a week until the late spring. After which it is regarded as a crim- ⁵ inal offense for the legislature not to be recessed well in advance of the closing days of the school year, thus giving legislators time to open summer houses, pack their kids' clothes for camp, and plan vacation trips. In Mas- ⁶ sachusetts, the legislators prefer to sit forever. They ⁷ usually have to be driven out of the building, practically at gunpoint. If a Massachusetts legislator is removed ⁸

from his game, his sport, his very life, then all that is left
for him to do is return home to his wife and family, and
in Massachusetts anybody can have a family but the
true goal of life is to be a politician; or, true term, a Pol.
It is not uncommon for the Massachusetts Pols to sit in 9
the State House throughout the summer, arguing,
spreading rumors, using the phones, and—true glory—
plotting against each other.

—Jimmy Breslin, *How the Good Guys Finally Won*

2.   Supper was at six and was over by half past. There 1,2
was still daylight, shining softly and with a tarnish, like
the lining of a shell; and the carbon lamps lifted at the
corners were on in the light, and the locusts were
started, and the fire flies were out, and a few frogs were
flopping in the dewy grass, by the time the fathers and
children came out. The children ran out first, hell bent 3
and yelling those names by which they were known;
then the fathers sank out leisurely in crossed suspen-
ders, their collars removed and their necks looking tall
and shy. The mothers stayed back in the kitchen wash- 4
ing and drying, putting things away, recrossing their
traceless footsteps like the life-time journeys of bees,
measuring out the dry cocoa for breakfast. When they 5
came out they had taken off their aprons and their
skirts were dampened and they sat in rockers on their
porches quietly.

—James Agee, *A Death in the Family*

3.   I do not know what it is to see into the heart of a 1
friend through that "window of the soul," the eye. I can 2
only "see" through my fingertips the outline of a face. I 3
can detect laughter, sorrow, and many other obvious
emotions. I know my friends from the feel of their 4
faces. But I cannot really picture their personalities by 5
touch. I know their personalities, of course, through 6
other means, through the thoughts they express to me,
through whatever of their actions are revealed to me.
But I am denied that deeper understanding of them 7
which I am sure would come through sight of them,
through watching their reactions to various expressed
thoughts and circumstances, through noting the immediate and fleeting reactions of their eyes and coun-
tenance.

—Helen Keller, "Three Days to See"

4

Convincing a Reader

In a way, all writing is arguing. You try to convince readers to accept your perspective on a topic, or at the very least you try to convince them that the time spent reading is not wasted. In exposition you try to convince readers to accept your explanation; in narration you attempt to convince them that your story is interesting; and in description you lead them to experience a scene or person as you did. Of course, convincing readers is fundamental in argumentation, when your purpose is always to obtain readers' agreement with your ideas.

To convince readers that your idea is sound, or even to get them to take your argument seriously, you have to follow certain well-established practices of essay development. Your idea will probably be stated in your thesis sentence, which narrows your topic to a single, specific assertion that reflects your viewpoint (see 1d). You will be expected to support your thesis sentence with more specific assertions, perhaps the topic sentences of your paragraphs (see 3a). And you will be expected to support these assertions with very concrete and specific evidence. This is the general structure of a well-ordered argument. In this chapter we'll examine the steps involved in putting together such an argument and the hazards to avoid along the way.

4a
Sounding moderate

Chapter 1 talked about considering your audience when you write—about using details and tone to gain the interest and the support of your readers, no matter what kind of writing you're doing. (See 1e.) When arguing about ideas, you have a special problem with audience. Readers are naturally (and appropriately) skeptical

° *log*
4a

of what they read, and they often resist being convinced of anything at all. Thus you have a much better chance of convincing them to accept your idea if you *under*play it than you do if you *over*play it. The best way to get readers to listen to your arguments is to write reasonably, moderately, and calmly.

The writer of the following introductory paragraph is not likely to put to rest the wariness or resistance of his audience.

> Pornography is vile and putrid, the cause of all moral decay and violence in America. It unleashes ugly desires and reduces men and women to their sex organs! It separates the human bond between love and sex. Consequently, it calls for the death of humanity. Pornography must not be tolerated!

No one could doubt the writer's sincerity, but his shrill tone is repellent. He uses absolute words like *all* that allow no exceptions. He punctuates sentences with exclamation marks instead of allowing the strength of his ideas to convey his meaning. And he employs words and phrases like *putrid, ugly,* and *death of humanity* that have strong emotional connotations but little rational appeal. No matter how well reasoned the rest of his argument is, his readers are unlikely to appreciate it.

Compare the wild and alienating tone of the preceding paragraph with the more moderate, inviting tone of the one that follows.

> Pornography is a form of free expression that causes a serious social and moral problem. Pornography may well help cause sexual crimes, and it certainly damages the moral tone of society. In addition, it degrades sexual relationships between men and women, substituting mechanical action for love. Because pornography is detrimental to society and to personal relations, it should be strictly controlled, even if free expression must be curtailed.

The writer's ideas haven't changed, just his way of expressing them.

As this revised paragraph suggests, a reasonable tone assures your audience that you have weighed all the alternatives before arriving at your idea. To this end you may want to acknowledge an opposing view and then show that it *isn't* reasonable. For example, an argument against expensive athletic programs might begin:

> Athletic directors often claim that athletic programs contribute money to academic programs; in fact, sports *cost* money, they don't make money.

Another way to show your objectivity is to admit that an opposing view *is* reasonable but insist (and demonstrate) that your point is more compelling.

> An atomic power plant will benefit the economy of this town. Granted, there are dangers associated with nuclear power. But the advantages outweigh the risks.

log

4b

A moderate tone and an acknowledgment of opposing views give the *appearance* of being reasonable and fair, and to some extent you are what you show yourself to be. However, being reasonable involves not only appearances but also substance. Attending to the substance of an argument is the subject of the following sections.

EXERCISE 1

Revise the following paragraph to make its tone moderate and appealing. Delete or add material as you think necessary to achieve moderation.

> Drugs and alcohol are two really stupid ways to escape from reality. Everyone knows they're both bad for you. People even die from using them. That's escape, all right! The best these excuses for thinking can do is give a minute of relief from disappointment and frustration. Big deal. People are pretty sick to think they're getting anything more.

EXERCISE 2

Introduce moderation into the following sentences by acknowledging a likely opposing view or by acknowledging the given view while asserting the opposite.

1. Fulfilling a science requirement (or an English requirement) is a waste of time.
2. The best way to solve the energy shortage is to perfect our use of solar energy.
3. In a society as advanced as ours, mail service should be free.
4. The federal and local governments should do more to regulate the quality of children's television.
5. All people convicted of a crime should be jailed for a definite time.

4b
Making assertions believable

Assertions are fundamental to your argument. Thus you want your readers to suspend their natural skepticism and to believe your assertions, even before they read the supporting evidence. In part, the tone you use and your openness to opposing views will influence your readers' acceptance of your assertions. But to write believable assertions, you need to be mindful of other factors as well: distinctions between fact, opinion, and prejudice; clearly defined terms; and straightforward confrontation of the issue.

1
Distinguishing fact, opinion, and prejudice

Most assertions you make will be statements of fact, opinion, or prejudice. Whether readers find your assertions believable or convincing will depend on which category they fall into.

A **fact** is a verifiable statement—that is, one can determine whether or not it is true. It may involve numbers or dates. (*A football field is 100 yards long. They were married in 1945.*) Or the numbers may be implied. (*George's family is larger than mine. The earth is closer to the sun than Saturn is.*) Or the fact may involve no numbers at all. (*Judith was hospitalized yesterday. The forecaster said to expect a tornado.*) If we assume that measuring devices or records or memories are correct, then the truth of the fact is beyond argument. And its truth won't change unless its elements change—for example, if your family increases in number and thus becomes larger than George's.

An **opinion,** on the other hand, is a judgment *based* on facts— an honest attempt to draw a reasonable conclusion from evidence. For example, you know that millions of people go without proper medical care because they can't afford it, and so you form the opinion or judgment that national health insurance should be the nation's top priority. This opinion is a viewpoint. It is contestable, because other facts might lead another person to a different opinion— for instance, that because national health insurance would cost billions of dollars, the country simply can't afford it. And an opinion is changeable. With more evidence you might conclude that other national problems such as inflation or unemployment seem as pressing as inadequate medical care. Then you would need to revise your opinion to rank national health insurance as *one of* the nation's top priorities.

Opinions are not the same as expressions of personal likes and dislikes, such as *I enjoy jazz more than rock music.* These statements can't be contested (would someone say, "No you don't"?), nor are they based on factual evidence. Statements of preference become opinions only when they're reworded to allow the possibility of argument or change. For instance, *Jazz is more complex than rock music* is an opinion.

Stated by itself, an opinion has little power to convince. Let your readers know what your evidence is and how it led you to arrive at your opinion. If, for example, several facts have contributed to your opinion, you should list them. And you should be careful never to let a prejudice pass as an opinion. A **prejudice** (or prejudgment) is a conclusion for which you have made little or no examination of the evidence. Very often prejudices are attitudes we acquire from others—parents, friends, the communications media— without thinking. *Women belong in the home. Men shouldn't cry. Fat people are jolly.* At best, such assertions oversimplify. *Some* women might be excellent housekeepers, but so might *some* men. Then the statement should read, *Some women and some men belong in the home.* Why bother to say it at all? At its worst, prejudice is narrow-minded and reflects a simplistic view of the world. And writers who are perceived as narrow-minded aren't likely to impress their readers with their reasonableness.

2
Defining terms

In any argument, but especially in arguments about abstract ideas, clear and consistent definition of terms is essential to a shared understanding of what the argument is about. In order to be understood, the writer of the following sentences needs to make clearer what she means by *justice*.

> What has happened to justice in this country over the past few decades? It seems less often applied than it was when my grandparents were young. In their day, both criminal and victim were treated justly. Today, however, neither receives justice.

We know that the writer regrets some change in the way criminals and their victims are dealt with, but other than that we don't know exactly what she's saying. She doesn't tell us what *justice* means to her. The word is abstract—it does not refer to anything concrete and in fact has different meanings for everyone. Compare the previous paragraph with the one following, in which the writer is careful to define the abstract word.

> If by "justice" we mean treating people fairly, punishing those who commit crimes and protecting the victims of those crimes, then justice has deteriorated in this country over the past decades. Criminals now receive more explicit protection from the laws— when they are arrested and tried and even if they are imprisoned— than their victims do. Thousands of criminals go free every year because an arresting policeman forgot to say a sentence or a prosecuting attorney decided another case was more important. Meanwhile, the victims are ignored.

We may need to see how this writer supports her ideas before we can accept them, but at least we have a clearer sense of what her terms mean.

3
Facing the question

log

4b

Almost every argument centers on an issue or question: "Is jazz more complex than rock music?" "Should the country adopt a national health insurance plan?" "Should the town allow an atomic power plant to be built nearby?" An effective argument deals squarely with the central issue—it faces the question. But facing the question can be difficult. It's often easier to oversimplify complex issues, or to argue superficially about them, than it is to grapple with all the evidence. Sometimes, too, a favored opinion dies hard, though the evidence fails to support it. These circumstances can cause two common faults: begging the question (also called circular reasoning) and ignoring the question by appealing to readers' emotions.

Avoid begging the question

You **beg the question** when you deal with a complex assumption that is open to question as if it were already proved or disproved. (In essence, you are begging your readers to accept your ideas from the start.) For example, if you argue that jazz is more complex than rock music because it's harder to play, then you're begging the question. You're using complexity—as measured by playing difficulty—to establish complexity. Not having proved that jazz is more complex, you now have to prove that jazz is harder to play. In the meantime your readers may lose patience with your failure to prove your point.

The following sentence begs the question of why teenage girls should be prevented from having abortions.

> Teenagers would not become pregnant in the first place if they weren't allowed to terminate their "mistakes" through abortion.

The writer assumes—and asks us to agree—that the option of having an abortion leads teenagers to unwanted pregnancies; therefore, removing the option will remove the problem. But how can we agree when we still have no proof for the fundamental assertion? The writer has merely substituted one debatable assumption for another.

Avoid ignoring the question

Writers sometimes attempt to gain agreement with their arguments not by making reasonable assertions and supporting them with evidence but by appealing to their readers' emotions. The effect is to obscure or skip over the real question.

One way to ignore the question is to touch on readers' fear of a situation or to appeal to their sense of decency or pity. The following sentences do not appeal to reason.

> If the government doesn't stop controlling the prices charged by domestic oil companies, the country will soon run out of oil. [Trades on people's fear of an oil shortage.]
>
> Dr. Bowen must be a good man because he attends church regularly and participates in community activities. [Appeals to people's sense of decent behavior.]
>
> She should not have to pay taxes because she's a lonely widow with no friends or relatives. [Touches on people's pity for the old and lonely.]

Another way to ignore the question is to appeal to readers' sense of what other people believe or do. One approach is **snob appeal,** leading people to accept what you say because they want to be identified with others they admire.

> As any literate person knows, James Joyce is the best twentieth-century novelist.
>
> The true sports fan prefers baseball to football.
>
> The fact that national congressmen are jogging daily should convince every chair-bound person to get out and run.
>
> Paul Newman's support for the governor is proof that the governor's doing a good job.

Writers sometimes ignore the question by trying to convince readers to agree with them because everybody else does. This is the **bandwagon approach.**

> As everyone knows and has experienced at least once, liquor is the most effective social mixer.
>
> No one in this town would consider voting for him.

Yet another diversion involves flattering your readers—in a way, inviting them to conspire with you on your views.

> Since you are thoughtful and intelligent, you will see what I mean by corruption among the insurance commissioners.
>
> We all understand campus problems well enough to see the disadvantages of such a backward policy.

All these sentences resort to appeals having nothing to do with the issues they raise. A careless reader might be momentarily swayed by snob appeal, the bandwagon approach, or flattery. But a careful reader is more likely to be repelled by the writer's insincerity.

log
4b

One final kind of emotional appeal is to address *not* the pros and cons of the issue itself but the real or imagined negative qualities of the people who hold the opposing view. This kind of argument is called *ad hominem,* Latin for "to the man."

> We needn't listen to her arguments against national health insurance because she's wealthy enough to afford private insurance. [Her wealth does not necessarily discredit her views on medical insurance.]

> The dean proved his inability to carry out his promises once before, so we shouldn't act on them now. [The dean's previous broken promise does not necessarily invalidate his current one.]

You'll recognize most of these tricks for ignoring the question from advertising and political campaigns. Are your children's teeth cavity-free? Is your kitchen floor as spotless as your neighbor's? Are you the only person who doesn't eat a certain brand of cereal? Is that candidate as incompetent as his opponent says? You should be wary of these pitches in what you read and hear, and you should avoid them in your own writing. A thoughtful audience is unlikely to be persuaded by them.

EXERCISE 3

Identify the uses of facts (verifiable statements), opinions (judgments based on facts), statements of personal preference, and assertions of prejudice in the following paragraphs.

1.   People probably weren't as interesting before electricity was discovered as they are today. They had many fewer contacts with others outside their immediate circle because printed matter wasn't so widely circulated, and radio and television weren't invented. They knew nothing about the arts except what they could see and hear firsthand at museums and concerts. They must have led deprived lives.

2.   I have always been a simple man. My pleasures consist of stargazing, walking in the woods, and eating homemade ice cream. The frantic pace and the constant bombardment of information experienced by most people are boring to me. I like to live as my grandparents lived.

EXERCISE 4

Identify the problems with definition in the following paragraph, which fails to define important words well enough for us to pin down the meaning intended. Revise the paragraph to eliminate the problems.

The best solution to current problems is one you don't hear very often: self-sufficiency. If we made for ourselves more of the things we use, we wouldn't have to rely so much on using scarce resources to satisfy basic needs. Sure, people play at gardening, sewing, and other skills, but very few of them try to free themselves of the grocery store's vegetables or the department store's clothes. If people were more self-sufficient, there would be less unhappiness, because independence ultimately creates a bond between individuals.

EXERCISE 5

Identify the question raised by each of the following sentences and evaluate the writer's effectiveness in facing the question.

1. Many women are bored with their lives because their jobs are tedious.
2. Steven McRae spends too much time making himself look good to be an effective spokesman for the student body.
3. Teenagers should not be allowed to drink because they are too young.
4. Giving nuclear capability to emerging nations is dangerous, since they will probably use it to wage war on their larger neighbors.
5. Our souls are immortal because they are not made of matter and thus are indestructible.

EXERCISE 6

Leaf through a magazine or watch television for half an hour, looking for advertisements that attempt to sell a product not on the basis of its worth but by snob appeal, flattery, or appeals to emotions. Be prepared to discuss the advertisers' techniques.

4c

Supporting the assertions

Making your assertions believable—by distinguishing among fact, opinion, and prejudice, by defining your terms, and by facing the question—is only the first step in conducting a convincing argument. The next step is to support your assertions with evidence—the substance of any argument. Making reasonable assertions keeps your readers' minds open only long enough to get them to the evidence. If the evidence proves unsatisfactory, then your cause will be lost.

The kinds of evidence available to writers came up earlier in the context of paragraph development (see 3c-1). There you saw how to use concrete and specific details, examples, and reasons to support general or abstract assertions so that your readers become interested in your ideas, identify with them, and come away convinced of them. Consider how the author of the following paragraph uses details, examples, and reasons to support his assertion (second sentence) about shopping malls.

> Customers come to malls from every possible place, walk of life, economic bracket. But if malls have a mind set, a spiritual epicenter, it's not the city, the suburb, or rural America, but out *there*, in between, just off the highway, where you find all the new Naugahyde and hanging-plant bars, with fancily named and priced drinks, foreign beers, wines and goods which 10 years ago were the exclusive preserve of big city life. Easy and quick isn't enough any more; the Highway Comfort Culture has gone beyond hamburgers and wash 'n' wear to a veneer of sophistication. It's Lobster and Löwenbräu, even though the lobster is microwaved and the beer is made in Texas. The stores and restaurants have dressed up their interiors with motifs that suggest haute cuisine and high fashion, while trying to keep the same streamlined delivery system as McDonald's. In retrospect, it seems inevitable that these highway stops would draw together and unite under one roof, the one-stop oasis of splendor, the mall.
> —William Severini Kowinski, "The Malling of America"

To work effectively in convincing a reader, the evidence you use must meet four criteria: it must be accurate, relevant, representative, and adequate.

Accurate evidence is usually drawn from reliable sources, quoted exactly, and used in an appropriate context that does not distort it. For an essay in favor of gun control, you might consult the anti-control National Rifle Association as well as pro-control groups to ensure that your evidence is accurate from both perspectives. In quoting excerpts as evidence, be careful to take their true meaning, not just a few words that happen to support your argument. For instance, you would distort the writer's meaning if you used the first sentence in the following passage as evidence of the positive effects of television.

> Television can be an effective force for education and understanding, for appreciation of people and their troubles and accomplishments. But it assumes that role so rarely that we have only fleeting glimpses of the possibilities. We know better the dull-witted, narrow-minded fare that monopolizes the set from one year to the next.

(See Appendix A for more information on quoting from sources.)

Relevant evidence comes from sources with authority on your

topic and relates directly to your point. Unless your uncle is a recognized expert on the Central Intelligence Agency, or you can establish his expertise, his opinion of whether the CIA meddles illegally in other countries' affairs is not relevant to your paper on the subject. On the other hand, if your uncle is a member of the town council, his views may very well be relevant evidence in your essay on how a new shopping mall will hurt the town merchants.

Evidence is representative when it reflects the sample from which it is said to be drawn. For instance, in an essay arguing that dormitories should stay open during school holidays, you might want to cite the opinions of the school's 5000 students. But you would mislead readers if, on the basis of a poll among your roommates and dormitory neighbors, you reported as evidence that "the majority of students favor leaving the dormitories open." A few dormitory residents could not be said to represent the entire student body, particularly the nonresident students. To be representative, your poll would have to take in many more students in proportions that reflect the numbers of resident and nonresident students on campus.

Evidence is adequate when there is enough of it to support your point. To convince readers of your view, you must tell them what you know. If you decide to write an essay against animal abuse, you will probably base your decision on information you have about abuse of animals as pets, in entertainment, and in scientific experiments. But you can't assume that your readers have the same information, so you can't hope to win them over with a statement like *Too many animals are deliberately injured or killed by humans every year.* You need to supply statistics instead of the vague *too many:* How many animals are injured? How many die? And you need to create for readers some of your feelings by supplying specific examples of animal abuse. Adequate, well-selected evidence and a controlled tone are crucial to an effective argument.

EXERCISE 7

Supply at least two specific details, examples, or reasons to support each of the following general assertions.

1. A college education shouldn't cost so much.
2. _____ is the television program (or movie, or both) that best shows life as it really is.
3. _____ is an example of a good teacher (or doctor, lawyer, politician, or parent).
4. Americans are energy spendthrifts.
5. Superman is a great hero.

EXERCISE 8

Identify the kinds of evidence (details, examples, and reasons) used in the following paragraphs, and evaluate the quality of the evidence against the four criteria of accuracy, relevancy, representativeness, and adequacy.

1.   Our rivers and streams are becoming choked by pollution. For example, swimming is now prohibited along stretches of the Mississippi River. The "big muddy" is now not only muddy but, in places, white and black as well. My minister says there are portions of the river where fish can't survive. Are we a nation that doesn't care enough about its resources to conserve them?

2.   Crime is out of control in this city. Three months ago my parents' house was burglarized. The thieves stole their food processor and their vibrating bed as well as their television and stereo. Then a month ago my roommate had her pocket picked on the subway. And last week I saw a confused old man trying to describe to the police how muggers had stolen his wallet and his groceries.

4d
Reasoning effectively

Our discussion so far in this chapter has been about the specific attributes of any reasonable argument. In fact, however, we tend to reason in one of two ways—inductively or deductively. We use these methods not only in our formal writing but also in our everyday activities, as the following slow-motion example will illustrate.

You want to give your father a birthday present. In thinking of what to buy you follow specific steps of reasoning: (1) You've given your father birthday presents before. (2) You've found that he appreciates books. (3) He has liked novels better than books about politics. (4) He especially enjoyed the two novels you gave him by John Updike. (5) He likes to receive Updike's novels. So far, your reasoning is **inductive.** You make a series of observations about the presents your father appreciates. And you induce, or infer, from those observations the generalization that he appreciates John Updike's novels. The **generalization** is a conclusion that what is applicable in one set of circumstances is also applicable in a similar set of circumstances. Having reasoned inductively to arrive at an idea for a birthday present, you then decide to follow through on the idea. This second line of reasoning, from a generalization to particular circumstances, is **deductive.** You take a conclusion that you know from the evidence to be true (your father likes to receive Updike's novels), apply it to a new situation (a birthday never before experienced, a novel never before read), and reach a new conclusion (that your father would like Updike's new novel for his birthday).

As this example illustrates, induction and deduction are fundamental to our thought. They ensure that our experience of the world is coherent, with one event related to another, and not fragmented. In the daily business of living we use these reasoning processes effortlessly and habitually. But we need to use them consciously and methodically in dealing with complex ideas—for instance, when evaluating the thinking of others or when trying to convince others to accept our view of an issue.

1

Using induction

Induction is the dominant method of reasoning in two situations: generalizing from observations and attributing a cause to a set of observed circumstances.

We saw an example of generalizing from observations in the process of choosing a present for your father. In another situation you observe that your English professor drives a Volkswagen, your psychology professor drives a Pinto, and your chemistry professor drives a Toyota. From these observations you infer that many faculty members drive small cars. The more faculty you observe, the more certain you can be that your generalization is true.

Attributing a cause to circumstances is essentially the same process as generalizing from observations. Over the course of a year you observe not only that your English professor drives a Volkswagen but also that his Volkswagen is beat up, he always eats his lunch out of a brown bag in his office, he wears shabby clothes, and he lives in a run-down section of town. From these observations you conclude that he is poorly paid. It is true that with a little imagination you could also conclude that he's well paid but must support a terminally ill and hospitalized Russian ballerina whom he is in love with. But as a rule, an explanation of cause is more reasonable when it is based exclusively on what you can observe than it is when you have to invent facts to support it.

The more evidence you have, the more likely it is that your generalizations are valid, but you can't know for certain that they are correct. You can only ensure that your generalizations are reasonable—sound conclusions based on sound evidence—and that your readers perceive them as such.

2
Using deduction

You reason deductively when you use some assertions to arrive at others. As when you determined that your father would like Updike's new novel for his birthday, in deduction you apply generalizations or conclusions that are accepted as true to slightly different but similar situations or issues. For example, if you know that all male members of your psychology class are on the football squad, and Albert is in the psychology class, then you conclude that Albert must be on the football squad. If you know that sentence fragments get poor grades on English papers, and you use sentence fragments, then you can expect a poor grade on your English paper. If inflation is caused in part by rising energy costs, and energy costs rise, then inflation will probably also increase.

Deductive reasoning is part of many arguments you read or try to write. The force of such arguments depends on the reliability of the initial assumptions and the care with which you apply them in drawing new conclusions. Two common sources of difficulty with deduction are unstated assumptions and overstated assumptions.

In many deductive arguments the basic assumption is not explicitly stated but is understood. For instance:

> Harold lived in Boston for several years, so he should know how to get to the ball park. [Assumption: Anyone who lived in Boston should know the way to the ball park.]
>
> As student-government president, Jordan will have to deal with conflicting demands from all sides. [Assumption: A student-government president must deal with conflicting demands.]

Problems arise when the unstated assumption is wrong or unfounded, as in the following sentences:

> Since Jane Lightbow is a senator, she must receive money illegally from lobbyists. [Assumption: All senators receive money illegally from lobbyists.]
>
> Now that Sally Matlock's mother is in jail, Sally will become a behavior problem. [Assumption: All children whose mothers are jailed become behavior problems.]

As these sentences show, when reasoning deductively you must carefully examine your basic assumptions, even when they are implied.

The second common problem in deduction—using overstated assumptions—comes from the difficulty in making a generalization that will apply to all instances, when ordinarily we must base any generalization on only a few instances. In reasoning from such generalizations, it's necessary to use or imply words like *some, many,* and *often,* rather than absolute words like *all, no one, never,* or *always.* Compare the difference in reasonableness in the following pairs of sentences.

OVERSTATED	Parents are *always* too busy to help their children solve problems.
MODIFIED	Parents are *often* too busy to help their children solve problems.
OVERSTATED	Movie theater ushers are a thing of the past: you *never* see them in the big cinema complexes.
MODIFIED	Movie theater ushers may be a thing of the past: you *rarely* see them in the big cinema complexes.

Remember, too, that modifying an assertion to make it sound more reasonable doesn't mean the assertion can be applied indiscriminately. For instance, modifying the unstated assumption about Senator Lightbow might result in this sentence:

> Since Jane Lightbow is a senator, she might receive money illegally from lobbyists. [Assumption: Some senators receive money illegally from lobbyists.]

But it does not necessarily follow that Senator Lightbow is one of the "some." The sentence is still not reasonable unless evidence demonstrates that Senator Lightbow should be linked with illegal activities.

3
Avoiding faulty reasoning

Some kinds of faulty inductive and deductive reasoning—errors called **fallacies**—are common in all sorts of writing. Like begging the question or appealing to emotions rather than reason, these fallacies weaken an argument.

Hasty generalization

A **hasty generalization** is one based on too little evidence or on evidence that is unrepresentative (see 4c). For example:

> The only major worth pursuing is business; others don't train you for work. [The writer's opinion of what's best for him is generalized to include everyone else.]

> When attendance is down and the team is losing, the basketball coach should be fired. [The sentence doesn't allow for other influences on the team's performance.]

A variation of the hasty generalization is the use of absolute words like *all, always, never,* and *no one* when what you mean is *some, sometimes, rarely,* and *few* (see also 4d-2).

Another common hasty generalization is the **stereotype,** a conventional and oversimplified characterization of a group of people. The ideas that the French are good lovers, the British reserved, and the Italians emotional are stereotypes. When you apply such a characterization to an individual Frenchman or Briton or Italian, you extend a prejudice, a judgment not based on evidence (see 4b-1). Here are several other stereotypes:

> City people are unfriendly.
> Country people are hicks.
> Californians are fad-crazy.
> Women are emotional.
> Men are less expressive than women.

Oversimplification

A frequent fallacy in all writing is **oversimplification** of the relation between causes and their effects. The fallacy (sometimes called the **reductive fallacy**) often involves linking two events as if one caused the other directly, whereas the causes may be more complex or the relation may not exist at all. For example:

> Poverty causes crime. [If so, then why do people who are not poor commit crimes? And why aren't all poor people criminals?]

> The better a school's athletic facilities are, the worse its academic programs are. [The sentence seems to assume a direct cause-and-effect link between athletics and scholarship.]

Post hoc *fallacy*

A fallacy related to oversimplification of cause and effect is assuming that because one thing followed another, it was caused by the other. This fallacy is called in Latin *post hoc, ergo propter hoc,* which means "after this, therefore because of this," or the ***post hoc* fallacy** for short. Here are a definition and example from the humorist Max Shulman, followed by two more examples of the fallacy at work.

> "Next comes Post Hoc. Listen to this: Let's not take Bill on our picnic. Every time we take him out with us, it rains."
> "I know somebody just like that," she exclaimed. "A girl back home—Eula Becker, her name is. It never fails. Every single time we take her on a picnic—"
> "Polly," I said sharply, "it's a fallacy. Eula Becker doesn't

cause the rain. She has no connection with the rain. You are guilty of Post Hoc if you blame Eula Becker."

—Max Shulman, "Love is a Fallacy"

Ever since they were married, Julie has been out of work. [Is Julie out of work because she got married?]

The city became one big parking lot because Mayor Braithwaite was elected. [Was the mayor responsible for building the parking lots?]

Either . . . or fallacy

You fall into the **either . . . or fallacy** when you assume that a complicated question has only two answers, one good and one bad, or both bad.

City policemen are either brutal or corrupt.

Either we institute national health insurance or thousands of people will become sick or die.

Like the illustrations of the previous fallacies, these sentences oversimplify complex issues and relationships so that the writer's perspective looks good. But no careful reader would be fooled. Many city policemen are neither brutal nor corrupt. And allowing people to sicken or die isn't the only alternative to national health insurance.

Non sequitur

A **non sequitur** occurs when no logical relation exists between two or more connected ideas. In Latin non sequitur means "it does not follow." In the sentences below the second thought does not follow from the first.

If high school English were easier, fewer students would have trouble with the college English requirement. [Presumably, if high school English were easier, students would have *more* trouble.]

Kathleen Newsome has my vote for mayor because she has the best-run campaign organization. [Shouldn't one's vote be based on the candidate's qualities, not the campaign organization's?]

False analogy

An **analogy** is a comparison between two essentially unlike things for the purpose of definition or illustration. (We saw analogy used in paragraph development; see 3c-2.) Arguing by using analogy is a kind of inductive reasoning, since you draw a likeness between things based on a single shared feature. But analogy can only illustrate a point, never prove it. And it can trick you into assuming that because things are similar in one respect, they *must* be alike in other respects. Here is an example of this fallacy, which is called **false analogy.**

> The nonhuman primates care for their young, clean and groom each other, and defend themselves and sometimes the group from attack. Why, then, must the human primates go so much further—Medicare, child care, welfare, Social Security, and so on—to protect the weak? [Taken to its logical extreme, this analogy would lead us to ask why we speak to each other when gorillas don't.]

EXERCISE 9

The following sentences contain either generalizations based on inadequate or invented evidence or deductions based on faulty unstated assumptions or overstated assumptions. Determine where each sentence goes wrong and revise it to be more effective.

1. Since capital punishment prevents murder, it should be the mandatory sentence for all murderers.
2. With a mayor who was once the president of a manufacturing company, our city will experience increased air pollution because environmental controls will not be enforced.
3. The only way to be successful in the United States is to make money, because Americans measure success by income.
4. Keeping the library open until midnight has caused the increase in late-night crime on the campus.
5. Government demands so much honesty that we should not leave it to lawyers and professional politicians.

EXERCISE 10

The following sentences are examples of the fallacies discussed in the text: hasty generalization, oversimplification, *post hoc* fallacy, either . . . or fallacy, non sequitur, and false analogy. Identify the fallacy that each sentence illustrates, and revise the sentence to eliminate that fallacy.

1. No one can appreciate marriage before the age of twenty-four.
2. Students' persistent complaints about the grading system prove that it is unfair.
3. The United States got involved in World War II because the Japanese bombed Pearl Harbor.
4. People watch television because they are too lazy to talk or read or because they want mindless escape from their lives.
5. Working people are slaves to their corporate masters: they have no freedom to do what they want, and they can be traded to other companies.

6. The stories about welfare chiselers show that the welfare system supports only shirkers and cheats.

7. Mountain climbing is more dangerous than people think: my cousin has fainted three times since he climbed Pike's Peak.

8. Racial tension is bound to occur when people with different backgrounds are forced to live side by side.

9. If our country tries to avoid becoming involved in conflicts like the one in Vietnam, we'll eventually be subjected to Communism.

10. She admits to being an atheist, so how can she be a good philosophy teacher?

EXERCISE 11

Evaluate the following brief essay for its effectiveness in convincing you (or any reader) to accept the writer's argument. Look especially for moderation in tone, the believability of assertions, adequate support for assertions, and sound inductive or deductive reasoning. Identify the writer's generalizations and evaluate their reasonableness. Do you see examples of any of the faults discussed in this chapter, such as begging or ignoring the question, overstating assumptions, or slipping into faulty reasoning?

Let's Hear It for Asphalt!

The truly disadvantaged students on this campus are the commuters. We pay our money and work hard for our degrees, yet we can't find a place to park our cars! Commuters are regularly treated as second-class citizens compared to resident students. But nowhere is the discrepancy more noticeable than in the parking situation.

The fact is, there aren't enough parking spaces for half the cars on campus. Students are lucky to make their classes at all after driving around for hours looking for a place to stop their car. If it were easier to park, students would get better grades, and the school administrators would probably have the higher enrollments they're so desperate for.

The really maddening thing is that we have to pay good money for parking tickets on top of tuition and everything else. The money probably goes toward a new faculty office building or dormitory or one of the other building projects that eat up what little parking space there is. Meanwhile, we commuters are pushed further and further away from the center of campus. But, then, why should the rich folks in charge of things care what happens to a few struggling students, some with families to support while they seek to better themselves?

The commuting students are like the Jews wandering in the wilderness. We need homelands for our cars and freedom from persecution by campus cops.

II
Grammatical Sentences

5
Understanding Sentence Grammar

Grammar describes how language works and helps us to talk about it. People who know a great deal about grammar don't always write well, and many people who write very well no longer think consciously about grammar and would have difficulty explaining in grammatical terms how their sentences work. But when something has gone wrong in your sentences, a knowledge of grammar will help you to recognize your problems and provide a language for discussing them.

You already know more grammar than you think you do, as you can see by looking at a sentence made up partly of nonsense words:

The rumfrum biggled the pooba.

You don't know what that sentence means. But you do know that something called a *rumfrum* did something to a *pooba*. He (or she, or it) *biggled* it, whatever that means. You know this because you understand the basic grammar of simple English sentences. You understand that this sentence sounds like *The boy kicked the ball, The man paid the bill,* or *The student wrote the paper.* As in those sentences, a single word following *the* names something; words with *-ed* endings usually denote action of some sort, especially when they fall in patterns like *the rumfrum biggled;* and word groups beginning with *the* and *that,* coming after words like *biggled,* usually name something that receives the action indicated.

In the sense that you understand *The rumfrum biggled the pooba,* you can understand even more complex sentences such as the following:

The stintless rumfrums biggled the jittish poobas who were kerpesting the gloots.

You don't know what *stintless* and *jittish* mean, but you do know that they describe *rumfrums* and *poobas,* respectively, and that the *poobas were kerpesting* (doing something to) *the gloots,* probably more than one *gloot.* You understand these things because you recognize familiar structures that recur in everyday talking and writing. Each statement about rumfrums is a **sentence,** the basic unit of the language. Grammar systematically describes the words that make up sentences and the way those words work together.

EXERCISE 1

Substitute English words for the nonsense words to make meaningful sentences of the following:

1. The floots spletted the fraz.
2. A merly sprot is a fris kroot.
3. Two whatly sprugs fristed a markley cree mot.
4. Frit is the wumple?
5. Glock me prack frusky claz prat, freeb.

5a
Understanding the basic sentence

Sentences are the basic units of writing, and good writing begins with sentences that are grammatical and clear. But to understand the grammar of sentences, we need to know what they do, in what patterns they typically appear, and how to describe the words that make them up.

1
Identifying subjects and predicates

Some sentences ask questions such as *Where is Bertram?* and *Who shouted?* Some sentences give commands such as *Close the door* and *Turn in your paper.* But most sentences make statements. First they name something; then they make an assertion about or describe an action involving that something. These two components are called the **subject** and the **predicate.**

SUBJECT	PREDICATE
Amanda	took the money to the bank.
Leroy	rode his bicycle down the middle of the street.
Erica	told Gerald she didn't want to see him anymore.
All the members of my family	were churchgoers from their earliest years.

2

Identifying the basic words: Nouns and verbs

gr

5a

If we study the five simple sentences below, we can learn a great deal about the words that make them up and the ways those words are put together.

SUBJECT	PREDICATE
The earth	trembled.
The earthquake	destroyed the city.
The result	was chaos.
The government	sent the city aid.
The citizens	declared the earthquake a disaster.

Words like *earth, earthquake, government,* and *citizens* name things, whereas words like *trembled, destroyed,* and *sent* express actions. (The word *the* appears several times but has no apparent meaning, at least not in the way that *earthquake* and *citizens* have meaning. Rather, *the* only points to the naming word that follows it; and the word *a* acts the same way.) Further, we can have *one earthquake* or *several earthquakes, one citizen* or *many citizens*; but we can't have one or more *declares* or *destroys*. If we drop the *-ed* from *destroyed* and *declared,* we change the time of the action from the past to the present. But we can't add *-ed* to *citizen* and have a form *citizened.* The word *citizen* just doesn't work that way. Clearly, these words function in different ways. Grammar classifies these distinctions by identifying different **parts of speech** or **word classes.**

Except for the words *the* and *a,* our five sentences are made up of two parts of speech: **nouns,** words that name; and **verbs,** words that express action or occurrence or a state of being. These are the basic words in English; without them we cannot form even the simplest sentences. The nouns and verbs in our sample sentences are listed below.

NOUNS	VERBS
earth	trembled
earthquake	destroyed
city	was
result	sent
chaos	declared
government	
aid	
citizens	
disaster	

We can identify nouns and verbs by their meanings and their forms.

Nouns

MEANING

Nouns name. They may name a person (*Paul McCartney, Johnny Carson, father*), a thing (*chair, book, spaceship*), a quality (*pain, mystery, simplicity*), a place (*city, Washington, ocean, Red Sea*), or an idea (*reality, peace, success*). Whatever exists or might exist has a name. Its name is a noun.

gr

5a

FORM

Many nouns add an *-s* to distinguish between the singular, meaning "one," and the plural, meaning "more than one" (*earthquake, earthquakes; city, cities; citizen, citizens; idea, ideas*). Nouns can also form a possessive, which sounds the same as the plural form but in writing uses an apostrophe as well as an *-s* (*citizen, citizen's; city, city's; father, father's*). The possessive form indicates that the noun owns, or possesses, a thing or quality (*citizen's declaration*).

Some nouns in our sample sentences—*chaos* and *earth*—don't usually form plurals. These words belong to a subgroup called **mass nouns.** They name something that is not usually countable, like *sugar, silver,* and *gravel*; or they name qualities, like *courage, fortitude,* and *anger*. (Other important groups of nouns not illustrated in our sentences are **proper nouns** like *Betty, Detroit,* and *Amazon,* which name specific people, places, and things; and **collective nouns** like *army, family,* and *herd,* which name groups.)

NOUNS WITH *THE, A,* AND *AN*

Many nouns in the singular are commonly preceded by *the* or *a* (*an* before a vowel sound: *an apple*). These words are usually called **articles,** but they may be described as **noun markers** since they occur only when a noun follows.

Verbs

MEANING

Verbs express an action or occurrence (*bring, grow, tell*) or a state of being (*be, become, seem*).

FORM

Verbs change form to indicate a difference between an action occurring in the present time and one occurring in past time. Most verbs show the difference by adding *-d* or *-ed* to the present-time form (*tremble, trembled; destroy, destroyed; declare, declared*). Such verbs are said to be **regular.** A few verbs show the difference between present and past time by some other change (*send, sent; ring, rang; eat, ate; think, thought; sleep, slept*). These verbs are called **irregular.** The verb *be* is unique because it has a different set of forms for present and past time in the singular (*is, was*) and the plural (*are, were*).

All verbs except *be* use the plain form (*tremble, destroy, declare, send, go, run*) to express present time when combined with all plural nouns and the words *I* and *you.*

gr

5a

you	tremble
earthquakes	destroy
they	declare
I	send
cars	go
boys	run

But they add an *-s* to the plain form when used to express present time with all singular nouns and with the words *he, she,* and *it.*

it	trembles
earthquake	destroys
he	declares
company	sends
car	goes
boy	runs

The verb *be* has the present form *is* when used with singular nouns and the words *he, she,* and *it* (*earth is, it is*). *Are* is the present form used with plural nouns and the words *you, we,* and *they* (*cards are, they are*). *Was* and *were* are the comparable past forms (*truck was, she was; trucks were, you were*).

VERBS WITH AUXILIARIES

All verbs combine with a small group of words called **auxiliary verbs** or **helping verbs** to form **verb phrases** (*has destroyed, had sent, may be called, is dealing, will have arrived*). Such phrases express more complex time relationships, as well as voice and mood. (See Chapter 7 for discussion of these characteristics.)

NOTE: The words *result* and *aid,* used as nouns in the sentences *The result was chaos* and *The government sent the city aid,* illustrate a very important point about parts of speech in English. These words are clearly nouns. But they also have the qualities of verbs. We can say *The result aided the citizens* or *The aid resulted in relief.* Many other English words also fit into more than one class of words or can be used in several ways. Thus when we try to identify what part of speech a word is, we must always look at how the word works in the sentence we are examining. The *function* of a word in a sentence always determines its part of speech in that sentence.

3
Forming sentence patterns with nouns and verbs

Let's reexamine our five sample sentences, this time looking at how the words are put together in each sentence. Putting an *N* over each noun and a *V* over each verb gives us the following:

        N   V
1. The earth trembled.

          N   V   N
2. The earthquake destroyed the city.

        N   V   N
3. The result was chaos.

         N   V   N N
4. The government sent the city aid.

        N   V   N   N
5. The citizens declared the earthquake a disaster.

Kinds of predicates

In each sentence above the subject consists only of a noun, or naming word, and an article, or marker. But the predicates vary: sentence 1 has a verb only, sentences 2 and 3 have a verb followed by a noun, and sentences 4 and 5 have a verb followed by two nouns. Further, although sentences 2 and 3 are constructed in the same way, they are not quite the same. In sentence 2, *destroyed* indicates an action, and *city* names what was destroyed. In sentence 3, *chaos* is simply another name for *result,* and the two words are related by *was.* We could write the sentence *result = chaos.* Sentences 4 and 5 are also alike but different. Both have two nouns after the verb, but those nouns are not related in the same way either to the verbs or to each other. In sentence 4, *aid* describes what was sent (as *city* in the second sentence describes what was destroyed). *City* in sentence 4 describes to whom or for whom (or what) the *aid* was sent. In sentence 5, *earthquake* describes what was declared, whereas *disaster* is another name for *earthquake.* The relation between *earthquake* and *disaster* is the same as that between *result* and *chaos* in sentence 3: *earthquake = disaster.*

To describe and simplify the relations among words in these predicates, we need names for the different functions of the nouns following the verbs. Thus we need another set of grammatical terms.

A **direct object** (DO) is a word that indicates what or who receives the action of the verb.

                          DO
The earthquake destroyed the *city.*

gr

5a

DO
The government sent the city *aid.*

DO
The citizens declared the *earthquake* a disaster.

An **indirect object** (IO) is a word that indicates to whom or for whom the action of the verb is directed.

IO
The government sent the *city* aid. [The government sent aid to or for the city.]

A **subject complement** (SC) is a word that renames or describes the subject.

SC
The result was *chaos.*

Chaos is a noun, as we have seen, but words that function as complements may be either nouns or adjectives (see 5b-1). (When they are nouns, they are sometimes called **predicate nouns.)**

An **object complement** (OC) is a word that renames or describes a direct object.

OC
The citizens declared the earthquake a *disaster.*

Like subject complements, object complements may also be nouns or adjectives (see 5b-1).

With these terms we can now describe not only the noun and verb patterns of our five sample sentences but also the different functions of their predicates. Repeating our sentences once more with the new labels, we see their five different patterns.

S   V
The earth trembled.

S   V   DO
The earthquake destroyed the city.

S   V   SC
The result was chaos.

S   V   IO   DO
The government sent the city aid.

S   V   DO   OC
The citizens declared the earthquake a disaster.

Verbs that make complete statements without the use of an object or complement are called **intransitive verbs.** *Trembled* is intransitive, because it requires no object or complement to complete its action. Verbs that take objects are called **transitive verbs.**

Destroyed, sent, and *declared* are all transitive because they require objects to complete their action. Verbs that are followed by complements describing their subjects are called **linking verbs.** *Was* is a linking verb because the complement *chaos* describes the subject *result.*

The five sentence patterns above are the basic frameworks for most written English sentences. However long or complicated a sentence is, one or more of these basic patterns forms its foundation. A question may change the order of the subject and verb (*Is she a doctor?*), a command may omit the subject entirely (*Be quiet!*), and the order of the parts may be different in some statements (see 5e), but the same basic sentence parts will be present or clearly understood.

gr
5a

Pronouns

Before we look at the kinds of words and word groups we use to vary and expand these five basic sentence patterns, we need to look at a third small but important group of words, the pronouns.

> Susanne enlisted in the Air Force. *She* leaves for her training in two weeks. Susanne is one of the people *who* took advanced physics in high school.

Most **pronouns** substitute for nouns and function in sentences as nouns do. In the sentences above the pronoun *she* substitutes for *Susanne,* and the pronoun *who* substitutes for *people.*

Pronouns can be divided into several subclasses depending on their form or function. The **personal pronouns** refer to an individual or to individuals. They are *I, you, he, she, it, we,* and *they.* The **indefinite pronouns,** such as *everybody* and *some,* do not substitute for any specific nouns, though they function as nouns (*Everybody likes Tim*). The **demonstrative pronouns,** including *this, that,* and *such,* identify or point to nouns (*This is the gun she used*). The **relative pronouns** *who, which,* and *that* relate groups of words to nouns or other pronouns (*Jim spoke to the boys who broke the window*). Intensive and reflexive pronouns have different functions but the same form—a personal pronoun plus *-self* (*himself, yourself*). **Intensive pronouns** emphasize a noun or other pronoun (*She herself asked the question*). **Reflexive pronouns** refer to the noun or pronoun acting as the sentence subject (*You might hurt yourself*). Finally, **interrogative pronouns,** including *who, which,* and *what,* introduce questions (*Who will come to the concert?*).

The personal pronouns *I, he, she, we, they* and the relative pronoun *who* change form when they serve different functions in sentences. (For a discussion of these form changes, see Chapter 6.)

gr

5a

EXERCISE 2

Identify the subjects and predicates of the following sentences.

Example:

Several important people will speak at commencement.

SUBJECT | PREDICATE

Several important people |will speak at commencement.

1. The radio fell.
2. Summer ends too soon.
3. My brother's dog had fourteen puppies.
4. People should think carefully before joining cults.
5. The Aeronautics and Space Museum has a piece of moon rock for visitors to touch.

EXERCISE 3

Identify each of the following words as noun, verb, or both.

1. car
2. light
3. door
4. company
5. whistle
6. condition
7. sing
8. post
9. attic
10. glue

EXERCISE 4

Identify all nouns and verbs in the following sentences. Which nouns could also function as verbs, and which verbs as nouns, if they appeared in other sentences?

Example:

Seven visitors took the tour through the house.

     N   V   N   N

Seven *visitors took* the *tour* through the *house.*

Nouns that could also function as verbs: *tour, house.*

1. The trees behind our house are dying of Dutch elm disease.
2. Drivers should take a new test every ten years.
3. The new speed limit has saved many lives.
4. I received two records last Christmas.
5. Although I was absent for a month, I finished the semester with passing grades.

EXERCISE 5

Identify each direct object (DO), indirect object (IO), subject complement (SC), and object complement (OC) in the following sentences.

Example:
Parents offer their children not only love but also support.

                   IO   **DO**   **DO**
Parents offer their *children* not only *love* but also *support*.

1. My uncle walks his dog at seven o'clock.
2. We brought my aunt a new painting.
3. Marie calls her boyfriend a genius.
4. The dentist's bill was five hundred dollars.
5. I missed three tests last week.
6. Many adults find rock concerts strange.
7. I read my brother *Charlotte's Web*.
8. Then I bought him his own copy.
9. We thought tonight's sunset beautiful.
10. Moderate exercise is good for your heart.

gr
5b

EXERCISE 6

Write two sentences using each of the following verbs. In each sentence use a direct and an indirect object.

   Example: send

              IO   **DO**
Sue sent her *teacher* a *note*.

              IO   **DO**
Don sent *Sue* six *roses*.

1. buy   4. read
2. bring   5. give
3. throw

5b
Expanding the basic sentence with single words

We have been studying simple sentences and their basic structures. But most of the sentences we read, write, or use in ordinary speech are longer and more complex. Most sentences contain one or more of the following: (1) modifying words; (2) word groups, called phrases and clauses; or (3) combinations of two or more words or word groups of the same kind.

The simplest expansion of sentences occurs when we add modifying words to describe or limit the nouns and verbs. Modifying words add detail to the earthquake disaster:

Recently, the earth trembled.

The earthquake *nearly* destroyed the *old* city.

The *frantic* citizens *quickly* declared the earthquake a *complete* disaster.

1
Using adjectives and adverbs

The new words added to our basic sentences are *recently, nearly, old, frantic, quickly,* and *complete.* As we found with nouns and verbs, not all these words act the same way. *Old, frantic,* and *complete* modify nouns, but *recently, nearly,* and *quickly* do not. We don't speak of a *recently earthquake* or a *quickly citizen.* Nor do we say *frantic declared* or *complete destroyed.* Again, we are dealing with two different parts of speech: **adjectives,** which describe or modify nouns and pronouns; and **adverbs,** which describe the action of verbs and also modify adjectives, other adverbs, and whole groups of words.

In addition to the half-dozen examples in our three sentences, here are a few of the many adjectives and adverbs we use every day:

ADJECTIVES	ADVERBS
crazy	roughly
heartless	evenly
strong	angrily
happy	sadly
slow	openly
acceptable	never
foolish	always

Several of the adjectives could be made into adverbs if we added *-ly* (*heartlessly, strongly, foolishly,* for example). And we could make adjectives from several of the adverbs by removing the *-ly* (*rough, even, sad,* for example). But we can't add *-ly* to make an adverb of *old;* nor can we make *never* and *always* into adjectives. *Old* can only be an adjective, *never* and *always* only adverbs.

To determine whether a word is an adjective or an adverb, we must identify the word it modifies in a sentence. Although an *-ly* ending often signals an adverb, many adverbs—*never* and *always,* for example—have a different form. Moreover, some *adjectives* end in *-ly:* in *a gentlemanly person, a likely candidate,* and *a lovely breeze, gentlemanly, likely,* and *lovely* clearly modify nouns and are thus adjectives.

Adjectives modify nouns and pronouns. Adverbs modify verbs, but they also modify adjectives and other adverbs:

extremely unhappy [adverb-adjective]
bitterly cold [adverb-adjective]
very quickly [adverb-adverb]

Adverbs may also modify groups of words within a sentence. For example, in the sentence *She ran almost to the end of the street, almost* modifies *to the end.*

Adverbs usually indicate where, when, how, or to what extent, as in the following:

Send all the mail *here*. [*Here* is *where* the mail is to be sent.]

Fred will arrive *tomorrow*. [*Tomorrow* is *when* Fred will arrive.]

We are *completely* satisfied. [*Completely* indicates *to what extent* we are satisfied.]

Jeremy answered *angrily*. [*Angrily* is *how* Jeremy answered.]

gr
5b

Adjectives and adverbs appear in three forms distinguished by degree. The **positive degree** is the basic form of both parts of speech, the one listed in the dictionary: *good, green, angry: badly, quickly, angrily*. The **comparative** form indicates a greater degree of the quality named by the word: *better, greener, angrier; worse, more quickly, more angrily*. The **superlative** form indicates the greatest degree of the quality named: *best, greenest, angriest; worst, most quickly, most angrily*. (For further discussion of the forms and uses of comparatives and superlatives, see 9e.)

We can use adjectives to vary two of the basic sentence patterns that we constructed with nouns and verbs. Whenever a noun follows a linking verb or a direct object, we can substitute an adjective in the noun's place.

The result was *chaos*. [*Chaos* is a noun complement.]

The result was *chaotic*. [*Chaotic* is an adjective complement.]

The citizens declared the earthquake a *disaster*. [*Disaster* is a noun complementing the direct object *earthquake*.]

The citizens declared the earthquake *disastrous*. [*Disastrous* is an adjective complementing the direct object *earthquake*.]

EXERCISE 7

Identify each adjective and adverb in the following sentences.

Example:

The red barn looked oddly out of place amid the modern buildings.

    ADJ   ADV   ADJ

The *red* barn looked *oddly* out of place amid the *modern* buildings.

1. The frozen rain made the trees glisten.
2. Happy children used the glazed streets as playgrounds.
3. Fortunately, no cars ventured out that day.
4. Wise parents stayed indoors where they could be warm and dry.
5. Even the dogs slept soundly near the warm radiators, going outside only when pushed.

EXERCISE 8

Change each adjective below into an adverb, and change each adverb into an adjective. Then use each new modifier in a sentence.

  Example:

  sorrowful

  David watched *sorrowfully* as the firemen removed the charred remains of his furniture.

1. watchful	6. evenly
2. wisely	7. happy
3. new	8. painfully
4. bright	9. darkly
5. fortunately	10. sturdy

2
Using other modifying words

Although adjectives and adverbs are the most important single-word modifiers, both nouns and some verb forms also serve as single-word modifiers.

Nouns as modifiers

Nouns often modify other nouns, as in *morning shoppers, office buildings, Thanksgiving prayer, gasoline truck, shock hazard.* (See 9f for a comment on the overuse of awkward constructions like *employee relations interview program,* in which a series of nouns modify another noun.)

Verb forms as modifiers

All verbs have a form that ends in *-ing* (*using, smoking*), called a **present participle,** and a form that is usually the same as the past-time form (*used, smoked*), called the **past participle.** Just as some verbs make their past-time forms in irregular ways, some also make their past participles irregularly (*drink, drunk; eat, eaten; sleep, slept*). These present and past participles frequently function as modifiers.

PRESENT PARTICIPLE	PAST PARTICIPLE
closing time	written work
drinking men	corrected papers
singing birds	worn clothing
speaking voice	spoken word
acting president	broken finger

(See 5c-2 for more discussion of these verb forms.)

EXERCISE 9

Form the present and past participles of the following verbs. (If you need help, see 5c-2 and Chapter 7.) Then use both participles to modify nouns.

Example:

smoke, smoking, smoked
Only a *smoking cigar* remained.
No one tried the *smoked oysters*.

1. type
2. paint
3. write
4. pitch
5. charge

gr
5c

5c
Expanding the basic sentence with word groups

Nouns, verbs, adjectives, and adverbs carry the primary meaning of sentences. But relatively few sentences we read or write are made up only of these words and pronouns. Most sentences contain groups of words that *function* as nouns, verbs, adjectives, and adverbs. An example:

When the earth trembled slightly, the early morning shoppers were afraid of another disaster.

The skeleton of this sentence—the basic subject-predicate shape—is *the shoppers were afraid*. This, of course, is the basic sentence pattern of subject-verb-complement, with the adjective *afraid* in the complement position. The subject is expanded to *early morning shoppers:* the noun *morning* modifies *shoppers,* and the adjective *early* modifies *morning.* But connected to this basic sentence are two groups of words, *when the earth trembled slightly* and *of another disaster.* These groups function as modifiers in the sentence, just as single adverbs and adjectives do. The group beginning with *when* functions as an adverb modifying the entire structure that follows it. The group beginning with *of (of another disaster)* also functions as an adverb, modifying the adjective *afraid.* The two words *when* and *of* serve principally as connectors between the words that follow them and the basic structure. *Of* belongs to a class of words called **prepositions.** *When* belongs to a class called **subordinating conjunctions,** or, simply, **subordinators.** (We will look at another kind of conjunction, the **coordinating conjunction,** a little later in 5d-1.)

These connectors introduce two kinds of word groups, clauses and phrases. A clause (*when the earth trembled slightly* or *the shoppers were afraid*) is any group of related words that contains a subject and a predicate. An **independent** or **main clause** makes a complete statement by itself (*the shoppers were afraid*). A **dependent** or

subordinate clause is used as a single part of speech (*when the earth trembled slightly* functions as an adverb) and does not make an independent statement. A **phrase,** such as *of another disaster,* is any group of related words that is used as a single part of speech but lacks either a subject or a predicate or both. Besides verb phrases (see p. 112), there are also **prepositional phrases** and **verbal phrases.**

1

Using prepositional phrases

Prepositions are words that never change form. Although we use these words with great frequency, the entire list of prepositions is short. Some of the most common are:

about	beside	of
above	between	on
across	beyond	over
after	by	since
against	despite	through
along	down	to
among	except	toward
as	for	until
at	from	up
before	in	upon
behind	inside	with
below	into	within
beneath	near	without

Prepositions always connect a noun, a pronoun, or a group of words functioning as a noun—called the **object of the preposition**—to another word that usually precedes the whole group.

She went *to the store.* [*To* is the preposition; *store* is the object.]

We went *without him.* [*Without* is the preposition; *him* is its object.]

(Some of these words may occur without an object, as in *He went inside.* In such cases the words function as adverbs.) The entire group introduced by the preposition—consisting of the preposition itself, its object, and any modifiers of the object—is called a **prepositional phrase.** The objects of prepositions are usually nouns or pronouns, but they may be any group of words that functions as a noun (see verbal phrases and clauses in 5c-2). Typical prepositional phrases are:

PREPOSITION	OBJECT
before	college
of	spaghetti

PREPOSITION	OBJECT
on	the plain
with	great satisfaction
upon	entering the room [verbal phrase]
from	where you are standing [clause]

Prepositions normally come before their objects. But sometimes the preposition comes after its object, particularly in speech.

gr
5c

What do you want to see him *about?*
Which *apartment* does she live *in?*

Prepositional phrases usually function as adjectives (modifying nouns) or as adverbs (modifying verbs, adjectives, or other adverbs). Occasionally, prepositional phrases also function as nouns, though rarely in writing.

PREPOSITIONAL PHRASES AS ADJECTIVES

Terry is the boy *in the pink shirt.* [Phrase describes *boy.*]

Life *on a raft in the Mississippi* gave an opportunity *for adventure.* [*On a raft* describes *life*; *in the Mississippi* describes *raft*; and *for adventure* describes *opportunity.*]

PREPOSITIONAL PHRASES AS ADVERBS

She had driven steadily *for four hours from Baltimore.* [Both phrases describe *driven.*]

Our Great Dane Joshua buries his bones *behind the garage.* [Phrase describes *buries.*]

PREPOSITIONAL PHRASE AS NOUN

Across the river is too far to go for ice cream. [Phrase functions as sentence subject.]

EXERCISE 10

Identify the prepositional phrases in the following sentences. Indicate whether each phrase functions as an adjective, an adverb, or a noun. If the phrase is a modifier, name the word that it modifies.

Example:

After an hour I finally arrived at the home of my professor.

ADV PHRASE   ADV PHRASE   ADJ PHRASE
After an hour I finally arrived *at the home of my professor.*

[*After an hour* and *at the home* modify *arrived; of my professor* modifies *home.*]

1. You can make time for anything.
2. The lady in the blue socks ran from the police.

3. The test will be given on Tuesday.
4. We went over the hill, through the woods, and across the stream.
5. I am sick to death of my job.
6. I will be exactly ten minutes behind you.
7. An error of 10 percent is too large.
8. The book begins with a gruesome murder.
9. Even now, it sticks in my mind.
10. Nobody told us the class had been moved outdoors beside the gym.

EXERCISE 11

To gain experience in expanding sentences with prepositional phrases, write one complete sentence from each set of phrases below.

> *Example:*
> in pencil
> on white paper
> We are required to write the exam *in pencil* and *on white paper.*

1. for two hundred people
   before the concert
2. across the street
   inside the grocery store
   upon the counter
3. beneath the surface of the lake
   alongside the dock
4. of several weeks
   between semesters
   for three hundred dollars
5. despite what I said previously
   with those people
   on Friday

2
Using verbals and verbal phrases

All verbs have three forms that either combine with auxiliaries or function as nouns, adjectives, and adverbs. We have touched briefly on two of the forms: the present participle and the past participle. The third form is the infinitive. The **present participle** adds *-ing* to the plain form of the verb: *asking, being, beating, exciting, eating, singing, working.* The **past participle** of regular verbs adds *-d* or *-ed* to the plain form—*asked, excited, worked*—and thus is the same as the past-time form. Irregular verbs form their past participle by some other kind of change, usually by adding *-en* instead of *-ed*, by changing an internal vowel, or both: *been, beaten, eaten, sung.* (See

7a for more discussion and a list of irregular verbs.) The **infinitive** is the plain form of the verb, the form listed in the dictionary. As a verbal it is usually preceded by *to*, which is often called the **infinitive marker**: *to ask, to be, to beat, to excite, to eat, to sing, to work.*

When these forms combine with auxiliaries, they form verb phrases that have a variety of meanings.

> They *had asked* me to come.
> Without support our team *will be beaten* in every game.
> Jane *should have been working* harder.

When these verb forms function as nouns, adjectives, and adverbs, they are called **verbals.**

> He landed *running.* [Present participle as adverb.]
> The article presents *distorted* results. [Past participle as adjective.]
> The coach's goal was *to win.* [Infinitive as noun complement.]

Verbals may stand either alone or in combination with other words in verbal phrases. *But a verbal cannot stand alone as the predicate of a sentence.* For this reason verbals are sometimes called **nonfinite verbs** in contrast to **finite verbs,** which can make an assertion or express a state of being.

The following examples illustrate the common uses of verbals.

Participles

Both present and past participles function as adjectives to modify nouns, pronouns, or groups of words functioning as nouns.

> The *freezing* rain made the roads dangerous. [Present participle as adjective modifying *rain.*]
> The *exhausted* miners were rescued after four days. [Past participle as adjective modifying *miners.*]
> Oliver found his *typing* job *boring.* [Present participle *typing* as adjective modifying *job;* present participle *boring* as object complement modifying *job.*]
> *Disgusted,* he quit that night. [Past participle as adjective modifying *he.*]

Present participles can also function as nouns. When they function this way, they are often given the special name **gerund.**

> Unfortunately, *studying* always bored Michael. [Gerund, or present participle, as subject of sentence.]
> His sister Annie hated *swimming.* [Gerund as direct object of *hated.*]
> Both Michael and Annie preferred *loafing* to *working.* [Gerunds as objects: *loafing* as object of *prefer; working* as object of preposition *to.*]

In fact, their principal occupation was *loafing*. [Gerund as noun complement.]

Infinitives

Infinitives function as nouns, adjectives, and adverbs.

He is the man *to elect*. [Infinitive as adjective modifying *man*.]

He hoped *to go*. [Infinitive as noun object of *hoped*.]

This physics problem is difficult *to solve*. [Infinitive as adverb modifying *difficult*.]

Verbal phrases

Like verbs, verbals may take subjects, objects, and complements, and they may be modified by adverbs. The verbal and all the words immediately related to it make up a **verbal phrase. Participial phrases** function as adjectives and nouns. **Infinitive phrases** function as nouns, adjectives, and adverbs.

PARTICIPIAL PHRASES AS ADJECTIVES

Chewing his pencil steadily, Dick stared into the air. [Participial phrase describes *Dick*. It consists of the present participle *chewing*, its object *his pencil*, and the adverb *steadily*.]

He was frustrated by the paper *lying before him*. [Participial phrase describes *paper*. It consists of the present participle *lying* and its modifier, the prepositional phrase *before him*.]

Defeated by the same blank paper earlier in the day, Dick knew he must somehow write something. [Participial phrase describes *Dick*. It consists of the past participle *defeated* modified by two prepositional phrases.]

PARTICIPIAL PHRASES AS NOUNS

When participial phrases function as nouns, they are often called **gerund phrases.**

Eating an entire lemon pie for lunch was easy for Wesley. [Participial phrase as noun subject of the sentence. It consists of the present participle *eating*, its object *an entire lemon pie*, and the prepositional phrase *for lunch*, modifying *eating*.]

As might be expected, his mother was annoyed at *his eating the whole pie*. [Participial phrase as object of the preposition *at*. It consists of the participle *eating*, preceded by its subject *his*, and followed by its object *the whole pie*.]

But she had hidden a second pie because she anticipated *his doing it*. [Participial phrase as direct object of the verb *anticipated*.]

Notice that when a gerund phrase has a subject (as in *his eat-*

gr

5c

ing or *his doing*), the subject is usually in the possessive case. (See 6h.)

INFINITIVE PHRASES AS NOUNS

To play nursemaid to her brother was not exactly Melanie's idea of fun. [Infinitive phrase as subject of the sentence. It consists of the infinitive *to play* and the prepositional phrase *to her brother* (an adjective phrase modifying *nursemaid*).]

She had planned *to spend the afternoon at the pool.* [Infinitive phrase as object of the verb *had planned.* It consists of the infinitive *to spend,* its object *the afternoon,* and the prepositional phrase *at the pool* (an adverb phrase modifying the infinitive).]

To lie repeatedly is *to deny reality.* [Two infinitive phrases—one as subject and one as subject complement. *To lie repeatedly* consists of the infinitive plus an adverb modifying it. *To deny reality* consists of the infinitive plus its object.]

We wanted *him to go.* [Infinitive phrase as object of *wanted.* It consists of the infinitive and its subject *him.*]

Notice that when a pronoun is either the object of an infinitive or the subject (as in *him to go*), it is in the objective case. (See 6f.)

INFINITIVE PHRASES AS ADJECTIVES

Students were pleased at the decision *to dismiss classes.* [Infinitive phrase modifying *decision.*]

Amy is not a girl *to put off difficult decisions.* [Infinitive phrase modifying *girl.*]

The best place *to eat pancakes* is Jimmy's place. [Infinitive phrase modifying *place.*]

INFINITIVE PHRASES AS ADVERBS

Frank jogged *to keep himself in good condition.* [Infinitive phrase modifying *jogged.*]

The child was too young *to understand the story.* [Infinitive phrase modifying *young.*]

Glenda always drives too fast *to enjoy the country.* [Infinitive phrase modifying *fast.*]

NOTE: An infinitive or an infinitive phrase can't always be identified by the infinitive marker *to.* When the infinitive or the infinitive phrase is used as a noun after verbs like *hear, let, help, make, see,* and *watch,* the *to* is not expressed.

He made *her correct the paper.* [Compare *He made her to correct the paper. Her* is the subject of the infinitive; *the paper* is its object.]

We all heard *her tell the story.*

gr

5c

gr

5c

3
Using absolute phrases

Absolute phrases consist of a noun or pronoun and a participle.

> *Our rabbits having been sold,* we no longer needed their food.
> *The job done,* the men rested.
> The old tree stood alone, *its trunk slowly rotting.*

Such phrases are called *absolute* because they have no specific grammatical connection to any word in the rest of the sentence. This lack of grammatical connection distinguishes absolute phrases from participial phrases, which always modify a specific word or word group in the sentence. Compare these two sentences:

> *His arms thrashing,* the swimmer again rose to the surface. [Absolute phrase does not modify a word or words in the sentence.]
> *Thrashing his arms,* the swimmer again rose to the surface. [Participial phrase modifies *swimmer.*]

When the participle of an absolute phrase is some form of *to be,* it is often omitted. *Being* is omitted from the three absolute phrases in the last half of this sentence:

> The animal lay on its side, *its body stiff, its legs askew, its eyes wide open.*

EXERCISE 12

The following sentences contain participles, infinitives, and participial and infinitive phrases. Identify each verbal or verbal phrase and indicate whether it is used as an adjective, an adverb, or a noun.

Example:
Running wildly, the dog tried to rid herself of the aching cramp.

   ADJ   N   ADJ
Running wildly, the dog tried *to rid herself* of the *aching* cramp.

1. To dance with Bill is to dance well.
2. Jogging every day, I have lost five pounds this month.
3. Daily jogging can help other people lose weight, too.
4. Defeated at Waterloo, Napoleon was sent into exile.
5. We must be strong enough to face the death of loved ones.
6. Whimpering and moaning, my brother was finally dragged to be vaccinated.
7. Eating at a nice restaurant is a relaxing way to end a demanding week.

8. To fly was one of humankind's recurring dreams.
9. The dwindling water supply made the remaining vacationers decide to leave for another campground.
10. The hungry wolves were kept at bay by the periodic firing of a rifle.

EXERCISE 13

Use each of the following verbals or verbal phrases in a sentence, as specified by the directions in parentheses.

> *Example:*
> studying every night (*as the object of a preposition*)
> He objected *to studying every night.*

1. to hike (*as a direct object*)
2. falling far behind the other runners (*as an adjective*)
3. breathing rapidly (*as a noun*)
4. opened by mistake (*as an adjective*)
5. convicted of two robberies (*as an adjective*)
6. to earn a living (*as an adverb*)
7. shopping (*as a subject*)
8. thinking (*as a subject*)
9. to harass the neighbors (*as an adverb*)
10. to take long trips (*as a direct object*)

EXERCISE 14

Change the following sentences to make absolute phrases and include the phrases in your own sentences.

> *Example:*
> The flower's petals wilted.
> *Its petals wilted,* the flower looked pathetic.

1. Her face was pale.
2. He left his money to his younger daughter.
3. The steelworkers are on strike.
4. The hotel was destroyed by fire.
5. The thief's mouth twitched.

4
Using subordinate clauses

We began our discussion of word groups with this sentence:

When the earth trembled slightly, the early morning shoppers were afraid of another disaster.

Both parts of this sentence (on either side of the comma) are alike in that they have subjects (*the earth* and *the shoppers*) and predicates (*trembled* and *were afraid*). The main difference between them is that the first begins with *when* whereas the second does not.

Each part of this sentence is a **clause,** a word group containing a subject and á predicate. But each is a different kind of clause. **Main** or **independent clauses,** such as *the shoppers were afraid,* can stand alone as sentences. **Subordinate** or **dependent clauses,** such as *when the earth trembled slightly,* cannot stand alone as sentences. They depend for their meaning on the independent clause they are attached to. We could write *The shoppers were afraid* as a free-standing sentence and our readers would understand our meaning (though they might wonder why the shoppers were afraid). But if we were to write *When the earth trembled slightly* as a freestanding sentence, our readers would be left trying to complete our meaning, asking "What happened?"

We use two kinds of words to connect subordinate clauses with independent clauses. The first kind is **subordinating conjunctions** or **subordinators.** They always come at the beginning of subordinate clauses. Like prepositions, subordinating conjunctions are few in number and never change form in any way. Some of the most common subordinating conjunctions are:

after	since	when
although	so that	whenever
as	that	where
because	though	wherever
before	unless	while
if	until	why

NOTE: Some of these words—for instance, *after, before,* and *until*—function as prepositions when they are followed only by a noun or the equivalent of a noun. *After* is a subordinating conjunction in *He came after he had had dinner.* But *after* is a preposition in *He came after dinner.*

The second kind of connecting word is the **relative pronoun.** It also introduces a subordinate clause and serves to link it with an independent clause. The relative pronouns are:

which	what	who (whose, whom)
that	whatever	whoever (whomever)

These words function in exactly the same way as subordinating conjunctions, although *who* and *whoever* change form depending on their function in their own clauses (see 6g).

Like prepositional and verbal phrases, subordinate clauses function as adjectives, adverbs, and nouns and are described as adjective, adverb, or noun clauses according to their use in a particular sentence. Only by determining its function in a sentence can we identify a particular clause.

gr

5c

SUBORDINATE CLAUSES AS ADJECTIVES

Adjective clauses modify nouns, pronouns, or groups of words serving as nouns. They are usually introduced by relative pronouns. Sometimes they are introduced by subordinating conjunctions such as *where* and *when.*

> My family still lives in the house *that my grandfather built.* [Subordinate clause modifying *house.*]
>
> Dale is the girl *who always gets there early.* [Subordinate clause modifying *girl.*]
>
> My yellow Volkswagen, *which I bought seven years ago,* has traveled 78,000 miles. [Subordinate clause modifying *Volkswagen.*]
>
> There comes a time *when each of us must work.* [Subordinate clause modifying *time.*]

gr

5c

SUBORDINATE CLAUSES AS ADVERBS

Adverb clauses modify verbs, adjectives, and adverbs; that is, they function the same way as single-word adverbs. They usually tell how, why, when, under what conditions, with what result, and so on. They always begin with subordinating conjunctions.

> Calvin liked to go *where there was action.* [Subordinate clause modifying *go.*]
>
> Elaine is friendlier *when she's talking on the telephone.* [Subordinate clause modifying *friendlier.*]
>
> Donald failed *because he did not study.* [Subordinate clause modifying *failed.*]
>
> She came as quickly *as she could.* [Subordinate clause modifying *quickly.*]

SUBORDINATE CLAUSES AS NOUNS

Noun clauses function as subjects, objects, and complements. They usually begin with relative pronouns, but sometimes they begin with subordinating conjunctions like *when* and *where.*

> Everyone knows *what a panther is.* [Subordinate clause as the direct object of *knows.*]
>
> *Whoever calls the station first* will win a case of bean soup. [Subordinate clause as the subject of the sentence.]
>
> The station will send *whoever requests it* a full report. [Subordinate clause as indirect object of *will send.*]
>
> The truth was *that Abner lacked good judgment.* [Subordinate clause as subject complement of the linking verb *was.*]

ELLIPTICAL CLAUSES

A subordinate clause that is grammatically incomplete but clear in meaning is called an **elliptical clause** (*ellipsis* means "omission"). The meaning of the clause is clear because the missing element can be supplied from the context. Most often the elements omitted are the relative pronouns *that, which,* and *whom* from adjective clauses or the predicate from the second part of a comparison.

gr

5c

> Thailand is among the countries (*that or which*) he visited.
> Ellen dances better *than Martha* (*dances*).

Here are other typical elliptical clauses:

When (*she was*) *only a child,* Julia saw a great gray owl.
Though (*they are*) *rare south of Canada,* great gray owls sometimes appear in Massachusetts.
If (*it is*) *possible,* report sightings of rare birds to the Audubon Society.

EXERCISE 15

Identify the subordinate clauses in the following sentences and indicate whether each is used as an adjective, an adverb, or a noun. If the clause is a noun, indicate its function in the sentence.

Example:

The auctioneer opened the bidding when everyone was seated.

ADV

The auctioneer opened the bidding *when everyone was seated.*

1. That Stefanie did not go to college was a disappointment to her parents.
2. Ever since she was a small child, they had saved money for her education.
3. Stefanie decided, though, that she wanted to work a year or two before college.
4. Until she makes up her mind, Stefanie's education money is collecting interest.
5. Her parents are the kind who let their children think for themselves.

EXERCISE 16

Combine each of the following pairs of independent clauses into one sentence by using a subordinating conjunction or a relative pronoun.

Example:

Josh may not graduate. He has bad grades.
Josh may not graduate *because* he has bad grades.

1. I like swimming. I once almost drowned.
2. Those dogs have a master. He gives them equal discipline and praise.
3. The basketball team has had a losing season. The team once showed promise.
4. He didn't bother to undress for bed. He was too tired.
5. She is the teacher. She gives very few A's.

5
Using appositives

Appositives are usually nouns or word groups functioning as nouns that rename other nouns or word groups.

> His first love, *racing stock cars,* was his last love. [Gerund phrase as appositive.]
>
> Bizen ware, *a dark stoneware,* is a Japanese ceramic produced since the fourteenth century. [Noun phrase as appositive.]

Like adjectives, appositives relate to nouns, but, unlike adjectives, they can substitute for the nouns they relate to. Compare this sentence with the first one above.

> Racing stock cars was his last love.

Appositives are often introduced by words and phrases like *that is, or, such as, for example,* and *in other words.*

> Kangaroos, opossums, and wombats are all marsupials, *that is, mammals that carry their young in external abdominal pouches.*
>
> Jujitsu, *or judo,* is based on the principle that an opponent's strength may be used to defeat him.

Although most appositives are nouns that rename other nouns, they may also be and rename other parts of speech.

> My dog Licorice, *alive with fleas,* was scratching himself furiously. [Adjective phrase *alive with fleas* is appositive to *My dog Licorice.*]
>
> All papers should be proofread carefully, that is, *checked for spelling, punctuation, and mechanics.* [Appositive beginning *checked* renames and defines the verb *proofread.*]

Appositives are a kind of abbreviated or reduced clause because they can always be stated as clauses with some form of the verb *be.*

> Bizen ware, (which is) a dark stoneware, is a Japanese ceramic produced since the fourteenth century.
>
> My dog Licorice, (who is) alive with fleas, was scratching furiously.

Thus appositives are economical alternatives to adjective clauses with a form of *be.*

EXERCISE 17

Add to and change the following sentences to form sentences of your own that use appositives.

Example:

The largest land animal in the world is the elephant.

The largest land animal in the world, *the elephant,* is also one of the most intelligent.

1. Jerry's aim in life is to avoid all productive labor.
2. Christine's usual time for leaving work is 5:30.
3. The things people collect include Superman comics, Beatles memorabilia, and beer cans.
4. Growing cactus is a hobby that takes plenty of patience.
5. The little boy is a nasty, spoiled brat.

gr

5d

5d
Compounding words, phrases, and clauses

We've seen how to modify the nouns and verbs of our basic sentence patterns and how to use word groups in place of single nouns and modifiers. Now we'll see how to combine both single words and groups of words, as in these examples:

Bonnie spent the afternoon in the park. Her father spent the afternoon in the park.

Bonnie and her father spent the afternoon in the park.

Curt was tired. He was sick. He was depressed.

Curt was tired, sick, and depressed.

Brenda went to the drug store. She bought some vitamins. She returned as soon as possible.

Brenda went to the drug store, bought some vitamins, and returned as soon as possible.

In the first pair of examples we have joined the two different subjects, *Bonnie* and *her father,* into a **compound subject,** thus avoiding repetition of the same predicate in two sentences. In the second pair of examples we have joined the three adjective complements into a **compound complement** (*tired, sick,* and *depressed*) that describes the common subject *Curt* after the common linking verb *was.* And in the last pair of examples we have joined the three different predicates into a **compound predicate** (*went . . . , bought . . . ,* and *returned . . .*), using the common subject *Brenda.* In every example we have used *and* to join the parts.

1
Using coordinating conjunctions and correlative conjunctions

The word *and* is a **coordinating conjunction.** Like prepositions and subordinating conjunctions, coordinating conjunctions do not change form and are few in number.

and	for
but	so
nor	yet
or	

gr

5d

Coordinating conjunctions function to connect words or word groups of the same kind—that is, two or more nouns, verbs, adjectives, adverbs, phrases, clauses, or whole sentences.

Stewart *or* Janice will have to go.
The chair was unfashionable *yet* charming.
Lee wanted to go *but* stayed to finish her homework.

The conjunctions *and, or, nor,* and *but* pair with *both, either, neither,* and *not* to form a special kind of conjunction called a **correlative conjunction.**

Both Bonnie *and* her father went to the park.
The basketball is *either* on the shelf *or* in the closet.
The committee spoke *neither* before he came *nor* after he left.

We consume energy *not only* when we are awake *but also* when we are asleep.

2
Using conjunctive adverbs

One other kind of connecting word joins *only* main or independent clauses, not single words, phrases, or subordinate clauses. Called a **conjunctive adverb,** it differs from a coordinating conjunction in that it functions as a modifier while it joins. Conjunctive adverbs include:

accordingly	however	otherwise
also	indeed	still
besides	instead	then
consequently	moreover	therefore
furthermore	nonetheless	thus
hence		

Compare the use of coordinating conjunctions and conjunctive adverbs in the following pairs of sentences.

The game was long and boring, *but* we stayed to the end.
The game was long and boring; *however,* we stayed to the end.

gr

5d

The game was long but exciting, *so* we stayed to the end.
The game was long but exciting; *consequently,* we stayed to the end.

In the first sentence of each pair, the coordinating conjunctions *but* and *so* join two main clauses and indicate the relations between them, but neither word modifies the clause that follows. In contrast, the conjunctive adverbs *however* and *consequently* join two main clauses while at the same time acting as adverbs to modify the clauses following them. Because they are adverbs, conjunctive adverbs can also be moved around within their clauses, as in the following:

Consequently (or *however*), we stayed to the end.
We *consequently* stayed to the end.
We stayed to the end, *however.*

The coordinating conjunctions *but* and *so* cannot be moved this way. They must remain between the two clauses they join. These differences between coordinating conjunctions and conjunctive adverbs are important because they determine very different punctuation in the clauses introduced by one or the other (see Chapter 11).

EXERCISE 18

Make two sentences from each pair of sentences below by using a coordinating conjunction, a correlative conjunction, or a conjunctive adverb, as specified, to combine the given sentences in different ways.

Example:

The encyclopedia had some information. It was not detailed enough. (*Coordinating conjunction; conjunctive adverb.*)

The encyclopedia had some information, *but* it was not detailed enough.

The encyclopedia had some information; *however,* it was not detailed enough.

1. Geoffrey raked some leaves. He stopped raking before he had finished the job. (*Coordinating conjunction; conjunctive adverb.*)
2. Television news is going to have to get better. I might give up news programs for newspapers. (*Coordinating conjunction; correlative conjunction.*)
3. Physics is a difficult but enjoyable subject. I plan to major in it. (*Coordinating conjunction; conjunctive adverb.*)
4. Cigarette smoking is not healthy. Excessive drinking is not healthy. (*Coordinating conjunction; correlative conjunction.*)
5. The football team's morale was bad. It had a winning season. (*Coordinating conjunction; conjunctive adverb.*)

5e

Changing the usual order of the sentence

All the sentences used so far as examples of basic sentence grammar have been similar: the subject comes first, naming the performer of the predicate's action, and the predicate comes second. This arrangement of subject and predicate describes most sentences that occur in writing, but we need to look briefly at four other kinds of sentences that alter this basic pattern.

1

Forming questions

We form questions in one of several ways. We may invert the normal subject-verb arrangement of statements:

The dog is barking. Is the dog barking?

We may use a question word like *what, who, when, where, which,* or *why*:

What dog is barking?

Or we may use some combination of the two methods:

Why is the dog barking?

In each case a question mark signals that the sentence is a question.

2

Forming commands

We construct commands even more simply than we construct questions: we merely delete the subject of the sentence, *you.*

Open the window.
Go to the store.
Eat your spinach.

3

Writing passive sentences

In any sentence that uses a transitive verb—that is, in any sentence where the verb takes an object—we can move the object to the position of the subject and put the subject in the predicate. When we do this we create a **passive sentence,** using the **passive voice** of the verb rather than the **active voice.** (See Chapter 7, p. 161.)

Greg wrote the paper. [Active voice.]
The paper was written by Greg. [Passive voice: *the paper,* which

was the original object of *wrote,* becomes the sentence subject; and the original sentence subject, *Greg,* joins the predicate.]

Passive sentences are so-called because their subjects do not perform or initiate the action indicated by their verbs. Rather, their subjects are acted upon. In passive sentences the verb is always a phrase made up of some form of the verb *be* and the past participle of the main verb (*paper was written, exams are finished*). (See 18d for cautions against overuse of the passive voice.)

4
Writing sentences with postponed subjects

The subject follows the predicate in two sentence patterns that are neither questions, commands, nor passive voice. In one pattern the normal word order is reversed for emphasis. This pattern occurs most often when the normal order is subject–intransitive verb–adverb. Then the adverb is moved to the front of the sentence while subject and predicate are reversed:

Then came the dawn.
Up walked Henry.
There goes Kathy.

A second kind of sentence with a postponed subject begins with either *it* or *there,* as in the following:

There will be eighteen people at the meeting.

It is certain that they will be there.

The words *there* and *it* in such sentences are called **expletives.** Their only function is to postpone the sentence subject. Since expletive sentences do not give emphasis, they are usually more effective when restated in the usual subject-predicate order. (See also 18e.)

Eighteen people will be at the meeting.
That they will be there is certain.

EXERCISE 19

Form a question and a command from the following noun and verb pairs.

    Example:
    split, wood
    Did you *split* all this *wood?*
    Split the *wood* for our fire.

1. water, boil   4. blackboard, write
2. music, stop   5. telephone, use
3. table, set

EXERCISE 20

Rewrite each passive sentence below as active, and rewrite each expletive construction to restore normal subject-verb order.

gr
5f

1. The football was thrown by the quarterback for more than forty yards.
2. It is uncertain whether microwave ovens are dangerous.
3. Sixty people were killed in the plane crash.
4. The lives of over one hundred others were saved because of the pilot's skill.
5. There was an audience of nearly ten thousand at the concert.

5f
Classifying sentences

Sentences can be described and classified in two different ways: by the meaning they convey (statement, question, command, exclamation, and so forth) or by their structure. Four basic sentence structures are possible: simple, compound, complex, and compound-complex.

1
Writing simple sentences

Simple sentences consist of a single independent clause. The subject, the verb, and its objects may be compound, but the sentence is simple unless it contains two complete independent clauses (two subjects and two predicates) or a subordinate clause.

Last July was unusually hot.
In fact, both July and August were vicious months.
The summer either made people leave the area for good or reduced them to bare existence. [Two predicates but only one subject.]

2
Writing compound sentences

A **compound sentence** consists of two or more simple sentences joined by a coordinating conjunction or by a semicolon.

Last July was hot, but August was even hotter.

The hot sun scorched the land to powder; the lack of rain made it totally untillable.

The government later provided assistance; consequently, those who remained gradually improved their lot.

3
Writing complex sentences

A sentence is **complex** if it contains one or more dependent or subordinate clauses as well as one independent clause.

Rain finally came, although many had left the area by then.

When the rain came, people rejoiced.

Those who remained were able to start anew because the government came to their aid.

Notice that length does not determine whether a sentence is complex or simple; both kinds can be short or long.

4
Writing compound-complex sentences

A **compound-complex sentence** has the characteristics of both the compound sentence (two or more independent clauses) and the complex sentence (at least one subordinate clause).

Even though government aid finally came, many people had already been reduced to poverty, and others had been forced to leave the area. [Subordinate clause; independent clause; independent clause.]

Some of those who had left gradually moved back to their original homes, but years passed before the land became as fertile as before. [Independent clause containing subordinate clause; independent clause; subordinate clause.]

EXERCISE 21

Identify the following sentences as simple, compound, complex, or compound-complex. Indicate which clauses are independent, which subordinate.

Example:

The police began patrolling more often when crime in the neighborhood increased.

┌─────────── INDEPENDENT ───────────┐
Complex: The police began patrolling more often
┌─────────── SUBORDINATE ───────────┐
when crime in the neighborhood increased.

1. Winters in Vermont are beautiful.
2. Summers in Vermont, by the way, are no less beautiful.
3. Although the guest of honor arrived late, no one seemed to mind.
4. The police strike lasted a week, but no robberies occurred in that time.
5. Even though some say football has supplanted baseball as the national pastime, millions of people watch baseball every year and they don't seem ready to stop.

gr
5f

EXERCISE 22

Expand each of the following simple sentences into the kind of sentence specified in the parentheses.

> *Example:*
>
> The traffic never stopped. (*Complex sentence.*)
> The traffic that passed by her house never stopped.

1. Dinner was tasty and filling. (*Compound sentence.*)
2. The wolves retreated over the hill. (*Compound sentence.*)
3. The storm passed by quickly. (*Complex sentence.*)
4. A strange object filled the sky. (*Complex sentence.*)
5. To many historians, the war in Vietnam was a loss. (*Compound-complex sentence.*)

6

Case of Nouns and Pronouns

Case refers to the form of a noun or a pronoun that shows its function in a sentence. The pronouns *I, we, he, she, they,* and *who* have different forms for three cases: the subjective, the possessive, and the objective. All other pronouns and all nouns have only two forms: a possessive case and a plain case, the form listed in the dictionary which serves all functions except that of the possessive.

Since the pronouns *I, we, he, she, they,* and *who* change form for each case, they are the ones we'll focus on in this chapter. Their **subjective forms,** named in the last sentence, are the ones listed in the dictionary. These forms are used when the pronoun is the subject of a sentence or a clause or the complement of a subject.

SUBJECT OF SENTENCE	*She* and *I* skied three days last week. *They* tried to save the house.
SUBJECT OF SUBORDINATE CLAUSE	Give the money to the kids who cleaned up. He is the man *who* I thought would win.
SUBJECT OF UNDERSTOOD VERB	Sarah has more money than *he* (has). I am not as smart as *she* (is).
SUBJECT COMPLEMENT	The editors of the paper were *he* and *I*. They assumed it was *I*.

The **objective forms** of the pronouns are *me, us, him, her, them,* and *whom*. These forms are used when the pronoun is an object—the direct or indirect object of a verb or verbal, the object of a preposition—or the subject of an infinitive.

OBJECT OF VERB	Lisa likes both Tom and *him*. It was John *whom* they suspected. The exam gave *him* a headache.
OBJECT OF PREPOSITION	Most of *us* hated to get up. I didn't know *whom* they laughed at.

OBJECT OF VERBAL	Electing *her* was easy. [Object of gerund.]
	Having elected *her,* the committee adjourned. [Object of past participle.]
	Mary ran to help *him.* [Object of infinitive.]
SUBJECT OF INFINITIVE	We invited *them* to eat with us.
	They asked *me* to speak.

The **possessive forms** of the pronouns are *my, our, his, her, their,* and *whose.* (*You* becomes *your.*) These forms are used before nouns and gerunds.

BEFORE NOUNS	His sisters needed *our* bicycles.
BEFORE GERUNDS	*Their* flying to Nashville was my suggestion.

In addition, the possessive forms *mine, ours, yours, his, hers,* and *theirs* (and only those forms) may be used without a following noun, in the position of a noun.

IN NOUN POSITIONS	*Hers* is the racket on the table.
	The blue Pinto is *mine* (*ours, yours, his, theirs*).

(For the possessive forms of nouns, see 23a.)

6a

Use the subjective case for all parts of compound subjects and for subject complements.

SUBJECTS	*Joan* and *I* left, but *Bill* and *he stayed.*
	After she and *I* left, the fight started.
SUBJECT COMPLEMENTS	The ones who paid the bill were *you* and *I.*
	The object of her hatred was *he.*

In speech we often use objective forms in the subject complement position in expressions like *it's me, it's him, it's us,* and *it's them.*

6b

Use the objective case for all parts of compound objects.

OBJECTS OF VERBS	We wanted to beat *Larry* and *her* at table tennis. [Direct object.]
	The coach gave *her* and *me* new paddles. [Indirect object.]
OBJECTS OF PREPOSITIONS	Marty gave presents to *Gloria* and *me.*
	The $10 gift was divided between *him* and *me.*

ca
6b

EXERCISE 1

Select, from the pairs in parentheses, the appropriate subjective or objective pronoun(s) for each of the following sentences.

> *Example:*
>
> The correspondence between (*he, him*) and (*I, me*) continued for three years.
>
> The correspondence between *him* and *me* continued for three years.

1. After a lot of planning, (*he, him*) and Chuck took off for Canada.
2. The reward check was made out to my friend and (*I, me*).
3. We couldn't see whether it was (*they, them*) or another group.
4. My parents had wanted all the children home for Thanksgiving but could afford to bring only Susanne and (*I, me*).
5. No one told us that (*he, him*) and George had left.
6. The woman gave money to (*he and I, him and me*).
7. The guilty ones are (*she, her*) and Allen.
8. All through the night Jimmy and (*I, me*) heard moans and strange knocks.
9. The rangers closed the mountain road after Mark and (*I, me*) made it to the top.
10. My father brought Mother and (*I, me*) tartans from Scotland.

6c

Use the appropriate case form when the plural pronouns *we* and *us* occur with a noun.

The case of the first-person plural pronoun used with a noun depends on the use of the noun.

> Most of *us* skaters grew up together. [*Skaters* is the object of the preposition *of*.]
>
> *We* fishermen all have great patience. [*Fishermen* is the subject of the sentence.]

6d

In appositives the case of a pronoun depends on the function of the word it describes or identifies.

The class elected two representatives, Debbie and me. [*Representatives* is the object of the verb *elected*, so the words in the appositive, *Debbie and me*, are in the objective case.]

Two representatives, Debbie and I, were elected. [*Representatives* this time is the subject of the sentence, so the words in the appositive, *Debbie and I*, are in the subjective case.]

If you are in doubt about case in an appositive, try the sentence without the word the appositive identifies.

The class elected Debbie and *me*.
Debbie and *I* were elected.

(See 5c-2 for more examples using appositives.)

ca
6e

EXERCISE 2

Select, from the pairs in parentheses, the appropriate subjective or objective pronoun for each of the following sentences.

Example:

The legislation provides new opportunities for (*we, us*) handicapped people.

The legislation provides new opportunities for *us* handicapped people.

1. Many of (*we, us*) graduating seniors may never see each other again.
2. To (*we, us*) fishermen, peace and quiet are real pleasures.
3. (*We, Us*) students appreciate clear directions on tests.
4. The best hockey players, (*she, her*) and Christine, received the awards.
5. The neighborhood project was started by three of us, John, Deborah, and (*I, me*).

6e

The case of a pronoun after *than* or *as* expressing a comparison depends on the meaning.

When we use *than* and *as* in comparisons, we often do not complete the clauses they introduce. The case of a pronoun in such constructions depends on the completion of the clause. The pronoun is subjective if it would be the subject of the omitted verb.

Annie liked Ben more than *I* (liked Ben).

The pronoun is objective if it would be the object of the omitted verb.

Annie liked Ben more than (she liked) *me*.

Notice the difference:

Annie liked Ben as much as *I* (liked Ben).
Annie liked Ben as much as (she liked) *me*.

6f

Use the objective case for pronouns that are subjects or objects of infinitives.

SUBJECT OF INFINITIVE

We wanted *him* to lose the tennis match.

OBJECT OF INFINITIVE

We wanted Julie to beat *him*.

6g

The form of the pronoun *who* is determined by its function in its clause.

1

At the beginning of questions use *who* if the question is about a subject, *whom* if it is about an object.

Who left the freezer door open? She left it open. [Subject.]
Whom do you blame? I blame him. [Direct object.]
Whom is the pizza for? It is for her. [Object of preposition.]

In speech, however, the subjective case *who* is commonly used whenever it is the first word of a question.

SPOKEN	*Who* are you working for?
WRITTEN	*Whom* are you working for? [Object of preposition.]

2

In subordinate clauses use *who* and *whoever* for all subjects, *whom* and *whomever* for all objects.

Remember that subordinate clauses themselves function as subjects, objects, and modifiers (see 5c-4). The case of a pronoun in a subordinate clause depends on its function in the clause, whether the clause itself functions as a subject, an object, or a modifier.

Give the clothes to *whoever* needs them. [*Whoever* is the subject of the clause *whoever needs them*. The entire clause is the object of the preposition *to*.]

I don't know *whom* the mayor appointed. [*Whom* is the object of *appointed: the mayor appointed whom*. The whole clause *whom the mayor appointed* is the object of the verb *know*.]

Whom he appointed is not my concern. [Again, *whom* is the object of *appointed*. This time the clause is the subject of the sentence.]

Larry is the man *whom* most people prefer. [*Whom* is the object of *prefer: people prefer whom.* The clause *whom most people prefer* modifies the noun *man.*]

If you have trouble determining which form of *who* or *whoever* to use, substitute a personal pronoun (*he, him; they, them*) for the relative pronoun. The case of the personal pronoun that sounds right is probably the correct case for the relative pronoun. Change the order of the words in the clause if necessary. For instance:

ca

6g

> I don't know (*who, whom*) Polly sang to. She sang to *him*.
> I don't know *whom* Polly sang to.

Don't be confused when expressions like *I think* and *she says* come between *who* as a subject and its verb.

> He is the man *who* I think *was running away.* [*Who* is the subject of *was*, not the object of *think*.]
> I asked the mechanic *who* Barbara said *was her friend.* [*Who* is again the subject of *was*, not the object of *said*.]

To choose between *who* and *whom* in such constructions, put the interrupting phrase in parentheses:

> I asked the mechanic who (Barbara said) was her friend.

EXERCISE 3

Select, from the pairs in parentheses, the appropriate form of the pronoun in each of the following sentences.

> *Example:*
> The caller asked (*who, whom*) I intended to vote for.
> The caller asked *whom* I intended to vote for.

1. (*Who, Whom*) will you invite to the party?
2. (*Whoever, Whomever*) parked this Cadillac needs to learn how to drive.
3. There is a fifty dollar reward for (*whoever, whomever*) finds and returns my Saint Bernard.
4. (*Who, Whom*) is Elaine living with?
5. (*Who, Whom*) is that man at the end of the alley?
6. He is the kind of person (*who, whom*), my father says, will always be able to multiply his money.
7. There will be a five-minute break for (*whoever, whomever*) among you needs it.
8. To (*who, whom*) should I give this letter?
9. The parents of that baby, (*whoever, whomever*) they are, shouldn't leave it alone.
10. Can you tell (*who, whom*) she looks like?

6h

Ordinarily, use the possessive form of a pronoun or noun immediately before a gerund.

Remember that a gerund is the present participle of the verb used as a noun. (See 5c-2.)

The doctor disapproved of *their* jogging.
Jim's failing mathematics surprised us all.

Note that the possessive is *not* used when the present participle serves as an adjective to modify a noun.

We watched *him* taking pictures.
We often see *John* running to work.

Notice also that the possessive is not usually used with the gerund when it would create an awkward construction.

AWKWARD	I hadn't known about everybody's wanting to quit.
REVISED	I hadn't known about everybody wanting to quit.
BETTER	I hadn't known everybody wanted to quit.

EXERCISE 4

Correct all inappropriate case forms in the following sentences, and explain the function of each case form.

After class Tom and I drove to the warehouse to pick up Tom's trunk. Between he and I, we could just lift the trunk's lid, never mind the whole trunk. We looked around for someone who could help us, someone who we could count on to supply extra muscle. The man we found proved no stronger than us, but him pulling and us pushing were enough to get the trunk on a dolly and into our car. We left him to help the next weaklings who showed up.

7

Verb Forms, Tense, Mood, and Voice

VERB FORMS

All verbs have three forms called **principal parts:** an infinitive, a past tense, and a past participle. The **infinitive** (sometimes called the **plain form**) is the dictionary form of the verb. It is the form we use when the verb's action is occurring in the present and the subject is a plural noun or the pronouns *I, we, you,* or *they.*

> We *eat* chicken three times a week.
> Our friends *leave* today.
> Examinations *frighten* me.

The **past tense** is the verb form indicating that the verb's action occurred in the past.

> We *ate* chicken last night.
> Our friends *left* yesterday.
> The examination *frightened* me.

The **past participle** is the verb form (usually the same as the past-tense form) that we use with *have, has,* or *had.*

> We *have eaten* the chicken.
> Our friends *had left* the day before.
> The examination *has frightened* me.

Verbs are regular or irregular according to whether they form their principal parts in a typical pattern or in an unusual way. Most verbs are **regular;** that is, they form their past tense and past participle by adding *-d* or *-ed* to the infinitive.

Infinitive	Past tense	Past participle
live	lived	lived
act	acted	acted
frighten	frightened	frightened

About two hundred English verbs are **irregular;** that is, they form their past tense and past participle in some irregular way. Unlike regular verbs, irregular verbs give us no automatic way of knowing what their forms will be. We have to learn the parts of these verbs just as we learn new words.

Most irregular verbs form the past tense and the past participle by changing an internal vowel. '

INFINITIVE	PAST TENSE	PAST PARTICIPLE
begin	began	begun
come	came	come
ring	rang	rung
swim	swam	swum

Some irregular verbs change an internal vowel and add an *-n* in the past participle.

INFINITIVE	PAST TENSE	PAST PARTICIPLE
break	broke	broken
draw	drew	drawn
speak	spoke	spoken
grow	grew	grown

A few irregular verbs have the same form in both the past tense and the past participle—or in all three forms.

INFINITIVE	PAST TENSE	PAST PARTICIPLE
let	let	let
set	set	set
sleep	slept	slept
shoot	shot	shot
tell	told	told

(See 7a for a list of irregular verbs and their principal parts.)

Most verbs can add *-s* or *-es* to their plain form, as in *asks, does, eats, imagines, says,* and *thinks.* We use this *-s* form when the verb's action is occurring in the present and the subject is a singular noun, an indefinite pronoun (*everybody, someone*), or the personal pronouns *he, she,* or *it.* (See 8a-1 and 8a-5.) (We use the plain form of the verb to indicate present time with plural nouns and the pronouns *I, we, you,* and *they: people eat, we do.*) The only verbs that do not add *-s* to indicate present time are *be* and *have,* for which the *-s* forms are *is* and *has.*

All verbs can add *-ing* to their infinitive—as in *acting, eating, living*—to form a **present participle.** The present participle is never used as the main or only verb in a sentence but combines with auxiliary verbs to form verb phrases.

Auxiliary verbs, often called **helping verbs,** are used with main verbs to indicate tense and other kinds of meaning in the verb. Combinations of auxiliaries with main verbs are called **verb phrases.** The auxiliaries *shall* and *will; have, has,* and *had; do, does,* and *did;* and the forms of *be* (*am, is, are, was, were, been,* and *being*) combine with main verbs to indicate time and voice (see pp. 155 and 161).

> I *will go.*
> She *had run.*
> Sylvia *did* not *want* strawberries.
> The doors *were opened.*

Auxiliaries such as *can, could, may, might, must, ought, shall, should, will,* and *would* combine with main verbs to indicate necessity, obligation, permission, possibility, and the like.

> She *can write.*
> I *should study.*
> You *must go.*
> I *might come.*

The two kinds of auxiliaries sometimes work together to create complex verb phrases.

> You *might have told* me.
> I *may be sleeping.*
> You *ought to have eaten.*

vb

7a

7a
Use the correct form of irregular verbs.

Choosing the correct form for the past tense and the past participle of irregular verbs can be difficult. Check a dictionary if you have doubt about a verb's principal parts. The form listed there is the infinitive or plain form. If no other forms are listed, the verb is regular; that is, both the past tense and the past participle are formed by adding *-d* or *-ed* to the infinitive: *agree, agreed; sympathize, sympathized; talk, talked.* If the verb is irregular, the dictionary will list the past tense and the past participle in that order: *speak, spoke, spoken; go, went, gone.* If the dictionary gives only two forms—as in *hear, heard* or *think, thought*—then the past tense and the past participle are the same.

The most common irregular verbs are in the following list. (When a principal part has two possible forms, as with *dove* and *dived,* both are included.) Look over this list to find verbs whose parts you are unsure of. Then spend some time memorizing the parts and using them in sentences.

Infinitive	Past tense	Past participle
arise	arose	arisen
begin	began	begun
bid	bid	bid
bite	bit	bitten, bit
blow	blew	blown
break	broke	broken
bring	brought	brought
catch	caught	caught
choose	chose	chosen
come	came	come
cut	cut	cut
dive	dived, dove	dived
do	did	done
draw	drew	drawn
dream	dreamed, dreamt	dreamed, dreamt
drink	drank	drunk
drive	drove	driven
eat	ate	eaten
fall	fell	fallen
find	found	found
flee	fled	fled
fly	flew	flown
forget	forgot	forgotten, forgot
freeze	froze	frozen
get	got	got, gotten
give	gave	given
go	went	gone
grow	grew	grown
hang	hung, hanged (executed)	hung, hanged
hear	heard	heard
know	knew	known
lay	laid	laid
lead	led	led
let	let	let
lie	lay	lain
lose	lost	lost
pay	paid	paid
prove	proved	proved, proven
ride	rode	ridden
ring	rang, rung	rung
rise	rose	risen
run	ran	run
say	said	said
see	saw	seen
set	set	set
sing	sang, sung	sung
sink	sank, sunk	sunk

INFINITIVE	PAST TENSE	PAST PARTICIPLE
sit	sat	sat
slide	slid	slid
speak	spoke	spoken
stand	stood	stood
steal	stole	stolen
swim	swam	swum
take	took	taken
tear	tore	torn
throw	threw	thrown

vb
7b

EXERCISE 1

Fill in the blanks below with either the past tense or the past participle of the irregular verb shown in parentheses, and identify the form you used.

> *Example:*
> The cash box was _____ from the safe. (*steal*)
> The cash box was *stolen* from the safe. Past participle.

1. Every afternoon after work, we have _____ at the pool. (*swim*)
2. The minister _____ to the Kiwanis Club last night. (*speak*)
3. Because the day was so dark, it seemed as though the sun had never _____. (*rise*)
4. Before my aunt could stop him, my cousin had _____ all the chocolate milk. (*drink*)
5. The fans were encouraged because their team had not _____ a home game all season. (*lose*)
6. She wanted to be _____ for the lacrosse team. (*choose*)
7. The air was so cold that my hands almost _____. (*freeze*)
8. We were not allowed to leave the table until we had _____ all our food. (*eat*)
9. After three dry weeks, the rains _____ again. (*begin*)
10. The quarterback _____ the football nearly out of the stadium. (*throw*)

7b
Distinguish between *sit* and *set* and between *lie* and *lay*.

The principal parts of *sit* and *set* and of *lie* and *lay* are often confused, especially in speech. Here are the forms of the two verbs:

INFINITIVE	PAST TENSE	PAST PARTICIPLE
sit	sat	sat
set	set	set
lie	lay	lain
lay	laid	laid

Sit and *lie*, as in *Sit down* and *Lie down*, mean to "be seated" and to "recline," respectively. They are both **intransitive verbs:** they cannot take objects. *Set* and *lay*, as in *Set the eggs down carefully* and *Lay the floor boards there*, mean to "put" or "place" something. They are **transitive verbs** and usually take objects. (See 5a-3.)

Loretta *lies* down every afternoon. [No object.]
Clarence *laid* the plans on the table. [*Plans* is the object of *laid*.]
The dog *sits* by the back door. [No object.]
Mr. Flood *set* the jug down carefully. [*Jug* is the object of *set*.]

EXERCISE 2

Choose the correct verb form from each of the pairs in parentheses.

1. The spider (*set, sat*) in its web, (*laying, lying*) in wait for its prey.
2. Marcia (*lay, laid*) her purse on the table not five minutes before it was stolen.
3. The phone rang right after I had (*lain, laid*) down for a nap.
4. What do I do with the skunk that (*lies, lays*) asleep in the trap?
5. You can (*lie, lay*) down for a nap as soon as you finish the dishes.

7c

Use the *-s* and *-ed* forms of the verb when they are required.

In speech we hear the *-s* and *-ed* endings of verbs clearly when they form a syllable, as in *pleases, passes, finishes, spotted,* or *demanded.* But in many verbs the final *-s* or *-ed* sound is almost entirely lost. This is especially true if the ending does not form another syllable and if the verb's plain form ends in certain consonant sounds, as in *asks, adds, bagged, lived,* and *used.* The *-s* or *-ed* sound may also be lost if words immediately following the verb begin with the same or a similar sound, as in *asks Susan, used to, raced downtown,* and *supposed to.*

In your writing be sure all present-tense verbs end in *-s* when they follow a singular noun, *he, she,* or *it,* or an indefinite pronoun like *everybody* (for exceptions with indefinite pronouns, see 8a-5). Check all past-tense forms of regular verbs to be sure they end in *-d* or *-ed.* If you are in doubt about past-tense forms, consult a dictionary. Remember that if the dictionary lists no other forms with the plain form, the verb is regular and requires *-d* or *-ed* in the past tense and past participle.

TENSE

Tense is the form of a verb that shows the time of the verb's action. The **simple tenses** indicate that an action or state of being is present, past, or future. You have met present and past already in the verb's principal parts. The future is formed with the helping verbs *will* or *shall*. The **perfect tenses** indicate that an action was or will be completed before another time or action. They are formed with the helping verb *have*.

vb
7d

	REGULAR VERB	IRREGULAR VERB
SIMPLE TENSES		
Present	You *work*.	You *write*.
Past	You *worked*.	You *wrote*.
Future	You *will work*.	You *will write*.
PERFECT TENSES		
Present perfect	You *have worked*.	You *have written*.
Past perfect	You *had worked*.	You *had written*.
Future perfect	You *will have worked*.	You *will have written*.

In addition, all verbs have a **progressive form,** sometimes called the **progressive tense,** that indicates action continuing in the time shown. This form uses the helping verb *be* with the *-ing* form of the verb.

I *am working.*
He *had been working.*
You *were writing.*
She *will have been writing.*

We use the auxiliary *do* (*does*) and its past tense *did* in asking questions, making negative statements, and showing emphasis.

Does he *write* every day? [Question.]
He *did* not *write* every day. [Negation.]
He *does write* every day. [Emphasis.]

7d

Observe the special uses of the present tense and the uses of the perfect tenses.

The present tense generally indicates action occurring at the time of speaking, as in *She understands what you mean* or *From here I see the river and the docks.* It is also used in several special situations.

TO INDICATE HABITUAL OR RECURRING ACTION

Abby goes to New York every Friday.
The store opens at ten o'clock.

TO STATE A GENERAL TRUTH

The mills of the gods grind slowly.
The earth is round.

vb
7e

TO DISCUSS THE CONTENT OF LITERATURE, FILM, AND SO ON

Huckleberry Finn has adventures we all would like to experience.
In that article the author examines several causes of crime.

TO INDICATE FUTURE TIME

Our friends arrive the day after tomorrow.
Ted is going in the next half hour.

(Notice that in sentences like the last two, time is really indicated by the phrases *the day after tomorrow* and *in the next half hour.*)
    The perfect tenses generally indicate an action completed before another specific time or action. The present perfect tense is also used for action begun in the past and continued into the present.

PRESENT PERFECT	Hannah *has fed* the dog, so we can go. [Action is completed at the time of the statement.]
	Hannah *has* always *fed* the dog. [Action began in the past but continues now.]
PAST PERFECT	Harley *had finished* his work by the time his friends arrived. [Action was completed before another past action.]
FUTURE PERFECT	He *will have finished* his work by the time his friends arrive. [The present tense *arrive* with *by the time* indicates the future. The future perfect *will have finished* indicates that his work will be completed before the future arrival.]

7e
Use the appropriate sequence of verb tenses.

    The term **sequence of tenses** refers to the relation between the verb in a main clause and the verbs or verbals in subordinate clauses or verbal phrases (see 5c). In the sentence *He left after I arrived*, the past tense of the verb *arrived* is in sequence with the past tense of *left*. (For a discussion of keeping verb tenses consistent from one sentence to another, see 13b.)

1

When the verb in a main clause is in the present, future, present perfect, or future perfect tense, use a tense in the subordinate clause that clearly expresses your meaning.

It isn't necessary for the verbs in main and subordinate clauses to have identical tenses, but the tense in the subordinate clause should reflect your meaning. In the following sentences all the verb forms follow a clear and natural sequence, though the tenses in main and subordinate clauses are sometimes different.

vb

7e

> He *knows* that we *have been* in New Orleans for three weeks. [Present tense *knows* in main clause; present perfect *have been* in subordinate clause.]
>
> I *have known* for some time that you *will come* to our camp next summer. [Present perfect and future tenses.]
>
> David *will tell* you why he *changed* his plans. [Future and past tenses.]
>
> The employer *will increase* wages because he *realizes* that his workers *have needed* more money for the past year. [Future, present, and present perfect tenses.]

2

When the verb in a main clause is in the past or past perfect tense, use the past or past perfect tense in the subordinate clause.

> We *talked* for a long time after we *returned* home. [Past tense and past tense.]
>
> My friend *had left* before I *came.* [Past perfect and past tenses.]

EXCEPTION: When a subordinate clause expresses a general truth such as *The earth is round,* use the present tense even though the verb of the main clause is in the past or past perfect tense.

> I never *realized* that many marriages *are* genuinely happy ones.

3

Use a present infinitive to express action at the same time as or later than that of the main verb. Use a perfect infinitive to express action earlier than that of the main verb.

The **present infinitive** is the verb's plain form preceded by *to* (see 5c-2). In the following sentences the present infinitive shows action at the same time as or later than that of the main verb.

> I *like to go* to baseball games.
> Last year I *went to see* a World Series game.

I *have* always *preferred to watch* football games on television.
I *would have liked to watch* the Superbowl.

The verb's **perfect infinitive** is the perfect form of the verb preceded by *to.* In the following sentences the perfect infinitive shows action earlier than that of the main verb.

Sarah *would like to have heard* Sylvia Plath read her poetry.

Ptolemy *is known to have been* the first astronomer who classified stars by their brightness.

vb
7e

4

Use a present participle to express action at the same time as that of the main verb. Use a past participle or a present perfect participle to express action earlier than that of the main verb.

In the sentence below the present participle shows action occurring at the same time as that of the main verb.

Driving across the United States, he *was astonished* by the vast spaces.

In the following sentences the past participle and the present perfect participle, respectively, show action occurring earlier than that of the main verb.

Exhausted by overwork, Sheila *went* on a Caribbean cruise.

Having lived all his life in the city, he *was surprised* by the openness of plains and mountains.

EXERCISE 3

Revise the following sentences for the appropriate sequence of verb tenses.

Example:

Hedy had hoped to have been elected.
Hedy had hoped *to be elected.*

1. My grandfather died before I had arrived at the hospital.
2. The jury recommends leniency because the criminal was so young.
3. Myrna's brother would have liked to have gone.
4. I meant to have told you about the new assignment yesterday.
5. The archaeologists estimated that the skull is from the last ice age.
6. She was on the critical list since she fell yesterday.
7. The stage hands refused to put up the set for the play because they think the design is unsafe.

8. Enrolling in five courses this semester, I will find that I am very busy.
9. Having driven without my glasses on, I caused an accident.
10. The class was told that the instructor is sick.

MOOD

Mood in grammar refers to a verb form that indicates the writer's or speaker's attitude toward what he or she is saying. The **indicative mood** states a fact or opinion or asks a question. The **imperative mood** expresses a command or gives a direction. The **subjunctive mood** expresses a requirement, a desire, or a suggestion, or states a condition that is contrary to fact. The three moods are illustrated in these sentences:

INDICATIVE	They *need* our help. [Opinion.]
	Marie *works* only on Saturday. [Fact.]
	Why *does* she *work* on Saturday? [Question.]
IMPERATIVE	*Work* only on Saturdays. [Command.]
	Turn right at the light. [Direction.]
SUBJUNCTIVE	Her father urged that she *work* only on Saturdays. [Suggestion.]
	Regulations require that applications *be* in writing. [Requirement.]
	If she *were* to work more, her studies would suffer. [Condition contrary to present fact.]

The imperative is indicated by omitting the subject of the sentence: (*You*) *Work only on Saturdays.* In the present tense the subjunctive mood uses only the plain form of the verb no matter what the subject is, as in the first subjunctive sentence above. The present subjunctive form of *to be* is *be.* rather than *am, is,* or *are,* as in the second sentence above. In the past tense the only distinctive subjunctive verb form is *were* for all subjects, as in the third sentence above. (For a discussion of keeping mood consistent within and among sentences, see 13b.)

7f

Use the subjunctive verb forms appropriately.

Although in the past English used distinctive subjunctive verb forms in a number of constructions, such forms are used now in only two kinds of constructions and in a few idiomatic expressions.

1

Use the subjunctive form *were* in contrary-to-fact clauses beginning with *if* or expressing a wish.

If I *were* you, I'd see a doctor.
If there *were* a way to treat the rash, she would have treated it.
I wish Jeannie *were* my doctor.

NOTE: The indicative form *was* (*I wish Jeannie was my doctor*) is common in speech and in some informal writing, but the subjunctive *were* is usually retained in formal English.

2

Use the subjunctive in *that* clauses following verbs that demand, request, or recommend.

Verbs like *ask, insist, urge, require, recommend,* and *suggest* are often followed by subordinate clauses beginning with *that* and containing the substance of the request or suggestion. The verb in such *that* clauses should be in the subjunctive mood.

Felix urged that Carol *go* with me.
The law required that he *report* weekly.
Julie's mother insisted that she *stay* home.
Instructors commonly ask that papers *be finished* on time.

NOTE: These constructions have widely used alternate forms, such as *Felix urged Carol to go with me* or *Julie's mother insisted on her staying home.*

3

Use the subjunctive in some set phrases and idioms.

Several English expressions commonly use the subjunctive. For example:

Come rain or *come* shine.
Be that as it may.
The people *be* damned.

EXERCISE 4

Revise the following sentences for the appropriate use of the subjunctive verb forms.

> *Example:*
> I would help the old man if there was a way I could reach him.
> I would help the old man if there *were* a way I could reach him.

1. If I was you, I would arrive at the interview on time.
2. Marie moves that the motion is adopted.
3. The syllabus requires that each student writes three papers and takes two essay tests.
4. They treat me as if I was their son.
5. If there was a road between them, the two towns could do business with each other.

vb
7

VOICE

Verbs can show whether their subjects are acting or are acted upon. In the **active voice** the subject names the actor.

Jane Fonda acted in that role.
David wrote the paper.

In the **passive voice** the subject names the object or receiver of the action.

The role was acted by Jane Fonda.
The paper was written by David.

We form the passive voice of a verb with the appropriate form of the helping verb *be* plus the past participle of the main verb. Other helping verbs may be present, but some form of the verb *be* and the past participle of the main verb must be present.

Senators *are elected* for six-year terms.
Sarah *was married* three years ago.
Jerry *has been given* complete freedom.

To change a sentence from active to passive voice, we convert the direct object or the indirect object of the verb into the subject of the verb. Thus only verbs that can take objects form the passive voice.

ACTIVE	We *gave* Jerry complete freedom.
PASSIVE	Jerry *was given* complete freedom. [Indirect object becomes subject.]
PASSIVE	Complete freedom *was given* (to) Jerry. [Direct object becomes subject.]

To change a sentence from passive to active voice, we switch the verb's subject into a direct or an indirect object and use a new subject.

PASSIVE	Sally *was bitten* by her dog.
ACTIVE	Her dog *bit* Sally.

PASSIVE	The statement *was read* at a press conference.
ACTIVE	The company's representative *read* the statement at a press conference.

(See 13c for a discussion of keeping voice consistent among sentences. See 18d and 31c-3 for a discussion of avoiding unnecessary use of the passive voice—which can deprive writing of emphasis and make it sound formal and impersonal.)

vb

7

EXERCISE 5

Convert the following sentences from active to passive or from passive to active. (In converting passive to active you may have to supply a subject for the new sentence.)

Example:

The building was demolished last spring.

The *city demolished* the building last spring.

1. The student government was elected last spring.
2. Whales are still killed by foreign fishing fleets.
3. The plane crash killed over thirty people.
4. The survivors were discovered by a passing freighter.
5. The Church was thought very important by the people of the Middle Ages.

EXERCISE 6

Identify all the verbs in the following paragraph and correct their form, tense, or mood if necessary.

We use to know nothing about our earliest ancestors. Before Darwin's *On the Origin of Species* was published in 1859, people had thought humans are only thousands of years old. Now we know that the earliest animals to have walked upright on two legs (a sign of having been human) existed *millions* of years ago. Anthropologists in Africa discovered footprints almost like ours that were 3½ million years old. When the footprints had been excavated, they were seen to be laying beside the dried-up remains of an ancient river.

8

Agreement

Agreement refers to the correspondence in form between subjects and verbs and between pronouns and their **antecedents,** the nouns or other pronouns they refer to. Subjects and verbs agree in number (singular and plural) and in person (first, second, and third). Pronouns and their antecedents agree in person, number, and gender (masculine, feminine, and neuter).

The following sentences illustrate agreement between subject and verb and between pronoun and antecedent.

> *Sarah* often *speaks* up in class. [Both subject and verb are in the third-person singular form.]

> Even though *we understand, we* still *dislike* it. [Both subjects and verbs are in the first-person plural form.]

> *Claude* resented their ignoring *him.* [Both the pronoun *him* and its antecedent *Claude* are masculine, and the pronoun agrees with its antecedent's third-person singular form.]

> The *dogs* stand still while *they* are judged. [The pronoun agrees with the third-person plural form of its antecedent.]

8a
Subjects and verbs should agree in number.

Your meaning—what you want to say—will always determine the number of the subject you select. You aren't likely to use *boy* when you mean *boys.* Once you've selected a subject, it will determine the form of the verb you use: *the boy eats; the boys eat.* In the present tense all verbs except *be* and *have* add an *-s* or *-es* to show agreement with third-person singular nouns and pronouns. The third-person singular forms of *be* and *have* are *is* and *has*, respectively. In the past tense all verbs except *be* use the same form for all subjects. *Be* uses *was* for the third-person singular and *were* for all plural subjects. (See chapter 7 for further discussion of verb forms.)

Most subject-verb agreement problems arise either because the writer can't easily determine whether the subject is singular or plural or because words come between subject and verb and blur their relationship. The following conventions deal with these and other problems that affect subject-verb agreement.

1

Use the verb ending *-s* or *-es* with all singular nouns and third-person singular pronouns.

In nouns and verbs that end in combinations of sounds such as *-sks*, *-sps*, and *-sts*, the final *-s* sound is often not pronounced clearly in speech and thus is often wrongly omitted in writing.

| NONSTANDARD | Julie *ask* a lot of questions in class. |
| STANDARD | Julie *asks* a lot of questions in class. |

Another reason writers and speakers drop the appropriate singular verb ending is that it simply is not used regularly in some English dialects. However, the ending is required in both spoken and written standard English.

| NONSTANDARD | No matter what, she always *go* to class. |
| STANDARD | No matter what, she always *goes* to class. |

2

Subject and verb should agree even when other words come between them.

When the subject and verb are next to each other in a sentence, they usually agree naturally, because they sound right. But when other words come between the subject and verb—particularly other nouns—then agreement errors are likely to arise because the verb may be connected to the nearest noun rather than to the actual subject.

A catalog of courses and requirements often *baffles* (not *baffle*) students. [The verb must agree with the subject, *catalog*, not the nearer word *requirements.*]

The profits earned by the cosmetic industry *are* (not *is*) great. [The subject is *profits*, not *industry.*]

Notice that *as well as, together with, along with, in addition to,* and similar expressions are considered as prepositions rather than coordinating conjunctions (see 5c-1 and 5d-1). Thus the phrases they begin do not change the number of the subject.

> The governor, as well as his advisors, *has* (not *have*) agreed to attend the protest rally.

In these cases if you really mean *and* (*The governor and his advisors have agreed to attend*), you can avoid confusion and awkwardness (and extra words) by using *and*. Then the subject is compound, and the verb should be plural (see 8a-3).

agr
8a

3

Subjects joined by *and* usually take plural verbs.

Two or more subjects joined by *and* take a plural verb whether one or all of the subjects are singular.

> Frost and Roethke *are* her favorite poets.
> An extension cord and a plug *are* needed.
> The dog, the monkey, the children, and the tent *were* in the car.

EXCEPTIONS: When the two or more parts of the subject form a single idea or refer to a single person or thing, then they often take a singular verb.

> Avocado and bean sprouts *is* my favorite sandwich.
> The winner and new champion *was* in the shower.

When a compound subject is preceded by the adjectives *each* or *every,* then the verb is usually singular.

> At customs, every box, bag, and parcel *is* inspected.
> Each man, woman, and child *has* a right to be heard.

But when a compound subject is *followed* by *each,* the verb may be singular or plural.

> The man and the woman each *has* (or *have*) different problems to deal with.

4

When parts of a subject are joined by *or* or *nor,* the verb agrees with the nearer part.

When all parts of a subject joined by *or* or *nor* are singular, the verb is singular; when all parts are plural, the verb is plural.

Neither the teacher nor the student *knows* the answer.
The rabbits or the woodchucks *have eaten* my lettuce.

Problems with subjects joined by *or* or *nor* occur only when one subject part is singular and the other plural. In that case the verb agrees with the part of the subject closest to it.

Either the chairman or the committee members *were* late.
Neither the members nor the chairman *was* late.

The same is true when the subject is made up of nouns and pronouns of different person requiring different verb forms: *neither Jim nor I, either he or they*. In this case, too, the verb agrees with the nearer part of the subject.

Either he or they *are* late.
Neither Jim nor I *am* late.

Since using this convention with pronouns of different number and person often results in sentences that sound awkward, it's best to avoid the problem altogether by rewording the sentence.

AWKWARD   Either she or I *am* late. Either they or he *is* late.

IMPROVED   One of us *is* late. One of them *is* late.

5

Generally, use singular verbs with indefinite pronouns.

An **indefinite pronoun** is one that does not refer to a specific person or thing. The common indefinite pronouns include *all, any, anybody, anyone, anything, each, either, everybody, everyone, everything, neither, nobody, none, no one, one, some, somebody, someone,* and *something*. Most of these are singular in meaning (they refer to a single unspecified person or thing), and they take singular verbs.

The president said anyone *was* welcome to join.
Something *is* wrong with that man.

But a few indefinite pronouns like *all, any, none,* and *some* may be either singular or plural in meaning. The verbs you use with these pronouns depend on the meaning of the noun or pronoun they refer to.

All of the money *is* reserved for emergencies. [*All* refers to *money,* so the verb is singular.]

When the men finally arrive, all *go* straight to work. [*All* refers to *the men,* so the verb is plural.]

6

Collective nouns take singular or plural verbs depending on meaning.

A **collective noun** has singular form but names a group of individuals or things—for example, *army, audience, committee, crowd, family, group,* and *team.* When used as a subject, a collective noun may take a singular or plural verb, depending on the context in which it is used. When you are considering the group as one unit, use the singular form of the verb.

agr
8a

> Contrary to some reports, the American family *is* still strong.
> Any band *sounds* good in that concert hall.

But when you are considering the group's members as individuals who act separately, use the plural form of the verb.

> The old group *have* gone their separate ways.
> Since their last concert, the band *have* not agreed on where to play.

NOTE: Even when the plural verb form is properly used, as in these examples, it often sounds awkward. For this reason many writers prefer to rephrase such sentences with plural subjects, as in *The members of the old group have all gone their separate ways.*

Number, used as a collective noun, may be singular or plural. Preceded by *a*, it is always plural. Preceded by *the*, it is always singular.

> A number of my friends *have* decided to live off campus.
> The number of people in debt *is* very large.

7

The verb agrees with the subject even when the normal word order is inverted.

Most often, inverted subject-verb order occurs with the expletive construction of *there* and a form of *to be.* (See 5e-4.)

> There *are* too many students in that class. [*Students* is the subject; *are* is the verb. Compare *Too many students are in that class.*]
> After many years there *is* finally peace in that country. [*Peace* is the subject; *is* is the verb. Compare *Peace is in that country.*]

In this construction, *there is* may be used before a compound subject when the first element in the subject is singular.

> There *is* much work to do and little time to do it.

Word order may sometimes be inverted for emphasis, without

use of the expletive construction. The verb still agrees with its subject.

From the mountains *comes* an eerie, shimmering light.

8

A linking verb agrees with its subject, not the subject complement.

When using the construction in which a subject complement follows a linking verb, you should check to be sure that the verb agrees with its subject, not with the noun or pronoun that serves as a subject complement.

Henry's sole support *is* his mother and father.
Henry's mother and father *are* his sole support.

(See 5a-3 for review of linking verbs and subject complements.)

9

When used as subjects, relative pronouns take verbs that agree with their antecedents.

The relative pronouns *who, which,* and *that* do not have different singular and plural forms. When they serve as subjects, the verb should agree with the noun or other pronoun that the relative pronoun refers to (its antecedent).

Mayor Garber ought to listen to the people who *work* for her. [*Who* refers to *people*, so the verb is plural.]

Agreement problems often occur with relative pronouns when the sentence includes a phrase beginning with *one of the.*

He is one of the teachers who *have* a bad reputation. [The antecedent of *who* is *teachers*, not *one*, so the verb is plural.]

But he is the only one of the teachers who *has* paid attention to me. [The antecedent of *who* is *one*, because only one teacher has paid attention.]

10

Nouns with plural form but singular meaning take singular verbs.

Some nouns with plural form (that is, ending in -*s*) are usually regarded as singular in meaning. They include *athletics, economics, mathematics, means, measles, news, politics, physics,* and *statistics.*

Mathematics *seems* difficult, but it is fascinating.
After so long a wait, the news *has* to be good.

A few of these—especially the ones ending in *-ics*—may occasionally be regarded as plural in meaning when they describe individual activities or items rather than whole bodies of activity or knowledge.

> After mathematics, statistics *is* my favorite subject. [*Statistics* refers to an organized body of knowledge.]
>
> The statistics *prove* him wrong. [*Statistics* refers to facts.]

11

Titles and words named as words take singular verbs.

When your sentence subject is the title of a work (such as a book or a movie) or a word you are defining or describing, the verb should be singular whether the title or the word is singular or plural.

> *Dream Days remains* one of her favorite books.
> *Folks is* a down-home word for *people.*

EXERCISE 1

Revise the following sentences so that subjects and verbs agree in number.

> *Example:*
> Each of the goslings nibble at my ankles.
> Each of the goslings *nibbles* at my ankles.

1. A cluster of roses and azaleas are just outside my bedroom window.
2. Neither that drawing nor those paintings appeals to my friend.
3. Margaret Gayoso is among those who is going to Washington to lobby for antipollution legislation.
4. We hear that the end justifies the means; but does the means justify the end?
5. The board of directors, after meeting with a team of accountants, have decided to sell the company to its largest competitor.
6. The committee applaud the city council's decision to build a mall along a portion of North Street.
7. Mathematics are his special problem.
8. *Seminars* have a more elegant sound than *classes.*
9. Every Tom, Dick, and Harry seem to have an opinion on how the federal dollar should be spent.
10. The committee differs on whether to authorize more money for the spring concert.
11. He is one of those persons who promises more than can be delivered.
12. *The Eustace Diamonds* are one of Anthony Trollope's most famous novels.

13. Neither the chemistry instructor nor her lab assistants seems to know the assignment for today.
14. A new porch door, in addition to new windows, are needed.
15. Either the manager or his representative are responsible for handling complaints.

8b

Pronouns and their antecedents should agree in person and number.

The **antecedent** of a pronoun is the noun or other pronoun it refers to. (The word *antecedent* comes from the Latin *ante-*, meaning "before," and *cedere*, "to go.")

Mark thought everyone was avoiding *him*. [*Mark* is the antecedent of *him*.]

Every *dog* in that kennel has received *its* shots. [*Dog* is the antecedent of *its*.]

All home *owners* have received *their* tax bills. [*Owners* is the antecedent of *their*.]

As these examples show, a pronoun agrees with its antecedent in gender (masculine, feminine, neuter), person (first, second, third), and number (singular, plural). Since pronouns have no meaning of their own, but derive their meaning from their antecedents, pronoun-antecedent agreement is essential for the reader to understand what you are saying.

1

Antecedents joined by *and* usually take plural pronouns.

Two or more antecedents joined by *and* take a plural pronoun whether one or all of the antecedents are singular.

My adviser and I can't coordinate *our* schedules.
Their argument resolved, George and Jennifer had dinner together.

Exceptions: When the compound antecedent refers to a single idea, person, or thing, then the pronoun may be singular.

The athlete and scholar forgot both *his* javelin and *his* books.

When the compound antecedent is preceded by *each* or *every*, the pronoun is singular.

Every girl and woman took *her* seat.

2
When parts of an antecedent are joined by *or* or *nor*, the pronoun agrees with the nearer part.

When the parts of an antecedent are connected by *or* and *nor*, the pronoun's person and number should agree with the part closer to it.

> Steve or John should have raised *his* hand.
>
> Either consumers or car manufacturers will have *their* way.
>
> Neither the student nor the elderly people will retrieve *their* deposits from that landlord.

When one subject is plural and the other singular, as in the last example, the sentence will be awkward unless you put the plural subject second.

AWKWARD	The antelopes or the giraffe changes *its* location in the zoo next Thursday.
BETTER	The giraffe or the antelopes change *their* location in the zoo next Thursday.

3
Generally, use a singular pronoun when the antecedent is an indefinite pronoun.

Most **indefinite pronouns**—pronouns that do not refer to a specific person or thing—are third-person singular in meaning: for example, *anyone, each, everybody, none, no one, something*. When indefinite pronouns serve as antecedents to other pronouns, then, they take singular pronouns.

> Everyone on the team had *her* own locker.
> Each of the boys likes *his* teacher.
> Something made *its* presence felt.

In these examples the gender intended by the indefinite pronoun is known and reflected in the pronouns *her, his,* and *its.* However, the meaning of indefinite pronouns more often includes both genders or either gender, not one or the other. In such cases we traditionally use *he* (or *him,* or *his*) to refer to the indefinite antecedent. But some people see this usage, although standard, as unfairly excluding females. Thus many writers now avoid using *he* in these situations by rewriting their sentences.

ORIGINAL	Everyone brought *his* book to class.
BROADER	Everyone brought *his or her* book to class.

agr
8b

| INFORMAL | Everyone brought *their* books to class. |
| PLURAL | All the students brought *their* books to class. |

Sometimes using *he* to refer to an indefinite pronoun—even when the meaning is clearly masculine—can result in an awkward sentence when the indefinite pronoun clearly means "many" or "all."

| AWKWARD | After everyone left, I shut the door behind *him.* |

Either rewrite such sentences or, when informal usage is acceptable, use a plural pronoun.

| REWRITTEN | After all the guests left, I shut the door behind *them.* |
| INFORMAL | After everyone left, I shut the door behind *them.* |

4

Collective noun antecedents take singular or plural pronouns depending on meaning.

Collective nouns like *army, committee, family, group,* and *team* have singular form but may be referred to by singular or plural pronouns, depending on the meaning intended. When you are referring to the group as a unit—all its members acting together—then the pronoun is singular.

The committee voted to disband *itself.*
The team attended a banquet in *its* honor.

But when you are referring to the individual members of the group, the pronoun is plural.

The audience arose quietly from *their* seats.
The old group have gone *their* separate ways.

The last example demonstrates the importance of being consistent in verb use as well as pronoun choice when assigning a singular or plural meaning to a collective noun (see also 8a-6).

| INCONSISTENT | The old group *has* gone *their* separate ways. |
| CONSISTENT | The old group *have* gone *their* separate ways. |

EXERCISE 2

Revise the following sentences so that pronouns and their antecedents agree in person and number.

Example:

We knew every one of the puppies would thrive in their new homes.

We knew every one of the puppies would thrive in *its* new home.

1. Each parent visited their child's teacher.
2. Neither of the two candidates is especially well known for their honesty.
3. We don't know yet whether Jeffrey or Nancy got the higher score on their test.
4. Everyone on the women's basketball team brought their own equipment.
5. Each member of the class had private conferences with their teacher.
6. Neither the president nor the board of directors was willing to give his approval to the merger.
7. Summer jobs are necessary for anyone working their way through college.
8. The class decided to dismiss themselves after waiting thirty minutes for the instructor.
9. No one turned up to take advantage of their free passes.
10. The team had never won on their home court.

EXERCISE 3

Revise the sentences in the following paragraph to correct errors in agreement between subjects and verbs or between pronouns and their antecedents.

Everyone has their favorite view of professional athletes. A common view is that the athletes are like well-paid children who have no real work to do, have no responsibilities, and simply enjoy the game and the good money. But this view of professional athletes fail to consider the grueling training the athletes have to go through to become professionals. Either training or competing lead each athlete to take risks that can result in their serious injury. The athletes have tremendous responsibility to the team they play on, which need to function as a unit at all times to win their games. Most athletes' careers as active players on the team is over by the age of forty, when they are too stiff and banged-up to go on. Rather than just listening to any of the people who criticizes professional athletes, everyone interested in sports need to defend the athletes. They take stiff physical punishment so neither the sports fanatic nor the mildly interested observer are deprived of their pleasure.

9
Adjectives and Adverbs

Adjectives and adverbs both are modifiers that describe, restrict, or otherwise qualify the words to which they relate. **Adjectives** modify nouns and pronouns. **Adverbs** modify verbs, adjectives, and other adverbs.

ADJECTIVE-NOUN	ADJ N serious student
ADJECTIVE-PRONOUN	ADJ PRON ordinary one
	PRON ADJ something expensive
ADVERB-VERB	ADV V hurriedly seek
ADVERB-ADJECTIVE-NOUN	ADV ADJ N only three people
ADVERB-ADVERB	ADV ADV quite seriously

Adverbs may also modify phrases, clauses, or entire sentences.

> He drove *nearly* to the edge of the cliff. [*Nearly* modifies the phrase *to the edge.*]

> They arrived *just* when we were ready to leave. [*Just* modifies the clause *when we were ready to leave.*]

> *Fortunately,* she is no longer on the critical list. [*Fortunately* modifies the entire sentence that follows.]

Many of the most common adjectives are familiar one-syllable words such as *good, bad, strange, true, false, large, right,* and *wrong.* Many others are formed by adding endings such as *-al, -able, -ful, -less, -ish, -ive,* and *-y* to nouns or verbs: *optional, fashionable, beautiful, fruitless, selfish, expressive, dreamy.*

Most adverbs are formed by adding *-ly* to adjectives: *badly,* *strangely, falsely, largely, beautifully, selfishly*. But note that we cannot depend on *-ly* to identify adverbs, since some adjectives also end in *-ly* (*fatherly, lonely, silly*) and since some common adverbs do not end in *-ly* (*always, forever, here, not, now, often, quite, then, there*). Thus, although certain endings sometimes help us to distinguish between adjectives and adverbs, the only sure way to distinguish them is to determine how the individual word is used in a sentence. If a word modifies a noun or pronoun, it is an adjective; if it modifies a verb, an adjective, or another adverb, it is an adverb.

9a

Don't use adjectives to modify verbs, adverbs, and other adjectives

Dropping the *-ly* ending of adverbs—leaving an adjective form—is nonstandard.

NONSTANDARD	They took each other *serious*.
STANDARD	They took each other seriously.
NONSTANDARD	Jenny read the book *easy*.
STANDARD	Jenny read the book *easily*.

Similarly, the adjectives *good* and *bad* often appear where standard English requires the adverbs *well* and *badly*.

NONSTANDARD	Playing *good* is the goal of practicing baseball.
STANDARD	Playing *well* is the goal of practicing baseball.

Although in informal speech the adjectives *real* and *sure* are often used in place of the adverb forms *really* and *surely*, formal speech and writing still require the *-ly* adverb form.

INFORMAL	After a few lessons, Dan drove *real* well.
FORMAL	After a few lessons, Dan drove *really* well.
INFORMAL	I *sure* was shocked by his confession.
FORMAL	I *surely* was shocked by his confession.

9b

Use an adjective after a linking verb to modify the subject. Use an adverb to modify a verb.

A **linking verb** is one that links, or connects, a subject and its complement (see 5a-3). Some verbs may be linking or not linking, depending on their meaning. The verbs most often used as linking verbs are forms of *be* and verbs associated with our five senses (*look, sound, smell, feel, taste*), as well as a few others (*appear, seem, become, grow, turn, prove, remain*). When these verbs are used to link subject and modifier, they are followed by an adjective. When the modifier defines or describes the verb, then an adverb is used.

> Dick felt *strong* after his workout. [Adjective.]
> Dick felt *strongly* that he should not go. [Adverb.]
>
> The evidence proved *conclusive*. [Adjective.]
> The evidence proved *conclusively* that the defendant was guilty. [Adverb.]

ad
9d

9c

After a direct object, use an adjective to modify the object and an adverb to modify the verb.

This situation is similar to the one described in 9b. When the modifier describes the direct object (a noun or pronoun), it is an adjective. When it describes the action of a verb, it is an adverb.

> His instructor considered the student's work *thorough*. [Adjective.]
>
> His instructor considered the student's work *thoroughly* before failing him. [Adverb.]

9d

When an adverb has a short form and an *-ly* form, distinguish carefully between the forms.

Some adverbs have two forms, one with an *-ly* ending and one without. These include the following:

cheap, cheaply	near, nearly
close, closely	quick, quickly
high, highly	sharp, sharply
late, lately	slow, slowly
loud, loudly	wrong, wrongly

The two forms in some pairs are used interchangeably. But in other pairs the choice between the two forms is a matter of idiom. Although no general rule is possible, a few guidelines are useful.

In some adverb pairs the *-ly* form has developed an entirely separate meaning.

> He went *late*.
> *Lately* he has been eating more.
>
> Winter is drawing *near*.
> Winter is *nearly* here.

In general, when the long and short forms mean the same, the short forms occur more frequently with other short words and in informal speech and writing. The *-ly* forms are preferable in formal writing.

INFORMAL	Drive *slow.*
FORMAL	She drove *slowly* through the parking lot.
INFORMAL	Jones wants to get rich *quick.*
FORMAL	Harrison became rich *quickly* when he invested in the stock market.

ad
9d

EXERCISE 1

Identify the adjectives and adverbs in the following sentences, and determine what part of speech each one modifies.

Example:

The antique lantern sputtered noisily and went out.

ADJ ⟶ N   V ⟶ ADV   V ⟶ ADV
The *antique* lantern sputtered *noisily* and went *out.*

1. The sunbathers grabbed their sandy towels and retreated quickly from the tide.
2. Everyone in the class answered the hardest question wrong.
3. He was such an exciting person that everyone felt bad when he left.
4. Even in good weather, one of the surest ways to cause an accident is to follow another car too closely.
5. As the Ferris wheel slowly turned, raising him higher in the air, he became increasingly ill.

EXERCISE 2

Revise the following sentences so that adjectives are used to modify nouns and pronouns and adverbs are used to modify verbs, adjectives, and other adverbs.

Example:

The largest bell rang loud.
The largest bell rang *loudly.*

1. I was real surprised when Martin and Emily got a divorce.
2. If you practice the piano regular, you will soon be able to play real music.
3. Thinking about the accident, Jerry began to feel badly about it.
4. After playing poor for six games, the hockey team finally had a game that was good.
5. If people learned karate, they could stop would-be robbers quick, before the robbers could steal anything.

9e

Use the comparative and superlative forms of adjectives and adverbs appropriately.

Adjectives and adverbs can show different degrees of quality or amount with the endings *-er* and *-est* or with the words *more* and *most* (to compare upward) or *less* and *least* (to compare downward). Most modifiers have three forms. The **positive form** is the dictionary form and simply describes without comparing.

> a *big* book
> spoke *forcefully*

The **comparative form** compares the thing modified with one other thing.

> a *bigger* book
> spoke *more* (or *less*) *forcefully*

The **superlative form** compares the thing modified with two or more other things.

> the *biggest* book
> spoke *most* (or *least*) *forcefully*

1

When word length or sound requires, use *more* and *most* instead of the endings *-er* and *-est*.

For downward comparisons, all adjectives and adverbs use *less* for the comparative (*less open*) and *least* for the superlative (*least successfully*). For upward comparisons, most one-syllable adjectives and adverbs and many two-syllable adjectives take the endings *-er* and *-est*.

POSITIVE	COMPARATIVE	SUPERLATIVE
Adjectives		
red	redder	reddest
lucky	luckier	luckiest
Adverbs		
fast	faster	fastest
late	later	latest

Many two-syllable adjectives can either add *-er* and *-est* or use the words *more* and *most*. The use of *more* or *most* tends to draw the comparison out and so places more emphasis on it.

POSITIVE	COMPARATIVE	SUPERLATIVE
steady	steadier	steadiest
	more steady	most steady

Using *more* and *most* is the only way to form the comparative and superlative for most adverbs of two or more syllables (including nearly all ending in *-ly*) and for adjectives of three or more syllables.

Positive	Comparative	Superlative
Adjectives		
beautiful	more beautiful	most beautiful
interesting	more interesting	most interesting
Adverbs		
often	more often	most often
sadly	more sadly	most sadly

2

Use the correct form of irregular adjectives and adverbs.

The irregular modifiers change the spelling of their positive form to show comparative and superlative degrees.

Positive	Comparative	Superlative
Adjectives		
good	better	best
bad	worse	worst
little	littler, less	littlest, least
many some much }	more	most
Adverbs		
well	better	best
badly	worse	worst

3

Don't use double comparatives or double superlatives.

The comparative or the superlative is doubled when the *-er* or *-est* ending is combined with the words *more, most, less,* or *least.*

He was the *wisest* (not *most wisest*) man I ever knew.
My sister gets more privileges because she's *older* (not *more older*).

4

In general, use the comparative form for comparing two things and the superlative form for comparing three or more things.

She was the *taller* of the two girls [Comparative.]
Of all those books, *The Yearling* is the *best.* [Superlative.]

In conversation the superlative form is often used even though only two things are being compared.

5

In general, don't use comparative or superlative forms for modifiers that can't logically be compared.

ad

9e

Adjectives and adverbs that can't logically be compared include *perfect, unique, dead, impossible,* and *infinite.* These words are **absolute;** that is, they are not, strictly speaking, capable of greater or lesser degrees because their positive form describes their only state. Thus, although they can be preceded by adverbs like *nearly* or *almost* that mean "approaching," they can't logically be used with *more, most, less,* or *least* (as in *most unique* or *less infinite*).

This distinction is now made more often in formal than in informal usage.

FORMAL	He was a *unique* teacher.
INFORMAL	He was the *most unique* teacher we had.

EXERCISE 3

Write the comparative and superlative forms of each adjective or adverb below. Then use the form specified in parentheses in a sentence of your own.

Example:

heavy (*comparative*)
Comparative: heavier. Superlative: heaviest.
The magician's trunk was *heavier* than I expected.

1. beautiful (*comparative*)
2. great (*superlative*)
3. lively (*comparative*)
4. hasty (*superlative*)
5. some (*comparative*)
6. often (*superlative*)
7. good (*comparative*)
8. well (*superlative*)
9. majestic (*comparative*)
10. badly (*superlative*)

EXERCISE 4

Revise the following sentences so that the comparative and superlative forms of adjectives and adverbs are used appropriately.

Example:

Attending classes full time and working at two jobs was the most impossible thing I ever did.

Attending classes full time and working at two jobs was *impossible* (or *the hardest thing I ever did*).

1. If I study hard, I should be able to do more better on the next economics test.
2. Working last summer as an assistant to my congressman was one of the more unique experiences I have ever had.

3. My uncle is the younger of three brothers.
4. He was the most cruelest person I ever met.
5. Of the two major problems with nuclear power plants—waste disposal and radiation leakage—radiation leakage is the most terrifying.

9f
Avoid overuse of nouns to modify other nouns.

We often use one noun to modify another, especially when there is no appropriate adjective form to use instead of the noun. For example:

father figure	truth serum
flood control	child care
slave trade	security guard

Carefully used, such constructions can be both clear and concise: *child care center* seems preferable to *center for the care of children*, which requires two successive prepositional phrases. But overuse of nouns to modify other nouns can lead to writing that is flat, if not senseless. To avoid awkward or confusing constructions, keep two principles in mind. First, always use an adjective form as a modifier if there is one.

NOT   Glenn wanted to be a *dentist* technician.

BUT   Glenn wanted to be a *dental* technician.

Second, use only short nouns as modifiers and use them only in sequences of no more than two or three words.

CONFUSING   Maria was appointed to the *union strike investigation committee.* [A union committee to investigate strikes? A committee to investigate union strikes?]

CONFUSING   Mimimex maintains a *plant employee relations interview program.* [Who is interviewing whom, for what purpose, where?]

EXERCISE 5

Revise the following sentences so that adjectives modify nouns and pronouns; so that adverbs modify verbs, adjectives, and other adverbs; so that the comparative and superlative degrees are used appropriately; and so that nouns are not overused as modifiers.

Example:

The opening lines of the poem are the better ones.
The opening lines of the poem are the *best* ones.

1. She and her sisters argued over which of them was the smarter.
2. After writing twenty-five letters, my father finally began to receive his retirement investment payments.
3. He rehearsed long enough to do real well in his audition for a part in the play.
4. Jerry was not more mature than his brother, though he was more older.
5. As we huddled over our sick guinea pig, he seemed to grow more dead by the hour.
6. The student activities committee dance program never got off the ground.
7. Our dog smells well because we bathe him twice a month.
8. Taking twenty-one hours of classes has been the most impossible thing I've ever done.
9. Jessica spoke careful and calm to ensure she'd get her point across.
10. Harry knew he'd play good if he could only relax.

III
Clear
Sentences

10

Sentence Fragments

Written English ordinarily requires complete sentences. To be complete, a sentence must contain both a subject and a verb that asserts something about that subject (a predicate), and it must be able to stand alone. A phrase or a clause introduced by a subordinating word cannot be a sentence because such phrases and clauses are dependent; that is, they must always be connected to an independent clause and cannot stand alone. (See 5c.)

Sentence fragments are parts of sentences that are set off as whole sentences by the use of an initial capital letter and a final period or other end punctuation.

FRAGMENT	When it is time.
FRAGMENT	After all.
FRAGMENT	Because she wasn't feeling well.

Fragments are serious errors in writing. They often suggest that the writer has been careless or does not understand the structure of a sentence. If you have trouble with sentence fragments in your writing, study the rules below. (For the uses of commas, semicolons, and other punctuation marks in correcting sentence fragments, see Chapters 20, 21, 22, and 25.)

10a
Don't set off a subordinate clause as a sentence.

When they are used as connectors, subordinating conjunctions (such as *although, because, if, since, until,* and *while*) and relative pronouns (such as *who, which,* and *that*) always introduce subordinate clauses (see 5c-4). Although subordinate clauses usually have both subjects and predicates, they have meaning only if they are parts of sentences; they cannot stand alone as sentences. You can usually correct a subordinate clause set off as a sentence by combining it with the preceding or following main clause. Or you can remove the subordinating word and write a new sentence. These methods are illustrated in the following examples. (The fragments are in italics.)

FRAGMENT	Many pine trees bear large cones. *Which appear in August.*
REVISED	Many pine trees bear large cones, which appear in August.
FRAGMENT	Larry asked more questions than the others. *Because he had missed the meeting.*
REVISED	Larry asked more questions than the others because he had missed the meeting.
FRAGMENT	The decision seems perfectly correct and fair. *Although I can't say I like it.*
REVISED	The decision seems perfectly correct and fair, although I can't say I like it.
REVISED	The decision seems perfectly correct and fair. I can't say I like it.

frag
10a

(Notice that in the last example the second revision gives more emphasis to the writer's dislike of the decision.)

Once you have identified a sentence fragment and corrected it, reread the new sentence to be sure it is a grammatical unit.

EXERCISE 1

Correct the sentence fragments below by combining them with an independent clause or making them independent clauses.

Example:
Whenever you are ready. We can go.
Whenever you are ready, we can go.

1. Robert missed only one question on his chemistry quiz. Even though he had not studied the night before.
2. I enjoy New England more in the winter than in the summer. Especially now that I have learned to ski.
3. Ann was given the part of Olivia in *Twelfth Night*. Though she had not tried out for it.
4. Freshman English is not as difficult as people say. Unless someone is not willing to do the work.
5. Sarah worked many hours perfecting her double somersault. Which was her best dive.

10b

Don't set off a verbal phrase as a sentence.

A verbal phrase consists of an infinitive (*to run, to satisfy*), a past participle (*ran, satisfied*), or a present participle (*running, satisfying*), together with its objects and modifiers (see 5c-2). Since verbals alone are not capable of assertion, they have meaning only if they are parts of sentences. They cannot stand alone as the main verb in a predicate. Like fragments consisting of subordinate clauses, fragments of verbal phrases are most easily corrected by combining them with an independent clause. Unlike subordinate clauses, which usually have both a subject and a predicate, verbal phrases cannot be made into separate sentences without rewriting.

frag

10b

Fragment	One of my great desires is a very simple one. *To live close to the sea.*
Revised	One of my great desires is a very simple one, to live close to the sea.
Fragment	He backed closer and closer to the end of the diving board. *At last falling into the water.*
Revised	He backed closer and closer to the end of the diving board, at last falling into the water.
Revised	He backed closer and closer to the end of the diving board. At last *he fell* into the water.

EXERCISE 2

Correct the sentence fragments below by combining them with an independent clause or rewriting them as independent clauses.

Example:

Dancing has become very popular. Captivating all generations.

Dancing has become very popular. *It is* captivating all generations.

1. I've always felt I missed something important. Never living by the mountains or the ocean.
2. Skateboarding is a mixed pleasure. Being both exciting and dangerous.
3. Having a hobby can be important to a fulfilling life. Allowing people to keep interested in things outside their work.
4. Just to stay awake. That is the major challenge of long-distance driving.
5. That was one of my childhood dreams. To be able to fly a glider.

10c
Don't set off a prepositional phrase as a sentence.

Prepositional phrases consist of prepositions (such as *in, on, to, over, under,* and *with*) together with their objects and modifiers (see 5c-1). Like subordinate clauses and verbal phrases, prepositional phrases always serve as parts of sentences; they cannot stand alone as complete sentences.

FRAGMENT	More than anything else, I wanted to get away from the heat. *To someplace cooler.*
REVISED	More than anything else, I wanted to get away from the heat—to someplace cooler.
REVISED	More than anything else, I wanted to get away from the heat to someplace cooler.

frag
10d

(Notice that of the two revisions, the first, which uses the dash, gives the prepositional phrase greater emphasis.)

EXERCISE 3

Correct the sentence fragments below by combining them with an independent clause or rewriting them as independent clauses.

> *Example:*
> She was still beautiful two years later. After seven operations.
> She was still beautiful two years later, after seven operations.

1. My great-grandfather paid fifty dollars. For one hundred acres and a barn.
2. She felt bare and helpless. Without her purse.
3. The house will take at least three weeks to paint. Even with two painters.
4. This weekend we discovered a new leak under the house. In a space occupied by some rodents that had decided to live with us.
5. In moving heavy things. You should be careful to lift using your legs, not your back.

10d
Don't set off an appositive or a part of a compound predicate as a sentence.

Appositives are nouns, or nouns and their modifiers, that rename or describe other nouns (see 5c-5). They cannot stand alone as sentences.

FRAGMENT	All kinds of sports events are held in the gymnasium. *Basketball, boxing, swimming, and indoor track.*
REVISED	All kinds of sports events are held in the gymnasium—basketball, boxing, swimming, and indoor track.
FRAGMENT	When I was a child, my favorite adult was an old uncle. *A retired sea captain who always told me long stories of wild adventures in faraway places.*
REVISED	When I was a child, my favorite adult was an old uncle, a retired sea captain who always told me long stories of wild adventures in faraway places.

frag
10d

Compound predicates are predicates made up of two or more verbs and their objects, if any. A verb or its object cannot stand alone as a sentence without a subject.

FRAGMENT	If his friends were in trouble, Henry always offered them much advice and many good wishes. *But no real help.*
REVISED	If his friends were in trouble, Henry always offered them much advice and many good wishes—but no real help. [Compound object.]
FRAGMENT	Pat worked all day. *And then danced at night.*
REVISED	Pat worked all day and then danced at night. [Compound verb.]

EXERCISE 4

Correct the sentence fragments below by combining them with an independent clause or rewriting them as independent clauses.

Example:

Harry was unable to spell. But, surprisingly, could play Scrabble well.

Harry was unable to spell but, surprisingly, could play Scrabble well.

1. During World War II Jack Armstrong was a hero for young people. The all-American boy.
2. Lynn graduated from college in 1979. And in the same year received three job offers.
3. The college of business administration offers several degrees. And the opportunity to be an intern for one of many businesses.

4. In whatever form, tobacco is bad for one's health. Whether cigarettes, cigars, pipe tobacco, or chewing tobacco.
5. With the money her grandmother left her she bought a stereo. A component system.

10e

Be aware of the acceptable uses of incomplete sentences.

A few word groups lacking the usual subject-predicate combination are nonetheless standard sentence patterns. Such patterns are acceptable in all writing although they occur most often in speech or in writing that records speech. These include exclamations (*Watch it! Drop dead!*); questions and answers (*Where next? To Kansas. Why? To see my brother.*); and commands (*Move along. Shut the window. Finish your work.*). Commands are also used in written directions. Another kind of incomplete sentence is common to writing, though limited to special situations. This is the transitional phrase, such as *So much for the causes, now for the results,* and *One final point.*

Professional writers sometimes use sentence fragments and do so effectively, particularly in narrative and descriptive writing. But such sentences are very infrequent in expository writing. Unless you are experienced and thoroughly secure in your own writing, you should avoid all fragments and concentrate on writing clear, well-managed, standard sentences.

frag
10e

EXERCISE 5

Revise the following paragraph to eliminate sentence fragments by combining them with an independent clause or rewriting them as independent clauses.

Becoming an adult can mean moving into the best years of life. Or moving downhill from the "high" of adolescence. It depends on one's outlook. On one's experiences as a child and one's view of adulthood. Beginning at about age 20, people enter a new world. Released from the restrictions adults place on them. They are approaching their physical and mental peak. The world is ahead. Waiting to challenge and be challenged. If their experiences as children have made them secure with themselves and others, they may welcome the challenges of adulthood. But those challenges can also seem frightening and overwhelming. If childhood and adolescence have already presented too many battles to fight. Too little security.

11

Comma Splices and Run-on Sentences

In speaking and writing we often link two or more independent clauses into one sentence. In speaking we naturally pause between clauses or use a coordinating conjunction like *and* or *but* to link clauses. In writing we also use coordinating conjunctions, but the pauses in speech must be indicated by punctuation in writing. Two problems commonly occur in punctuating linked clauses. One is the **comma splice,** in which two or more independent clauses are joined only by commas. The second is the **run-on sentence** (sometimes called the **fused sentence**), in which two or more independent clauses are joined with no punctuation or conjunction between them.

CLAUSES AS SEPARATE SENTENCES

The ship was huge. Its mast was thirty feet high.

CLAUSES COMBINED IN ONE SENTENCE

The ship was huge; its mast was thirty feet high.

COMMA SPLICE

The ship was huge, its mast was thirty feet high.

RUN-ON SENTENCE

The ship was huge its mast was thirty feet high.

Like sentence fragments (see Chapter 10), comma splices and run-on sentences are serious errors because they often suggest the writer has been careless or does not understand the structure of a sentence. (For the uses of commas, semicolons, and other sentence punctuation, see Chapters 20, 21, 22, and 25.)

COMMA SPLICES

11a

Don't join two main clauses with a comma unless they are also joined by a coordinating conjunction.

When a comma is the only mark of punctuation between two main clauses and there is no other connector (such as a coordinating conjunction), the relation between the clauses is often unclear.

COMMA SPLICE   Rain had fallen steadily for sixteen hours, many basements were flooded.

COMMA SPLICE   Cars would not start, people were late to work.

cs

11a

You have four main options for correcting a comma splice: (1) make separate sentences of the independent clauses; (2) insert a coordinating conjunction preceded by a comma between the clauses; (3) insert a semicolon between the clauses; and (4) subordinate one of the clauses to the other. The option you choose depends on the relation you want to establish between the clauses. Some general principles will help you choose among the possibilities.

Revising a comma splice by making separate sentences from the independent clauses will always be correct.

Rain had fallen steadily for sixteen hours. Many basements were flooded.

The period is not only correct but preferable if the ideas expressed in the two main clauses are only loosely related.

COMMA SPLICE   Chemistry has contributed much to our understanding of foods, many foods like wheat, corn, and beans can be produced in the laboratory.

REVISED   Chemistry has contributed much .to our understanding of foods. Many foods like wheat, corn, and beans can be produced in the laboratory.

When the ideas in the independent clauses are closely related to each other, you may choose to correct a comma splice by inserting the appropriate coordinating conjunction between the clauses, after the comma.

Cars would not start, *and* people were late to work.

Notice that the relation indicated by a coordinating conjunction can be complementary (*and*), contradictory (*but, yet*), or alternate (*or, nor*).

COMMA SPLICE	He had intended to work all weekend, his friends arrived Friday and stayed until Sunday.
REVISED	He had intended to work all weekend, *but* his friends arrived Friday and stayed until Sunday.

If the relation between the ideas expressed in the main clauses is very close and obvious without a conjunction, you can connect the clauses with a semicolon. (See also 11b.)

cs

11a

Rain had fallen steadily for sixteen hours; many basements were flooded.

COMMA SPLICE	Rhoda and Nancy were close friends, they roomed together, ate meals together, and studied together.
REVISED	Rhoda and Nancy were close friends; they roomed together, ate meals together, and studied together.

When the idea in one clause is more important than that in the other, you can subordinate the less important idea in a dependent clause. Use a subordinating conjunction or a relative pronoun at the beginning of the new dependent clause.

After rain had fallen steadily for sixteen hours, many basements were flooded.

In the examples below notice that subordination is more effective than forming separate sentences, because it defines the relation between the clauses more sharply.

COMMA SPLICE	The examination was finally over, Becky could feel free to enjoy herself once more.
REVISED	The examination was finally over. Becky could feel free to enjoy herself once more. [Both ideas receive equal weight.]
IMPROVED	*When* the examination was finally over, Becky could feel free to enjoy herself once more. [Emphasis on the second idea.]
COMMA SPLICE	They had driven for nine hours without stopping, they were starved when they arrived home.
REVISED	They had driven for nine hours without stopping. They were starved when they arrived home.

IMPROVED   *Because* they had driven for nine hours without stopping, they were starved when they arrived home.

(See 16b for more discussion of effective use of subordination.)

EXCEPTIONS: Commas are sometimes used between three or more parallel main clauses or between two main clauses that are balanced, as in the following:

Paul dislikes sports, he dislikes work, he dislikes everything. [Parallel.]

Janet always studies, Tom never studies. [Balanced.]

11b

cs
11b

Use a period or semicolon to separate main clauses connected by conjunctive adverbs or transitional expressions.

Conjunctive adverbs are words like *also, consequently, however, nevertheless, then,* and *therefore* (see 5d-2). Typical transitional expressions are *for example, on the contrary,* and *that is* (see 3b-6). Conjunctive adverbs and transitional expressions frequently connect main clauses, and when they do the clauses must be separated by a period (forming two separate sentences) or by a semicolon. (The adverb or expression is also frequently followed by a comma; see 21b.)

COMMA SPLICE   Most Americans refuse to give up enjoyable habits that cause serious sickness, consequently our medical costs are higher than those of many other countries.

REVISED   Most Americans refuse to give up enjoyable habits that cause serious sickness. Consequently, our medical costs are higher than those of many other countries.

COMMA SPLICE   The cost of education has been rising steadily for several decades, moreover it will probably continue to rise in the future.

REVISED   The cost of education has been rising steadily for several decades; moreover, it will probably continue to rise in the future.

Like coordinating and subordinating conjunctions, conjunctive adverbs and transitional expressions help to link the two clauses they join. But they also serve as adverbs, modifying the clause in which they appear. And unlike conjunctions, which must be placed between the word groups they join (coordinating) or at the beginning of the word group they introduce (subordinating), conjunctive adverbs and transitional expressions may be placed at the beginning, middle, or end of the clause. No matter where in the clause a conjunctive adverb or transitional expression appears, however, the clause must be separated from another main clause by a period or a semicolon.

COMMA SPLICE	The increased time devoted to watching television is not the only cause of the decline in reading ability, it is one of the important causes.
COORDINATING CONJUNCTION	The increased time devoted to watching television is not the only cause of the decline in reading ability, *but* it is one of the important causes.
SUBORDINATING CONJUNCTION	*Although* the increased time devoted to watching television is not the only cause of the decline in reading ability, it is one of the important causes.
CONJUNCTIVE ADVERB	The increased time devoted to watching television is not the only cause of the decline in reading ability; *however,* it is one of the important causes.
CONJUNCTIVE ADVERB	The increased time devoted to watching television is not the only cause of the decline in reading ability; it is, *however,* one of the important causes.
CONJUNCTIVE ADVERB	The increased time devoted to watching television is not the only cause of the decline in reading ability; it is one of the important causes, *however.*
CONJUNCTIVE ADVERB	The increased time devoted to watching television is not the only cause of the decline in reading ability. *However,* it is one of the important causes.

cs

11b

EXERCISE 1

Revise the comma splices below by making separate sentences or by using coordinating conjunctions, semicolons, or subordinating words. Use each method of correction at least twice.

Example:

Judith slept deeply at night, she had worked hard all day.

Judith slept deeply at night *because* she had worked hard all day.

1. The election was held on a rainy day, the weather kept people away from the polls.
2. Marvin and Percy went to the concert, there were no tickets left.
3. My brother enlisted in the Marines for three years, he will probably reenlist when his hitch is up.
4. I will marry someday, I don't know when.
5. We were favored to win over Colliersville, however our center sprained his ankle and we lost.
6. Marian never seems to stop, she has so much energy.
7. Snow fell for three days in a row, consequently the superintendent had to shut down the schools.
8. My brother is spoiled, he gets whatever he wants.
9. Sean bought a new suit for the interview, he didn't get the job.
10. Little Orphan Annie used to be a comic-strip character, now she has become a character in a Broadway play.

run-on

11c

RUN-ON SENTENCES

11c

Don't run two main clauses together without using a connector or appropriate punctuation between them.

When two main clauses are joined without a word to connect them or a punctuation mark to separate them, the result is a **run-on sentence,** sometimes called a **fused sentence.** Run-on sentences are never acceptable.

RUN-ON	Many people would be lost without television they would not know how to amuse themselves.
RUN-ON	Our foreign policy is not well defined many countries are confused by it.

Run-on sentences may be corrected in the same way as comma splices (see 11a).

REVISED	Our foreign policy is not well defined. Many countries are confused by it. [Make separate sentences of the clauses.]
REVISED	Our foreign policy is not well defined, *and* many countries are confused by it. [Use coordinating conjunction and comma.]

Revised	Our foreign policy is not well defined ; many countries are confused by it. [Use semicolon.]
Revised	*Because* our foreign policy is not well defined, many countries are confused by it. [Use subordinating conjunction.]

EXERCISE 2

Revise the run-on sentences below.

Example:

People had often accused Tim of being shy he tried hard to be outgoing.

People had often accused Tim of being shy, *so* he tried hard to be outgoing.

1. The rain fell so hard that water started pouring into the kitchen from the back porch it blew in around the kitchen windows too.
2. Children sometimes misbehave just to test their elders parents should discipline them on those occasions.
3. The science club used to hold yearly competitions I had a lot of fun helping to organize them.
4. The skills center offers job training to people who need it it can't guarantee jobs, though.
5. The parking problem in the downtown area is getting out of hand the mayor suggests a new underground parking garage.

EXERCISE 3

Identify and revise the comma splices and run-on sentences in the following paragraph.

A pleasant, inexpensive treat is a weekend in a country inn. Inns are usually located in quaint villages, there is little noise during the night except for crickets. The surrounding area is countryside, often with historical sites to visit. The inn-keeper is sometimes a great cook. I have had delicious breakfasts at inns frequently they are included in the charge for the room. The rooms themselves are large and airy. The chairs are soft the beds are just right. The trip to the inn may take an hour and the weekend may cost as little as twenty dollars. It's a great break from school or work, I recommend it to everyone.

run-on
11c

12

*Pronoun
Reference*

Pronouns substitute for nouns, but in themselves they have no meaning. A pronoun must therefore refer clearly and unmistakably to the noun whose place it takes, called its **antecedent.** If the pronoun's antecedent is not clear, the sentence itself will not be clear. A sentence like *Mark and him went to the movies* is ungrammatical, but it is clear. In contrast, *He spoke to Mark; he didn't want to go* is not clear. The fault in the first sentence is the more obvious, but the fault in the second sentence may be the more serious because it violates the first rule of writing: that it be clear. One way to clarify the relation of a pronoun to its antecedent is to ensure that they agree in person and number (see 8b). The other way is to ensure that the pronoun can refer to only one antecedent.

12a
Make a pronoun refer clearly to one antecedent.

A pronoun may, of course, refer to two or more nouns in a compound antecedent, as in the following:

Jenkins and Wilson pooled *their* resources and became partners.

But when either of two nouns can be a pronoun's antecedent, the reference will not be clear.

CONFUSING	When Jenkins became partners with Wilson in April, he did not know he would be a failure. [The first *he* seems to refer to Jenkins, but who would be a failure?]
CLEAR	When Jenkins became partners with Wilson in April, he did not know Wilson would be a failure.

CLEAR   When Jenkins became partners with Wilson in April, Wilson did not know Jenkins would be a failure.

In sentences like those above, clarity requires that we replace pronouns with the appropriate nouns or restructure the sentence entirely. Sentences that report what someone said, using verbs like *said* or *told*, often require direct rather than indirect quotation.

CONFUSING   Oliver told Bill that he was mistaken.

CLEAR   Oliver told Bill, "I am mistaken."

CLEAR   Oliver told Bill, "You are mistaken."

ref

12b

NOTE: Avoid the awkward device of using a pronoun followed by the appropriate noun in parentheses.

WEAK   Mary should help Joan, but *she* (*Joan*) should help herself first.

IMPROVED   Mary should help Joan, but *Joan* should help herself first.

12b

Place a pronoun close enough to its antecedent to ensure clarity.

Even in relatively short sentences, a pronoun reference will not be clear if pronoun and antecedent are separated by other nouns that the pronoun could refer to.

CONFUSING   Jan held the sandwich in one hand and the telephone in the other, eating it while she talked. [Common sense tells us Jan was eating the sandwich, not the telephone. But we are distracted because *it* could refer to either.]

CLEAR   Jan held the sandwich in one hand and the telephone in the other, eating the sandwich while she talked.

When a relative pronoun introduces a clause that modifies a noun, the pronoun should generally be placed immediately after its antecedent to prevent possible confusion. (See also Chapter 14 on misplaced modifiers.)

CONFUSING   Jody found a dress in the attic that her aunt had worn. [Her aunt had worn the attic?]

CLEAR   In the attic Jody found a dress that her aunt had worn.

If no other likely antecedents come between a pronoun and its actual antecedent, the two may be some distance away from each other without causing confusion. In the following sentences, for example, the reference of *he* to Reggie is perfectly clear because no intervening noun could be called *he*.

> *Reggie* always went to great lengths to ensure that nothing interfered with personal pleasure, not study, not concern for others, and, above all, not work. *He* was, in short, completely selfish.

EXERCISE 1

Revise the following sentences so that the pronouns refer clearly to only one antecedent and fall close enough to their antecedents to ensure clarity.

ref
12c

> *Example:*
> The discouraged artist looked at his canvas and at the apple he was painting and then destroyed it.
> The discouraged artist looked at his canvas and at the apple he was painting and then destroyed *the apple.*

1. If your pet cheetah will not eat raw meat, cook it.
2. When hunters outnumber deer, they will no longer be a problem.
3. Dick and his cousin did not get along because he liked to have his own way.
4. The young priest was pleased to tell his bishop that the parishioners seemed to like him.
5. The danger of radiation leakage from the nuclear power plant leaves nearby residents in fear of it.
6. The postcard from Mother describing her visit to Geraldine never arrived because she forgot to mail it.
7. Alice told her sister that she was gaining weight.
8. Saul found an old gun in the rotting shed that was just as his grandfather had left it.
9. Camera in one hand and light meter in the other, Murray took pictures with it as fast as he could.
10. There is a difference between the heroes of today and the heroes of yesterday: they have flaws in their characters.

12c
Make a pronoun refer to a specific antecedent rather than to an implied one.

As a rule, the meaning of a pronoun will be clearest when it refers to a specific noun or other pronoun. When the antecedent is not specifically stated but implied by the context, the reference can only be inferred by the reader. Implied reference occurs frequently with the pronouns *this, that, which,* and *it.*

> He stole money, *which* disturbed his parents and his counselors. [*Which* refers to the whole preceding clause.]

In this sentence the implied reference is acceptable because the meaning is unmistakably clear. But even this kind of nonspecific reference can lead to vagueness, unless it is used very carefully. Other kinds of implied reference, such as reference to modifying words, are almost always confusing and unacceptable.

ref
12c

1

Use *this, that, which,* and *it* cautiously in referring to whole statements.

The most common kind of implied reference is that illustrated above: the pronouns *this, that, which,* and *it* refer to a whole idea or situation described in the preceding clause, sentence, or even paragraph. Such reference, often called **broad reference,** is acceptable only if the pronoun refers clearly to the clause preceding it.

If the reader could possibly be confused, the sentence should be recast to avoid using the pronoun or to provide an appropriate noun.

CONFUSING	I knew nothing about economics, *which* my instructor had not learned.
CLEAR	I knew nothing about economics, a fact my instructor had not learned.
CLEAR	I knew nothing about economics, because my instructor knew nothing about it.
CONFUSING	The faculty agreed that they wished to change the requirements, but *it* took time.
CLEAR	The faculty agreed that they wished to change the requirements, but agreeing took time.
CLEAR	The faculty agreed that they wished to change the requirements, but the change itself took time.
CONFUSING	They walked for blocks talking about the movie they had seen. *That* was what they needed.
CLEAR	They needed a long walk after the movie they had seen, and they talked about it while they walked.
CLEAR	They wanted to talk about the movie they had seen, so they walked for blocks.

2

Don't use a pronoun to refer to a noun implied by a modifier.

Adjectives, nouns used as modifiers, and the possessives of nouns or pronouns make unsatisfactory antecedents. Although they may imply a noun that could serve as an antecedent, they do not supply the specific antecedent needed for clarity.

WEAK	In the president's speech *he* outlined plans for tax reform.
REVISED	In his speech the president outlined plans for tax reform.
WEAK	Liz drove a red Toyota; *it* was her favorite color.
REVISED	Liz drove a red Toyota because red was her favorite color.
REVISED	Liz drove a Toyota that was red, her favorite color.

ref

12c

3

Don't use a pronoun to refer to a noun implied by some other noun or phrase.

WEAK	Jim talked at length about salesmanship, although he had never been *one*.
REVISED	Jim talked at length about salesmanship, although he had never been a salesman.
WEAK	Jake was bitten by a rattlesnake, but *it* was not serious.
REVISED	Jake was bitten by a rattlesnake, but the bite was not serious.

4

Don't use part of a title as an antecedent in the opening sentence of a paper.

The title of a paper is considered to be entirely separate from the paper itself, so a pronoun can't be used to refer to the title. If you open a paper with a reference to the title, repeat whatever part of the title is necessary for clarity.

TITLE	How to Row a Boat
NOT	This is not as easy as it looks.
BUT	Rowing a boat is not as easy as it looks.

12d

Avoid the indefinite use of *it* and *they*. Use *you* indefinitely only to mean "you, the reader."

In conversation we commonly use expressions like *it says in the paper* or *in Texas they say*. But indefinite use of *it* and *they* with no antecedents should be avoided in all but informal writing. The constructions are not only unclear but wordy.

WEAK	In chapter four of this book *it* describes the early flights of the Wright brothers.
REVISED	Chapter four of this book describes the early flights of the Wright brothers.
WEAK	In the average television drama *they* present a false picture of life.
REVISED	The average television drama presents a false picture of life.

Using *you* with indefinite reference to people in general is also well established in conversation: *You can never tell when it will rain. You can find what you want in the library.* The indefinite *you* frequently occurs in informal writing, too. But formal writing requires the pronoun *one* or a general noun such as *person* or *people* instead of *you*.

INFORMAL	In college you can take varied courses.
FORMAL	In college one can take varied courses.

You is well established in all but very formal writing when the meaning is clearly "you, the reader," as in *You can learn the standard uses of pronouns.* But the writer must consider whether the context is appropriate for such a meaning. Consider this example.

INAPPROPRIATE	In the fourteenth century *you* had to struggle simply to survive. [Clearly, the meaning cannot be "you, the reader."]
REVISED	In the fourteenth century *one* (or *a person* or *people*) had to struggle simply to survive.

In contrast, the following opening of a student paper uses *you* appropriately to mean "you, the reader."

If you want to live in the city today, you had better be alert and competitive. If you cross the street against traffic, you must meet the glares of drivers. If you squeeze onto an elevator, you must be prepared to get your feet stepped on and your shins kicked. If you try to hold your place when people are getting off a subway, you must put up with elbows in your stomach and ribs.

12e

Avoid using the pronoun *it* more than one way in a sentence.

We use *it* idiomatically in expressions like *It is raining* or *It is growing colder daily.* We use *it* to postpone the subject in sentences like *It is true that more jobs are available to women today.* And, of course, we use *it* as a personal pronoun in sentences like *Jon wanted the book, but he couldn't find it.* All these uses are standard. But when two of these uses occur in the same sentence, the reader can be confused.

CONFUSING	I forgot to wear my raincoat, and now that *it* is raining I need *it*. [The first *it* is idiomatic; the second refers to the raincoat.]
REVISED	I forgot to wear my raincoat, and now that the rain has begun I need it.
REVISED	Now that it is raining, I need the raincoat I forgot to wear.

ref
12f

12f

Be sure the relative pronouns *who, which,* and *that* are appropriate for their antecedents.

The relative pronouns *who, which,* and *that* are commonly used to refer to persons, animals, or things. *Who* refers most often to persons but may also be used to refer to animals that have names.

Jon is the boy *who* leads the other boys into trouble.
Their dog Wanda, *who* is growing lame, has difficulty running.

Which refers to animals and things.

The Orinoco River, *which* is 1600 miles long, flows through Venezuela into the Atlantic Ocean.

That refers to animals and things and sometimes to persons.

The jade tree *that* my grandmother gave me suddenly died.
Infants *that* walk need constant tending.

The possessive *whose* is often used to refer to animals and things to avoid awkward and wordy *of which* constructions.

The book *whose* binding broke had been my father's.

EXERCISE 2

Revise the following sentences so that all pronouns refer clearly to specific, appropriate antecedents.

Example:
In impressionist paintings, they used color to imitate reflected light.
Impressionist painters used color to imitate reflected light.

1. We receive warnings to beware of nuclear fallout, DDT, smog, and oil shortages, but I try not to think about it.
2. The merchants agreed to implement a new policy on outdoor signs, but it took longer than they thought.
3. In F. Scott Fitzgerald's novel he wrote about the Jazz Age.
4. Martina loves to try on mink coats because she likes the way it feels.
5. By the time the firemen arrived at the scene, it was blazing out of control.
6. Carl is a master carpenter because his father, a cabinetmaker, taught him about it when he was a teenager.
7. After the ice had caused a portion of the school roof to cave in, they had to hold classes in a nearby church.
8. Macbeth is a complicated and ambiguous hero, and that is one thing that makes it a good play.
9. After hearing Professor Eakins's lecture on marine biology, I think I want to become one.
10. Next summer John and I want to go to Canada, but we think it will be too expensive.
11. Smoking increases your risk of a heart attack.
12. In urban redevelopment projects they try to make neighborhoods safe and attractive.
13. In the nineteenth century you didn't have many options in motorized transportation.
14. It is difficult to see a chocolate eclair without wanting to eat it.
15. My car Harriet, who has no roof, is useless when it rains.

ref
12

13

Shifts

A sentence should be consistent: grammatical elements such as tense, mood, voice, person, and number should remain the same throughout the sentence, unless grammar or the meaning of the sentence requires a shift. Unnecessary shifts in these elements, either within a sentence or among related sentences, distract the reader and confuse meaning.

13a
Keep sentences consistent in person and number.

Person in grammar refers to the distinction between the person talking (first person), the person spoken to (second person), and the person, object, or concept being talked about (third person). **Number** refers to the distinction between one (singular) and more than one (plural). Both nouns and personal pronouns change form to show differences in number, but only the personal pronouns have distinctive forms for the three persons.

The most common faulty shifts in person are shifts from second to third and from third to second person. They occur because we can refer to people in general, including our readers, either in the third person (*a person, one; people, they*) or in the second person (*you*).

> *People* should not drive when *they* have been drinking.
> *One* should not drive when *he* (or *he or she*) has been drinking.
> *You* should not drive when *you* have been drinking.

Although any one of these possibilities is acceptable, a mixture of more than one is inconsistent.

> **INCONSISTENT**   If *a person* works hard, *you* can accomplish a great deal.

REVISED	If *you* work hard, *you* can accomplish a great deal.
REVISED	If *a person* works hard, *he* (or *he or she*) can accomplish a great deal.
BETTER	If *people* work hard, *they* can accomplish a great deal.

(For a discussion of avoiding the use of *he* to mean both *he* and *she*, see 8b-3.)

Inconsistency in number occurs most often between a pronoun and its antecedent (see 8b).

INCONSISTENT	If a *student* does not understand a problem, *they* should consult *their* instructor.
REVISED	If a *student* does not understand a problem, *he* (or *he or she*) should consult *his* (or *his or her*) instructor.
BETTER	If *students* do not understand a problem, *they* should consult *their* instructor.

EXERCISE 1

Revise the sentences below to make them consistent in person and number.

Example:

A plumber will fix burst pipes, but they won't repair waterlogged appliances.

Plumbers will fix burst pipes, but they won't repair waterlogged appliances.

1. If a person has just moved to the city, you have trouble knowing where to go.
2. When a taxpayer does not file on time, they have to pay a penalty.
3. Dr. Moran wanted everyone to live their own life.
4. Writers must know what they are writing about; otherwise one cannot write.
5. If a student misses too many classes, you may fail a course.

13b
Keep sentences consistent in tense and mood.

Some changes in verb tense are required by the meaning of a sentence or by the grammatical requirements of tense sequence. (See 7e.) Unless such changes are necessary, however, tense should be kept consistent.

INCONSISTENT	We *were walking* along slowly, when suddenly a motorcycle *races* in front of us and *skids* into a tree.
REVISED	We *were walking* along slowly, when suddenly a motorcycle *raced* in front of us and *skidded* into a tree.
INCONSISTENT	The main character in the novel *suffers* psychologically because he *has* a clubfoot, but he eventually *triumphed* over his handicap.
REVISED	The main character in the novel *suffers* psychologically because he *has* a clubfoot, but he eventually *triumphs* over his handicap.

shift

13b

(In the second example a consistent use of the present tense is desirable because the present tense is ordinarily used to describe the action of a novel, a play, or a movie. See 7d.)

Shifts in the mood of verbs occur most frequently in giving directions. (See 7f.) The shifts can usually be avoided (and the directions can be stated most directly and clearly) by consistent use of the imperative.

INCONSISTENT	*Cook* the mixture slowly, and *you should stir* it until the sugar is dissolved.
REVISED	*Cook* the mixture slowly, and *stir* it until the sugar is dissolved.

EXERCISE 2

Revise the sentences below to make them consistent in tense and mood.

Example:

Lynn ran to first, rounded the base, and keeps running until she slides into second.

Lynn ran to first, rounded the base, and *kept* running until she *slid* into second.

1. Soon after he joined the union, Lester appears at a rally and makes a speech.
2. If you saw yourself as I see you, you will understand why I get angry.
3. First sand down any paint that is peeling; then you should paint the bare wood with primer.
4. Rachel is walking down the street, and suddenly she stops, as a shot rang out.
5. I had hoped to see the doctor that afternoon, but she calls to say she won't be in.

13c

Keep sentences consistent in subject and voice.

Shifts in the sentence subject and the voice of the verb are sometimes necessary because of meaning:

> *Carter campaigned* vigorously in the primaries and *was nominated* on the first ballot.

But unnecessary shifts in subject and voice create confusing sentences and may cause other grammatical problems.

INCONSISTENT	In the morning *we rode* our bicycles for six miles; in the afternoon *our skateboards were given* a good workout.
REVISED	In the morning *we rode* our bicycles for six miles; in the afternoon *we gave* our skateboards a good workout.
INCONSISTENT	*Looking* out over the ocean, *ships can be seen* in the distance.
REVISED	*Looking* out over the ocean, *we can see* ships in the distance.

(Notice that in the second example the shift from active to passive voice creates a dangling modifier. See 14g.)

EXERCISE 3

Make the sentences below consistent in subject and voice.

> *Example:*
> At the reunion, they ate hot dogs and volleyball was played.
> At the reunion, they ate hot dogs and *played volleyball.*

1. If you take the expressway, much time will be saved.
2. Some arrowheads were dug up, and they found some pottery that was almost undamaged.
3. Our trip was concluded in Tulsa when we visited Tod's aunt.
4. They started the game after some practice drills were run.
5. The tornado ripped off the roof, and it was deposited in a nearby lot.

13d

Don't shift unnecessarily between indirect and direct discourse.

Direct discourse reports, in quotation marks, the exact words of a speaker. **Indirect discourse** reports what was said but not in the speaker's exact words.

DIRECT	He said, "I am going."
INDIRECT	He said that he was going.
INCONSISTENT	Sue asked whether we had repaired the car and "Is anything else likely to happen?"
REVISED	Sue asked, "Have you repaired the car? Is anything else likely to happen?"
REVISED	Sue asked whether we had repaired the car and whether anything else was likely to happen.

EXERCISE 4

Revise the sentences below to eliminate shifts between indirect and direct discourse.

shift

13d

> *Example:*
> Tom asked whether the guest host had arrived and "Are the cameras ready?"
> Tom asked whether the guest host had arrived and *whether the cameras were ready.*
> Tom asked, *"Has the guest host arrived?* Are the cameras ready?"

1. Coach Butler said that our timing was terrible and "I would rather cancel the season than watch you play."
2. Roger asked if we had finished our project and "When are we going to present it?"
3. The report concluded, "Drought is a serious threat" and that we must begin conserving water now.
4. My mother always tells me, "Be careful," and I should come in early.
5. Teachers who assign a lot of homework always say, "I'm doing this for your own good," and that they'd rather not hear any complaints.

EXERCISE 5

Identify each faulty shift in the following paragraph as inconsistent in person, number, tense, mood, subject, voice, or form of discourse. Revise the faulty sentences to eliminate the shifts.

> One is always urged to conserve energy, and we try to do that. However, saving energy requires making sacrifices. My children like baths, not showers, so how can I tell them that they must keep clean and then insist, "You must not use the bath"? They won't stay clean. I don't mind a cool house, but it has to be kept warm when you have the flu. Everyone enjoys a fire in the fireplace, but they fail to realize how much heat from the furnace was released up the chimney. Nonetheless, we have to learn to live with inconveniences or be introduced to real hardship later on.

14

Misplaced and Dangling Modifiers

When we read, we depend principally on the arrangement of the words in a sentence to tell us how they are related. When we write, we usually follow expected arrangements without thinking about it. But since written sentences are often more complex than those we use in speech, we may create confusing sentences if we fail to keep certain principles of arrangement in mind. The confusion is especially likely to occur with modifying words and groups of words.

MISPLACED MODIFIERS

We say that a modifier is **misplaced** if it appears to modify something that common sense tells us it can't, or if the reader cannot be certain what meaning the writer intended.

14a

Place prepositional phrases where they will clearly modify the words intended.

When prepositional phrases function as adjectives to modify nouns, they usually are positioned directly after the noun they modify.

The man *in the green hat* blew smoke in my face.

But prepositional phrases that function as adverbs are movable; that is, they can stand at the beginning, middle, or end of a sentence. Since many prepositional phrases can function as either adjectives or adverbs, confusion can result from their placement.

CONFUSING   She served hamburgers to the men *on paper plates.* [Surely the hamburgers, not the men, were served on paper plates.]

CLEAR	She served hamburgers *on paper plates* to the men.
CONFUSING	He was unhappy after failing to break the record *by a narrow margin*. [The sentence implies that he wanted to break the record only by a narrow margin.]
CLEAR	He was unhappy after failing *by a narrow margin* to break the record.

14b
Place subordinate clauses where they will clearly modify the words intended.

Like adjective phrases, adjective clauses modify nouns and ordinarily fall directly after the word or words they modify. Such clauses usually begin with the relative pronouns *who, which,* or *that.* Adverb clauses are usually marked by subordinating conjunctions like *after, because,* and *since.* (See 5c-4.) Like adverb phrases, they can stand at the beginning, middle, or end of a sentence.

CONFUSING	We returned the toy to the store *that was broken.* [The toy, not the store, was broken.]
CLEAR	We returned the toy *that was broken* to the store.
CONFUSING	The mayor was able to cut the ribbon and then the band played *because someone found scissors.*
CLEAR	*Because someone found scissors,* the mayor was able to cut the ribbon and then the band played.

EXERCISE 1

Revise the sentences below so that prepositional phrases and subordinate clauses clearly modify the word intended.

Example:

Sir Arthur Conan Doyle wrote a mystery about a hound on the moors in 1902.

In 1902 Sir Arthur Conan Doyle wrote a mystery about a hound on the moors.

1. We took several machines to the factory in our truck.
2. The magician made a rabbit disappear with a wink.
3. Vance tried heroically to rescue his dog for an hour.
4. The electric typewriter is running on the desk.

5. Marie opened the book given to her last Christmas by Charles Dickens.
6. We found the contact lens during lunch on the rug.
7. I remembered I had forgotten my keys after I got home.
8. I built the bookcase of white wood that you see over there.
9. The little girl fed her kitten in the kitchen that she had received for Christmas.
10. The bell is an heirloom that you hear chiming.

14c

Place limiting modifiers with care.

mm
14c

Limiting modifiers include *almost, even, exactly, hardly, just, merely, nearly, only, scarcely,* and *simply.* They modify the expressions that immediately follow them. Compare the uses of *just* in the following sentences:

The instructor *just nodded* to me as he came in.
The instructor nodded *just to me* as he came in.
The instructor nodded to me *just as he came in.*

In speech several of these modifiers frequently occur before the verb, regardless of what they are intended to modify. In writing it is usually best to place them immediately before the word or word group they modify in order to avoid any ambiguity.

SPOKEN	If you want more advice, you should *only* come to me.
WRITTEN	If you want more advice, you should come *only* to me.

NOTE: *Only* is acceptable immediately before the verb when it modifies a whole statement.

She *only* thought she would help him; in fact, she didn't.

But now I *only* hear its melancholy, long, withdrawing roar.
                                                        —Matthew Arnold

EXERCISE 2

Use each of the following limiting modifiers in two versions of the same sentence.

Example:
only
He is the *only* one I like.
He is the one *only* I like.

1. almost   4. simply
2. even   5. exactly
3. hardly

14d
Avoid squinting modifiers.

A **squinting modifier** is one that may refer to either the preceding or the following word, leaving the reader uncertain about which modification is intended. A modifier can modify only *one* grammatical element in a sentence. It cannot serve two elements at once.

SQUINTING	The work that he hoped would satisfy him *completely* frustrated him.
CLEAR	The work that he hoped would *completely* satisfy him frustrated him.
CLEAR	The work that he hoped would satisfy him frustrated him *completely.*
CONFUSING	Follow instructions *whenever possible* to avoid mistakes.
CLEAR	*Whenever possible,* follow instructions to avoid mistakes.
CLEAR	To avoid mistakes *whenever possible,* follow instructions.

mm
14e

EXERCISE 3

Revise the following squinting modifiers so they modify only one word.

> *Example:*
> Those who complain *often* get results.
> *Often,* those who complain get results.

1. The baseball team that wins championships most of the time has excellent pitching.
2. I told my son when the game was over I would play with him.
3. Anyone who thinks occasionally will make mistakes.
4. A person who skis often gets cold.
5. The man who was bald totally refused to seek a hair transplant.

14e
Avoid separating a subject from its predicate or a verb from its object or complement.

We expect the sentence subject together with its modifiers to be followed immediately by the predicate together with its modifiers. Within the predicate we expect the verb to be followed closely by its object or complement. As long as the subject with all its modifiers is followed by the predicate with all its modifiers, a sentence will be clear even when it is long.

> The men who were demolishing the old house discovered a large box of coins that had been hidden for decades. [The subject ends with *house;* the predicate begins with *discovered.*]

However, if movement from subject to verb to object is interrupted, especially by a long modifier, the resulting sentence is likely to be awkward and confusing.

<table>
<tr><td>**AWKWARD**</td><td>The men who were demolishing the old house, *soon after they began work on the first day,* discovered a large box of coins. [The clause beginning *soon after,* which modifies the whole sentence, interrupts the movement from subject to predicate.]</td></tr>
<tr><td>**REVISED**</td><td>Soon after they began work on the first day, the men who were demolishing the old house discovered a large box of coins. [The sentence modifier is placed first, where it clearly modifies the whole sentence.]</td></tr>
</table>

mm
14f

14f

Avoid separating the parts of a verb phrase or the parts of an infinitive.

Verb phrases are made up of auxiliaries plus a main verb, as in *will call, was going, had been writing.* Such phrases constitute close grammatical units. We regularly insert single-word adverbs in them without causing awkwardness.

> Joshua *had not* entirely *completed* his assignment.
> He *was* seriously *considering* asking for an extension.

But when longer word groups interrupt verb phrases, the result is almost always awkward.

<table>
<tr><td>**AWKWARD**</td><td>Many students *had,* by spending most of their time on the assignment, *completed* it.</td></tr>
<tr><td>**REVISED**</td><td>By spending most of their time on the assignment, many students *had completed* it.</td></tr>
<tr><td>**REVISED**</td><td>Many students *had completed* the assignment by spending most of their time on it.</td></tr>
</table>

When infinitives consist of the marker *to* plus the plain form, as in *to produce* or *to enjoy,* the two parts of the infinitive are widely regarded as a grammatical unit that should not be split.

| **AWKWARD** | The weather service expected temperatures *to,* within the next week, *rise.* |
| **REVISED** | The weather service expected temperatures *to rise* within the next week. |

Note, however, that a split infinitive may sometimes be natural and preferable, though it will still bother some readers.

Her brother wanted *to* fully *understand* wood carving.

If *fully* were placed so that it did not interrupt the infinitive (for instance, *wanted fully to understand* or *wanted to understand fully*), the sentence would be unnecessarily formal or awkward.

dm
14g

EXERCISE 4

Revise the sentences below to connect separated parts of sentences (subject-predicate, verb-object-complement, verb phrase, infinitive).

> *Example:*
> Most children have by the time they are seven lost a tooth.
> *By the time they are seven,* most children have lost a tooth.

1. In a stream by my house some beavers who let me play with them live.
2. The lieutenant had given, even though he was later accused of dereliction of duty, the correct orders.
3. The girls loved to daily sun beside the pool.
4. Ballet will, if the present interest continues to grow, be one of the country's most popular arts.
5. The police gave, after holding on to it for two days, the story to the press.

DANGLING MODIFIERS

14g
Avoid dangling modifiers.

A **dangling modifier** is one that cannot sensibly modify any word in its sentence. The sentences below illustrate typical dangling modifiers.

| **DANGLING** | *Passing the building,* the vandalism was clearly visible. [The modifying phrase seems to modify *vandalism.* The writer hasn't expressed the noun to be modified.] |

DANGLING   *When only a few minutes from Boston,* the accident happened. [The modifying clause seems to modify *accident.*]

When certain kinds of word groups stand at the beginning of a sentence, readers take them to modify the subject of the main clause immediately following. These word groups include participial phrases, infinitive phrases, prepositional phrases in which the object of the preposition is a gerund, and elliptical clauses in which the subject is understood. (See 5c.) All the modifying word groups beginning the following sentences modify *Morton,* the subject of the main clause.

dm

14g

PARTICIPIAL PHRASE	*Being very tired,* Morton slept through the alarm.
	Exhausted, he could not be awakened.
INFINITIVE PHRASE	*To get up on time,* Morton had to make a great effort.
PREPOSITIONAL PHRASE	*After getting up,* Morton needed coffee to wake himself up.
ELLIPTICAL CLAUSE	*When finally awake,* Morton could easily work hard all day.

But notice what happens when the opening modifier cannot sensibly relate to the subject of the sentence.

DANGLING	*Being very tired,* the alarm was not heard.
DANGLING	*To get up on time,* a great effort was necessary.
DANGLING	*After getting up,* coffee was needed.
DANGLING	*When finally awake,* hard work was easy.

The initial word groups in these sentences modify the subjects of the following main clauses, but the subjects can't sensibly be related to them. Alarm clocks don't get tired, effort and coffee don't get up, and hard work doesn't awake.

We correct dangling modifiers by recasting the sentences they appear in. We can change the subject of the main clause to the word the introductory modifier properly relates to. Or we can recast the introductory modifier as a complete clause. The examples below illustrate these revisions.

DANGLING	*Being crowded in the car,* the trip was uncomfortable. [Dangling participle.]
REVISED	*Being crowded in the car, we* were uncomfortable.
REVISED	*Because we were crowded in the car,* the trip was uncomfortable.

DANGLING	*After roasting for three hours,* we turned the oven off. [Dangling prepositional phrase.]
REVISED	*After the meat had roasted for three hours,* we turned the oven off.
DANGLING	*To walk a high wire,* a pole is needed for balance. [Dangling infinitive phrase.]
REVISED	*To walk a high wire, a person* needs a pole for balance.
REVISED	*For a person to walk a high wire,* a pole is needed for balance.
DANGLING	*Only a few days out of the hospital,* the stitches were removed. [Dangling elliptical clause.]
REVISED	*Only a few days out of the hospital, he* had his stitches removed.
REVISED	*When he was only a few days out of the hospital,* the stitches were removed.

dm

14g

EXERCISE 5

Revise the sentences below to eliminate any dangling modifiers.

Example:

Having let out all the string, our kite sailed dangerously near the wires.

Having let out all the string, we watched our kite sail dangerously near the wires.

1. Staring at the ceiling, the idea became clear.
2. Once revised and corrected, I got an A.
3. Sagging and needing a new coat of paint, Mr. Preston called the house painter.
4. After studying for two days, the test was easy.
5. By repairing the transmission, our car began to run again.
6. Without accomplishing anything, Monday passed me by.
7. To swim well, good shoulder muscles help.
8. While on the telephone, the water in the pot boiled over.
9. To avoid collecting unemployment, a job is required.
10. When only a ninth grader, my grandmother tried to teach me double-entry bookkeeping.

15

Mixed and Incomplete Sentences

MIXED SENTENCES

All **mixed sentences** contain two or more parts that are incompatible—that is, the parts do not fit together. The misfit may be in grammar or in meaning.

MIXED GRAMMAR	After watching television for twelve hours was the reason his head hurt.
MIXED MEANING	The work involved in directing the use of resources is the definition of management.

15a
Be sure that your sentence parts, particularly subjects and predicates, fit together grammatically.

Many mixed sentences occur when we start a sentence with one grammatical plan or construction in mind but lose sight of that plan and continue with a different one. Such sentences often result from a confusion between two ways of making a statement.

MIXED	In all his efforts to please others got him into trouble.
REVISED	In all his efforts to please others he got into trouble.
REVISED	All his efforts to please others got him into trouble.

In the mixed sentence the writer starts with a modifying prepositional phrase but then tries to make it work as the subject of *got*. But prepositional phrases can rarely function as sentence subjects. The second revision makes *all his efforts* the subject of *got*. The first keeps *all his efforts* in a prepositional phrase but supplies the necessary subject *he* for the main clause. Either sentence works well for what the writer wants to say.

The following sentences illustrate similar confusions between two sentence plans, as well as ideas for revision.

MIXED	By increasing the amount of money we spend will not solve the problem of crime. [Prepositional phrase as subject of *will*.]
REVISED	Increasing the amount of money we spend will not solve the problem of crime.
REVISED	We cannot solve the problem of crime by increasing the amount of money we spend.
MIXED	Although he was seen with a convicted thief does not make him a thief. [Adverb clause as subject of *does*. An adverb clause cannot serve as a subject.]
REVISED	That he was seen with a convicted thief does not make him a thief. [*That* changes the clause into a noun clause, a grammatical subject.]
REVISED	Although he was seen with a convicted thief, he is not necessarily a thief.
MIXED	Among those who pass the entrance examinations, they do not all get admitted to the program. [The sentence subject *they* is not an appropriate subject for the modifying phrase beginning with *among*. A subject like *all* or *many* is needed.]
REVISED	Among those who pass the entrance examinations, not all get admitted to the program.
REVISED	Among those who pass the entrance examinations, many do not get admitted to the program.
REVISED	Not all those who pass the entrance examinations get admitted to the program.

mixed
15b

15b
Be sure that the subjects and predicates of your sentences fit together in meaning.

The mixed sentences we examined above were confusing because their parts did not fit together grammatically. Another kind of mixed sentence fails because its subject and predicate do not fit together in meaning. Such mixtures are sometimes called **faulty predications.**

The most common form of faulty predication occurs when the linking verb *to be* connects a subject and its complement. Since such a sentence forms a kind of equation, the subject and complement must be items that can be sensibly equated. If they are not, the sentence goes awry.

> **FAULTY** A *compromise* between the city and the town would be a nice *place* to live.

In this sentence the subject *compromise* is equated with the complement *place.* Thus the sentence says that *a compromise is a place,* clearly not a sensible statement. Sometimes such mixed sentences seem to result from the writer's effort to compress too many ideas into a single word or phrase. The sentence above can be revised to state the writer's meaning more exactly.

> **REVISED** A *place* that offers the best qualities of both city and town would be the ideal *place* to live.

Faulty predications are not confined to sentences with *to be.* In the following sentences the italicized subjects and verbs highlight the misfit between the two.

> **FAULTY** The *use* of emission controls *was created* to reduce air pollution. [The controls, not their use, were created.]
>
> **REVISED** Emission *controls were created* to reduce air pollution.
>
> **FAULTY** The *area* of financial management *poses* a threat to small businesses. [Management, not the area, poses the threat.]
>
> **REVISED** (Poor) financial *management poses* a threat to small businesses.

A special kind of faulty predication occurs when a clause beginning with *when* or *where* forms the subject complement in a definition using *to be,* or when a *because* clause forms the subject complement of the subject-verb pattern *the reason is.* Definitions require nouns in both the subject and complement positions. Sentences beginning *the reason is* require a *that* clause as complement.

> **FAULTY** An *examination* is *when you are tested* on what you know.
>
> **REVISED** An *examination* is *a test* of what you know.
>
> **REVISED** *In an examination you are tested* on what you know.

FAULTY	*A prison* is *where people are sent* when they are convicted of a crime.
REVISED	*A prison* is *a place* where people are sent when they are convicted of a crime.
FAULTY	The *reason* we are late *is because* we had an accident.
REVISED	The *reason* we are late *is that* we had an accident.

In some mixed sentences the combination of faults is so confusing that the writer has little choice but to start over.

MIXED	The hours of work spent in preparing your report will finally boil down to the readability of the words on your page.
POSSIBLE REVISION	The hours you spend preparing your report will make your words more readable.
MIXED	My long-range goal is through law school and government work I hope to deal with those problems I now deal with more effectively.
POSSIBLE REVISION	My long-range goal is to go to law school and then work in government so I can deal more effectively with problems I now face.

mixed
15b

EXERCISE 1

Revise the sentences below so their parts fit together gramatically and in meaning.

Example:

When they found out how expensive pianos are is why they were discouraged.

They were discouraged because they found out how expensive pianos are.

1. By wrapping tape around the muffler will keep us from having to replace it just yet.
2. Because of a broken leg is the reason Vance left the football team.
3. After mowing the backyard was the right time for a glass of iced tea.
4. Among the gems on the counter, they had none that I could afford.
5. Any government that can support an expedition to Mars, they should be able to solve their country's social problems, too.
6. A famous painting has always been a secret dream of mine.
7. The different tastes of different beers is in how they are brewed.

8. A divorce is when a judge dissolves a marriage contract.
9. The reason many people still don't accept the theory of evolution is because it goes contrary to their religious beliefs.
10. My room is where I go to feel happy and secure.

INCOMPLETE SENTENCES

inc

15c

The most serious kind of incomplete sentence is the fragment (see Chapter 10), but sentences or parts of sentences are sometimes incomplete simply because the writer has omitted one or more necessary words. The omissions sometimes result from the writer's haste or carelessness. More often they result from the writer's failure to see that a word is needed to clarify meaning or to complete an idiom (see 31b-3).

15c

Omit words from the second part of a compound construction only when the omission is consistent with grammar or idiom.

Both speech and writing commonly use **elliptical constructions,** constructions that omit words not necessary for meaning (see 5c-4). In the following sentences the words in parentheses are ordinarily omitted.

My car has been driven 80,000 miles; his (has been driven) only 20,000 (miles).

Some people heat by oil, some (heat) by gas, others (heat) by electricity.

She had great hope for her sons and (for) their future.

Such omissions are possible only when the words omitted are common to all the parts. When the parts differ in grammar or idiom, all words must be included in all parts. (See also 17a.) In the following sentences the italicized words differ and must be included.

My car *has been driven* 80,000 miles; their cars *have been driven* only 20,000 miles.

I *am* firm; you *are* stubborn; he *is* pigheaded.

All members of the committee *were important* and *were consulted.* [The first *were* is a linking verb with the complement *important.* The second *were* is an auxiliary in the passive verb phrase *were consulted.*]

She had faith *in* and hopes *for* the future. [Idiom requires *in* after the noun *faith* but *for* after *hopes.* Thus both must be present.]

Notice that in the sentence *My friend and partner moved to Dallas,* the omission of *my* before *partner* indicates that *friend* and *partner* are the same person. If two different persons are meant, the modifier or article must be repeated, as in *My friend and my partner moved to Dallas.*

15d
Be sure that all comparisons are complete and logical.

Comparisons make statements about the relation between two or more things, as in *Tom is richer than Mary* or *Tom is the richest of my friends.* Unless we are particularly careful to make such statements complete, they can be ambiguous or illogical.

inc

15d

1
Be sure that a comparison is complete enough to ensure clarity.

UNCLEAR	Boston is nearer to New York than Washington.
CLEAR	Boston is nearer to New York than *Washington is.*
CLEAR	Boston is nearer to New York than *it is to Washington.*
UNCLEAR	He likes Susan better than Marie.
CLEAR	He likes Susan better than *Marie likes her.*
CLEAR	He likes Susan better than *he likes Marie.*

2
Be sure that the items compared belong to the same class of things.

UNCLEAR	The human heart is bigger than a dog.
CLEAR	The human heart is bigger than a *dog's* (heart).

3
After a comparative, make sure that the subject of the comparison is *excluded* from the class to which it is being compared.

ILLOGICAL	Los Angeles is larger than *any city* in California.
LOGICAL	Los Angeles is larger than *any other city* in California.

4

After a superlative, make sure that the subject of the comparison is *included* in the comparison.

ILLOGICAL	Your car is the best of *any other* I have driven.
LOGICAL	Your car is the best of *all cars* I have driven.
BETTER	Your car is the best car I have driven.

5

Avoid comparisons that do not state what is being compared.

inc
15d

Brand X gets clothes *whiter*. [Whiter than what?]
Brand Y is so much *better*. [Better than what?]

EXERCISE 2

Revise the sentences below to complete constructions or comparisons as necessary for clarity.

Example:

Our house is closer to the courthouse than the subway stop.

Our house is closer to the courthouse than *it is to* the subway stop.

Our house is closer to the courthouse than the subway stop *is*.

1. My dog is just a puppy; their cats a great deal older.
2. Both of them not only believe but work for energy conservation.
3. The union's new leaders were partly elected, partly appointed, and trying to figure out which group was more important.
4. The legal question raised by the prosecution was relevant, complex, and considered by the judge.
5. Football interested Ralph more than his friends.
6. His tip was larger than any customer I waited on last night.
7. I enjoy country music more than my son.
8. This book is the best of any one I have read this year.
9. My test grade was higher than any in the class.
10. With an altitude of 6288 feet, Mount Washington is higher than any mountain in New Hampshire.

IV
Effective Sentences

16

Using Coordination and Subordination

To communicate effectively, you must fit thoughts together according to their relative importance, much as you assemble the pieces of a jigsaw puzzle. You **coordinate** the facts and ideas that you wish to give equal emphasis to, such as the ideas about insurance in the sentence *Car insurance is costly, but medical insurance is almost a luxury.* You **subordinate** your lesser facts and ideas to the ones you wish to emphasize. In the sentence *Car insurance is expensive because accidents and theft are frequent,* the clause beginning *because* is subordinate to the main clause. Subordinated information may be very important to the total meaning of the sentence, but readers will always see it as less important than the subject and predicate in the main clause of the sentence.

You coordinate words, phrases, and clauses by connecting them with the coordinating conjunctions *and, but, or, nor, for, so,* and *yet;* by connecting them with conjunctive adverbs such as *however, moreover,* and *therefore;* and by expressing them in the same kind of grammatical construction (see Chapter 17 on parallelism). You subordinate ideas by expressing them in clauses introduced by subordinating conjunctions (such as *although, because, if, when, where, while*) or relative pronouns (*who, which, that*), or by expressing them in phrases and single words.

The sections that follow provide some guidelines for managing coordination and subordination effectively.

16a
Coordinating to relate equal ideas

Two or more simple sentences in a row will seem to have roughly equal importance. Thus the reader must detect whatever specific relation exists between them. Using coordinating conjunctions to link related sentences and ideas enables the reader to see the relations easily. Compare the following passages.

> We have a large resource in the moving waters of our rivers. Smaller streams also add to the total volume of water. Much of this water resource is not developed. Coal and oil do not renew themselves. The same is true of uranium. Also, water is always there. In addition, the cost of water stays the same.

> The moving waters of our rivers and streams provide a resource substantial in volume, yet more than half of it is still to be developed. The water resource renews itself, unlike coal and oil and uranium; and its cost will not rise as the years go by.

The details in both passages are essentially the same, but the second passage is considerably more informative and easy to follow. Whereas the first passage strings ideas together in simple sentences without relating them, the second passage relates coordinate points about the water in rivers and streams as a resource: this water is plentiful, it is largely undeveloped, it renews itself, and its cost is constant. By bringing together four closely related facts about water as a resource, the writer has shown us its advantages more immediately and clearly.

coord

16a

1
Avoiding faulty coordination

Faulty coordination occurs when no sensible connection seems to exist between two coordinated statements or when the stated connection contradicts common sense. Sometimes faulty coordination occurs because the writer omits necessary information, as in this example:

FAULTY	Jacob is a foster child and has to go to the dentist often.
REVISED	Jacob is a foster child *whose real parents neglected his teeth; consequently,* he has to go to the dentist often.
REVISED	*Because* Jacob is a foster child *whose real parents neglected his teeth,* he has to go to the dentist often.

Often, as the last example above shows, the intended relation between clauses can be made clear by subordinating one of the ideas if it is supplemental. Here are some other examples.

FAULTY	Folk ballads are created by unknown writers, and they often deal with tragedies that may or may not actually have occurred.

REVISED	*Created by unknown writers,* folk ballads often deal with tragedies that may or may not actually have occurred.
FAULTY	John Stuart Mill was a utilitarian, and he believed that actions should be judged by their usefulness or by the happiness they cause.
REVISED	John Stuart Mill, *a utilitarian,* believed that actions should be judged by their usefulness or by the happiness they cause.

2
Avoiding excessive coordination

Writers who lack confidence in writing complex sentences sometimes rely heavily on simple sentences. The easiest way to escape the stop-go-stop-go effect of simple sentences is to link the sentences with *and* to show that the details are related. But hooking simple sentences together in a loose and-and-and sequence is little improvement.

coord

16a

EXCESSIVE COMPOUNDING	We were near the end of the trip, and the storm kept getting worse, and the snow and ice covered the windshield, and I could hardly see the road ahead, and I knew I should stop, but I kept on driving, and once I barely missed a truck.

Such loosely compounded sentences need subordination so relationships are distinct. (In the following example the main clauses are italicized.)

REVISED	As we neared the end of the trip, *the storm kept getting worse,* covering the windshield with snow and ice until I could barely see the road ahead. Even though I knew I should stop, *I kept on driving,* once barely missing a truck.

Be careful not to overuse *so* as a coordinating connector.

EXCESSIVE COMPOUNDING	Jim had an examination that day, *so* he came home late, *so* he missed seeing the fire, *so* he wasn't able to describe it to us.

As with other varieties of excessive coordination, the best way to revise such sentences is to separate the central statement from dependent details.

REVISED   *Jim wasn't able to describe the fire to us,* be-
                     cause he had an examination that day and ar-
                     rived home too late to see the fire.

Excessive compounding is not always so obvious as it is in the
two examples above. The passage below contains only two compound sentences, but they still relate facts so loosely that the reader
is left to distinguish their importance.

**EXCESSIVE
COMPOUNDING**   A man came out of the liquor store. He wore a
                     pair of frayed corduroy pants, and he wore a
                     brown sweater. He started toward a blue car,
                     and the police arrested him.

Using subordination to rewrite this passage shows clearly which
ideas are important and which less important. The central fact that
the police arrested the man becomes the main clause, and all other
details are incorporated into a single subordinate *when* clause.

REVISED   When a man wearing frayed corduroy pants
                     and a brown sweater came out of the liquor
                     store and started toward a blue car, *the police
                     arrested him.*

coord
16a

EXERCISE 1

Rewrite each pair of simple sentences below as one coordinate
sentence by inserting a coordinating conjunction (*and, but, or, nor,
yet*) and substituting a comma for the first period.

> *Example:*
> I applied to my mother's college. I was rejected.
> I applied to my mother's college, *but* I was rejected.

1. In June we have little rain. The haze makes it seem always
   cloudy.
2. People in Vermont care a lot about their environment. Their
   legislation proves their concern.
3. We did not want to go dancing. We did not want to stay home.
4. Spring rains damaged the roof. Water in the ground seeped
   into the cellar.
5. Air traffic in and out of major cities is becoming dangerously
   congested. The current regulations cannot adequately control
   even the present traffic.

EXERCISE 2

Revise the passage below to coordinate related ideas.

> Everyone read fairy tales as a child. Everyone remembers

some. Most people think they are only for children. They express the deepest fears and desires of children. They also express the deepest fears and desires of adults. Adults read them *to* children. They should read them *for* themselves.

EXERCISE 3

Revise the following sentences to eliminate faulty or excessive coordination. Add or subordinate information or form more than one sentence to relate ideas effectively.

Example:

My dog barks at the slightest noise, and I have to move out of my apartment.

My dog's barking at the slightest noise *has disturbed my neighbors,* and I have to move out of my apartment.

1. Michelangelo was a great architect of the Renaissance, and he designed the dome of St. Peter's in Rome.
2. Daylight saving time starts soon, and I will start playing tennis again, but I need to buy a new racket, and I need tennis shoes.
3. My clock radio has been repaired, and now I should sleep better, and I will be on time for class.
4. The dean was adamant, and she maintained that city police had no business on the campus.
5. I would have tipped the waiter, but he gave us bad service, and he was surly to us.
6. The dogs escaped from the pen because the keeper forgot to secure the latch, and the dogs wanted freedom, and they got it by running away, and it took the rest of the day to find them all.
7. The weather in March is cold and rainy, and sometimes it is warm and sunny.
8. The gun sounded, and I froze, but an instant later I was running with a smooth, pumping motion, and I knew I would win the race.
9. Registering for classes the first time is confusing, and you have to find your way around and deal with a lot of strangers.
10. The Chinese are communists, and they believe in the common ownership of goods and the means to produce them.

sub
16b

16b
Subordinating to distinguish the main idea

In any series of statements you make, some will be more important to you than others. Subordination enables you to distinguish the principal points you wish to make from your lesser but closely related ideas. The following passage makes little use of subordination.

> In recent years prices have constantly increased, and housing prices have increased more rapidly, and more people have bought houses for financial protection.

The writer gives three facts—constantly increasing prices, larger increases in housing prices, increased purchasing of houses for protection. By loosely coordinating these three facts, the writer suggests some relation among them. But *in recent years* provides the only explicit relation. We do not know which fact the writer sees as central or how the remaining facts relate to it. Look at the improvement in these revisions.

> *Because* housing prices have increased more rapidly than other prices, more people have bought houses to protect themselves financially.
>
> *When* housing prices increase more rapidly than others, more people buy houses for financial protection.
>
> *Although* all prices have constantly increased, housing prices have increased even more rapidly, *so that* more people have bought houses for financial protection.

sub
16b

In each of these revisions the words *because, when, although,* and *so that* indicate specific cause-and-effect relations among the three facts. Although the emphasis differs from one version to another, each sentence makes clear that people are more likely to buy houses when housing prices increase more rapidly than other prices.

No rules can specify what information in a sentence should be central and what subordinate, for the decision is dictated in every instance by your intentions. But, in general, details of time, cause, condition, concession, purpose, and identification (size, location, and the like) belong in subordinate clauses or other dependent constructions. Consider the following pairs of sentences (some of the appropriate subordinating conjunctions and relative pronouns are listed in parentheses).

> Tɪᴍᴇ (*after, before, since, until, when, while*)
> The mine explosion killed six men, and the owners adopted safety measures.
> *After* the mine explosion killed six men, the owners adopted safety measures.
>
> Cᴀᴜsᴇ (*because, since*)
> Jones has been without work for six months. He is having trouble paying his bills.
> *Because* Jones has been without work for six months, he is having trouble paying his bills.

CONDITION (*if, provided, since, unless*)

Mike doesn't attend lectures and he studies irregularly. He has little chance of passing his biology examination.

Unless Mike attends lectures and studies regularly, he has little chance of passing his biology examination.

CONCESSION (*although, as if, even though, though*)

The horse looked very gentle. It proved high-spirited and hard to manage.

Although the horse looked very gentle, it proved high-spirited and hard to manage.

PURPOSE (*in order that, so that, that*)

Congress passed legislation, and many Vietnamese refugees could enter the United States.

Congress passed legislation *so that* many Vietnamese refugees could enter the United States.

IDENTIFICATION (*that, when, where, which, who*)

The old factory now manufactures automobile transmissions. It stands on the south side of town and covers three acres.

The old factory, *which* stands on the south side of town and covers three acres, now manufactures automobile transmissions.

Using subordinate clauses to distinguish your main ideas from lesser ideas is the first and most important step toward writing effective sentences. But skillful subordination depends also on recognizing other grammatical constructions that help to subordinate information. Many times a verbal or prepositional phrase, an appositive, an absolute phrase, or even a single-word modifier will be sufficient to give all the weight needed to subordinate information. In general, a subordinate clause will give greatest importance to subordinate detail; verbal phrases, appositives, and absolute phrases will give somewhat less weight; prepositional phrases still less; and single words the least. We can see the differences among alternate subordinate constructions if we study the changes in a single sentence.

Old barns, *which are often painted red,* are common in New England. [Subordinate clause.]

Old barns, *often painted red,* are common in New England. [Single phrase.]

Old *red* barns are common in New England. [Single word.]

Notice how different grammatical constructions give different weights to the information in some of the sentences we looked at above.

Because Jones has been without work for six months, he is having trouble paying his bills. [Subordinate clause.]

Having been without work for six months, Jones is having trouble paying his bills. [Verbal phrase.]

Out of work for six months, Jones is having trouble paying his bills. [Prepositional phrase.]

Although the horse looked very gentle, it proved high-spirited and hard to manage. [Subordinate clause.]

The horse, *a gentle-looking animal,* proved high-spirited and hard to manage. [Appositive.]

The *gentle-looking* horse proved high-spirited and hard to manage. [Single word.]

Congress passed legislation *so that many Vietnamese refugees could enter the United States.* [Subordinate clause.]

Congress having passed enabling legislation, many Vietnamese refugees could enter the United States. [Absolute phrase.]

With enabling legislation from Congress, many Vietnamese refugees could enter the United States. [Prepositional phrase.]

The old factory, *which stands on the south side of town and covers three acres,* now manufactures automobile transmissions. [Subordinate clause.]

The *three-acre* factory *on the town's south side* now manufactures automobile transmissions. [Single word and prepositional phrase.]

sub

16b

1
Avoiding faulty subordination

Faulty subordination occurs when the idea expressed in a subordinate clause seems clearly to be more important than that expressed in the main clause. Sometimes faulty subordination merely reverses the dependent relation the reader expects.

FAULTY	Ms. Angelo was in her first year of teaching, *although* she was a better instructor than others with many years of experience. [Sentence suggests that Ms. Angelo's inexperience is the central idea, whereas the writer almost certainly intended to stress her skill *despite* her inexperience.]
REVISED	Although Ms. Angelo was in her first year of teaching, she was a better instructor than others with many years of experience.

FAULTY	Marty's final interview *that* was to determine his admission to law school began at two o'clock.
REVISED	Marty's final interview, *which* began at two o'clock, was to determine his admission to law school.

2

Avoiding excessive subordination

Excessive subordination sometimes occurs when a writer tries to jam too much loosely related detail into a single sentence.

OVERLOADED	The boats that were moored at the dock when the hurricane, which was one of the worst in three decades, struck were ripped from their moorings because their owners had not been adequately prepared, since the weather service had predicted the storm would blow out to sea, which is normal for this time of year.

sub
16b

Since such sentences usually have more than one idea that deserves a main clause, they are best revised by sorting their detail into more than one sentence.

REVISED	Struck by one of the worst hurricanes in three decades, *the boats at the dock were ripped from their moorings. The owners were unprepared* because the weather service had said that hurricanes at this time of year normally blow out to sea.

A special kind of excessive subordination occurs in a series of adjective clauses, as in the following:

EXCESSIVE **SUBORDINATION**	Every Christmas we all try to go to my grandfather's house, which is near Louisville, which is an attractive city where my parents now live.

These sentences can often be revised by choosing alternative modifying structures for some of the dependent clauses. In the revision below, for example, the clause *which is near Louisville* has been reduced to a simple modifier, and the clause *which is an attractive city* has been changed to an appositive.

REVISED	Every Christmas we all try to go to my grandfather's house *near Louisville, an attractive city* where my parents now live.

EXERCISE 4

Rewrite each compound sentence or pair of sentences below as one sentence, using a subordinate clause to subordinate one idea to another.

Example:

My father worked for years as a traveling salesman. He will not stay in motels.

Because he worked many years as a traveling salesman, my father will not stay in motels.

1. I will take a Shakespeare course next semester. I need the course for graduation.
2. Susan will graduate in two years, and she plans to travel to the Middle East.
3. The chemical company upriver installed waste control devices. The government said it had to.
4. The lake gleamed. It reflected the moon.
5. The final exam will count 30 percent of the grade, but it will consist only of two essay questions.

EXERCISE 5

sub

16b

Rewrite each pair of sentences below as one or two sentences that subordinate the second idea to the first. Use the grammatical construction or constructions indicated in parentheses.

Example:

During the late eighteenth century, workers carried beverages in beautiful colored bottles. The bottles had cork stoppers. (*Subordinate clause beginning that. Prepositional phrase.*)

Subordinate clause: During the late eighteenth century, workers carried beverages in beautiful colored bottles *that had cork stoppers.*

Prepositional phrase: During the late eighteenth century, workers carried beverages in beautiful colored bottles *with cork stoppers.*

1. In World War I, German forces set out to capture Verdun. Verdun was a fortress in northeastern France. (*Subordinate clause beginning which. Appositive.*)
2. One of the largest salt mines in the world lies under a city in Poland. It yields an average of 60,000 tons of salt yearly. (*Participial phrase.*)
3. Bertrand Russell was raised by his grandparents. He had been orphaned in early childhood. (*Subordinate clause beginning because or since. Subordinate clause beginning who.*)
4. James Joyce is one of the most controversial writers of the twentieth century. He has been praised as the greatest writer since Milton and condemned as a writer of "latrine literature." (*Subordinate clause beginning who. Participial phrase.*)

5. The Amish live peaceful but austere lives. Most of them refuse to use modern technology. (*Absolute phrase.*)

EXERCISE 6

Revise the paragraph below to subordinate the less important ideas to the more important ones. Use subordinate clauses or other subordinating constructions as appropriate.

Many students today are no longer majoring in the liberal arts. I mean by "liberal arts" such areas as history, English, and the social sciences. Students think a liberal arts degree will not help them get jobs. They are wrong. They may not get practical, job-related experience from the liberal arts, but they will get a broad education. It will never again be available to them. Many employers feel that a technical, professional education makes an employee's views too narrow. The employers want employees with the ability to think about problems from many angles. We must maintain the vitality of a liberal arts curriculum. We may become a society directed by technicians.

EXERCISE 7

Revise the following sentences to eliminate faulty or excessive subordination by reversing main and subordinate ideas, by using coordination, or by making separate sentences.

Example:

Scarred for life, he was severely injured in a car crash.
Severely injured in a car crash, he was scarred for life.

1. The car that my boss parked behind the delivery truck, which rolled into my bike, was the car that he had just bought.
2. The best plays in basketball are sometimes made at the last minute because it is a game of surprises.
3. A woman who wants a career in the armed forces is better off now than she used to be, because reasonable people no longer think that there's anything wrong with women who want to become career officers, which used to be a problem.
4. Children should understand that many good television shows that take some thought to enjoy are worth watching, because true entertainment doesn't occur unless people have to think about what they see.
5. Although my brother is still hospitalized, the war in Vietnam has been over for many years.
6. I was tending the cash register, which the thief emptied.
7. The speaker from the Sierra Club, whom we had invited on short notice, when our planned speaker canceled, nonetheless gave an informative and moving talk about the need to preserve our wilderness areas, which he said were in danger of extinction.

8. Even though he would not fly anywhere near Hurricane Dorothy, my uncle had been a pilot for twenty years.
9. They looked closely at the decorated saucer, which they believed was used by prehistoric Indians whom they thought did not make such implements.
10. I was surprised to hear that I had been left money by my great-aunt, who had always seemed to favor my cousin, who had visited her often in Happy Days Rest Home, where I could never bear to go because the cruel nurses upset me.

16c
Choosing clear connectors

Most coordinating and subordinating conjunctions indicate specific and unambiguous relationships. Among the coordinating conjunctions, *and* indicates simple addition or an and-then relation; *but* and *yet* indicate contrast; *or* and *nor* indicate an alternative. Among the subordinating conjunctions, *after, before,* and *until* indicate time; *if* and *unless,* condition; *because,* cause; *so that,* result; *although* and *even though,* concession. Some other subordinating conjunctions like *since* can indicate more than one relation, but context almost always makes the intended meaning clear. A few connectors, however, require cautious use, either because they are ambiguous in many contexts or because they are often misused in current English.

sub
16c

1
Avoiding ambiguous connectors: *as* and *while*

The subordinating conjunction *as* can indicate several kinds of adverbial relations including time, cause, and comparison.

TIME	The instructor finally arrived *as* the class was leaving.
CAUSE	*As* their plane was delayed, our friends were late.
COMPARISON	He was working *as* rapidly as he could.

As is always the correct conjunction in comparisons such as the last example above. But the variety of its meanings often makes *as* ambiguous for other relationships, so a more exact connector should be substituted.

AMBIGUOUS	*As* I was in town, I visited some old friends. [Time or cause intended?]
CLEAR	*When* I was in town, I visited some old friends. [Time.]

CLEAR

Because I was in town, I visited some old friends. [Cause.]

The subordinating conjunction *while* can indicate either time or concession. Unless context makes the meaning of *while* unmistakably clear, use a more exact connector.

AMBIGUOUS

While we were working nearby, we did not hear the burglars enter. [Time or concession?]

CLEAR

When we were working nearby, we did not hear the burglars enter. [Time.]

CLEAR

Although we were working nearby, we did not hear the burglars enter. [Concession.]

2

Avoiding misused connectors: *as, like,* and *while*

The use of *as* as a substitute for *whether* or *that* is nonstandard.

NONSTANDARD

He was not sure *as* he could come.

REVISED

He was not sure *whether* (or *that*) he could come.

Although *like* is often used as a conjunction in speech and in advertising (*Dirt-Away works like a soap should*), writing and standard speech continue to require the conjunction *as if* or *as though*.

INFORMAL SPEECH

The examination seemed *like* it would never end.

WRITING

The examination seemed *as if* (*as though*) it would never end.

The subordinating conjunction *while* is sometimes carelessly used in the sense of *and* or *but,* creating false subordination.

FAULTY

My sister wants to study medicine *while* I want to study law.

REVISED

My sister wants to study medicine, *and* I want to study law.

FAULTY

He found mathematics difficult *while* he found economics still more difficult.

REVISED

He found mathematics difficult, *but* he found economics still more difficult.

EXERCISE 8

Substitute a clear or correct connector in the sentences below where *as, while,* and *like* are ambiguous or misused.

Example:
He looked to me like he'd slept in his clothes.
He looked to me *as if* he'd slept in his clothes.

1. As I was going home for Thanksgiving, my mother cooked a squash pie for me.
2. From where I was sitting, the car looked like it was going to hit the baby carriage.
3. Busing school children is a major issue in many cities, while in others it doesn't seem to be very important.
4. As teachers and legislators worry about the literacy of high school students, the situation may improve.
5. Many states give minimum competency tests for graduation from high school, like there weren't enough hurdles to jump over to get a high school diploma.

EXERCISE 9

Identify each use of faulty, excessive, or ineffective coordination or subordination in the paragraph below. Revise the paragraph so that coordination and subordination are used correctly and effectively.

sub

16c

    Many people claim that chemical fertilizers and insecticides are essential for a healthy and productive vegetable garden, although they are wrong. You don't need chemicals to have a healthy garden. In fact, your garden—and you—will become healthier as you practice organic-gardening methods. Good, nutritious soil will give any plant a head start on healthy growth, and the most necessary soil element is nitrogen, which can be supplied by several organic sources, which include animal manure and fish meal. The soil must be well aerated with decaying matter, mosses, bark, and the like. Aerating the soil allows roots room to grow. It also allows water to drain easily. Pests like mites and beetles have their place in the food chain. Using insecticides to kill them can result in larger populations of the more troublesome pests that they sometimes feed on. A strong plant in good soil will resist attack from pests. A strong plant is the best defense against pests. If they're still doing damage, you can make exotic concoctions of strong-smelling ingredients like beer, onions, and red peppers, which will discourage many pests, which react much as we do to the strong odors. And practiced gardeners know that growing certain plants next to others also discourages pests. For example, eggplants grown near green beans will be less susceptible to beetles. Leeks keep flies away from carrots.

17
Using Parallelism

Parallelism is a similarity of grammatical form between two or more coordinated elements.

The air is dirtied by || factories || belching || smoke
           and || cars || spewing || exhaust.

Coordination between words, phrases, and clauses indicates that they are equal in importance. Parallelism confirms and clarifies that equality by placing all coordinate structures in the same or closely similar grammatical form. In the sentence below the two parts of the compound predicate are both coordinate and parallel.

The movement to recycle old buildings both *conserves our resources* and *preserves the grace and charm of our past.*

The principle underlying parallelism is that form follows meaning. Since the parts of a compound subject, predicate, object, or modifier have the same function and importance, they must have the same grammatical form.

In one sense parallelism is a grammatical requirement. But it is also a device for giving emphasis, clarity, and coherence to ideas and sentences. In the following sections we will look at parallelism both as a grammatical requirement and as a rhetorical device.

17a
Using parallelism for coordinate elements

Parallel structure is needed wherever coordination exists: wherever elements are connected by coordinating conjunctions or by correlative conjunctions, wherever elements are compared or contrasted, and wherever items are arranged in a list or outline.

1

Using parallelism for elements linked by coordinating conjunctions

The coordinating conjunctions *and, but, or, nor,* and *yet* are always identifying marks of parallelism, as the following sentences show.

> *In the kitchen* and *on the patio,* Miracle Grill will cook your food *safer, faster,* and *cheaper.* [Parallel phrases as adverbs; parallel single-word adverbs.]

> Political candidates *often explain what they intend to do* but *rarely explain how they are going to do it.* [Parallel predicates, each consisting of an adverb, a verb, and a noun clause serving as direct object of the verb.]

> In Melanie's home, children had to account for *where they had been* and *what they had been doing.* [Parallel clauses serving as objects of the preposition *for.*]

When elements linked by coordinating conjunctions are not parallel in structure, their coordination is weakened and the reader is distracted.

17a

> **FAULTY**   The disadvantages of nuclear reactors are *their great danger* and *that they are very expensive.* [A noun and a noun clause are joined as a compound subject complement.]

> **REVISED**   The disadvantages of nuclear reactors are *their great danger* and *their great expense.*

Do not hesitate to repeat words like *to, in, the,* and *that* when the repetition can save your readers from confusion. Such words often signal parallelism, stress relationships, and help keep meanings clear.

> **CONFUSING**   Thoreau stood up for his principles *by not paying* his taxes and *spending* a night in jail. [Did he spend a night in jail or not?]

> **REVISED**   Thoreau stood up for his principles *by not paying* his taxes and *by spending* a night in jail.

Be sure that clauses beginning with *and who* or those beginning with *and which* are coordinated only with preceding *who* and *which* clauses.

> **FAULTY**   Marie is a young woman *of great ability* and *who wants* to be a lawyer.

> **REVISED**   Marie is a young woman *who has* great ability and *who wants* to be a lawyer.

Note that such constructions are often improved by omitting the conjunction.

Marie is a young woman *of great ability who wants* to be a lawyer.

2
Using parallelism for elements linked by correlative conjunctions

Correlative conjunctions are pairs of connectors like *both . . . and, either . . . or, not only . . . but also.* Since these pairs emphasize the equality and balance between the two elements they connect, those elements should be parallel.

Ernest is addicted not only *to drinking* but also *to gambling.*

Off-road bikes are not only *interrupting the peacefulness of the desert* but also *destroying its vegetation.*

// **17a**

The common error in parallelism with correlative conjunctions is the omission of words like prepositions or the infinitive marker *to* after the second connector.

NONPARALLEL	He told the boy either *to brush* the horse or *feed* the chickens.
REVISED	He told the boy either *to brush* the horse or *to feed* the chickens.

3
Using parallelism for elements being compared or contrasted

Elements being compared or contrasted should ordinarily be cast in the same grammatical form.

It is better *to live rich* than *to die rich.*
—Samuel Johnson

WEAK	Jody wanted *a job* rather than to *apply for welfare.*
REVISED	Jody wanted *a job* rather than *welfare payments.*
REVISED	Jody wanted *to find a job* rather than *to apply for welfare.*

4
Using parallelism for items in lists or outlines

The elements of a list or outline that shows a division of a larger point are coordinate and should be parallel in structure.

FAULTY	**IMPROVED**
The Renaissance in England was marked by:	The Renaissance in England was marked by:
1. an extension of trade routes	1. the extension of trade routes
2. merchant class became more powerful	2. the increasing power of the merchant class
3. the death of feudalism	3. the death of feudalism
4. upsurging of the arts	4. the upsurge of the arts
5. the sciences were encouraged	5. the encouragement of the sciences
6. religious quarrels began	6. the rise of religious quarrels

EXERCISE 1

Identify the parallel elements in the following sentences. How does parallelism contribute to the effectiveness of each sentence?

1. Tonight a Santa Ana will begin to blow, a hot wind from the northeast whining down through the Cajon and San Gorgonio Passes, blowing up sandstorms out along Route 66, drying the hills and the nerves to the flash point.
   —Joan Didion

2. The faster the plane, the narrower the seats.
   —John H. Durrell

3. [The afternoon] was gray, deadened, and wintry, with a slow, moist, heavy coldness sinking in and deadening all the faculties.
   —D. H. Lawrence

4. The mornings are the pleasantest times in the apartment, exhaustion having set in, the sated mosquitoes at rest on ceiling and walls, sleeping it off, the room a swirl of tortured bedclothes and abandoned garments, the vines in their full leafiness filtering the hard light of day, the air conditioner silent at last, like the mosquitoes.
   —E. B. White

5. Aging paints every action gray, lies heavy on every movement, imprisons every thought.
   —Sharon Curtin

17a

EXERCISE 2

Revise the sentences below to make coordinate, compared, or listed elements parallel in structure. Add words or rephrase as necessary to increase the effectiveness and coherence of each sentence.

> *Example:*
>
> After waiting for hours, pacing the floor, and having bitten her nails to the quick, Sherry was frantic with worry.
>
> After waiting for hours, pacing the floor, and *biting* her nails to the quick, Sherry was frantic with worry.

1. For exercise I prefer swimming and to jog.
2. After a week on a construction job, Leon felt not so much exhausted as that he was invigorated by the physical labor.
3. To lose weight, cut down on what you eat, eat fewer calories in the food you do consume, and you should walk or jog.
4. All persons are entitled both to equal educational opportunities and employment opportunities.
5. I see three advantages to warm climates: (1) heating bills are low; (2) you don't need two wardrobes for cold and hot weather; and (3) outdoor sports can be enjoyed year round.

17b
Using parallelism to increase coherence

Parallelism not only ensures that coordinated structures are alike in form but also helps bring opposed or paired units into line with each other and helps clarify their relation. Failing to recognize parallel units is closely related to mixing constructions within a sentence (see Chapter 15). Consider this sentence:

NONPARALLEL   During the early weeks of the semester, the course reviews fundamentals, whereas little emphasis is placed on new material or more advanced concepts.

Here "the course" is doing two things—or doing one thing and not doing the other—and these are opposites. But this fact is not quickly apparent from the construction of the sentence. Rather it is obscured by the use of the active voice in the first clause (*the course reviews*) and the passive voice in the second (*little emphasis is placed*). Revised to bring these two ideas in line—to make them parallel—the sentence reads:

REVISED   During the early weeks of the semester, the course *reviews fundamentals* but *places little emphasis* on new material or more advanced concepts.

Effective use of parallelism will enable you to combine in a single, well-ordered sentence related ideas that you might have expressed in two or three separate sentences. Compare the following three sentences with the original single sentence written by H. L. Mencken.

Slang originates in the effort of ingenious individuals to make language more pungent and picturesque. They increase the store of terse and striking words or widen the boundaries of metaphor.

Thus a vocabulary for new shades and differences in meaning is provided by slang.

Slang originates in the effort of ingenious individuals to make the language more pungent and picturesque—to increase the store of terse and striking words, to widen the boundaries of metaphor, and to provide a vocabulary for new shades and differences in meaning.

—H. L. Mencken

Just as parallel structure works to emphasize the coordination of elements within a single sentence, it can also help achieve coherence among sentences in a paragraph. Consider the use of parallelism in the first part of a paragraph by Gilbert Highet.

> Style is an extraordinary thing. It is one of the subtlest secrets of all art. . . . *In painting, it is* composition, colour-sense, and brushwork. *In sculpture, it is* the treatment of depths and surfaces and the choice of stones and metals. *In music, it is* surely the melodic line, the tone-colour, and the shape of the phrase. . . . *In prose and poetry, it is* the choice of words, their placing, and the rhythms and melodies of sentence and paragraph.
>
> —Gilbert Highet

// 17b

Here, Highet clarifies and emphasizes his point that style is common to all forms of art by using the same structure in four successive sentences (*In . . . , it is . . .*).

(See 3b-2 for further discussion of using parallelism within paragraphs to achieve coherence.)

EXERCISE 3

Combine each group of sentences below into one sentence in which parallel elements are in parallel structure.

Example:

Christin sorted the books neatly into piles. She was efficient about it, too.

Christin sorted the books neatly *and efficiently* into piles.

1. The class is held on Wednesday afternoons. Sometimes it meets on Saturday mornings.
2. Dick finally held onto a job after lasting three weeks at his previous job. He had worked at an earlier job for two weeks. And the one before that had lasted three days.
3. After making several costly mistakes, he stopped to consider the jobs available to him. He thought about his goals for a job.
4. To make a good stew, marinate the meat. There should be plenty of vegetables added. Wine should be included for flavor. Simmer the whole thing for at least two hours.
5. Joan preferred the courses that challenged her. She did not like the boring courses.

18

Emphasizing Main Ideas

Well-managed sentences relate ideas and details clearly through coordination, subordination, and parallelism. They also emphasize central points by making them stand out within a sentence. You can control emphasis within your sentences in three ways: by placing the most important ideas in the strongest position; by using repetition carefully; and, when a statement is important enough, by separating it from surrounding information.

18a
Arranging ideas effectively

Arranging ideas within sentences for emphasis involves two principles. First, the most emphatic positions within a sentence are the beginning and the ending, the ending being the more emphatic of the two. Second, parallel series of words, phrases, or clauses will be most emphatic if the elements fall in order of their increasing importance.

1
Using sentence beginnings and endings

The most emphatic position in a sentence is the ending; the next most emphatic position is the beginning. Thus qualifying words and word groups coming after a main statement tend to weaken it, for they distract readers' attention.

UNEMPHATIC   Education remains the most important single means of economic advancement, in spite of all of its shortcomings.

REVISED

In spite of all of its shortcomings, education remains the most important single means of economic advancement.

REVISED

Education remains, in spite of all its shortcomings, the most important single means of economic advancement.

In the first sentence above our final attention rests on education's shortcomings rather than on its central importance, even though the latter is clearly what the writer wished to emphasize. The first revision, by placing the qualifying phrase at the beginning of the sentence, emphasizes education's importance. The second revision de-emphasizes the qualifying phrase even further by inserting it in the middle of the sentence, leaving education and its central importance at the emphatic points of the sentence.

Arranging the elements of a sentence so that all the qualifying details precede the main subject and predicate produces a **periodic sentence.**

emph
18a

PERIODIC

In three years, two months, and seven days, according to his view, the world will end.

PERIODIC

Though his lawyer defended him eloquently and he himself begged for leniency in a moving plea, he was convicted and sentenced to life in prison.

The emphasis of a periodic sentence comes from the suspense it creates by delaying the important point of the sentence until the end.

The **loose sentence,** the opposite of the periodic sentence, completes its main statement early and follows it with modifiers or other elements that explain and amplify.

LOOSE

It is green high summer everywhere you look: on the hills that shoulder down to the river, the rich maples in their fullness, the plain, the playing field, the turf of the stadium.
                    —Josiah Rounting III

PERIODIC

Everywhere you look—on the hills that shoulder down to the river, the rich maples in their fullness, the plain, the playing field, the turf of the stadium—it is green high summer.

LOOSE

The old man bitterly hated all social planning, having lived most of his life when complicated social problems either did not exist or could be ignored, and firmly believing that they still did not exist or, if they did, still could be ignored.

PERIODIC   Having lived most of his life when complicated social problems either did not exist or could be ignored, and firmly believing that they still did not exist or, if they did, still could be ignored, the old man bitterly hated all social planning.

Loose sentences are far more common than periodic sentences. The movement of a loose sentence—starting with the subject, then proceeding to the verb and object, and letting modifiers accumulate around each part of the sentence—parallels our natural habits of thinking and writing. The long periodic sentence requires planning, thinking through the sentence before beginning to write. Precisely because it must be carefully planned, it is relatively infrequent and highly emphatic. Thus you should save it for the times when climactic emphasis will truly contribute to your writing.

emph
18a

2

Arranging parallel elements effectively

Series

Parallelism requires that you use the same grammatical structure for coordinate ideas of equal importance (see Chapter 17). But a series of grammatically parallel elements can still be weak if you arrange the elements randomly.

UNEMPHATIC   The storm ripped the roofs off several buildings, killed ten people, and knocked down many trees in town.

In this sentence the three kinds of damage are named without concern for their relative importance: trees knocked down, the least serious damage, concludes the series, and people killed, certainly the most serious damage, is buried in the middle of the sentence. The revised sentence below arranges the items in the order of their increasing importance so that the most important item comes at the end, the most emphatic point.

EMPHATIC   The storm knocked down many trees in town, ripped the roofs off several buildings, and killed ten people.

Here are some additional examples.

UNEMPHATIC   Unless we have rain soon, we will have no water, no flowers, and no grass.

EMPHATIC	Unless we have rain soon, we will have no flowers, no grass, and no water.
UNEMPHATIC	After years of teaching, Anna decided to quit when she realized that she actually disliked children, that her fellow teachers bored her, and that she didn't have enough time for her hobbies.
EMPHATIC	After years of teaching, Anna decided to quit when she realized that she didn't have enough time for her hobbies, that her fellow teachers bored her, and that she actually disliked children.

You may want to use an unexpected item at the end of a series for humor or for another special effect.

Early to bed and early to rise makes a man healthy, wealthy, and dead.
                                                                    —James Thurber

But be careful not to use such a series unintentionally. If the writer of the following sentence intended to be humorous, the attempt is not successful.

emph

18a

UNEMPHATIC	After Terry had been late to work twenty times and had called in sick just as often, the personnel director threatened him with demotion, with reduction in salary, and with the loss of his parking space.
EMPHATIC	After Terry had been late to work twenty times and had called in sick just as often, the personnel director threatened him with the loss of his parking space, demotion, and reduction in salary.

(See 1f-1 and 3b-1 for discussion of arranging details in essays and paragraphs in increasing order of importance.)

Balanced sentences

The **balanced sentence** is a compound or a compound-complex sentence in which the coordinate clauses are parallel.

The fickleness of the women I love is equalled only by the infernal constancy of the women who love me.
                                                                    —George Bernard Shaw

In a pure balanced sentence the two clauses are exactly parallel: they match item for item.

A man should seek to know in order to live, not seek to live in order to know.

But the term is commonly applied to sentences that are only approximately parallel or that have only some parallel parts.

> He [man] has got a fine Geneva watch, but he has lost the skill to tell the hour by the sun.
>
> —Ralph Waldo Emerson

Balanced sentences are heavily emphatic but require thoughtful planning. If used carefully, they can be an especially effective way to emphasize the contrast between two ideas.

emph

18a

EXERCISE 1

Revise the sentences below so that their most important ideas are placed for maximum emphasis, either at the beginning or at the end of the sentence.

Example:

Of all waterfalls, the tallest one in the United States is Yosemite in California, which is 2425 feet high.

The tallest waterfall in the United States, 2425 feet high, is Yosemite in California.

1. Every day Charles worried that he would have an accident, even though he had a perfect safety record at the plant where he worked.
2. Books will remain the most effective medium for transferring knowledge for years to come.
3. The law limiting the weight of trucks on state highways was passed by a large majority, as we expected it would be.
4. Bill says that because he travels in a wheelchair, he finds it difficult to get taxis to stop for him when he hails them.
5. Our per capita income has risen steadily, but poverty remains a great burden for many people in various parts of the country.

EXERCISE 2

Identify each of the following sentences as loose or periodic. Then rewrite each loose sentence as a periodic one and each periodic sentence as a loose one.

1. One of the most disastrous cultural influences ever to hit America was Walt Disney's Mickey Mouse, that idiot optimist who each week marched forth in Technicolor against a battalion of cats, invariably humiliating them with one clever trick after another.

   —James A. Michener
2. From time immemorial man has been made in such a way that his vision of the world, so long as it has not been instilled under hypnosis, his motivations and scale of values, his actions

and intentions, are determined by his personal and group experience of life.

—Aleksander I. Solzhenitsyn

3. At length, in the beginning of May, with the help of some of
   my acquaintances, rather to improve so good an occasion for
   neighborliness than from any necessity, I set up the frame of
   my house.

   —Henry David Thoreau

4. Because they wanted a fair price for their crops and felt the
   government was not doing enough for them, the farmers
   marched on Washington.
5. Matthew's children worked two years to get him out of jail—
   writing letters, seeing lawyers, attending meetings—because
   they knew him to be honest and believed him to be innocent.

EXERCISE 3

Revise the sentences below so that elements in a series or balanced elements are arranged to give maximum emphasis to main
ideas.

emph
18b

   Example:

   The campers were stranded without matches, without food or
   water, and without a tent.

   The campers were stranded without matches, without a tent,
   and without food or water.

1. The explosion at the chemical factory blew up half a city
   block, killed six workers, and started a fire in an apartment
   building.
2. In the 1950s Americans wanted to keep up with the Joneses;
   keeping up with change will be what America wants in the
   1980s.
3. People view heaven in several ways—as the presence of God,
   as a myth, as just another world, or as the promise of future
   happiness.
4. Claire smiled at the thought of her old friend Carl, and when
   she thought of her husband she shivered.
5. The football players marched into the locker room, victorious,
   battered, and bruised.

18b
Repeating ideas

Although careless repetition results in weak and wordy sentences, judicious repetition of key words and phrases can be an effective means of emphasis. Such repetition often combines with
parallelism. It may occur in a series of sentences within a paragraph

(see 3b-3). Or it may occur in a series of words, phrases, or clauses within a sentence, as in the examples below.

> We have the tools, all the tools—we are suffocating in tools—but we cannot find the actual wood to work or even the actual hand to work it.
>
> —Archibald MacLeish

> Government comes from below, not above; government comes from men, not from kings or lords or military masters; government looks to the source of all power in the consent of men.
>
> —Henry Steele Commager

| 18c

| Separating ideas

You can emphasize a statement or a part of a statement by setting it off from others to which it is closely related. The second example below illustrates how putting an important idea in a separate sentence can highlight it.

> Boys are wild animals, rich in the treasures of sense, but the New England boy had a wider range of emotions than boys of more equable climates because he felt his nature crudely, as it was meant.

> Boys are wild animals, rich in the treasures of sense, but the New England boy had a wider range of emotions than boys of more equable climates. He felt his nature crudely, as it was meant.
>
> —Henry Adams

You can vary the degree of emphasis by varying the extent to which you separate one idea from the others. Separating two ideas with a semicolon provides more emphasis than separating them with a comma and a coordinating conjunction. And separating them with a period provides still greater emphasis. Compare the following sentences.

> Most of the reading which is praised for itself is neither literary nor intellectual but narcotic.

> Most of the reading which is praised for itself is neither literary nor intellectual; it is narcotic.

> Most of the reading which is praised for itself is neither literary nor intellectual. It is narcotic.
>
> —Donald Hall

Sometimes a dash or a pair of dashes will isolate and thus emphasize a part of a statement.

> His schemes were always elaborate, ingenious, and exciting—and wholly impractical.

Athletics—that is, winning athletics—have become a profitable university operation.

EXERCISE 4

Revise the sentences below to emphasize their main idea by using repetition or by separating the main idea from the rest of the sentence.

Example:

I try to listen to other people's opinions. When my mind is closed, I find that other opinions open it. And they can change my mind when it is wrong.

I try to listen to other people's opinions, for they can open my mind when it is closed and they can change my mind when it is wrong.

1. Without rain our seeds will not germinate. We will have no crops this year if it doesn't rain.
2. Roger worked hard to win the prize in chemistry. It was a respected prize. His father had also won it.
3. Men, that is, those who used to be thought of as men, were supposed to have muscles like an ox, eat nails, and fundamentally dislike women.
4. By the time the rescuers reached the crash site, the wind had nearly covered the small plane with snow and no one had survived.
5. The key to staying happy is staying free. Keep out of debt. Don't do other people's work. Avoid relationships that only entangle.

emph
18d

18d
Using the active voice

In the active voice the subject acts (*I peeled the onions*). In the passive voice the subject is acted upon and the actor is either reduced to a phrase (*The onions were peeled by me*) or omitted entirely (*The onions were peeled*). The passive voice is thus indirect, obscuring the actor or burying him or her entirely. The active voice is more natural, direct, vigorous, and emphatic. Further, all sentences turn on their verbs, which give sentences their motion, pushing them along. And active verbs push harder than passive ones.

Passive	For energy conservation it is urged that all lights be turned off when not being used. [Who is urging? Who is to turn the lights off?]
Active	To save energy, students should turn off all lights they are not using.

Passive	The new cost-of-living increase was announced just when the tax revolt was being spread nationwide by the press.
Active	The government announced the new cost-of-living increase just when the press was spreading the tax revolt nationwide.

Sometimes the subject of an active statement is unknown or unimportant, and then the passive voice can be useful.

The flight was canceled.
Wellington was called the "Iron Duke."
Thousands of people are killed annually in highway accidents.

Except in these situations, however, rely on the active voice. It is economical and creates movement.

18e

Being concise

Conciseness—brevity of expression—aids emphasis no matter what the sentence structure. Unnecessary words detract from necessary words. They clutter sentences and obscure ideas.

One common structure that may contribute to wordiness is the expletive construction, which inverts the normal subject-verb order by beginning a sentence with *there* or *it* and a form of the verb *be* (see 5e-4).

Weak	*There are* likely to be thousands of people attending the rally against nuclear power plants.
Emphatic	*Thousands of people are* likely to attend the rally against nuclear power plants.

Some frequently used qualifying phrases such as *in my opinion, more or less,* and *for the most part* are also unnecessarily wordy. They can always be reworded more concisely and can often be omitted entirely.

Weak	*In my opinion,* the competition for grades distracts many students from their goal of obtaining a good education.
Emphatic	*I think* the competition for grades distracts many students from their main goal of obtaining a good education.
Emphatic	The competition for grades distracts many students from their goal of obtaining a good education.

(See 31c for further discussion of strengthening sentences through conciseness.)

EXERCISE 5

Revise the sentences below to make them more emphatic by converting passive voice to active voice, by eliminating expletive constructions, or by eliminating unnecessary words and phrases.

Example:

Under certain atmospheric conditions, the moon can be seen as purple, in a manner of speaking.

Under certain atmospheric conditions, the moon *appears almost* purple.

1. The residents were told by the government to evacuate their homes when the government discovered dangerous amounts of contaminants in their water.
2. There must be a way we can get out of this predicament, whether legally or illegally.
3. The problem in this particular situation is that we owe more taxes than we can afford to pay.
4. The paintings were looked over by the art dealers before the auction began.
5. After all these years there is still not a good road running between Springfield and Lyndon.

EXERCISE 6

Revise the following paragraph to add emphasis to weak sentences. Rearrange, repeat, or separate main ideas from supporting ideas. Eliminate instances of the passive voice or wordiness.

The most famous fairy tale, "Cinderella," is also the most popular. As we all know, the tale is about a girl who is badly treated by her stepmother and stepsisters. They make her do all the chores. Finally, her fairy godmother rescues her, and she is married to a handsome prince. The story was originated in ninth-century China, which shows up in the episode of the glass slipper that the prince can fit only on Cinderella's tiny, delicate foot. Small feet were a mark of special beauty for Chinese women at that particular time. We are still fascinated by Cinderella's story, although we do not remain so fascinated by small feet. In Europe and the United States alone, the tale exists in over 500 versions down to this day.

19
Achieving Variety

By using coordination and subordination effectively or by controlling parallelism and emphasis, you can make clear and forceful the ideas within individual sentences. But in a paragraph or an essay, sentences do not stand one by one. Rather, each stands in relation to those before and after it. Making sentences work together effectively requires varying their length, word order, structure (simple, compound, complex, compound-complex), and type (statement, question, command, exclamation).

A series of sentences that are similar in length, structure, order, and type will be monotonous and ineffective, as this passage illustrates.

> Ulysses S. Grant and Robert E. Lee met on April 9, 1865. Their meeting place was the parlor of a modest house at Appomattox Court House, Virginia. They met to work out the terms for the surrender of Lee's Army of Northern Virginia. One great chapter of American life ended with their meeting, and another began. Grant and Lee were bringing the Civil War to its virtual finish. Other armies still had to surrender, and the fugitive Confederate government would struggle desperately. It would try to find some way to go on living with its chief support gone. Grant and Lee had signed the papers, however, and in effect it was all over.

These eight sentences are perfectly clear and well detailed. But together they are dull. Their length is roughly the same—ranging from twelve to sixteen words. Each begins with its subject. And all are either simple or compound. At the end of the passage we have a sense of names, dates, and events, but we are beginning to doze. Since the sentences are similar in length and structure, no one idea stands out as more important than the others.

Now compare the sentences above with the actual passage written by Bruce Catton.

When Ulysses S. Grant and Robert E. Lee met in the parlor of a modest house at Appomattox Court House, Virginia, on April 9, 1865, to work out the terms for the surrender of Lee's Army of Northern Virginia, a great chapter in American life came to a close, and a great new chapter began.

These men were bringing the Civil War to its virtual finish. To be sure, other armies had yet to surrender, and for a few days the fugitive Confederate government would struggle desperately and vainly, trying to find some way to go on living now that its chief support was gone. But in effect it was all over when Grant and Lee signed the papers.

—Bruce Catton, "Grant and Lee"

The information in these two passages is almost the same. The differences lie chiefly in the sentence variety of the second and the sharp focus on the end of war which that variety underscores. Catton's four sentences range from eleven to fifty-five words. His first sentence is compound-complex, bringing together in one long *when* clause all the details contained in the first three sentences of the first passage. The very brief second sentence is simple; the third sentence is compound-complex; and the final sentence is complex. The subject occurs first only in the second sentence. And whereas the first passage is a blurred series of statements without sharp focus, the brevity of Catton's second and fourth sentences highlights an unmistakable central idea: the meeting marked a turning point in American history.

While using the following advice on how to vary sentences, keep in mind that experienced writers do not set out to vary their sentences as an end in itself. They let length, structure, and arrangement take care of themselves, varying naturally with the relative complexity of the ideas and their relation to each other.

var
19a

| 19a

| Varying sentence length and structure

The sentences of a good essay will differ most obviously in their length. Looking more closely, you would see that some sentences are simple, some compound, some complex, and some both compound and complex. Although short sentences can be grammatically complex and long sentences can be grammatically simple, length and structure often go hand in hand.

Neither short sentences nor long sentences are intrinsically better. But in most contemporary writing, sentences tend to vary from between 10 and 15 words on the short side to between 35 and 40 words on the long, with an average of between 15 and 25 words depending on the writer's purpose and style. If your own sentences are all at one extreme or the other, you should ask yourself whether you have depended too much on either simple or complex sentences, or have thought too much about separate sentences at the expense of variety. If most of your sentences have fewer than 10 or 15 words, you probably need to use more coordination and subordination to relate ideas. If most of your sentences are 35 words or more, you probably need to break some up into short, simple sentences.

1
Avoiding strings of brief and simple sentences

var
19a

A series of very brief and simple sentences is especially weak and monotonous. If you find yourself depending on simple sentences, work to increase variety by combining some of the sentences into compound, complex, or compound-complex sentences. (See also 16a and 16b.)

WEAK	The moon is presently moving away from the earth. It moves away at the rate of about one inch a year. Our days on earth therefore get longer. They grow a thousandth of a second longer every century. We might eventually lose the moon altogether. Or a month will be 47 of our present days long. Such great planetary movement rightly concerns astronomers. It needn't worry us. The movement will take 50 million years.
REVISED	The moon is presently moving away from the earth at the rate of about one inch a year. As it moves away, our days on earth are getting longer, a thousandth of a second or so every century. If we don't eventually lose the moon altogether, a month will someday be 47 of our present days long. Such great planetary movement rightly concerns astronomers. But it needn't worry us; it will take 50 million years.

In the first passage the choppy movement of the nine successive simple sentences leaves the reader with nine independent facts and a lame conclusion. The revision retains all the facts of the original but compresses them into five sentences, the first one simple, the next two complex, the next one simple, and the last one two simple main clauses tied by a semicolon. Notice how combining the last two sentences of the first version emphasizes the dramatic fact that all this movement is 50 million years away.

2
Avoiding excessive compounding

A series of compound sentences will be as weak as a series of brief simple sentences, especially if the clauses of the compound sentences are all of about the same length. Notice the seesaw effect of the first passage below, and consider how the use of participial phrases, rather than independent clauses, strengthens the revised passage.

WEAK	It was Sunday afternoon and we were on the hotel beach. The beach faces the south and the main street runs along the north side of the hotel. The main street is heavily traveled and often noisy, but the beach is always quiet and sunny. We lay stretched out on the sand, and the sun poured down on us.
REVISED	The main street, heavily traveled and often noisy, runs along the north side of the hotel. But on the south side, the hotel beach is always quiet and sunny. On Sunday we lay there stretched out on the sand, letting the sun pour down on us.

var
19a

(See 16a-2 for discussion of how to avoid excessive coordination within sentences.)

EXERCISE 1

Revise the following paragraphs to increase variety in sentence structure and length. Use subordination or coordination to break up strings of simple sentences. Use subordination or simple sentences to break up sentences with excessive compounding.

1. I hate fairy tales. They are either dull or distasteful. Little Miss Muffet's whey makes me ill. Pinocchio can keep his nose long or short. Cinderella can have her glass slipper and her prince. The prince has a thing about feet. Little Red Riding Hood can be as foxy as she wants. Walt Disney can have them all. Disney and fairy tales go together. I prefer Doonesbury and Spider Man. They reflect the real world. They contain real characters and real action.

2. Popular music today sounds like warmed-over Rolling Stones or double-time Perry Como, and I'm tired of it. The only new music to come along in the last several years is dance music, but it all sounds the same and doesn't hold up to repeated listening. I tried to listen to the radio, but it only plays what performers put out. I'm looking for a new interest, and I think I've found one. Now I just tune it all out and read.

3. Nathaniel Hawthorne was one of America's first great writers, and he was descended from a judge. The judge had presided at some of the Salem witch trials, and he had condemned some men and women to death. Nathaniel Hawthorne could never forget this piece of family history, and he always felt guilty about it. He never wrote about his ancestor directly, but he did write about the darkness of the human heart. He wrote *The Scarlet Letter* and *The House of Seven Gables,* and in those books he demonstrated his favorite theme of a secret sin.

19b
Varying sentence beginnings

The standard English sentence begins with the subject, followed by the verb and its complement or object, if any. Modifiers either immediately precede or follow the words they modify. For example:

The defendant's lawyer relentlessly cross-examined the witness for two successive days.

The majority of sentences follow this standard pattern. But, as shown by the altered passage on Grant and Lee at the start of this chapter (p. 256), an unbroken sequence of sentences beginning with the subject blurs relationships and quickly becomes dull. You can vary the subject-first pattern by shifting adverb modifiers to the beginning of the sentence, by starting with a participial phrase, by starting with a coordinating conjunction or a transitional expression, and, sometimes, by resorting to an expletive construction.

Adverb modifiers, unlike adjective modifiers, can often be placed at different spots in a sentence without affecting meaning. When they fall at the beginning of a sentence, they delay the subject and verb.

The defendant's lawyer *relentlessly* cross-examined the witness *for two successive days.*

For two successive days, the defendant's lawyer *relentlessly* cross-examined the witness.

Relentlessly, the defendant's lawyer cross-examined the witness *for two successive days.*

Notice that moving both modifiers to the beginning creates a periodic and thus more emphatic sentence (see 18a-1).

Relentlessly, for two successive days, the defendant's lawyer cross-examined the witness.

Beginning with a participial phrase may also create a periodic sentence.

The lawyer thoroughly cross-examined the witness and then called the defendant herself to testify.

Having thoroughly cross-examined the witness, the lawyer called the defendant herself to testify.

When the relation between two successive sentences allows, begin the second with a coordinating conjunction or a transitional expression such as *for instance, thus,* or *moreover.* (See 3b-6 for a longer list of transitional expressions.)

The witness expected to be dismissed after his first long day of cross-examination. He was not; the defendant's lawyer called him again the second day.

The witness expected to be dismissed after his first long day of cross-examination. *But* he was not; the defendant's lawyer called him again the second day.

The prices of clothes have risen astronomically in recent years. The cotton shirt that once cost $6.00 and now costs $15.00 is an example.

The prices of clothes have risen astronomically in recent years. *For example,* a cotton shirt that once cost $6.00 now costs $15.00.

var

19b

Occasionally, an expletive construction—*it* or *there* plus a form of *be*—may be useful to delay the subject of the sentence.

A paper on why bell-bottoms became popular would be pointless. People don't care why. They no longer wear them.

There is no point in writing a paper on why bell-bottoms became popular. People don't care why, because they no longer wear them.

However, expletive constructions are more likely to harm writing by adding extra words than they are to help it by adding variety. You should use them deliberately and carefully. (See 18e.)

EXERCISE 2

Revise each pair of sentences below, following the instructions in parentheses to make one of the two sentences begin with a coordinating conjunction or transitional expression, or to make a single sentence that begins with an adverb modifier or a participial phrase.

Example:

The *Seabird* left to take its place in the race. It moved quickly in the wind. (*Participial phrase; one sentence.*)

Moving quickly in the wind, the *Seabird* left to take its place in the race.

1. We thought certainly that the Equal Rights Amendment

would be ratified by 1978. It required an act of Congress to extend the period for ratification. (*Coordinating conjunction; two sentences.*)
2. Robert crawled through the store window. He did not think that he would be seen. (*Participial phrase; one sentence.*)
3. Gasoline prices are driven up by international conditions we cannot control. They may not stabilize for several years. (*Transitional expression; two sentences.*)
4. The ski patrol lowered the frightened climber from the ledge. They were careful. (*Adverb modifier; one sentence.*)
5. I have gone white-water canoeing. I can tell you how exhilarating it is. (*Participial phrase; one sentence.*)

EXERCISE 3

Revise the passage below to vary sentence beginnings by using each of the following at least once: an adverb modifier, a participial phrase, a coordinating conjunction, and a transitional expression.

> Fred found himself cut off from the rest of the campers. He sat down to try to get his bearings. He watched the movement of the sun carefully. He thought he would find his way before nightfall. He was still lost when the stars came out. He admitted he was lost. He covered himself in leaves for warmth.

var

19c

| 19c
Inverting the normal word order

Inverted sentences such as *Up came the dawn* and *Mutton he didn't like* are infrequent in modern prose. Because the word order of subject, verb, and object or complement is so strongly fixed in English, inverted sentences can be emphatic.

> Harry had once been a dog lover. Then his neighbors' barking dogs twice raced through his flowers. Now Harry detests all dogs, especially barking dogs.

> Harry had once been a dog lover. Then his neighbor's barking dogs twice raced through his flowers. Now *all dogs*, especially barking dogs, *Harry detests.*

Inverting the normal order of subject, verb, and complement can be useful in two successive sentences when the second expands on the first.

> Critics have not been kind to Presidents who have tried to apply the ways of private business to public affairs. Particularly *explicit was the curt verdict* of one critic of President Hoover: Mr. Hoover

was never President of the United States; he was four years chairman of the board.

> —Adapted from Emmet John Hughes,
> "The Presidency vs. Jimmy Carter"

Inverted sentences used without need are artificial. Avoid descriptive sentences such as *Up came Larry, and down went Cindy's spirits.*

| 19d
| Mixing types of sentences

Except in dialogue, most sentences in writing are statements. Occasionally, however, questions, commands, or, more rarely, exclamations may be useful to achieve variety. Questions may point the direction of a paragraph, as in *What does a detective do?* or *How is the percentage of unemployed workers calculated?* More often, though, the questions used in exposition or argumentation do not require an answer. These so-called **rhetorical questions** are illustrated in the following passages.

> Another word that has ceased to have meaning due to overuse is *attractive*. *Attractive* has become verbal chaff. Who, by some stretch of language and imagination, cannot be described as attractive? And just what is it that attractive individuals are attracting?
>
> —Diane White
>
> Politicians could run Pennsylvania and Ohio, and if they could not run Chicago they could at least deliver it. But politicians run the world? What did they know about the Germans, the French, the Chinese? He [John Kennedy] needed experts for that, and now he was summoning them.
>
> —David Halberstam, *The Best and the Brightest*

Imperative sentences occur frequently in a description of a process, particularly in directions. In such writing they are often the principal type of sentence rather than a means to variety, as this passage on freewriting illustrates.

> The idea is simply to write for ten minutes (later on, perhaps fifteen or twenty). Don't stop for anything. Go quickly without rushing. Never stop to look back, to cross something out, to wonder how to spell something, to wonder what word or thought to use, or to think about what you are doing.
>
> —Peter Elbow, *Writing Without Teachers*

Notice that the authors of all these examples use questions and commands for some special purpose, not merely to vary their sentences. Variety occurs because a particular sentence type is effective for the context, not because the writer set out to achieve variety for its own sake.

EXERCISE 4

Imagine that you are writing an essay on the parking problem at your school. Practice writing different sentence types by composing a sentence or passage to serve each purpose listed below.

1. Write a question that could open the essay.
2. Write a command that could open the essay.
3. Write an exclamation that could open the essay.
4. For the body of the essay, write a short paragraph including a rhetorical question.

EXERCISE 5

Examine the paragraphs below for their authors' use of variety in sentence length and structure. In each paragraph what are the longest and shortest sentences? What is the structure of each sentence? How does the author vary the beginnings of his or her sentences, and how does this variation contribute to the effectiveness of the paragraph?

var

19d

1. Love. We are early taught to say it. I love you. We are trained to the thought of it as if there were nothing else, or nothing else worth having without it, or nothing worth having which it could not bring with it. Love is taught, always by precept, sometimes by example. Then hate, which no one meant to teach us, comes of itself. It is true that if we say I love you, it may be received with doubt, for there are times when it is hard to believe. Say I hate you, and the one spoken to believes it instantly.
—Katherine Anne Porter, "The Necessary Enemy"

2. That night in my rented room, while letting the hot water run over my can of pork and beans in the sink, I opened [H. L. Mencken's] *A Book of Prefaces* and began to read. I was jarred and shocked by the style, the clear, clean, sweeping sentences. Why did he write like that? And how did one write like that? I pictured the man as a raging demon, slashing with his pen, consumed with hate, denouncing everything American, extolling everything European or German, laughing at the weaknesses of people, mocking God, authority. What was this? I stood up, trying to realize what reality lay behind the meaning of the words. Yes, this man was fighting, fighting with words. He was using words as a weapon, using them as one would use a club. Could words be weapons? Well, yes, for here they were. Then, maybe, perhaps, I could use them as a weapon? No. It frightened me. I read on and what amazed me was not what he said, but how on earth anybody had the courage to say it.
—Richard Wright, *Black Boy*

V

Punctuation

20

End Punctuation

THE PERIOD

20a

Use the period to end sentences that are statements, mild commands, or indirect questions.

STATEMENTS

These are exciting and trying times.

Some African revolutionaries use mercenary soldiers to help them fight.

MILD COMMANDS

Please take your feet off the furniture.

Turn to page 146.

Tell her to close the window.

If you are unsure whether to use an exclamation point or a period after a command, use a period. The exclamation point should be used only rarely. (See 20f.)

An **indirect question** reports what someone has asked but does not use the original speaker's own words.

INDIRECT QUESTIONS

The judge asked why I had been driving with my lights off.

Carla's brother asked her when she planned to look for work.

Students sometimes wonder whether teachers read their papers.

See 25e for the use of three spaced periods—an ellipsis (. . .)—to indicate omissions from quotations.

20b

Use periods with most abbreviations.

Ordinarily, use periods with abbreviations.

p.	Ph.D.	P.M.
D.C.	e.g.	Mr.
M.D.	B.C.	Mrs.
Dr.	A.D.	Ms.
B.A.	A.M.	

The periods are usually dropped from abbreviations for organizations and for national and international agencies when more than two words are being abbreviated. For example:

IBM	NFL
EEOC	AFL-CIO

Check a dictionary for the preferred form of such abbreviations, and see Chapter 28.

Note that **acronyms**—pronounceable words, such as UNESCO, NATO, VISTA, and WHO, formed from the initial letters of the words in a name—never require periods. (See 28c.)

EXERCISE 1

Revise the sentences below so that periods are used correctly.

> *Example:*
> Several times we asked whether Julie could go with us?
> Several times we asked whether Julie could go with us.

1. Watch Sheryl do a back flip
2. The police asked whose dog was barking?
3. Class begins at 3:00 PM sharp
4. The new house had 2200 sq ft of heated space
5. The Roman Empire collapsed in 476 AD

THE QUESTION MARK

20c

Use the question mark after direct questions.

DIRECT QUESTIONS

Who will follow her?
Can we get there from here?
Why doesn't anyone ever listen to me?

?
20c

After indirect questions, use a period: *My mother asked why I came in so late.* (See 20a.)

Questions in a series are each followed by a question mark.

The officer asked how many times the suspect had been arrested. Three times? Four times? More than that?

The use of capital letters for questions in a series is optional. (See 26a.)

NOTE: Question marks are never combined with other question marks, periods, or commas.

FAULTY	I finally asked myself, "Why are you working at a job you hate?."
REVISED	I finally asked myself, "Why are you working at a job you hate?"
FAULTY	"When will you sign the divorce papers?," Joyce asked her husband.
REVISED	"When will you sign the divorce papers?" Joyce asked her husband.

20d

Use a question mark within parentheses to indicate doubt about the correctness of a number or date.

The Greek philosopher Socrates was born in 470 (?) B.C. and died in 399 B.C. from drinking poison after having been condemned to death.

NOTE: Don't use a question mark within parentheses to express sarcasm or irony. Express these attitudes through sentence structure and diction. (See Chapters 18 and 31.)

FAULTY	The boy claimed he was innocent (?) of the theft.
REVISED	*Though none of us believed him,* the boy claimed he was innocent of the theft.

EXERCISE 2

Revise the sentences below so that question marks (along with other punctuation marks) are used correctly.

Example:

When Joey found out he was going to die, he asked, "Can I take my dog with me?".

When Joey found out he was going to die, he asked, "Can I take my dog with me?"

1. Parents often wonder whether their children are getting anything out of college?
2. "What does *ontogeny* mean?," the biology instructor asked?
3. The candidate for Congress asked whether there was anything
   he could do to help us?
4. Will little children always ask, "Well, if God made everything,
   who made God?"?
5. Ulysses and his mariners took seven years to travel from Troy
   to Ithaca. Or was it six. Or eight?

THE EXCLAMATION POINT

20e

Use the exclamation point after interjections and after
emphatic statements and commands.

Come here!
When she saw her rain-soaked term paper, she gasped, "Oh, no!"
Can we let the Republicans win the next election? No!

Follow mild interjections and commands with periods or commas, as appropriate.

When you take the car to the service station, have the oil checked.
"Dear me," Frances thought.

NOTE: Exclamation points are never combined with other exclamation points, periods, or commas.

FAULTY	My father was most emphatic. "I will not give you any more money!," he roared.
REVISED	My father was most emphatic. "I will not give you any more money!" he roared.

!
20f

20f

Avoid overusing exclamation points.

Don't express sarcasm, irony, or amazement with the exclamation point. Rely on sentence structure and diction to express these
attitudes. (See Chapters 18 and 31.)

FAULTY	My instructor told me I got an "A" (!) on the exam.
REVISED	*To my surprise*, my instructor told me I got an "A" on the exam.

Frequent use of the exclamation point for emphasis is like crying wolf: the mark loses its power to impress the reader. Overused exclamation points can also make the tone of your writing seem immoderate. (See 4a.) In the passage below the writer could have conveyed her ideas more effectively by punctuating sentences with periods. The several exclamation points convey an intensity that is out of proportion to the facts provided.

> Our city government is a mess! After just six months in office, the mayor has had to fire four city officials! The city council can't agree on anything! Every time they meet, they just argue!

EXERCISE 3

Revise the sentences below so that exclamation points (along with other punctuation marks) are used correctly.

> *Example:*
> What a shock it was to hear her scream, "Stop!"!
> What a shock it was to hear her scream, "Stop!"

1. The policeman told the fleeing criminal to stop immediately!
2. Close your books and take out a clean piece of paper!
3. Watch out.
4. "Well, now!", I said.
5. As the fire fighters moved their equipment into place, police walked through the crowd shouting, "Move back!".

EXERCISE 4

Write sentences according to the instructions given below. Be certain that end punctuation is correct.

1. a sentence that makes a statement
2. a sentence that makes a mild command
3. an indirect question
4. a sentence with one or more abbreviations using periods
5. a direct question
6. a sentence followed by questions in a series
7. a statement that contains a direct question
8. a question that includes a direct question
9. a sentence that makes an emphatic statement or a command
10. a statement that contains an emphatic quotation

!
20f

21
The Comma

The comma is the most frequently used—and misused—mark of internal punctuation. In general, commas function within sentences to indicate pauses and to separate elements; they also have several conventional uses, as in dates. Omitting needed commas or using needless ones can confuse the reader, as the following sentences show.

COMMA NEEDED	Though very tall Abraham Lincoln was not an overbearing man.
REVISED	Though very tall, Abraham Lincoln was not an overbearing man.
UNNEEDED COMMAS	The hectic pace of Beirut, broke suddenly into frightening chaos when the city became, the focus of civil war.
REVISED	The hectic pace of Beirut broke suddenly into frightening chaos when the city became the focus of civil war.

21a
Use the comma before a coordinating conjunction linking main clauses.

The coordinating conjunctions are *and, but, or, nor,* and sometimes *yet, so,* and *for.* They should be preceded by a comma when they link main clauses.

> She was perfectly at home in what she knew, *and* what she knew has remained what all of us want to know.
> —Eudora Welty on Jane Austen

> He would have turned around again without a word, *but* I seized him.
> —Fyodor Dostoyevsky

> Seventeen years ago this month I quit work, *or,* if you prefer, I retired from business.
>> —F. Scott Fitzgerald

> They made their decision with some uneasiness, *for* they knew that in such places any failure to conform could cause trouble.
>> —Richard Harris

EXCEPTIONS: Some writers prefer to use a semicolon before *so* and *yet.*

> Many people say that the institution of marriage is in decline; *yet* recent evidence on the number and stability of marriages suggests that the institution is at least holding steady.

When the main clauses in a sentence are very long or grammatically complicated, or when they contain internal punctuation, use a semicolon before the coordinating conjunction so that the division between clauses is clear.

> Without risks or prizes for the darer, history would be insipid indeed; *and* there is a type of military character which everyone feels that the race should never cease to breed, for everyone is sensitive to its superiority.
>> —William James

When the main clauses are short and closely related in meaning, you may omit commas if the resulting sentence is clear.

21a

> She opened her mouth *but* no sound came out of it.
>> —Flannery O'Connor, "Revelation"
> The gain in precision is illusory *but* the loss of clarity is real.
>> —Bruce Price
> My heart raced *and* I felt ill.

EXERCISE 1

Insert a comma before each coordinating conjunction that links main clauses in the sentences below.

> *Example:*
> I would have dropped out of school but my physics teacher talked me into staying.
> I would have dropped out of school, but my physics teacher talked me into staying.

1. Kampala is Uganda's capital and largest city and it serves as the nation's social and economic center.
2. I am looking for a job but the ones I find either pay too little or require too many skills that I don't have.
3. Rising prices and rising interest rates are making it difficult for

people to buy houses yet the real estate market seems to improve every year.
4. Jill wanted to go out for the tennis team but she strained a tendon in her right ankle.
5. The hikers had come a long way and they could not summon the energy for the final mile to the river and a comfortable campsite.

21b

Use the comma to set off introductory phrases and clauses.

Introductory phrases and clauses always modify a word or words in the main clause that follows. They usually function as adverbs but may function as adjectives modifying sentence subjects.

Because the human intelligence is weak and because the pressure of events is always forcing it to choose some method and some principle for dealing with its problems, it is perpetually tempted to simplify too much. [Adverb clause.]
—Joseph Wood Krutch

From Columbus and Sir Walter Raleigh onward, America has been traveling the road west. [Prepositional phrase as adverb.]
—Peter Davison

Exhausted from the long race, the runner collapsed at the finish line. [Participial phrase as adjective.]

Take care to distinguish verbals used as subjects (gerunds or gerund phrases) from verbals used as modifiers. The former never take a comma; the latter usually do.

Jogging through the park has become a popular form of recreation for city dwellers. [Gerund phrase used as subject.]

Jogging through the park, I was unexpectedly caught in a downpour. [Adjective phrase used as modifier.]

Short introductory phrases and clauses need not be followed by a comma if its omission does not create confusion.

CLEAR	By the year 2000 the world population will be more than 6 billion.
CLEAR	In Rome the traffic is laughable as long as you don't have to drive in it.
CONFUSING	When eighteen children are considered young adults.
REVISED	When eighteen, children are considered young adults.

EXERCISE 2

Insert commas where needed after introductory elements in the sentences below. Circle the number preceding each sentence in which the punctuation is correct as given.

Example:

Not long after the rally ended a fight erupted.
Not long after the rally ended, a fight erupted.

1. Gasping for breath the firemen staggered out of the burning building.
2. Because of the late morning rain the baseball game had to be canceled.
3. Collecting old Marvel comics is his favorite hobby.
4. Without even saying goodbye Phyllis slammed the door and left.
5. Before you make any more mistakes read the directions.
6. Closing the shop was the hardest thing she had to do.
7. Even though Regina was sick last week she attended every rehearsal.
8. Tomorrow morning Mark will drive the children to the bus depot.
9. When young Robert was tall for his age.
10. In both the North and the South schools are more integrated now than they were fifteen years ago.

21c

Use the comma to set off nonrestrictive elements.

Restrictive elements limit, or restrict, the meaning of the nouns they apply to; they identify and define. **Nonrestrictive elements** give additional information about nouns; they describe.

RESTRICTIVE ELEMENT	The state law *that allowed juries to decide on capital punishment* was reexamined after the 1972 Supreme Court ruling. [The clause beginning *that* restricts the subject to a specific law.]
NONRESTRICTIVE ELEMENT	The new state law, *which was passed by one vote,* makes capital punishment mandatory for certain crimes. [The clause beginning *which* adds information but does not restrict the subject.]

To determine whether a sentence element is restrictive or nonrestrictive, read the sentence without it. If the sentence's meaning changes, the element is restrictive. If the meaning remains essentially the same, the element is nonrestrictive. Never set off restrictive elements with commas. Always set off nonrestrictive elements. (You may occasionally use dashes or parentheses rather than commas to indicate greater separation between nonrestrictive elements and other sentence parts. See 25b-2 and 25c for examples.)

1
Use the comma to set off nonrestrictive clauses and phrases.

NONRESTRICTIVE CLAUSES

The President of the United States is to have the power to return a bill, *which shall have passed the two branches of the legislature,* for reconsideration.

—Alexander Hamilton

This interest of a male, *who wishes to ripen a growing thing too soon,* could mean no good to her.

—Jean Toomer

NONRESTRICTIVE PHRASE

Large organisms, *like large churches,* have very few options open to them.

—Stephen Jay Gould

RESTRICTIVE CLAUSES

Every question *that has a reasonable answer* is justifiable.

—Konrad Lorenz

It is very difficult for someone *who doesn't have experience of working in the world of affairs* to realize the demands there and to judge what is done objectively.

—Elizabeth Janeway

RESTRICTIVE PHRASE

As an observer *from outside* I take a grave view *of the plight of the press.*

—A. J. Liebling

Notice that restrictive clauses often begin with *that.* *Which* often begins nonrestrictive clauses. See the Glossary of Usage, page 498, for advice on the use of *that* and *which.*

2
Use the comma to set off nonrestrictive appositives.

An **appositive** is a noun or noun substitute that identifies or describes in different words another noun immediately preceding it. (See 5c-5.) Many appositives are nonrestrictive; thus they are set off, usually with commas. Take care *not* to set off restrictive appositives, which give readers information they need.

NONRESTRICTIVE APPOSITIVES

The Chapman lighthouse, *a three-legged thing erect on a mud-flat,* shone strongly.

—Joseph Conrad

Winter, *ancient operator,* deaf and blind to his mood, lingered long after Maud had gone.

—Bernard Malamud

RESTRICTIVE APPOSITIVES

The philosopher *Alfred North Whitehead* once wrote that the history of philosophy was a series of footnotes to Plato.

The clipper ship *The Anne McKin* is said to have been the first of its kind.

3

Use the comma to set off parenthetical expressions.

Parenthetical expressions are explanatory or transitional words or phrases that interrupt the sentence structure. Transitional expressions include *however, indeed, consequently, as a result, of course, for example, in fact,* and *on the other hand* (see 3b-6). They are usually set off by commas.

> The Cubist painters, *for example,* were obviously inspired by the families of crystals.
>
> —Jacob Bronowski

Afterthoughts and phrases supplying supplementary information are also parenthetical and usually should be set off with commas. (For the use of dashes and parentheses with such elements, see 25b-2 and 25c.)

> It was an old store even then, *forty-five years ago,* and its wide oak floor boards had been worn pleasantly smooth by the shoe soles of three generations of customers.
>
> —James Thurber

> Any writer, *I suppose,* feels that the world into which he was born is nothing less than a conspiracy against the cultivation of his talent.
>
> —James Baldwin

4

Use the comma to set off *yes* and *no*, words of direct address, and mild interjections.

YES AND NO

Yes, I understand the assignment.

No, I won't have time to wash the car today.

DIRECT ADDRESS

Cody, please bring me the newspaper.
With all due respect, *sir,* I will not do that.

MILD INTERJECTIONS

Well, I don't think I'd better go out tonight.
Oh, she forgot to tell me.

NOTE: You may want to use exclamation points or dashes to set off forceful interjections. See 20e and 25b for examples.

EXERCISE 3

Insert commas in the sentences below to set off nonrestrictive elements. If the sentence is correct as given, circle the number preceding it.

> *Example:*
> The doctor who attended medical school in the 1920s was one of the first women heart surgeons.
> The doctor, who attended medical school in the 1920s, was one of the first women heart surgeons.

1. *Moby Dick* a novel by Herman Melville is thought by some critics to be America's finest novel.
2. Our modern ideas about civil liberties can be traced back to the Magna Carta which was written in 1215.
3. Several bystanders who had witnessed the robbery identified the thief.
4. We have used the Gregorian calendar named after Pope Gregory XIII since 1582.
5. Legionnaire's disease a recently discovered illness has been responsible for the deaths of many people.
6. We can make the trip in three days of course if we don't stop to rest.
7. Yes I always vote no matter who's running.
8. Bear with me George while I finish my story.
9. The report concluded that Americans who pay property taxes are the most disgruntled citizens.
10. The port of New York which was once the busiest in the nation is not nearly as active as it was.

21d

21d

Use the comma to set off absolute phrases.

Absolute phrases modify whole sentences rather than an individual word or group of words, but they are not grammatically related to the rest of the sentence by any connecting word. (See 5c-3.)

Absolute phrases usually consist of a noun or pronoun and a participle, as in the following:

> *Their work finished,* the men quit for the day.

But infinitive phrases, like *to be truthful,* and participial phrases, like *considering all things,* may also be absolute. Absolute constructions can occur at almost any point in the sentence. Whatever their position, they are always set off by commas.

> *Her homework done,* my sister can watch whatever she wants on television.
>
> After reaching Eagle Rock, we pointed our canoes toward shore, *the rapids ahead being rough.*
>
> *Considering the difficulty of the exam,* he was lucky to pass the course.

EXERCISE 4

Insert commas in the sentences below to set off absolute constructions.

> *Example:*
>
> Prices having risen steadily the government instituted a price freeze.
>
> Prices having risen steadily, the government instituted a price freeze.

1. The shooting having started the set was quiet except for the actors' voices.
2. Their exams finished the students had a party to celebrate.
3. The painters quit work early the house painted and the supplies put away.
4. The police drove away from the accident their job done.
5. Spring coming nearer the ground felt damp and the air smelled fresh.

/\
21e

21e

Use the comma to set off phrases expressing contrast.

Style is the manner of a sentence, *not its matter.*

—Donald Hall

> It was Saturday, *not Sunday,* when the burglary occurred.
>
> Trout are found in fresh water, *not in salt water.*

NOTE: Experienced writers do not always use commas to set off contrasting phrases containing *but.*

It is not light that is needed, *but fire*; it is not the gentle shower, *but thunder.*

—Frederick Douglass

He longed for the stereotype, not to embrace *but to be.*

—Germaine Greer

EXERCISE 5

Insert commas in the sentences below to set off phrases that express contrast.

Example:

Susan not her sister was the one who succumbed to the disease.

Susan, not her sister, was the one who succumbed to the disease.

1. I schedule all my classes in the mornings never in the afternoons.
2. The humidity not just the heat makes some summer days unbearable.
3. I forgot that it was William Faulkner not F. Scott Fitzgerald who won the Nobel Prize.
4. World War II ended with the surrender of the Japanese in September of 1945 not with the earlier surrender of the Germans in May.
5. My family attends church in Cromwell not Durben because we know the minister in Cromwell.

21f

Use the comma between words, phrases, and clauses forming a series and between coordinate adjectives not linked by conjunctions.

Place commas between all elements of a **series**—three or more items of equal importance.

The names *Belial, Beelzebub, and Lucifer* sound ominous.

He felt cut off from them *by age, by understanding, by sensibility, by technology, and by his need to measure himself against the mirror of other men's appreciation.*

—Ralph Ellison

It *was solid black, stood five feet high at the shoulder, had a five-foot span of horns, and must have weighed 1,200 pounds on the hoof.*

—Richard B. Lee

The comma between the last two items in a series always helps the reader see the two items as separate.

CONFUSING	After the storm, the downtown streets were littered with branches, broken glass from windows and signs advertising businesses.
CLEAR	After the storm, the downtown streets were littered with branches, broken glass from windows, and signs advertising businesses.

EXCEPTIONS: When short items are linked in a series, some writers omit the comma before the *and* connecting the last two items.

> For his second birthday, I'd like to buy my son a plastic hammer, a punching bag *and* a brass collar.

When items in a series are long and grammatically complicated, composed of clauses or phrases with modifiers, they may be separated by semicolons. If the items have internal punctuation, they *must* be separated by semicolons for clarity. (See 22d.)

Coordinate adjectives are two or more adjectives that modify the same noun or pronoun. The individual adjectives are separated by coordinating conjunctions or commas.

> Nothing is more essential to *intelligent, profitable* reading than sensitivity to connotation.
> —Richard Altick

> The *sleek* and *shiny* car was a credit to the neighborhood.
> The *dirty, rusty, dented* car was an eyesore.

21f

Coordinate adjectives can be rearranged without changing meaning, and the word *and* can be substituted for commas separating them. If neither of these changes is possible, then the adjectives aren't coordinate and should not be separated by commas.

> The ceiling beams were made of *fake hand-hewn* wood.
> The house overflowed with *ornate electric* fixtures.

Notice in the following example that numbers are not coordinate with other adjectives.

FAULTY	Among the junk in my grandmother's attic I found *one, lovely* vase.
REVISED	Among the junk in my grandmother's attic I found *one lovely* vase.

Notice also that a comma is not used between the final coordinate adjective and the noun.

FAULTY	Spring evenings in the South are *warm, sensuous,* experiences.
REVISED	Spring evenings in the South are *warm, sensuous* experiences.

EXERCISE 6

Insert commas in the sentences below to separate elements in series or coordinate adjectives. Circle the number preceding each sentence whose punctuation is already correct.

Example:

The paved road became a soft sticky goo when the sun shone on it.

The paved road became a soft, sticky goo when the sun shone on it.

1. After working hard saving his money and investing it carefully, my grandfather was able to live comfortably in retirement.
2. Neither personal loss business setbacks nor illness could keep my grandfather down.
3. The school bought a fine old Victorian house to use as a faculty and alumni club.
4. That morning, fresh crisp and clear, turned out to be memorable.
5. Television newscasters rarely work full time as reporters investigate only light stories if any and rarely write the copy they read on the air.
6. That was the second frightening experience I had that day.
7. Several stores opened new larger branches in the shopping mall outside the city.
8. The suspect was brought in kicking hitting and cussing.
9. She was a Bostonian by birth a farmer by temperament and a worker to the day she died.
10. The unset leg fracture she had had as a child caused her annoying painful trouble all her life.

21g

Use the comma according to convention in dates, addresses, place names, and long numbers.

DATES

July 4, 1776
December 7, 1941

ADDRESSES

5262 Laurie Lane, Memphis, Tennessee
Box 3862, Pasadena, California

NAMES OF GEOGRAPHICAL LOCATIONS

Columbus, Ohio
Garden City, Long Island, New York

Commas are not used between state names and zip codes in addresses nor between the parts of a date in inverted order.

Berkeley, California 94720
Boston, Massachusetts 02106
28 March 1971
15 December 1979

Use the comma to separate the figures in long numbers into groups of three, counting from the right.

5,265   191,386
73,421   93,000,000

The comma with numbers of four digits is optional.

5,000   5000

EXERCISE 7

Insert commas as needed in the following dates, addresses, place names, or numbers.

Example:
$10624
$10,624

1. 127436211 people
2. Denver Colorado
3. Boston Suffolk County Massachusetts U.S.A.
4. P.O. Box 725 Asheville North Carolina 28803
5. January 1 2000

21h

Use the comma with quotations according to standard practice.

1

Ordinarily, use a comma to separate introductory and concluding explanatory words from quotations.

General Sherman summed up the attitude of all thoughtful soldiers when he said, "War is hell."

"Good fences make good neighbors," Robert Frost wrote.

EXCEPTIONS: When a quotation followed by explanatory words ends with an exclamation point or a question mark, do not use the comma: *"Claude!" Mrs. Harrison called.* (See 20c and 20e.) Use a colon to separate explanatory words and a quotation when there is an emphatic break between them in meaning or in grammar or when the quotation is very formal or longer than a sentence. (See 25a.)

> The first article of the Bill of Rights is unambiguous: "Congress shall make no law respecting an establishment of religion, or prohibiting the free exercise thereof; or abridging the freedom of speech, or of the press; or the right of the people peaceably to assemble, and to petition the government for a redress of grievances."

2

Use the comma after the first part of a quotation interrupted by explanatory words. Follow the explanatory words with the punctuation required by the quotation.

"This is the faith with which I return to the South," Martin Luther King, Jr., proclaimed. "With this faith we will be able to hew out of the mountain of despair a stone of hope." [The explanatory words fall at the end of a sentence in the quotation and thus end in a period.]

"When you got nothin'," Kris Kristofferson sings, "you got nothin' to lose." [The explanatory words interrupt a sentence in the quotation and thus end with a comma.]

3

Place commas that follow quotations within quotation marks.

"That's my seat," she said coldly.
"You gave it up," I replied evenly, "so you have no right to it."

For complete instructions on punctuating quotations, see 24g.

EXERCISE 8

Insert commas in the sentences below to correct punctuation with quotations.

Example:

When asked to open her bag, the shoplifter exclaimed "I didn't steal anything."

When asked to open her bag, the shoplifter exclaimed, "I didn't steal anything."

1. "The mass of men lead lives of quiet desperation" Henry David Thoreau wrote in *Walden.*
2. "I'll be on the next bus for Cleveland" the woman promised.
3. In a sentence that has stirred generations of readers, Jean-Jacques Rousseau announced "Man was born free, and everywhere he is in chains."

21h

4. "We must face reality" the president said sternly "while we have time."
5. After trying for half an hour to revive the little girl, the doctor announced sadly "She's dead."

21i

Use the comma to prevent misreading.

The comma tells the reader to pause slightly before moving on. In some sentences words run together in unintended ways and create confusion unless a comma separates them. Use a comma in such sentences even though no rule requires one.

CONFUSING	Soon after she left town for good. [A short introductory phrase doesn't require a comma, but clarity requires it in this sentence.]
REVISED	Soon after, she left town for good.
CONFUSING	The students who can usually give some money to the United Fund. [Without a comma the sentence seems incomplete.]
REVISED	The students who can, usually give some money to the United Fund.

21j

EXERCISE 9

Insert commas in the sentences below to prevent misreading.

Example:

At twenty-one children have usually left their parents' homes.
At twenty-one, children have usually left their parents' homes.

1. Beginning tomorrow afternoon practice will be canceled.
2. Though old Grandfather was still spry.
3. Happy and prosperous Dan loved his work.
4. Of the fifty six boys can't go.
5. Those who can't regret it.

21j

Avoid overusing or misusing the comma.

Although commas are useful and often necessary to signal pauses in sentences, they can make sentences choppy and even confusing if they are used more often than needed or in violation of rules 21a through 21h. Examine every sentence you write to be sure you have used commas sparingly and properly.

/

1

Don't use the comma to separate a subject from its verb, nor a verb or a preposition from its object, unless the words between them require punctuation.

FAULTY

The returning *soldiers, expected* a warmer welcome than they received. [Separation of subject and verb.]

REVISED

The returning *soldiers expected* a warmer welcome than they received.

FAULTY

After deciding that she could do one but not both, my sister *chose, to have children* rather than pursue a career. [Separation of verb and object.]

REVISED

After deciding that she could do one but not both, my sister *chose to have children* rather than pursue a career.

FAULTY

I was amazed when the refund from the utility company came *in, only three weeks.* [Separation of preposition and object.]

REVISED

I was amazed when the refund from the utility company came *in only three weeks.*

In the sentence below, commas are needed to set off the nonrestrictive adjective clause that interrupts subject and verb.

21j

Americans, who are preoccupied with football, baseball, basketball, and hockey, have not developed a strong interest in professional soccer.

2

Ordinarily, don't use the comma with words or phrases joined by coordinating conjunctions.

FAULTY

Television advertising is *expensive, and slick, and sometimes very effective.*

REVISED

Television advertising is *expensive and slick and sometimes very effective.*

FAULTY

The sale of *handguns, and other weapons* is increasing alarmingly.

REVISED

The sale of *handguns and other weapons* is increasing alarmingly.

(See 21a for the appropriate use of commas with coordinating conjunctions linking main clauses.)

3

Don't set off restrictive elements.

FAULTY	The land, *that both the Arabs and Israelis claim is theirs,* is mostly arid and unpopulated. [The clause beginning *that* restricts the meaning of the sentence.]
REVISED	The land *that both the Arabs and Israelis claim is theirs* is mostly arid and unpopulated.
FAULTY	Hawthorne's work, *The Scarlet Letter,* was the first major American novel. [The title of the novel is essential to distinguish the novel from the rest of Hawthorne's work.]
REVISED	Hawthorne's work *The Scarlet Letter* was the first major American novel.
FAULTY	We stayed, *at the beach,* for two days. [The phrase *at the beach* limits the verb *stayed.*]
REVISED	We stayed *at the beach* for two days.
FAULTY	My father, *often,* thought of moving us all to Australia. [*Often* limits the verb *thought.*]
REVISED	My father *often* thought of moving us all to Australia.

21j

(See 21c for further discussion of identifying and punctuating nonrestrictive and restrictive elements in sentences.)

4

Don't use the comma before the first or after the last item in a series unless a rule requires it.

FAULTY	The *forsythia, daffodils, and tulips,* turned my aunt's garden into a rush of color. [The comma after *tulips* separates subject and verb.]
REVISED	The *forsythia, daffodils, and tulips* turned my aunt's garden into a rush of color.
FAULTY	Europeans brought the New World, *writing, advanced technology, and disease.* [The comma after *World* separates verb and object.]
REVISED	Europeans brought the New World *writing, advanced technology, and disease.*

The commas before the first and after the last item in the following series are necessary because the series functions as an appositive.

Two names for the Mississippi River, *Old Man River* and *the Father of Rivers,* show both affection and respect.

(See 21f for further discussion of punctuating elements in a series.)

5

Don't set off indirect quotations or a single quoted word unless it is a nonrestrictive appositive.

INDIRECT QUOTATION

FAULTY	The students asked, why they had to take a test the day before vacation.
REVISED	The students asked why they had to take a test the day before vacation.

QUOTED WORD

FAULTY	Joyce's story, "Araby," was assigned last year, too. [Restrictive appositive.]
REVISED	Joyce's story "Araby" was assigned last year, too.

The sentence below requires a comma because *abracadabra* is a nonrestrictive appositive.

To make something happen, repeat the magician's word, "abracadabra."

(See 21c for more on punctuating appositives.)

⋏
21j

EXERCISE 10

Revise the sentences below by inserting commas where they are needed or by eliminating needless or misused commas. Circle the number preceding each sentence that is already punctuated correctly.

> *Example:*
> The mirror, that I broke, had been my aunt's.
> The mirror that I broke had been my aunt's.

1. We stayed, with my grandparents, for a week last summer.
2. Because it ran out of money the team had to cancel the rest of its games.
3. The campers, later, decided they had taken a wrong turn.
4. *David Copperfield,* by Charles Dickens, is still a favorite of generations of readers.
5. My best friend, Dave, thinks he will be an Olympic swimmer.

6. The Yankees, the Red Sox, and the Royals, all had a chance at the pennant in 1978.
7. The coach said, that next year we would have a winning season.
8. We brought to the lake, a canoe, a rowboat, and lots of fishing gear.
9. The instructor asked for our papers but I had forgotten mine.
10. The tennis term, *love*, meaning, "zero," comes from the French word, *l'oeuf*, meaning, "the egg."
11. A baseball game, usually has nine innings.
12. An experienced painter it seems to this novice can complete the inside of a house without much effort.
13. Cheese eggs and milk are high in cholesterol.
14. Mary bought some of her course books but she couldn't afford to buy all of them.
15. The house which is downtown has been designated a National Historic Landmark.
16. After the New Hampshire primary, which eliminates some candidates, the presidential race calms down somewhat.
17. My cat brought home a dirty smelly sock.
18. The point, of many of Scott Fitzgerald's stories, is that having money doesn't guarantee happiness.
19. He wanted a raise, yet didn't expect to receive one.
20. Forest fires often benefit, the woods they burn.

⋏
21j

22

The Semicolon

22a

Use the semicolon to separate main clauses not joined by a coordinating conjunction.

Main clauses are often linked by a comma and a coordinating conjunction (*and, but, or, nor,* and sometimes *yet, for,* and *so*). (See 21a.) If the coordinating conjunction is omitted, the clauses should be linked with a semicolon.

> I was not led to the university by conventional middle-class ambitions; my grip on the middle class was more tenuous than that on the school system.
>
> —Robin Fox

> Nobody can be promoted to a job until the person who occupies it has left. ... If that person is about to be fired, then it is sensible to make yourself as different as you can from him; if he is about to be promoted, then it makes sense to pattern your behavior on his; if he is about to retire, you're on your own.
>
> —Michael Korda

(If, instead of substituting a semicolon for an omitted conjunction, you use a comma or no punctuation at all, you will produce a comma splice or a run-on sentence. See Chapter 11.)

EXCEPTION: If one or both main clauses are very short, a comma is permissible.

> The poor live, the rich just exist.

EXERCISE 1

Insert semicolons or substitute them for commas in the sentences below to separate main clauses.

Example:

One man guided the group another brought up the rear.
One man guided the group; another brought up the rear.

1. Karate is not just a technique for self-defense, like a religion, it teaches inner calm.
2. He is still playing baseball at the age of sixty-three he is still no good.
3. The Himalayas are the loftiest mountain range in the world, they culminate in the highest mountain in the world, Mount Everest.
4. Subways in New York City are noisy, dirty, and dangerous they are also a superbly efficient means of transportation.
5. The pony express was slow but competent the Postal Service is just slow.

22b

Use the semicolon to separate main clauses joined by a conjunctive adverb.

Conjunctive adverbs include *however, indeed, moreover,* and *therefore.* (See 5d-2 for a complete list.)

The Labor Department lawyers will be here in a month; *therefore,* the grievance committee should meet as soon as possible.

For the first time in twenty years, the accident rate in St. Louis did not rise; *indeed,* it actually declined.

The position of the semicolon between main clauses never changes, but the conjunctive adverb may appear in several positions within a clause. When the adverb immediately follows the semicolon, follow it with a comma. Put commas before and after conjunctive adverbs farther away from the semicolon.

Blue jeans have become fashionable all over the world; *however,* the American originators still wear more jeans than anyone else.

Blue jeans have become fashionable all over the world; the American originators, *however,* still wear more jeans than anyone else.

EXERCISE 2

Insert semicolons and commas in the following sentences to separate main clauses linked by conjunctive adverbs and to set off the conjunctive adverbs from the rest of the clause they appear in.

Example:

She had heard that the auditions were going to be mobbed she went early to the gym therefore and was one of the first to try out.

> She had heard that the auditions were going to be mobbed; she went early to the gym, therefore, and was one of the first to try out.

1. There are fewer than three weeks until Thanksgiving vacation still I haven't made any plans for the big turkey dinner.
2. Environmentalists are trying to preserve the meadow outside town moreover they sued some land developers who were trying to build in the city park.
3. The elevator shakes when it goes down the inspector says it is safe however.
4. We must cut down on our fuel consumption otherwise we'll find ourselves with *no* fuel, not just less.
5. The air was suddenly calm consequently we had to paddle our sailboat to shore.

22c

Use the semicolon to separate main clauses if they are very long and complex or if they contain commas, even when they are joined by a coordinating conjunction.

You would normally use a comma with *and, but, or, nor,* and *for* between main clauses. But using semicolons between clauses punctuated with commas, or between clauses that are long and grammatically complicated (containing several phrases and modifiers), makes the clauses easier to identify and the sentence easier to read.

> It is this largess that accounts for the presence within the city's walls of a considerable section of the population; *for* the residents of Manhattan are to a large extent strangers who have pulled up stakes somewhere and come to town, seeking sanctuary or fulfillment or some greater or lesser grail.
> —E. B. White

> The calling song of the *Gryllus pennsylvanicus,* the northern fall field cricket of the United States, consists of a series of chirps at the rate of about four per second; *but* in fact each chirp consists of four pulses so close together that to a human ear they sound like a single chirp.
> —Howard E. Evans

Many writers prefer to use a semicolon between main clauses joined by the conjunctions *so* and *yet,* even when the clauses are not internally punctuated or complicated.

> It was a blustery day; *so* I decided to walk to class rather than ride my bicycle.

> Three truckloads of supplies arrived at the construction site; *yet* we still did not have enough cement.

EXERCISE 3

Substitute semicolons for commas in the following sentences to separate main clauses that are long or grammatically complicated or that are internally punctuated.

> *Example:*
>
> She enjoyed dancing to popular music, often joined a group for square dancing, and even danced the fox trot with her father and brothers, but she preferred ballet.
>
> She enjoyed dancing to rock music, often joined a group for square dancing, and even danced the fox trot with her father and brothers; but she preferred ballet.

1. By evening, having looked at every house on the realtor's list, the Morianis were exhausted and crabby, but they still hadn't found anything they could afford to buy.

2. James did whatever he wanted, without regard for the feelings or welfare of those around him or for the harm he was doing to himself, and eventually he got in trouble.

3. Seeking lower taxes, businesses moved to the suburbs, and merchants closed their downtown stores in favor of new ones in the shopping mall, and the city's center died.

4. She had a challenging job, a decent income, and good prospects for the future, but she remained miserable.

5. I will have to attend classes more regularly, do more of the required reading, and learn better ways to study for exams, or I will flunk out at the end of the semester.

;

22d

22d

Use the semicolon to separate items in a series if they are long or contain commas.

Though commas normally punctuate items in a series, using semicolons for long or internally punctuated items helps the reader identify them.

> To the winners, we give prizes; to the losers, consolation; and to the spectators, a good show.
>
> One may even reasonably advance the claim that the sort of communication that really counts, and is therefore embodied into permanent records, is primarily written; that "words fly away, but written messages endure," as the Latin saying put it two thousand years ago; and that there is no basic significance to at least fifty per cent of the oral interchange that goes on among all sorts of persons, high and low.
>
> —Mario Pei

EXERCISE 4

Substitute semicolons for commas in the following sentences to separate long or internally punctuated items in a series.

Example:

Buses are cheap, but they take time, planes are fast, but they cost too much, and trains both take time and cost too much.

Buses are cheap, but they take time; planes are fast, but they cost too much; and trains both take time and cost too much.

1. Julie brought beach blankets, chairs, and a beach ball, Brian brought beer, potato salad, and hot dogs, and I forgot my bathing suit.
2. The convocation droned on as the college president spoke of the challenges of education, the dean, first thanking the president, spoke of the joys of education, and the student government president, thanking both the president and the dean, spoke of students' responsibilities to the college.
3. We have a cat who is the size of a cocker spaniel, with a bark to match, a dog who is so big we can't trust him in the house, and neighbors who, for some reason, won't speak to us.
4. The car, with its headlights out, swerved into oncoming traffic, narrowly missed a large oil truck, and headed, nose first, into a deep, muddy ditch.
5. The farm we visited has a clear, fast-moving brook, a shallow but clear pond, and trees, hundreds of trees that keep the waters and the house delightfully cool.

;
22e

22e
Avoid overusing or misusing the semicolon.

The semicolon signals a long pause in a sentence. Overused or misused, it will halt the flow of a sentence and often confuse the reader.

1
Don't use the semicolon to link subordinate clauses or phrases to main clauses.

FAULTY According to African authorities; only about 35,000 Pygmies exist today, and their number is dwindling.

REVISED According to African authorities, only about 35,000 Pygmies exist today, and their number is dwindling.

FAULTY	The world would be less interesting; if clothes were standardized.
REVISED	The world would be less interesting if clothes were standardized.

2
Don't use the semicolon to introduce a list.

Colons and dashes, not semicolons, introduce explanations, lists, and so forth. (See 25a and 25b.)

FAULTY	Whatever the little reasons for doing poorly in a course, they usually add up to one big one; not doing the work.
REVISED	Whatever the little reasons for doing poorly in a course, they usually add up to one big one: not doing the work.
REVISED	Whatever the little reasons for doing poorly in a course, they usually add up to one big one— not doing the work.

3
Don't overuse the semicolon.

; 22e

Use the semicolon only occasionally, and only when required by a rule. Even when semicolons are required by rule, too many of them often indicate repetitive sentence structure. Compare these two versions of the same paragraph. In the first the semicolon is overused. In the second fewer semicolons are used, and the paragraph is clearer and the sentences more varied.

We live in an industrialized and urbanized society; men and women no longer share in tasks of production in accordance with strength and ability. The man disappears to the factory or office; the woman concentrates exclusively on managing consumption. This is a conventional arrangement; it is not an efficiently necessary division of labor; at a simple level of consumption it is perfectly possible for one person to do both. The family retains other purposes, including those of love, sex, and child rearing; however, it is no longer an economic necessity.

With industrialization and urbanization, men and women no longer share in tasks of production in accordance with strength and ability. The man disappears to the factory or office; the woman concentrates exclusively on managing consumption. This is a conventional arrangement, not an efficiently necessary division of labor; at a simple level of consumption it is perfectly possible for one person to do both. Without denying that the family retains other purposes, including those of love, sex, and child rearing, it is no longer an economic necessity.

—John Kenneth Galbraith

EXERCISE 5

Revise the sentences or groups of sentences below to eliminate misused or overused semicolons.

> *Example:*
> The table was ready for refinishing; all the old finish had been removed, the raw wood had been sanded smooth, and the dust had been wiped off with a clean rag.
>
> The table was ready for refinishing: all the old finish had been removed, the raw wood had been sanded smooth, and the dust had been wiped off with a clean rag.

1. Thinking of her future; Marie decided to major in economics.
2. The bus line finally went out of business; because more and more students drove themselves to school.
3. Even though the American League won the World Series; I continue to root for the National League.
4. The older I get, the more I realize the truth of the saying that only two things are inevitable; death and taxes.
5. Walking is great fun; we don't do enough of it. You see things when you're walking that you don't see when you're driving; you can smell and feel different things, too. Walking makes you a part of life; driving just races you through it.

22e

EXERCISE 6

Revise the sentences below to insert semicolons where they are needed or to eliminate needless or misused semicolons. Circle the number preceding each sentence that is already punctuated correctly.

> *Example:*
> The plan for gas rationing gained wider acceptance, however, people still didn't believe it would apply to them.
>
> The plan for gas rationing gained wider acceptance; however, people still didn't believe it would apply to them.

1. The weather was suited to a horror movie, the air was chilled and thick with fog.
2. Never had she seen so many smiling, contented faces as when she entered the lecture hall, but the message of the speaker, while pleasing the other members of the audience, terrified her.
3. Joel felt himself losing energy and saw himself gaining weight; he decided, consequently, to start exercising and dieting.

4. The end of the civil war seemed to be near; when the government agreed to negotiate with the rebels.

5. The suspect was tall, but not over six feet, heavy, but not fat, and bearded.

6. I want to take a course in Shakespeare's plays because I've only read a couple of them, but, according to my adviser, I have to take an introductory drama course as preparation.

7. The vacuum cleaner company did not send a brochure as it had promised it would, instead, it sent a salesperson to see us.

8. I don't understand economics; the theory doesn't seem to relate to practical problems.

9. Disputing your gas bill involves at least one and possibly two steps; calling or writing the gas company with your complaint and, if that doesn't work, requesting a hearing before the public utilities commission.

10. The bookstore should sell us books at its cost, it's in business to serve students, not make a profit.

23

The Apostrophe

23a
Use the apostrophe to indicate the possessive case for nouns and indefinite pronouns.

The **possessive case** shows ownership or possession of one person or thing by another. (See Chapter 6.) Possession may be shown with an *of* phrase (*the hair of the dog*) or, often, with the addition of an apostrophe and usually an *-s* (*the dog's hair*).

1
Add *-'s* to form the possessive case of singular or plural nouns or indefinite pronouns not ending in *-s*.

The *cat's* paw was mangled.
The *children's* parents performed *Snow White*.
Laura felt she was *no one's* friend.

2
Add *-'s* to form the possessive case of singular words ending in *-s*, unless adding another *s* makes pronunciation difficult.

Henry *James's* novels reward the patient reader.

Doris's term paper was read aloud in our English class.

BUT

For *goodness'* sake, don't holler.

Jesus' moral principles guide the behavior of people even today.

3

Add only an apostrophe to form the possessive case of plural words ending in -*s*.

The *teachers'* association called a strike.
Workers' incomes have risen over the past decade but not fast enough.
The *Murphys'* car was stolen.

4

Add -*'s* only to the last word to form the possessive case of compound words or word groups.

My *father-in-law's* birthday was yesterday.
The *council president's* address was a bore.
Go bang on *somebody else's* door.

5

When two or more words show individual possession, add -*'s* to both. Add -*'s* to only the last word if they show joint possession.

INDIVIDUAL POSSESSION

Harry's and Gerry's dentists both use laughing gas.
The committee's and the lawyer's reports contained obvious contradictions.

JOINT POSSESSION

Merrill, Lynch, Pierce, Fenner, and Smith's stock market report is encouraging.
That living room is an example of *John and Martha's* bad taste.

23a

EXERCISE 1

Use each word or word group below in a complete sentence after forming its possessive case as instructed in parentheses.

    Example:
    man *(plural possessive)*
    The *men's* team lost to the women's.

  1. mayor *(singular possessive)*
  2. garbage collector *(plural possessive)*
  3. John Adams *(singular possessive)*
  4. sister-in-law *(singular possessive)*
  5. everyone *(singular possessive)*
  6. somebody *(singular possessive)*

7. child *(plural possessive)*
8. Marvin and Sarah *(joint possession)*
9. Tom and Jerry *(individual possession)*
10. utility company *(plural possessive)*

23b

Don't use the apostrophe in forming the possessive case of personal pronouns.

His, hers, its, ours, yours, theirs, and *whose* are the possessive forms; they don't need apostrophes.

FAULTY	Credit for discovering this house is really *her's.*
REVISED	Credit for discovering this house is really *hers.*

NOTE: Don't confuse the personal pronouns *its, their,* and *whose* with the contractions *it's* ("it is"), *they're* ("they are"), and *who's* ("who is"). (See 23c, below.)

EXERCISE 2

Revise the sentences below to correct mistakes in the formation of the possessive case of personal pronouns. Circle the number preceding any sentence that is already correct.

Example:
"Who's book is this?" she asked.
"Whose book is this?" she asked.
1. The tennis racket was her's.
2. We hear they're buying a house.
3. The dog darted suddenly from it's resting place.
4. Its not fair that he lost.
5. That's the lady who's house I'm going to buy.

23c

Use the apostrophe to indicate the omission of one or more letters, numbers, or words in standard contractions.

it's	it is
who's	who is
they're	they are
class of '79	class of 1979
o'clock	of the clock
ma'am	madam

EXERCISE 3

Form correct contractions from each set of words below. Use each contraction in a complete sentence.

> *Example:*
> we are
> *we're*
> *We're* open to ideas.

1. they are
2. he is
3. she will
4. is not
5. cannot

6. should not
7. hurricane of 1962
8. we would
9. they will
10. are not

23d

Use the apostrophe plus -*s* to form the plurals of letters, numbers, and words named as words.

That sentence has too many *but*'s.
At the end of each chapter the author had written two *3*'s.
Remember to dot your *i*'s and to cross your *t*'s, or your readers may not be able to distinguish them from *e*'s and *l*'s.

V
23d

Notice that the letters, numbers, and words are italicized (underlined in typed or handwritten copy) but that the apostrophe and added -*s* are not. (See 27e on this use of italics or underlining.)
EXCEPTION: References to the years in a decade are not italicized and often omit the apostrophe. Thus 1960's and 1960s are both acceptable.

EXERCISE 4

Form the plural of each letter, number, or word by using an apostrophe and -*s* and by underlining (italicizing) appropriately. Use the new plural in a complete sentence.

> *Example:*
> x
> Erase or white out typing mistakes. Do not use x's.

1. and
2. k
3. which

4. 4
5. stop

24
Quotation Marks

The principal use of quotation marks is to enclose direct quotations from speech and from writing. Always use quotation marks in pairs, one at the beginning of a quotation and one at the end. They may be double (" ") or single (' ') depending on their use. (For the use of brackets within quotations to separate your own comments from the words of the author you quote, see 25d. For the use of the ellipsis mark (. . .) to indicate an omission from a quotation, see 25e.)

24a
Use double quotation marks to enclose direct quotations.

When Einstein's father asked the headmaster what calling young Albert should pursue, the reply was, "It doesn't matter; he'll never make a success of anything."

—Lincoln Barnett

Indirect quotations—statements reporting what has been said, but not in the speaker's exact words—are not enclosed in quotation marks.

Albert Einstein's headmaster predicted that Albert would never be a success.

24b
Use single quotation marks to enclose a quotation within a quotation.

When you quote a writer or speaker, use double quotation marks (see 24a). When the material you quote contains yet another quotation, enclose the second quotation in single quotation marks.

"In formulating any philosophy," Woody Allen writes, "the first consideration must always be: What can we know? . . . Descartes hinted at the problem when he wrote, 'My mind can never know my body, although it has become quite friendly with my legs.'"

Notice that two quotation marks appear at the end of the sentence—one single (to finish the interior quotation) and one double (to finish the main quotation).

EXERCISE 1

Insert single and double quotation marks as needed in the following sentences. Circle the number preceding each sentence that is already correct.

Example:

Shakespeare's phrase salad days to describe youth means more to me as I grow older, Mr. Bowman said.

"Shakespeare's phrase 'salad days' to describe youth means more to me as I grow older," Mr. Bowman said.

1. She tells us Dance is poetry, Marsha said, but I don't understand what she means.
2. Mark Twain quipped, Reports of my death are greatly exaggerated.
3. We shall overcome, sang the civil rights workers of the 1960s. I think we should still be singing those words.
4. After a long pause he said that the man in the red shirt had stolen the car.
5. Now that spring is here, Ms. Radley said, we can hold classes on the lawn.

" "
24c

24c

Set off quotations of dialogue, poetry, and long prose passages according to standard practice.

Dialogue

When quoting conversations, begin a new paragraph for each speaker.

"Say something, son," the detective said.
"I didn't hold this guy up," said the suspect in a dead voice.
—Bernard Malamud

NOTE: When you quote a single speaker for more than one paragraph, put quotation marks at the beginning of each paragraph but at the end of only the last paragraph. The absence of quotation marks from the end of each paragraph but the last tells readers that the speech is continuing.

Poetry

Poetry quotations of one line are normally run in to the text and enclosed by quotation marks.

> Shakespeare's most famous line, "To be or not to be: that is the question," pinpoints the dilemma of the person who contemplates suicide.

Quotations of two lines may be run in or set off. If you run in a two-line quotation, enclose it in quotation marks, and indicate the end of the first line with a slash.

> Robert Frost's incisiveness shows in two lines from "Death of the Hired Man": "Home is the place where, when you have to go there, / They have to take you in."

If you set off the quotation, indent it from the left, single-space it, and omit quotation marks.

> Robert Frost's incisiveness shows in two lines from "Death of the Hired Man":
>> Home is the place where, when you have to go there,
>> They have to take you in.

" "

24c

Always set off and indent quotations of more than two lines of poetry.

> Shakespeare evoked old age in "That Time of Year":
>> That time of year thou mayst in me behold
>> When yellow leaves, or none, or few, do hang
>> Upon those boughs which shake against the cold,
>> Bare ruined choirs, where late the sweet birds sang.

Be careful when quoting poetry to reproduce unusual capitalization, punctuation, spelling, and line indentions faithfully in handwriting or typing.

Long prose passages

Set off a prose quotation of more than four lines from the body of your paper and indent it from the left margin. Don't add quotation marks. Also, single-space the quotation unless you are preparing the copy for publication, in which case double-space it.

While deploring the effects of the social sciences on English prose style, Malcolm Cowley can still use his sense of humor:

> Considering this degradation of the verb, I have wondered how one of Julius Caesar's boasts could be translated into Socspeak. What Caesar wrote was *"Veni, vidi, vici"*—only three words, all of them verbs. The English translation is in six words: "I came, I saw, I conquered," and three of the words are first-personal pronouns, which the sociologist is taught to avoid. I suspect that he would have to write: "Upon the advent of the investigator, his hegemony became minimally coextensive with the areal unit rendered visible by his successive displacements in space."

EXERCISE 2

Practice using quotation marks in quoted dialogue, poetry, and long prose passages by completing each of the exercises below.

1. Write a short stretch of dialogue between two people.
2. Write a sentence that quotes a single line of poetry.
3. Write two sentences that quote two lines of poetry. In one sentence run the poetry lines in to the text. In the other sentence set the two lines off.
4. Write a sentence introducing a prose passage of over four lines, and then set up the quotation appropriately for its length.

24d

Put quotation marks around the titles of songs, short poems, articles in periodicals, short stories, essays, episodes of television and radio programs, and the subdivisions of books.

SONGS

"Lucy in the Sky with Diamonds"
"Mr. Bojangles"

SHORT POEMS

"Stopping by Woods on a Snowy Evening"
"Sunday Morning"

ARTICLES IN PERIODICALS

"Comedy and Tragedy Transposed" (in *The Yale Review*)
"Does 'Scaring' Work?" (in *Newsweek*)

SHORT STORIES

"The Battler"
"The Gift of the Magi"

Essays

"Politics and the English Language"
"Joey: A 'Mechanical Boy' "

Episodes of television and radio programs

"The Mexican Connection" (on *60 Minutes*)
"Cooking with Clams" (on *Eating In*)

Subdivisions of books

"Voyage to the Houyhnhnms" (Part IV of *Gulliver's Travels*)
"The Mast Head" (Chapter 35 of *Moby Dick*)

See 27a on the use of italics (or underlining) for all other titles. And see 26b for guidelines on the use of capital letters in titles.

24e

Occasionally, quotation marks may be used to enclose words used in a special sense and in definitions.

An architect refers to one view of a building as its "aspect."
Pardon my pun, but I find that lawyer "appealing."
By "charity," I mean the love of one's neighbor as oneself.

Note: In definitions, italics (or underlining) are more common than quotation marks. (See 27d.)

By *charity*, I mean the love of one's neighbor as oneself.

" "
24e

EXERCISE 3

Insert quotation marks as needed for titles and words in the sentences below. If quotation marks should be used instead of italics, insert them.

Example:

How can you call him sir when he doesn't show any respect for you?

How can you call him "sir" when he doesn't show any respect for you?

1. The song Old Man River comes from the musical *Showboat.*
2. A Rose for Emily is a touching story by William Faulkner.
3. E. B. White's famous essay Farewell, My Lovely! is about his old Model T Ford.
4. Joyce Kilmer's poem Trees has to be the worst poem I've read.
5. Doom means simply judgment as well as unhappy destiny.

24f

Avoid using quotation marks where they are not required.

Don't use quotation marks in the titles of your papers unless they contain or are themselves direct quotations.

NOT	"The Death Wish in One Poem by Robert Frost"
BUT	The Death Wish in One Poem by Robert Frost
OR	The Death Wish in "Stopping by Woods on a Snowy Evening"

Don't enclose common nicknames and technical terms in quotation marks.

NOT	"Jimmy" Carter prefers to use his nickname.
BUT	Jimmy Carter prefers to use his nickname.
NOT	The "mitosis" of a cell is fascinating to watch.
BUT	The mitosis of a cell is fascinating to watch.

Don't use quotations marks in an attempt to justify or apologize for the use of slang and trite expressions that are inappropriate to your writing. If slang is appropriate; use it without quotation marks.

NOT	Everybody was "doing his own thing," but nobody was making any "bread."
BUT	Everybody was doing what he wanted, but nobody was making any money.
NOT	Since it was "raining cats and dogs," we canceled our softball game.
BUT	Since it was raining so hard, we canceled our softball game.

(See 31a-1 and 31b-5 for a discussion of how to avoid slang and trite expressions.)

24g

Place other marks of punctuation inside or outside quotation marks according to standard practice.

1

Place commas and periods inside quotation marks.

"One broken leg is enough. I will never go skiing again."
"Your first check will come next month," the social worker said.

2

Place colons and semicolons outside quotation marks.

A few years ago the slogan in elementary education was "learning by playing"; now educators are concerned with teaching basic skills.

We all know what is meant by "inflation": more money buys less.

3

Place dashes, question marks, and exclamation points inside quotation marks only if they belong to the quotation.

When a dash, question mark, or exclamation point applies to the quotation, put it inside quotation marks.

"But must you—" Marcia hesitated, afraid of the answer.
"Who is she really?" he mused.
"Go away!" I yelled.

When a dash, question mark, or exclamation point applies only to the larger sentence, and not to the quotation, place it outside quotation marks.

One of the most evocative lines in English poetry—"After many a summer dies the swan"—was written by Alfred, Lord Tennyson.

Who said, "Now cracks a noble heart"?

Believe it or not, she even boasted, "I'll have you fired"!

" "

24g

EXERCISE 4

Revise the sentences below for the proper use of quotation marks. Insert quotation marks where they are needed, remove them when they are not needed, and be sure that other marks of punctuation are correctly placed inside or outside the quotation marks. Circle the number preceding each sentence that is already punctuated correctly.

Example:

In America the signs say, Keep off the grass; in England they say, Please refrain from stepping on the lawn.

In America the signs say, "Keep off the grass"; in England they say, "Please refrain from stepping on the lawn."

1. In *King Richard II* Shakespeare calls England This precious stone set in the silver sea.
2. The doctors gave my father an "electrocardiogram" but found nothing wrong.
3. The commercial says, Aspirin will relieve the pain of neuritis and neuralgia; but what are they?

4. In his three-piece suit he looked like a real "man about town."
5. Anyone who failed to read today's story, The Tell-Tale Heart, raise your hand, the instructor ordered.
6. Years ago, an advertising campaign said, The family that prays together stays together; today, born-again Christians are saying the same thing.
7. You—come here! David cried.
8. Land development is slowly depriving us of our forests—in Longfellow's words, "The murmuring pines and the hemlocks."
9. Must we regard the future with what Kierkegaard called fear and trembling?
10. What sort of person would hurt an animal? my son asked.

25

Other Punctuation Marks

THE COLON

25a

Use the colon to introduce and to separate.

1

Use the colon to introduce summaries, explanations, series, appositives ending sentences, long or formal quotations, and statements introduced by *the following* or *as follows*.

SUMMARY

The facts can lead us to only one conclusion: we're putting more cancer-causing chemicals into our bodies and they're doing their work superbly.

EXPLANATION

The conditioning starts very early: with the girl child who wants the skin that Ivory soap has reputedly given her mother, with the nine-year-old who brings back a cake of Camay instead of the male deodorant her father wanted.

—Marya Mannes

SERIES

It is impossible to dissociate language from science or science from language, because every natural science always involves three things: the sequence of phenomena on which the science is based; the abstract concepts which call these phenomena to mind; and the words in which the concepts are expressed.

—Antoine Lavoisier

FINAL APPOSITIVE

Two chief elements make work interesting: first, the exercise of skill, and second, construction.

—Bertrand Russell

LONG OR FORMAL QUOTATIONS

Scarcely had the moon flight been achieved before one U.S. senator boldly announced: "We are the masters of the universe. We can go anywhere we choose."

—Loren Eiseley

STATEMENT INTRODUCED BY *THE FOLLOWING* OR *AS FOLLOWS*

The relation between leisure and income is as follows: the quality of play depends on the quantity of pay.

NOTE: Usage varies on whether to begin a complete sentence following a colon with a capital letter or a lowercase letter. Either is acceptable.

2
Use the colon to separate subtitles and titles, the subdivisions of time, and the parts of biblical citations.

TITLES AND SUBTITLES

Charles Dickens: An Introduction to His Novels
Eros and Civilization: A Philosophical Inquiry into Freud

25a

TIME

1:30
12:26

BIBLICAL CITATIONS

Isaiah 28:1–6
1 Corinthians 3:6–7

3
Avoid misusing the colon.

Use the colon only at the end of an independent clause. Avoid using it between a verb or a preposition and its object or when formal introduction is lacking.

NOT	My three favorite movies are: *The Great Gatsby, Star Wars,* and *The Godfather.*
BUT	My three favorite movies are *The Great Gatsby, Star Wars,* and *The Godfather.*
NOT	Shakespeare showed the qualities of a Renaissance man, such as: humanism and a deep interest in classical Greek and Roman literature.

BUT	Shakespeare showed the qualities of a Renaissance man, such as humanism and a deep interest in classical Greek and Roman literature.

EXERCISE 1

Insert colons as needed in the sentences below.

Example:

You can find the state park as follows get on the expressway going south, take Exit 27, and drive 20 miles due east.

You can find the state park as follows: get on the expressway going south, take Exit 27, and drive 20 miles due east.

1. Let me conclude with this word either improve the mass transit system or look forward to the decay of your downtown area.
2. He based his interpretation of the Second Coming on John 21 17–30.
3. He left his cottage at 800 in the morning with only one goal in mind to murder the man who was blackmailing him.
4. Two lethal influenza strains have hit the United States in recent years Asian flu and swine flu.
5. The Pilgrims had one major reason for coming to the New World they desired religious freedom.

25b

THE DASH

25b

Use the dash or dashes to indicate sudden changes in tone or thought and to set off some sentence elements.

1

Use the dash or dashes to indicate sudden shifts in tone, new or unfinished thoughts, and hesitation in dialogue.

On the mosquito's sides had been two flattened sacs, and from them she now pulled out—wings!

—Sally Carrigher

"I was worried you might think I had stayed away because I was influenced by—" he stopped and lowered his eyes.

Astonished, Howe said, "Influenced by what?"

"Well, by—" Blackburn hesitated and for answer pointed to the table.

—Lionel Trilling

2

Use the dash or dashes to emphasize parenthetical expressions.

I meet this American government, or its representative, the state government, directly, and face to face, once a year—no more—in the person of its tax-gatherer.

—Henry David Thoreau

At any given time there exists an inventory of undiscovered embezzlement in—or more precisely not in—the country's businesses and banks. This inventory—it should perhaps be called the bezzle—amounts at any moment to millions of dollars.

—John Kenneth Galbraith

(See also 25c-1.)

3

Use the dash or dashes to set off introductory series, summaries, and appositives.

It was love on the run, love on the lam, love in a pressure cooker, love on the barricades, love all mixed up with political passion and suicidal despair, love born of broken hearts and cracking brains—for all of them the most intense emotional experience of their short lives.

—Shana Alexander

Shortness of breath, skin discoloration or the sudden appearance of moles, persistent indigestion, the presence of small lumps—all can be signs of cancer.

The qualities Monet painted—sunlight, rich shadows, deep colors—were abundant around the rivers and gardens he used as subjects.

25b

4

Avoid misusing or overusing the dash.

Don't use the dash when commas, semicolons, and periods are more appropriate. And don't use too many dashes. They—and the expressions they set off—can create an unpleasant jumpy or breathy quality in writing.

Not   In all his life—eighty-seven years—my great-grandfather never allowed his picture to be taken—not even once. He claimed the "black box"—the camera—would steal his soul, but he couldn't fool us—we knew the real problem—he was just too vain to entrust his likeness to a machine.

BUT	In all his eighty-seven years my great-grandfather did not allow his picture to be taken even once. He claimed the "black box"—the camera—would steal his soul, but we knew he was just too vain to entrust his likeness to a machine.

EXERCISE 2

Insert dashes as needed in the sentences below.

Example:
What would we do if someone like Adolf Hitler that monster appeared among us?
What would we do if someone like Adolf Hitler—that monster—appeared among us?

1. The religious I should say fanatic quality of their belief was almost frightening.
2. The three cats on the ledge one Persian, one Siamese, and one Manx make a pleasant late-afternoon picture.
3. Carnivals, circuses, rodeos, amusement parks all the wonders of childhood Joey had seen.
4. It was the recurring dream the one in which she floated in space that she wanted to talk to her doctor about.
5. To feed, clothe, and find shelter for the needy these are real achievements.

( )
25c

PARENTHESES

25c

Use parentheses to enclose nonessential elements within sentences.

1

Use parentheses to enclose parenthetical expressions.

Parenthetical expressions include explanations, examples, and minor digressions that may aid understanding but are not essential to meaning.

He drove trucks (tractor-trailers, actually) to earn money for college.

Queen Victoria's death in 1901 (a traumatic event for the British people) more or less officially ended the historical period since named for her.

See 21c-3 and 25b-2 for the uses of commas and dashes, respectively, to set off parenthetical expressions. Both emphasize parenthetical expressions more than parentheses do, and the dash is more emphatic than the comma.

NOTE: Don't put a comma before a parenthetical expression enclosed in parentheses.

NOT	In the smallest of these huts lived old Berl, a man in his eighties, and his wife, who was called Berlcha, (wife of Berl).
BUT	In the smallest of these huts lived old Berl, a man in his eighties, and his wife, who was called Berlcha (wife of Berl).

—Isaac Bashevis Singer

2

Use parentheses to enclose letters and figures labeling items in lists within sentences.

My father could not, for his own special reasons, even *like* me. He spent the first twenty-five years of my life acting out that painful fact. Then he arrived at two points in his own life: (1) his last years, and (2) the realization that he had made a tragic mistake.

—Ray Weatherly

When lists are set off from the text, the numbers or letters labeling them are usually not enclosed in parentheses.

( )
25c

EXERCISE 3

Insert parentheses as needed in the sentences below.

Example:

The Hundred Years' War 1337–1453 between England and France was not a continuous war but a series of widely spaced battles.

The Hundred Years' War (1337–1453) between England and France was not a continuous war but a series of widely spaced battles.

1. Our present careless use of coal and oil will lead to a series of unpleasant events: 1 all of us will have to cut back drastically on our use of resources; 2 only the rich will have access to these resources; and 3 no one will have access to them for they will be exhausted.

2. We have received numerous requests 125 to be exact for transcripts of last Wednesday's town council meeting.

3. Charles Darwin's *On the Origin of Species* 1859 remains a controversial book to this day.

4. The Rocky Mountains and they are rocky are as ominous as they are beautiful.

5. The life of the English dramatist Christopher Marlowe 1564–1593 was short but intense.

BRACKETS

25d

Use brackets within quotations to separate your own comments from the words of the writer you quote.

If you need to explain, clarify, or correct the words of the writer you quote, place your additions in brackets.

"That Texaco station [just outside Chicago] is one of the busiest in the nation," said a company spokesman.

The word *sic* (Latin for "in this manner") in brackets indicates that an error in the quotation appeared in the original and was not introduced by you.

According to the newspaper report, "The car slammed thru [*sic*] the railing and into oncoming traffic."

```
. . .
25e
```

THE ELLIPSIS MARK

25e

Use the ellipsis mark to indicate omissions within quotations.

The **ellipsis mark** consists of three spaced periods (. . .). It is used most often to show that something has been left out of a quotation.

ORIGINAL QUOTATION

"It took four years for Bernice Gera to walk onto that ball field, four years of legal battles for the right to stand in the shadow of an 'Enjoy Silver Floss Sauerkraut' sign while the crowd cheered and young girls waved sheets reading 'Right On, Bernice!' and the manager of the Geneva Phillies welcomed her to the game. 'On behalf of professional baseball,' he said, 'we say good luck and God bless you in your chosen profession.' And the band played and the spotlights shone and all three networks recorded the event. Bernice Gera had become the first woman in the 133-year history of the sport to umpire a professional baseball game."

—Nora Ephron

OMISSION OF PART OF A SENTENCE

"Bernice Gera had become the first woman . . . to umpire a professional baseball game."

OMISSION OF TWO SENTENCES

"It took four years for Bernice Gera to walk onto that ball field, four years of legal battles for the right to stand in the shadow of an 'Enjoy Silver Floss Sauerkraut' sign while the crowd cheered and young girls waved sheets reading 'Right On, Bernice!' and the manager of the Geneva Phillies welcomed her to the game. . . . Bernice Gera had become the first woman in the 133-year history of the sport to umpire a professional baseball game."

Notice that when the ellipsis mark follows a sentence, as in the example immediately above, four equally spaced periods result: the sentence period (closed up to the last word of the sentence) and the three periods of the ellipsis mark. Notice also that although Ephron's essay goes on after the quoted paragraph, an ellipsis mark is not used at the end of the quotation.

. . .

25e

If you omit one or more lines of poetry or paragraphs of prose from a quotation, use a separate line of ellipsis marks across the full width of the quotation to show the omission.

NOTE: Pauses and unfinished statements in quoted speech may be indicated with the ellipsis mark. (See 25b-1 for the use of the dash for this purpose.)

"I know the game," he said. "Five times in one day is a little bit . . . Well, you better look sharp and get a copy of our correspondence to the Delacour case for Mr. Allyne."

—James Joyce

EXERCISE 4

To practice using ellipsis marks to show omissions from quotations, follow each instruction below using the following paragraph by Stewart Udall.

The most common trait of all primitive peoples is a reverence for the life-giving earth, and the native American shared this elemental ethic: the land was alive to his loving touch, and he, its son, was brother to all creatures. His feelings were made visible in medicine bundles and dance rhythms for rain, and all of his religious rites and land attitudes savored the inseparable world of nature and God, the master of life. During the long Indian tenure the land remained undefiled save for scars no deeper than the scratches of cornfield clearings or the farming canals of the Hohokams on the Arizona desert.

—Stewart Udall

1. Quote the first sentence from this paragraph, but omit the words *its son* (plus punctuation as necessary) and show the omission with an ellipsis mark.
2. Quote this paragraph, but omit the second sentence and show the omission with an ellipsis mark.

THE SLASH

25f

Use the slash between options and to indicate the end of a line of poetry when two lines are run in to the text.

OPTION

I don't know why some teachers oppose pass/fail courses.

POETRY

More than fifty years after its introduction, people are still baffled by e. e. cummings's unique form of expression, as in lines like "next to of course god america i / love you land of the pilgrims' and so forth oh."

/
25f

(See 24c for more on quoting poetry.)

EXERCISE 5

Insert colons, dashes, parentheses, brackets, ellipsis marks, or slashes as needed in the sentences below, or remove them where they are not needed. When two or more different marks would be appropriate in the same place, be able to defend the choice you make. Circle the number preceding each sentence that is already correct as written.

Example:

Suddenly a voice boomed "The court is in session. All rise."

Suddenly a voice boomed: "The court is in session. All rise." [Colon before formal quotation.]

1. The sidewalks of Venice some as old as the city are regularly immersed in water from flooded canals.
2. She looked just like her sister lean and mean.
3. We took a carful of camping equipment, including: a large tent, two cots, two sleeping bags, a stove, pots and pans, and enough food and clothing for a year.

4. "Barbra Streisand's sole talent . . . . is singing."
5. I used *Ernest Hemingway A Reconsideration* for my English paper.
6. "Buy the new Universal Dictionery *sic,*" the ad said. But how could anybody buy a dictionary that can't spell *dictionary?*
7. "Do you think—?" Artie didn't need to finish his question.
8. James Joyce's *Ulysses* first published in 1922 but not published in the United States until 1933 is a beautiful, shocking novel.
9. The sudden warmth, the palest green, the splashy, cleansing rain these signs of an eastern spring were what she missed most in California.
10. In the letter he quoted two lines John Donne once wrote in a letter of his own: "Sir, more than kisses, letters mingle souls; For thus friends absent speak."

25

VI
Mechanics

26
Capitals

Writers generally agree on when to use capitals, but the conventions are constantly changing. Consult a dictionary if you have any doubt about whether a particular word should be capitalized.

26a
Capitalize the first word of every sentence.

Every writer should own a good dictionary.
Will this rain ever stop?
Watch out!

NOTE: Capitalization of the questions in a series is optional. Both of the following sentences are correct.

Is this paper supposed to be four hundred words long? Five hundred words? Six hundred words?

Is this paper supposed to be four hundred words long? five hundred words? six hundred words?

26b
In titles of your papers and of books, plays, and all other works of art, capitalize the first and last words, any word after a colon or semicolon, and all other words except articles and prepositions and conjunctions of less than five letters.

"The Love Song of J. Alfred Prufrock"
The Sound and the Fury
"Courtship Through the Ages"
Pamela: Or Virtue Rewarded
"Industry Since World War II"

NOTE: Always capitalize the first word in hyphenated words. Capitalize the second word only if it is a noun, an adjective, or as important as the first word.

"How to Apply Stage Make-up"
The Pre-Raphaelite Imagination
Through the Looking-Glass

26c

Always capitalize the pronoun *I* and the interjection *O*. Don't capitalize *oh* unless it begins a sentence.

Oh, I never do well on multiple-choice tests.
Praise be, O God, for all these gifts.
I love to stay up at night, and, oh, how I hate to get up in the morning.

26d

Capitalize proper nouns, proper adjectives, and words used as essential parts of proper nouns.

1

Capitalize proper nouns and proper adjectives.

Common nouns name general classes of persons, places, and things. **Proper nouns** name specific persons, places, and things. **Proper adjectives** are formed from some proper nouns. Capitalize all proper nouns and proper adjectives but not the articles (*a, an, the*) that precede them.

cap

26d

COMMON NOUNS	PROPER NOUNS	PROPER ADJECTIVES
state	California	Californian
man	Shakespeare	Shakespearean
building	Radio City Music Hall	—

SPECIFIC PERSONS AND THINGS

Jimmy Carter	the Leaning Tower of Pisa
Napoleon Bonaparte	Boulder Dam
Jane Fonda	the Empire State Building

SPECIFIC PLACES AND GEOGRAPHICAL REGIONS

New York City	the Mediterranean Sea
China	Lake Victoria
Europe	the Northeast

DAYS OF THE WEEK, MONTHS, HOLIDAYS

Monday	Yom Kippur
May	Christmas
Thanksgiving	Columbus Day

HISTORICAL EVENTS, DOCUMENTS, PERIODS, MOVEMENTS

World War II	the Romantic Movement
the Treaty of Ghent	the Age of Reason
the Constitution	the Renaissance

ORGANIZATIONS, ASSOCIATIONS, AND GOVERNMENT OFFICES OR DEPARTMENTS

Girl Scouts of America	Department of Defense
Young Men's Christian Association	Social Security Administration
B'nai B'rith	Postal Service

RACES, NATIONALITIES, AND THEIR LANGUAGES

Native American	Germans
Asian	Swahili
Afro-American	Italian
But: blacks, whites	

POLITICAL, SOCIAL, ATHLETIC, AND OTHER GROUPS AND THEIR MEMBERS

Republican Party	Elks
Democrats	Eastern Star
Rotary Club	Junior League
Daughters of the American Revolution	Boston Celtics

RELIGIOUS TERMS FOR SACRED PERSONS AND THINGS

God	Buddha
Allah	the Bible
Christ	the Koran

RELIGIONS AND THEIR FOLLOWERS

Hinduism	Judaism
Hindus	Jews
Christianity	Islam
Christians	Moslems

cap

26d

NOTE: Capitalization of pronouns referring to God is optional in most contexts, but it is required in religious texts and where necessary to avoid confusion.

CORRECT	Through holy books people have come to believe they know who God is and what *He* is.
CORRECT	Through holy books people have come to believe they know who God is and what *he* is.

AMBIGUOUS	Our minister spoke of God as though *he* loved every member of our congregation.
REVISED	Our minister spoke of God as though *He* loved every member of our congregation.

2
Capitalize common nouns used as essential parts of proper nouns.

The common nouns *street, avenue, park, river, ocean, lake, company, college, county,* and *memorial* are capitalized when they are part of proper nouns.

Main Street	Lake Superior
Park Avenue	Ford Motor Company
Central Park	Madison College
Mississippi River	Kings County
Pacific Ocean	George Washington Memorial Park

3
Capitalize trade names.

Trade names identify individual brands of certain products. When a trade name loses its association with a brand and comes to refer to a product in general, it is not capitalized. Refer to a dictionary for current usage when you are in doubt about a name.

Scotch tape
Chevrolet
Xerox
Bunsen burner
But: nylon, thermos

cap
26e

26e
Capitalize titles when they precede proper names but generally not when they follow proper names or are used without them.

Professor Otto Osborne	Otto Osborne, a professor of English
Doctor Jane Covington	Jane Covington, a medical doctor
Senator Jacob Javits	Jacob Javits, the senator from New York
Ambassador Ruth Golden	Ruth Golden, the ambassador to Holland

EXCEPTION: Many writers capitalize a title without a proper name if it denotes very high rank.

the President of the United States
the Chief Justice of the Supreme Court

26f
Avoid unnecessary capitalization.

In general, modern writers capitalize fewer words than earlier writers did. Don't capitalize a word unless a rule says you must.

1
Don't capitalize common nouns used in place of proper nouns.

UNNECESSARY	By the time I graduate from College, I will have taken six economics courses.
REVISED	By the time I graduate from college, I will have taken six economics courses.
REVISED	By the time I graduate from Madison College, I will have taken six economics courses.

2
Don't capitalize compass directions unless they refer to specific geographical areas.

northeast	the Northeast
west	the West
south	the South
northwest	the Northwest

3
Don't capitalize the names of seasons or the names of academic years.

spring	winter quarter
fall	freshman year
autumn	summer term

4

Don't capitalize the names of relationships unless they form part of or substitute for proper names.

my mother
John's brother
the father of my friend

BUT

I remember how Father scolded us.
Aunt Annie, Uncle Jake, and Uncle Irvin died within two months of each other.

EXERCISE

Capitalize words as needed in the sentences below, or lowercase capital letters where they are not needed. Consult a dictionary if necessary. If the capitalization in a sentence is already correct, circle the number preceding the sentence.

> *Example:*
>
> The last book i read, *The american way of death,* is about American burial customs.
>
> The last book I read, *The American Way of Death,* is about American burial customs.

1. "It's bitter cold. better play inside today."
2. The grand canyon is in arizona, not too far from phoenix.
3. According to his card, he was a doctor of medicine, but I could tell he had a lousy bedside manner.
4. My Grandmother died before I was born.
5. The bible, koran, and bhagavad gita are the holy books of jews and christians, muslims, and hindus, respectively.
6. The text for my psychology course, *A study of psycho-social development,* opened my eyes about how children learn.
7. Our scavenger-hunt map directed us two blocks Southeast and two blocks Northeast to find an old sink.
8. The Suwannee river rises in the Okefenokee swamp and moves through Georgia and Florida to the gulf of Mexico.
9. The new Saunders theater is an acoustical triumph, but, Oh, it was expensive to build.
10. Never one to take sides, father says that both general Douglas MacArthur and president Harry Truman were fine men and it's just too bad they had to argue.

cap
26f

27
Italics

Type that slants upward to the right is known as *italic type.* We use italics to distinguish or emphasize certain words and phrases. In your handwritten or typed papers, <u>underline</u> to indicate material that would be italicized if set into type.

27a

Underline the titles of books, long poems, plays, periodicals, pamphlets, published speeches, long musical works, movies, television and radio programs, and works of visual art.

As a rule, underline the titles of long poems, essays, and short stories only if they were originally published as an entire volume. (See 24d for the use of quotation marks with all other titles.)

BOOKS

Catch-22
War and Peace
The Promise

LONG POEMS

Beowulf
The Song of Roland
Paradise Lost

PLAYS

Equus
Hamlet
Summer and Smoke

PERIODICALS

Time
Philadelphia *Inquirer*
Yale Law Review

PAMPHLETS

The Truth About Alcoholism
On the Vindication of the Rights of Women

PUBLISHED SPEECHES

Lincoln's *Gettysburg Address*
Pericles' *Funeral Oration*

LONG MUSICAL WORKS	**MOVIES**
Swan Lake	*Gone with the Wind*
Sergeant Pepper's Lonely	*Star Wars*
Hearts Club Band	*An Unmarried Woman*

TELEVISION AND RADIO PROGRAMS	**WORKS OF VISUAL ART**
All in the Family	Michelangelo's *David*
The Shadow	the *Mona Lisa*

NOTE: Be careful to underline articles and marks of punctuation only if they are part of the title (the *Reader's Digest*, not *The Reader's Digest*). In titles of newspapers the initial *the* and the name of the city in which the paper is published may or may not be part of the title.

the Manchester *Guardian*
The New York Times

EXCEPTIONS: Legal documents, the Bible, and their parts are generally not italicized.

NOT	They registered their *deed*.
BUT	They registered their deed.

NOT	We just studied the *Bible's* book of *Revelation*.
BUT	We just studied the Bible's book of Revelation.

27b

Underline the names of ships, aircraft, spacecraft, and trains.

Queen Elizabeth II
Spirit of St. Louis
Apollo XI
Orient Express

27c

Underline foreign words and phrases that are not part of our language.

English tends to absorb foreign words and phrases that speakers and writers find useful. The French expression *bon voyage*, for example, is now part of our language and need not be underlined. If a foreign word or phrase has not been absorbed into our language, it should be underlined. A good dictionary will tell you whether or not the words you wish to use should be underlined.

ital
27c

The scientific name for the brown trout is *Salmo trutta.*

What a life he led! He was a true *bon vivant.*

The Latin *De gustibus non est disputandum* translates roughly as "There's no accounting for taste."

27d
Underline words, letters, numbers, and phrases named as words.

Some people pronounce *th,* as in *thought,* with a faint *s* or *f* sound.

Carved into the middle of the column, twenty feet up, was a mysterious 7.

Try pronouncing *unique New York* ten times fast.

Italics may also be used instead of quotation marks in definitions. (See 24e.)

The word *syzygy* refers to a straight line formed by three celestial bodies, as in an eclipse of the sun or moon.

27e
Occasionally, underlining may be used for emphasis.

Compare these sentences:

I thought you had the key.
I thought you had the key.
I *thought* you had the key.
I thought *you* had the key.

In the absence of clues from context, the first sentence doesn't tell us where the emphasis should lie. The three following sentences, however, tell us exactly what word to emphasize, and the different emphases create different meanings. In this way italics (or underlining) can be useful to stress an important word or phrase, especially in reporting how someone said something. But such emphasis should be used sparingly. Excessive underlining will make your writing sound immature or hysterical, as the following example illustrates.

The hunters had *no* food and *no* firewood. But they were *too* tired to do anything more than crawl into their *sopping* sleeping bags. Had it been ten degrees colder, *they might have frozen to death.*

If you find that you rely too much on underlining to achieve emphasis, consult Chapter 18 for other techniques to help you accent your writing.

EXERCISE

Underline (italicize) words and phrases as needed in the following sentences, or circle any unnecessarily italicized words or phrases.

Example:

Eric Clapton's album Layla shows his superb guitar style.
Eric Clapton's album <u>Layla</u> shows his superb guitar style.

1. The clock has long since been stolen, but the sign below its old spot still reads tempus fugit.
2. The lecture made me so *angry* that I had to leave in the middle of it.
3. Esquire was the forerunner of magazines like Playboy, Penthouse, and GQ.
4. No matter how many times I say it, the word euphemism comes out wrong.
5. The Chronicle and the Examiner are San Francisco's major newspapers.
6. The *liqueur* smelled of almonds and tasted sweet and strong.
7. When Elizabeth Taylor and Richard Burton fell in love on the set of Cleopatra, their romance was described as une grande passion.
8. According to the Chronicle of Higher Education, enrollments in business courses are climbing rapidly, whereas enrollments in the social sciences and humanities are plummeting.
9. The mountains were *so* beautiful that I had to *force* myself to leave them.
10. Whether he's watching 60 Minutes, Wide World of Sports, or the silliest situation comedy, Larry is happy in front of the television.

ital

27

28

Abbreviations

Everyone uses certain standard abbreviations because they're convenient and readily understood. Nevertheless, only a few abbreviations are acceptable in general writing. For a list of abbreviations used in footnotes and bibliographies, see 35h.

28a

Use standard abbreviations for titles immediately before and after proper names.

BEFORE THE NAME	AFTER THE NAME
Dr. James Hsu	James Hsu, M.D.
Mr., Mrs., Ms., Hon.,	D.D.S., D.V.M., Ph.D.,
St., Rev., Msgr., Gen.	Ed.D., O.S.B., S.J., Sr.

Use abbreviations such as *Mr., Mrs., Ms., Rev., Hon., Prof., Rep., Sen., Dr.,* and *St.* (for *Saint*) only if they appear with a proper name. Spell them out in the absence of a proper name.

FAULTY	By then my head hurt so badly that I was forced to call the *Dr.*
REVISED	By then my head hurt so badly that I was forced to call the *doctor.*
REVISED	By then my head hurt so badly that I was forced to call *Dr. Kaplan.*

NOTE: The title *Ms.,* used before a name instead of *Mrs.* or *Miss* when a woman's marital status is unknown or irrelevant, is not actually an abbreviation, though it is followed by a period: *Ms. Judith Boyer.*

The abbreviations *Jr., Sr., Esq., M.D., D.D., Ph.D., S.J.,* and so

on, which generally fall after proper names, are usually not spelled
out.

> Rose Simonton, *Ph.D.*
> Edward James Giordano, *Jr.*

NOTE: You may use abbreviations for academic degrees without proper names.

> After seven years my brother finally received his *Ph.D.* in
> biochemistry.

28b

Familiar abbreviations and acronyms for the names of
organizations, corporations, people, and some countries
are acceptable in most writing.

An **acronym** is an abbreviation that spells a pronounceable
word. *Radar,* which we no longer capitalize, is an acronym for *"radio detecting and ranging."* Other acronyms include WHO,
UNESCO, and NATO. These abbreviations, written without periods,
are acceptable in most writing as long as they are familiar. So are
several familiar abbreviations of the names of organizations, corporations, people, and countries. When these abbreviate three or more
words, they are often written without periods.

ORGANIZATIONS	CIA, FBI, YMCA
CORPORATIONS	IBM, CBS, ITT
PEOPLE	JFK, LBJ, FDR
COUNTRIES	U.S.A. (or USA), U.S.S.R. (or USSR)

(See 20b for more information on when to use periods in
abbreviations.)

NOTE: If a name or term (such as *operating room*) is used often
in a piece of writing, then its abbreviation (*O.R.*) may be useful to
cut down on extra words. Spell out the full name at its first appearance, indicate its abbreviation in parentheses, and use the abbreviation from then on. However, if the term is used only once or twice,
the abbreviation will serve no useful purpose and may even confuse
readers. In that case spell out the name or term each time it occurs.

> In the fall of 1975 a group of colleges and universities in the
> Southeast began to work together under the leadership of the
> Project on Institutional Renewal through the Improvement of
> Teaching (PIRIT). The following year another group of colleges
> and universities, these from the Midwest, also joined the project.
> By 1977 PIRIT included sixteen colleges and universities spread
> out over a large geographical area.

ab
28b

28c

Use the abbreviations B.C., A.D., A.M., P.M., *no.*, and the symbol *$* with specific dates and numbers only.

Notice that B.C. ("before Christ") always follows a date, whereas A.D. (*anno Domini,* Latin for "year of our Lord") always precedes a date.

44 B.C.	8:05 P.M.	no. 36
A.D. 1492	11:26 A.M.	$7.41

NOTE: As shown here, B.C., A.D., A.M. and P.M. are set in small capital letters, which is a printer's convention. In handwriting and typewriting, use capitals for B.C. and A.D. (B.C., A.D.) and either capitals or lowercase letters for A.M. and P.M. (A.M., a.m., P.M., p.m.). The abbreviation for *number* may be either capitalized or not (No., no.).

28d

Generally, reserve common Latin abbreviations such as *i.e., e.g.,* and *etc.* for use in footnotes, bibliographies, and comments in parentheses.

i.e.	that is (*id est*)
c.f.	compare (*confer*)
e.g.	for example (*exempli gratia*)
et al.	and others (*et alii*)
etc.	and so forth (*et cetera*)
N.B.	note well (*nota bene*)

He said he would be gone a fortnight (i.e., two weeks).
Bloom et al., editors, *Anthology of Light Verse*
Trees, too, are susceptible to disease (e.g., Dutch elm disease).

ab
28e

28e

Don't use *Inc., Bros., Co.,* or the ampersand (*&* for *and*) except when they are part of the official name of a business firm.

FAULTY   *The Santini bros.* operate a large moving firm in New York City.

REVISED   *Santini Bros.* is a large moving firm in New York City.

REVISED	*The Santini brothers* operate a large moving firm in New York City.
FAULTY	As a child I read every story about the Hardy Boys & Nancy Drew.
REVISED	As a child I read every story about the Hardy Boys *and* Nancy Drew.

28f

In most writing don't abbreviate units of measurement; geographical names; names of days, months, and holidays; names of people; courses of instruction; and labels for divisions of written works.

UNITS OF MEASUREMENT

The dog is thirty *inches* (not *in.*) high.
Dig a hole six *feet* (not *ft.*) deep.

EXCEPTIONS: Long phrases such as *miles per hour* (m.p.h.) or *cycles per second* (c.p.s.) are conventionally abbreviated and may or may not be punctuated with periods: *The speed limit on that road was once 75 m.p.h.* (or *mph*).

GEOGRAPHICAL NAMES

The publisher is in *Massachusetts* (not *Mass.* or *MA*).
He came from Aukland, *New Zealand* (not *N.Z.*).
She lived on Morrissey *Boulevard* (not *Blvd.*).

EXCEPTIONS: The United States is conventionally referred to as the U.S.A. (USA) or the U.S., and the Soviet Union as the U.S.S.R. (USSR).

ab
28f

NAMES OF DAYS, MONTHS, AND HOLIDAYS

The truce was signed on *Tuesday* (not *Tues.*), *January* (not *Jan.*) 16.

NAMES OF PEOPLE

James (not *Jas.*) Bennett ran for that seat.
Robert (not *Robt.*) Frost writes accessible poems.

COURSES OF INSTRUCTION

I'm majoring in *political science* (not *poli. sci.*).
Economics (not *econ.*) is a tough course.

LABELS FOR DIVISIONS OF WRITTEN WORKS

The story begins on *page* (not *p.*) 15.
Read *Chapter* (not *Ch.*) 6.
We finally finished *Volume* (not *Vol.*) I of our history text.

EXERCISE

Revise the following sentences as needed to correct faulty use of abbreviations. Circle the number preceding each sentence in which the abbreviations are already correct as written.

Example:

Our English prof. told us that the novelist George Eliot was a woman.

Our English *professor* told us that the novelist George Eliot was a woman.

1. They bought a house with 100 ft. of lake frontage.
2. Mount Vesuvius erupted in *anno Domini* 79 and buried Pompeii.
3. Mr. and Mrs. Harold Marsh, Jr., donated a new wing for the library.
4. The city built a new office building at the corner of Juniper and Cowen Sts.
5. A good dictionary, e.g., *Webster's New Collegiate Dictionary* or *The American Heritage Dictionary,* will tell you whether to punctuate an abbreviation with periods.
6. FDR died on Thurs., Apr. 12, 1945, in Warm Springs, Ga.
7. The Lynch bros., Wm. & Robt., went bankrupt in the same year.
8. The Cold War between the U.S. and the U.S.S.R. dominated international affairs in the 1950s.
9. They asked the rev. to marry them on horseback.
10. There, in the middle of Ch. 6, between pp. 128 & 129, was a leaf my mother had pressed as a child.

ab
28

29

Numbers

Writers vary in their choice between writing numbers out and using figures. In scientific and technical writing, numbers are usually written as figures. In general writing, numbers are more often spelled out. The rules below give conventions for general writing.

29a

Use figures for any number that requires more than two words to spell out.

The leap year has *366* days.
The population of Minot, North Dakota, is about *32,500*.

A hyphenated number can be considered as one word.

The ball game drew *forty-two thousand* people.

Spell out numbers of two words or less. (See also 29b.)

That hotel can accommodate no more than *seventy-five* people.
The first writing we know of was done over *six thousand* years ago.
The museum's collection included almost *twelve hundred* drawings and paintings.

29b

Use figures for days and years; numbers of pages, books, volumes, acts, scenes, and lines; numbers containing decimals, percentages, and fractions; addresses; scores and statistics; exact amounts of money; and the time of day.

DAYS AND YEARS

June 18, 1981   A.D. 12   456 B.C.

EXCEPTION: The day of a month may be expressed in words (*June fifth; October first*) when it is not followed by a year.

NUMBERS OF PAGES, BOOKS, VOLUMES, ACTS, SCENES, LINES	NUMBERS CONTAINING DECIMALS, PERCENTAGES, AND FRACTIONS
page 123	22.5
Encylopaedia Britannica, Volume 14	48% (or 48 percent)
Hamlet, Act V, Scene 3, lines 35–40.	3½

ADDRESSES	SCORES AND STATISTICS
355 Clinton Avenue	21 to 7
419 Stonewall Street	a mean of 26
Washington, D.C. 20036	a ratio of 8 to 1

EXACT AMOUNTS OF MONEY	THE TIME OF DAY
$4.50	9:00
$3.5 million	3:45
$2,763.00 (or $2763.00)	2:30

EXCEPTIONS: Round dollar or cent amounts of only a few words may be expressed in words: *seventeen dollars; fifteen hundred dollars; sixty cents.* When the word *o'clock* is used for the time of day, also express the number in words: *two o'clock; twelve o'clock.*

29c

Always spell out numbers that begin sentences.

num
29c

We are so accustomed to seeing a capital letter at the beginning of a sentence that a number there can make reading difficult. Therefore, always spell out any number that begins a sentence. If the number requires more than two words, avoid further awkwardness by rewording the sentence so the number falls later and can be expressed as a figure.

AWKWARD	*1974* was the climax of the Watergate scandal.
AWKWARD	*Nineteen hundred and seventy-four* was the climax of the Watergate scandal.
REVISED	*The year 1974* was the climax of the Watergate scandal.

EXERCISE

Revise the following sentences to correct the use of numbers. Circle the number preceding each sentence in which numbers are already used appropriately.

Example:

The 15 texts for my courses cost me one hundred and twelve dollars.

The *fifteen* texts for my courses cost me *$112.00.*

1. A meter is equal to just over thirty-nine inches.
2. Turn to page ninety-nine, and study the figure there.
3. I was born on May fifteenth, six days after my dog.
4. Peter Minuit bought Manhattan Island from the Indians for twenty-four dollars.
5. The school had to rent two buses, since the largest one they had seated only sixty (60) people.
6. 166 people this year installed our solar-heating system in their homes.
7. He ran several 2-mile laps.
8. A disappointing fifty-two percent of the voters showed up at the polls.
9. The new school cost a million and three-quarters dollars.
10. Because of the snow, only two hundred and ten students attended the dance.

num
29

30

Word Division

As much as possible, avoid dividing words. If you must divide a word between the end of one line and the beginning of the next, do so between syllables. Put a hyphen at the end of the first line—never at the beginning of the second. Never divide the last word on a page, because in the act of turning the page the reader may forget the beginning of the word. If you are in doubt about how to break any word into syllables, consult a dictionary. Note, however, that not all syllable breaks are appropriate for word division. Use the following rules to decide when and how to divide words.

30a
Don't make a division that leaves a single letter at the end of a line or fewer than three letters at the beginning of a line.

FAULTY	She called me late last night to ask *a- bout* today's assignment.
REVISED	She called me late last night to ask *about* today's assignment.
FAULTY	Counseling is required for every child *abus- er.*
REVISED	Counseling is required for every child *abuser.*

30b
Don't divide one-syllable words.

Since one-syllable words have no break in pronunciation, they should not be divided.

FAULTY	The shiny, spinning space capsule *dropped* suddenly from the clouds.
REVISED	The shiny, spinning space capsule *dropped* suddenly from the clouds.

30c
Divide compound words only between the words that form them or at fixed hyphens.

Compound words are words made up of two or more words (*drawback, homecoming*). Their component words may be hyphenated (*well-paying, cross-reference*), in which case the hyphen is called **fixed.**

FAULTY	If you want to have friends, be *good-natured.*
REVISED	If you want to have friends, be *good-natured.*
FAULTY	Sherlock Holmes exemplifies the *mastermind.*
REVISED	Sherlock Holmes exemplifies the *mastermind.*

(See 34d for guidelines on when to use hyphens in compound words.)

30d
Avoid confusing word divisions.

div
30d

Some word divisions may momentarily confuse the reader because the first or second part by itself forms a pronounceable (or unpronounceable) unit that does not fit with the whole. For example: *poi-gnant, read-dress, in-dict.* Avoid word divisions like these.

CONFUSING	Her walking out of class was an act of *heroism.*
CLEAR	Her walking out of class was an act of *heroism.*
CONFUSING	He claims that stealing never bothered his *conscience.*
CLEAR	He claims that stealing never bothered his *conscience.*

EXERCISE

Revise the sentences below so that words are divided properly. Circle the number preceding each sentence in which word division is correct as given.

> *Example:*
>
> I thought Harry's joke was sidesplit-
> ting, but no one else even smiled.
>
> I thought Harry's joke was *side-*
> *splitting,* but no one else even smiled.

1. Instead of going to college, she joined the arm-
   y.
2. Each of the twenty-three apartments he looked at was rented before he could make a deposit on it.
3. Americans find any number of ways to keep from feeling mid-
   dle-aged.
4. While the photographers snapped pictures, Dan blush-
   ed with embarrassment.
5. After she had heard the answer, Dotty felt like an i-
   diot for asking her question.

VII
Effective Words

31

Controlling Diction

Diction is the choice and use of words. Controlling diction means using words that fit your purpose and express your meaning accurately and clearly. It means pruning all words that don't make your meaning more exact. Because the substance and the effectiveness of what you say come down to the words you choose, you will waste much of your effort at writing unless you develop a respect for words and a curiosity about their shades of meaning. The following sections describe criteria for choosing the appropriate and exact word, but they cannot cover all instances. You must rely on your own judgment to select words that fit into the context of what you are writing. The first rule, perhaps, is to be suspicious of the first word that comes to mind. The chances are good that you can discover another one with a shade of meaning that will sharpen your writing.

31a
Choosing the appropriate word

Words are appropriate when they suit the purpose of your writing, the image of yourself that you want to project, and the readers you are writing for. We all use different kinds of language—different sets of words—depending on the context in which we are speaking or writing. Talking to friends, for example, you might say of the new dean, *He can stand the heat from students, but he sure can't get his act together on the curriculum.* Writing an editorial for the college newspaper, however, you would say the same thing quite differently, perhaps writing, *Dean Albertazzi dealt with the recent student demonstration calmly and fairly, but his plans for curriculum reform are seriously muddled.* In each case the diction fits the occasion: you are relaxed and informal, using words like *sure*, *heat*, and *act*, when you talk to people you know well and share experiences with; and you are more formal, using words like *demonstration* and *seriously muddled*, when you write to a general audience.

Most of your writing in college and after will be analyzing, discussing, explaining, and sometimes defending your understanding and interpretation of events and ideas. The words appropriate to such writing, like the conventions of grammar and usage described earlier in this handbook, are those which educated readers and writers understand and use widely. The huge vocabulary in what is called educated English excludes words that only limited groups of people use and understand: slang, colloquial language, regional words and expressions, nonstandard language, obsolete words, technical terms, and pretentious words. These more limited vocabularies, discussed below, should be avoided or used only cautiously and in special contexts. If you are in doubt about the status of a word you want to use, always consult a dictionary (see 32c-2).

1
Avoiding slang

All groups—from musicians and computer scientists to vegetarians and gangsters—invent **slang,** novel and colorful expressions that reflect the group's special experiences and set it off from others. Unless we know the language of the underworld (or have a dictionary of such language), we will have trouble with a statement such as *Bang the fink if he won't chill,* which means, "Shoot the informer if he won't be intimidated by threats."

Slang displays endless inventiveness. Some gives new meanings to old words. The 1950s gave *cool* a meaning of "self-controlled" (*Stay cool*) or "pleasing, excellent" (*The movie was cool*). The 1960s adopted *freak* to describe a person on drugs (*a speed freak*) and, later, to describe anyone with long hair, patched jeans, and a fondness for drugs (*He's a freak, so I think you'll like him*). More recently, *into* has described personal commitment (*I'm really into plants*), and *get off* has meant "to become excited" (*I really get off on old Rolling Stones records*). Some slang borrows from other languages: our word *chow* ("food" or "a meal") comes from the Chinese *chao,* meaning "to stir or fry"; *hoosegow* ("jail") comes from the Spanish *juzgado,* "courtroom"; and *schlep* ("to lug" or "a clumsy person") comes from the Yiddish *schleppen,* "to drag." Sometimes the slang of a particular ethnic group is widely adopted by the rest of the population. *Out to lunch, put on ice,* and *pad,* for example, are contributions of black slang.

Among those who understand it, slang may be vivid, lively, and forceful. And some slang, such as *dropout* (*She was a high school dropout*), has proven so useful that it has passed into the general vocabulary. But most slang is flippant, short-lived, and meaningful only to a narrow audience. In addition, it is generally too vague and imprecise to communicate effectively. The writer who says that *many students start out pretty straight but then turn into freaks* not only has deprived her writing of seriousness but also hasn't said much about what specifically happens to the students. The same is true of this sentence: *The mayor has put out some new hype for the city.* In each case, avoiding slang and including specific detail would strengthen the sentence.

2
Avoiding colloquial language

Colloquial language designates the words and expressions that are appropriate to spoken language. Regardless of our backgrounds and how we live, we all try to *get along with* each other. We sometimes *get together with* our neighbors. We play with *kids*, *go crazy* about one thing, *crab* about something else, and in our worst moments try to *get back at* someone who has made us do the *dirty work*. These italicized words and expressions are not "wrong"; quite the contrary, more formal language would sound stilted and pompous in casual conversation.

Some informal writing that tries to create the casual, relaxed effect of conversation uses the language of speech intentionally. And some formerly colloquial words (*rambunctious*, *trigger* as a verb) have gained acceptance in more formal, written English. But the colloquial language so natural to conversation does not suit the exactness and precision needed in more formal college, business, and professional writing. In such writing you should generally avoid those words and expressions labeled "informal" or "colloquial" in your dictionary. Be especially careful to avoid mixing the different levels of diction.

appr
31a

MIXED DICTION	According to a Native American myth, the Great Creator *had a dog hanging around with him* when he created the earth.
CONSISTENT	According to a Native American myth, the Great Creator *was accompanied by a dog* when he created the earth.
MIXED DICTION	The events of Watergate were too complex to keep track of, but Nixon's resignation was *really wild*.
CONSISTENT	The events of Watergate were too complex to keep track of, but Nixon's resignation was *extraordinary* (or *exciting*).

3
Avoiding regional words and expression

All languages vary slightly from one area to another. In American English, regional differences are most marked in pronunciation. A Texan overhearing a conversation between a Bostonian and a Georgian will not mistake either of the speakers for a fellow Texan. But some regional differences also occur in vocabulary. Southerners may describe something as *right nice,* an expression rarely heard elsewhere. People in Maine invite their Boston friends to come *down* rather than *up* (north) to visit. In the Northeast, people *catch a cold* and *get sick,* but in some other parts of the country they *take a cold* and *take sick.* Regional expressions are perfectly appropriate in writing that addresses local readers and may give color and realism to regional description, but they should be avoided in writing intended for a general audience.

REGIONAL	My uncle was so angry I had to *general him around* for an hour.
GENERAL	My uncle was so angry I had to *avoid him* for an hour.

4
Avoiding nonstandard language

Words and grammatical forms called **nonstandard** never (or very rarely) occur in even the relaxed conversation of educated speakers, and they are entirely avoided in writing other than dialogue. Dictionaries label such words "nonstandard," "illiterate," or "substandard." Examples are *nowheres;* such pronoun forms as *hisn, hern, hisself,* and *theirselves;* *them* as an adjective, as in *them dishes, them courses;* the expressions *this here* and *that there,* as in *that there elevator;* verb forms such as *knowed, throwed, hadn't ought,* and *could of;* and double negatives such as *didn't never* and *haven't no.* Avoid nonstandard expression in both speech and writing.

appr
31a

5
Avoiding obsolete or archaic words and neologisms

Since our surroundings and the lives we lead are constantly changing, some words gradually pass out of use and others are created to fill new needs. **Obsolete** and **archaic** are dictionary labels for words or meanings of words that we no longer use but that appear in older documents and literature still read today. The label *obsolete* indicates that the word or a particular meaning is no longer used at all. Thus *enwheel,* meaning "to encircle," and *cote,* meaning "to pass," are now obsolete. The label *archaic* indicates that the word or meaning now occurs rarely and then only in special contexts, often poetic. The sense of *fast* meaning "near" (*fast by the school house*) and *belike,* meaning "perhaps," are archaic.

Whereas obsolete and archaic words have passed out of use, **neologisms** are words created (or coined) so recently that they have not come into established use. Some neologisms do become accepted as part of our general vocabulary. *Motel,* coined from *motor* and *hotel,* and *brunch,* meaning a combination of breakfast and lunch, are examples. But most neologisms pass quickly from the language. Newsmagazines have recently coined the words *equalimony* and *palimony* to refer to changing attitudes and court interpretations of alimony rights, but these words are unlikely to gain any wide use. Unless such words serve a special purpose in your writing and are sure to be understood and appreciated by your readers, you should avoid them.

6
Using technical words with care

All subjects from accounting to zoology use special words or give common words special meanings. Chemists speak of *esters* and *phosphatides,* geographers and mapmakers refer to *isobars* and *isotherms,* and literary critics write about *motifs* and *personae.* Golfers talk about *mashies* and *niblicks.* Printers use common words like *cut, foul,* and *slug* in special senses. Such technical language allows specialists to communicate precisely and economically with other specialists who share their vocabulary. But without explanation these words are meaningless to the nonspecialist. When you are writing for a general reader, avoid unnecessary technical terms. If your subject requires words the reader may not understand, be careful to define them. (See 31c-4 for a discussion of jargon, overly technical and inflated language.)

appr
31a

7
Avoiding pretentious writing

Any writing that is more elaborate and ornate than its subject requires will sound pretentious, that is, excessively showy. Good writers choose their words for their exactness and economy. Pretentious writers choose them in the belief that fancy words will impress readers. They won't.

PRETENTIOUS	Many institutions of higher education recognize the need for youth at the threshold of maturity to confront the choice of life's endeavor and thus require students to select a field of concentration.
REVISED	Many colleges and universities force students to make decisions about their careers by requiring them to select a major.

When either of two words will say what you mean, prefer the small word to the big one, the common word to the uncommon one. If you want to say *It has begun to rain,* say so. Don't say *I perceive that moisture has commenced to precipitate earthward.*

EXERCISE 1

Insert words appropriate for educated written English in the sentences below to replace slang, colloquialisms, regionalisms, nonstandard expressions, obsolete or archaic words, neologisms, technical words, or pretentious expressions. Consult a dictionary as needed to determine a word's appropriateness and to find suitable substitutes.

Example:

We did not tell our father we were going to the demonstration because we were afraid he'd get bent out of shape.

We did not tell our father we were going to the demonstration because we were afraid he'd *get angry.*

1. I had to stop reading A. Alvarez's book about suicide because it got too heavy.
2. A few stockholders have been down on the company ever since it refused to stop conducting business in South Africa.
3. The most stubborn members of the administration still will not hearken to our pleas for a voice in college doings.
4. My new quadraphonic stereo system, which plays music out of four speakers, is quadriffic.
5. I almost failed Western Civ, because the jerk who borrowed my notes lost them.
6. We realized after we asked him to cut class with us that he might queer the afternoon by ratting on us.
7. Her arm often aches, but she says it doesn't bother her none.
8. Because he understands the finest intricacies of democratic management and can covertly manipulate the most recalcitrant legislator, we should return the governor to his position as chief executive of our fair state.
9. Whenever I hear someone boast about the famous people he or she knows, I suspect a put-on.
10. The lecture on Charlemagne was fantastic, but I missed some of it because the mike kept going on the blink.

appr

31a

31b
Choosing the exact word

Good writers labor to find the word within the large vocabulary of educated English that fits their meaning, that says precisely what they want to say and with exactly the overtones they intend. Inexact or fuzzy or inappropriate words weaken writing and often confuse readers.

1
Understanding denotation and connotation

A word's **denotation** is the thing or idea it refers to, the meaning listed in the dictionary without reference to any of the emotional associations it may arouse in a reader. Using words according to their established denotations is the first rule of clear diction. The person who writes *My dog is inflicted with fleas* or *Older people must often endure infirmaries* has, in mistaking *inflicted* for *afflicted* and *infirmaries* for *infirmities,* said something different from what was intended. The writer who says *The divergence between the estimate and the stadium's actual cost is surprising* has also missed the mark, though not as widely. The word needed is *discrepancy,* not *divergence.* The two words are second or third cousins, but they are not interchangeable. Some mistakes in word use occur because of confusion of **homonyms,** words that sound alike but have different spellings and meanings (for instance, *principle/principal* or *rain/reign/rein*). See 34a-1 for an extensive list of commonly confused homonyms and their meanings.

Writers miss the exact word they want more often by misjudging its connotation than by mistaking its denotation. **Connotation** refers to the association a word carries with it. Personal connotations derive from one's particular experiences. A person whose only experience with dogs was being bitten three times will have a different reaction to the word *dog* than will someone who lives with the warm memories of a childhood pet. People whose family lives are punctuated by quarrels and bitterness will react to the word *home* far differently than those who find their homes secure and comfortable. But in spite of such personal associations, most people agree about the favorable or unfavorable connotations of a word. To most readers, the connotations of *love, home,* and *peace* are favorable, whereas those of *lust, shack,* and *war* are unfavorable. Most of us would prefer to be described as *slim* rather than *skinny* or as *stout* rather than *fat.* And we would prefer to have our tastes described as *inexpensive* rather than *cheap.*

Synonyms are words with approximately, but often not exactly, the same meanings. Frequently, the differences in meaning are matters of connotation. *Cry* and *weep* are similar words, both denoting the shedding of tears; but *cry* connotes more of a sobbing sound accompanying the tears. *Sob* itself connotes broken, gasping crying, with tears, whereas *wail* connotes sustained sound, rising and falling in pitch, perhaps without tears. Used to fill in the blank in the sentence *We were disturbed by his _____ing*, each of these words would call forth different sounds and appearances. Tracking down the word whose connotation is exactly what you want can take time and effort. The best resource is the dictionary, particularly the discussions of synonyms and their shades of meaning at the end of many entries (see 32c-2 and 33c-2 for samples).

EXERCISE 2

Revise the sentences below to replace words that are not used according to their established denotations. If all the words in a sentence are used correctly, circle the number preceding the sentence. Consult a dictionary as needed.

Example:

Sam and Dave are going to Bermuda and Mattapan, respectfully, for spring vacation.

Sam and Dave are going to Bermuda and Mattapan, *respectively,* for spring vacation.

1. The enormity of the beached whale—and its horrible stench—both amazed and repulsed us.
2. My parents have the allusion that I will enter the family business when I graduate.
3. The ashen color of my father's face when he caught my brother shoplifting has convinced me never to steal.
4. The pond's water was always defiled, so we had to keep from imbibing it when we swam.
5. When students boycotted the school cafeteria, I was disinterested in their childish protest.
6. We've been without furniture for days, but now the movers are due to arrive momentously.
7. The sight for the new bank had formerly held apartments for seventy-five elderly people.
8. After trying continually to see my teacher for two weeks, I finally complained to the dean.
9. The affect of the town's hasty determination to close the library this summer has been to deprive poor people, expressly children, of books to read.
10. Having been deferred from acting on impulse, she felt paralyzed by indecision.

exact

31b

EXERCISE 3

Describe how the connotations of the italicized words in each sentence below contribute to the writer's meaning.

1. Hollywood, only four years away from the status of a *sheeptown without a Post Office*, was already the world's motion-picture *factory*.
   —Alistair Cooke

2. I want to tell you what she looked like and how she carried herself and how she sounded standing balanced *lightly* on her aluminum crutches, whistling to her peacocks who came *floating* and *rustling* to her, calling in their *rusty* voices.
   —Katherine Anne Porter on Flannery O'Connor

3. The song ended on a *long low* note, and then everything was silent except the sea, whose *shallow silver* waves made a little *hushing* sound, and were silent for an instant, and said *Hush!* again.
   —Randall Jarrell

4. *Totalitarian* countries preserve their secrecy by *regimenting* their people, giving them neither freedom of travel, freedom of the press, freedom of conscience, nor freedom of opinion.
   —I. I. Rabi

5. After a long straight *swoop* across the *pancakeflat* prairies, hour after hour of harvested land *streaked* with yellow *wheatstubble* to the horizon, it's exciting to see hills ahead, *dark* hills under clouds against the west.
   —John Dos Passos

2

Balancing the abstract and concrete, the general and specific

Abstract words name qualities and ideas—*inflation, depression, labor, management, beauty, truth, culture, integration, liberal, conservative.* **Concrete words** name things we can know by our senses—*bacon, apple, brick, grass, sweat, weeds, wood, stone, stove, pencil, book, mosquito, woodpecker.*

exact

31b

General words name classes or groups of things, such as *professional people*, and include all the varieties of the class. **Specific words** limit a general class like *professional people* by naming one of its varieties, such as *doctors, scientists, teachers,* or *public accountants*. The general term *bad weather* includes the specific varieties *rain, blizzard, windstorm, hurricane, tornado,* and *cyclone*. The class of *birds* includes *sparrows, eagles, geese, parrots, bobolinks,* and *vultures*. But *general* and *specific* are relative terms. *Doctor* becomes a general word in relation to *radiologist* and *surgeon,* and *surgeon* is general in relation to *neurosurgeon* and *orthopedic surgeon*. *Rain* is the general class for *drizzle, sprinkle,* and *downpour,* and *downpours* can be *continuous* or *sudden*. You become more and more specific as you move from a general class to a unique item, from *bird* to *pet bird* to *parrot* to *my parrot Moyshe.*

Good writing requires abstract and general words as well as concrete and specific ones. The abstract and general words are useful in the broad statements that set the course for your writing and tell readers what to expect.

> The wild horse in America has a *romantic* history.
>
> We must be *free* from *government interference* in our lives and affairs.
>
> My aunt was a *gentle, generous,* and *compassionate* woman.

But statements like these, which rely heavily on abstract and general words, mean little to a reader unless they are developed and supported by concrete and specific detail. Writing seldom fails because it lacks abstraction and general words. It fails because it lacks the concrete and specific words that nail down meaning and make writing vivid, real, and clear. In your own writing choose the concrete and specific word over the general and abstract. When your meaning does call for an abstract or general word, make sure you define it, explain it, and narrow it with concrete and specific words. Look at how concrete and specific detail turns vague sentences into exact ones in the example below.

Vague	The size of his hands made his smallness real.
Exact	Not until I saw his white, doll-like hands did I realize that he stood at least a full head shorter than most other men.
Vague	The long flood caused a lot of awful destruction in the town.
Exact	The flood waters, which rose swiftly and then stayed stubbornly high for days, killed at least six townspeople and made life a misery for the hundreds who had to evacuate their ruined homes and stores.

exact

31b

EXERCISE 4

For each abstract or general word below, give at least two other words or phrases that illustrate increasing specificity or concreteness. Consult a dictionary as needed. Use the most specific or concrete word from each group in a sentence of your own.

> *Example:*
>
> tired, *sleepy, droopy-eyed*
>
> We stopped for the night when I became so *droopy-eyed* that the road blurred.

1. cloth
2. delicious
3. car
4. narrow-minded
5. reach (*verb*)
6. green
7. walk (*verb*)
8. flower
9. serious
10. pretty

3

Using idioms

Idioms are expressions whose meanings can't be determined simply from the words in them or whose component words can't be predicted by any rule of grammar; often they violate conventional grammar. Examples are *put up with, plug away at,* and *make off with.* People learn the common idioms of their language naturally, just as they learn other common words, and generally they pose no problem for writers. But even experienced writers of English have difficulty with some idiomatic combinations of an adjective or verb and a preposition. For instance, *conform to the rules* is idiomatic, whereas *conform with the rules* is not. Some typical idioms are listed below for reference. Be sure to check a dictionary if you are unsure of what preposition to use with an idiom (see 32c-2).

in accordance *with*
according *to*

accuse *of* a crime

agree *with* a person
agree *to* a proposal
agree *on* a plan

angry *with*

capable *of*

charge *for* a purchase
charge *with* a crime

concur *with* a person
concur *in* an opinion

contend *with* a person
contend *for* a principle

differ *with* a person
differ *from* in appearance
differ *about* or *over* a question

independent *of*

impatient *at* her conduct
impatient *of* restraint
impatient *for* a raise
impatient *with* a person

inferior *to*

occupied *by* a person
occupied *in* study
occupied *with* a thing

part *from* a person
part *with* a possession

prior *to*

rewarded *by* the judge
rewarded *for* something done
rewarded *with* a gift

superior *to*

wait *at* a place
wait *for* a train, a person
wait *on* a customer

EXERCISE 5

Insert the preposition in each sentence below that correctly completes the idiom. Consult the preceding list or a dictionary as needed.

> *Example:*
>
> I disagree _____ many feminists who say women should not be homemakers.
>
> I disagree *with* many feminists who say women should not be homemakers.

1. He had waited for years, but as the time came nearer he grew impatient _____ the money that she would leave to him.
2. Sarah felt that her success was a fluke, that she was incapable _____ pleasing an audience.
3. They agreed _____ most things, but they differed consistently _____ how to raise their child.
4. I was rewarded _____ my persistence _____ an opportunity to meet the senator.
5. Compared _____ her old Volkswagen, her new car looks quite sporty.

4
Using figurative language

Figurative language expresses or implies comparisons between different ideas or objects. The sentence *As I try to write, I can think of nothing to say* is a literal statement. The sentence *As I try to write, my mind is a blank slab of black asphalt* is a figurative statement. The abstract concept of having nothing to say has become concrete, something the reader can visualize. The blank slab of black asphalt is bare, hard, and unyielding, just as the frustrated writer's mind seems bare, resisting all attempts to write.

Figurative language is commonplace. We sprinkle our conversation with figures: Having *slept like a log*, we get up to find it *raining cats and dogs* but have to *pluck up our courage* and *battle the storm*. The sports pages abound in figurative language: The Yankees *shell* the Royals, the Cowboys *embark* on another season, and basketball players make *barrels* of money. Slang is largely figurative: You get *bent out of shape* by math, so the whole course is *a bad trip*.

Speech gives little time for inventiveness, and most figures of daily conversation, like hastily written news stories, are worn and hackneyed. But writing gives you time to reject the tired figure and to search out the fresh words and phrases that will carry meaning concretely and vividly.

The two major figures of speech are the **simile** and the **metaphor.** Both compare two things of different classes, often one

exact
31b

abstract and the other concrete. A simile makes the comparison explicit, usually beginning with *like* or *as*.

> We force their [children's] growth as if they were chicks in a poultry factory.
>
> —Arnold Toynbee

> When he tried to think of the future he was like some blundering insect that tries, again and again, to climb up the smooth wall of a dish into which it has fallen.
>
> —Robert Penn Warren

> To hold America in one's thoughts is like holding a love letter in one's hand—it has so special a meaning.
>
> —E. B. White

Rather than stating it, the metaphor implies the comparison, omitting such words as *like* or *as*.

> Heavy and dragging at its end, at its outset every war means an explosion of imaginative energy. The dams of routine burst, and boundless prospects open.
>
> —William James

> A school is a hopper into which children are heaved while they are young and tender; therein they are pressed into certain standard shapes and covered from head to heels with official rubber stamps.
>
> —H. L. Mencken

> Cape Cod is the bared and bended arm of Massachusetts: the shoulder is at Buzzard's Bay; the elbow or crazy bone at Cape Mallebarre; the wrist at Truro; the sandy fist at Provincetown.
>
> —Henry David Thoreau

Metaphors can be extended into a whole paragraph, as Lewis Thomas does below in comparing a society of ants to an intelligent organism.

> A solitary ant, afield, cannot be considered to have much of anything on his mind; indeed, with only a few neurons strung together by fibers, he can't be imagined to have a mind at all, much less a thought. He is more like a ganglion on legs. Four ants together, or ten, encircling a dead moth on a path, begin to look more like an idea. They fumble and shove, gradually moving the food toward the Hill, but as though by blind chance. It is only when you watch the dense mass of thousands of ants, crowded together around the Hill, blackening the ground, that you begin to see the whole beast, and now you observe it thinking, planning, calculating. It is an intelligence, a kind of live computer, with crawling bits for its will.
>
> —Lewis Thomas

Two other common figures of speech, **personification** and **hy-**

perbole, are less common than metaphor and simile. Personification treats ideas and objects as if they were human.

> The economy digests my money faster than I can feed it.
> I could hear the whisper of snowflakes, nudging each other as they fell.

Hyperbole deliberately exaggerates.

> Absolutely anyone can set a world record.   —William Allen

> I'm going to cut him up in small cubes and fry him in deep fat.

To be successful, figurative language must be fresh and unstrained, calling attention not to itself but to the writer's meaning. If readers reject the language as trite or overblown, they will reject the message. One kind of figurative language gone wrong is the **mixed metaphor,** in which the writer combines two or more incompatible figures of speech.

> **MIXED**   He often hatched new ideas, using them to unlock the doors of opportunity.

Since metaphors often generate visual images in the mind of the reader, a mixed metaphor can create a ludicrous scene.

> **MIXED**   Various thorny problems that one would prefer to sweep under the rug continue to bob up all the same.

To revise a mixed metaphor, follow through consistently with just one metaphor.

> **IMPROVED**   Various thorny problems that one would prefer to weed out continue to sprout up all the same.

exact
31b

EXERCISE 6

Identify each figure of speech in the sentences below as a simile or a metaphor, and analyze how it contributes to the writer's meaning.

1. All artists quiver under the lash of adverse criticism.
   —Catherine Drinker Bowen
2. Louisa spends the entire day in blue, limpid boredom. The caressing sting of it appears to be, for her, like the pleasure of lemon, or the coldness of salt water.   —Elizabeth Hardwick
3. Every writer, in a roomful of writers, wants to be the best, and the judge, or umpire, or referee is soon overwhelmed and

shouted down like a chickadee trying to take charge of a caucus of crows.

—James Thurber

4. See enough and write it down, I tell myself, and then some morning when the world seems drained of wonder, some day when I am only going through the motions of doing what I am supposed to do, which is write—on that bankrupt morning I will simply open my notebook and there it all will be, a forgotten account with accumulated interest, paid passage back to the world out there. . . .

—Joan Didion

5. At best today it [the railroad in America] resembles a fabled ruin, a vast fallen empire. More commonly it suggests a stodgy and even dirtier-looking subway; a sprawling anachronism that conveys not ruin but mess, not age but senility, not something speeding across continents but stalled between stations.

—Louis Kronenberger

EXERCISE 7

Invent appropriate figurative language of your own (simile, metaphor, hyperbole, or personification) to describe each scene or quality below, and use the figure effectively in a sentence.

Example:

the attraction of a lake on a hot day
The waves *like fingers beckoned* us irresistibly.

1. the sound of a kindergarten classroom
2. people waiting in line to buy gasoline
3. the politeness of strangers meeting for the first time
4. a streetlight seen through dense fog
5. the effect of watching television for ten hours straight

5
Avoiding trite expressions

exact

31b

Trite expressions, or **clichés,** are phrases so old and so often repeated that they have become stale. They include worn figures of speech, such as *heavy as lead, thin as a rail, wise as an owl;* stale scraps from literature, such as *to be or not to be, trip the light fantastic, gone with the wind;* adjectives and nouns that have become inseparable, such as *acid test, crushing blow, ripe old age;* and simply overused phrases, such as *point with pride, easier said than done, better late than never.* Many of these expressions were probably once fresh and forceful, but constant use has dulled them. They slide almost automatically into your writing unless you are alert to them. If you let a few slip through, they will weaken your writing by suggesting that you have not thought about what you are saying and have used the easiest expression.

The following list contains some of the trite expressions you should work to avoid.

add insult to injury	ladder of success
beyond the shadow of a doubt	moving experience
brought back to reality	needle in a haystack
cool, calm, and collected	sadder but wiser
diabolical skill	on a silver platter
dyed in the wool	sneaking suspicion
face the music	sober as a judge
gentle as a lamb	stand in awe
hard as a rock	strong as an ox
hit the nail on the head	tried and true
hour of need	tired but happy

EXERCISE 8

Revise the sentences below to eliminate trite expressions.

> *Example:*
> The basketball team had almost seized victory, but it faced the test of truth in the last quarter of the game.
> The basketball team seemed *about to win*, but the last quarter of the game *tested it further.*

1. These disastrous consequences of the war have shaken the small nation to its roots.
2. The handwriting is on the wall: either cut the federal government down to size or face the music of having more bureaucrats than citizens.
3. When my father retired from the gas company after thirty long years, he was honored to receive a large clock in recognition of his valued service.
4. Sam shouldered his way through the crowd, hoping to catch a glimpse of the actress who had become the woman of his dreams.
5. After years of unprecedented prosperity and nearly uninterrupted peace and quiet, Americans have been brought back to reality by internal strife and economic confusion.

con

31c

31c
Being concise

The word *concise* comes from a Latin word meaning "to cut," and being concise in writing means cutting whatever adds nothing to your meaning. In revising your sentences, search for forceful and exact words and details that are essential to your meaning. Cross out all the empty words; cut out repetition that neither clarifies nor emphasizes your meaning; and be sure you have used the most direct grammatical form to express your ideas. Don't mistake brevity for conciseness; they are not the same thing. Concise writing states without wasting words but does not exclude the concrete and specific details that make meaning clear and exact.

1

Cutting empty words and phrases

Some words and phrases serve no purpose beyond filling space. Avoid these **filler phrases** and **all-purpose words,** or cut them when they sneak into your writing.

For each of the following filler phrases, a single simple word serves just as well.

For	Substitute
at all times	always
at the present time	now
in the nature of	like
for the purpose of	for
in order to	to
until such time as	until
for the reason that	because
due to the fact that	because
because of the fact that	because
by virtue of the fact that	because
in the event that	if
by means of	by
in the final analysis	finally

Some filler phrases—such as *all things considered, as far as I'm concerned,* and *for all intents and purposes*—can be cut entirely with no loss in meaning.

Wordy	For all intents and purposes, few women have yet achieved equal pay for equal work.
Concise	Few women have yet achieved equal pay for equal work.

All-purpose words such as *angle, area, aspect, case, character, factor, field, kind, situation,* and *type* almost always lead to wordy and unnecessarily complicated sentences.

Wordy	Because of the fact that I chose the area of chemistry as my major, the whole character of my attitude toward learning has changed.
Concise	My choice of chemistry as a major has changed my attitude toward learning.

WORDY	The type of large expenditures on advertising that manufacturers must make is a very important aspect of the cost of detergent cleansers.
CONCISE	Large advertising expenditures increase the cost of detergents.

EXERCISE 9

Revise the following sentences as necessary to achieve conciseness. Concentrate on cutting filler phrases and all-purpose words.

> *Example:*
>
> I came to college because of many factors, but most of all because of the fact that I want a career in medicine.
>
> I came to college *primarily because* I want a career in medicine.

1. When making plans of any sort, one cannot discount the element of chance.
2. The fact is that people are too absorbed in their own lives to care much what happens to others.
3. The baseball situation I like best is when the game seems to be over, for all intents and purposes, and the home team's slugger hits the winning run out of the park.
4. The nature of cooking—the attention to detail it demands and the creativity it allows—is what drew me into cooking school.
5. One aspect of majoring in Asian studies is a distinct drawback: except for a few rare teaching and curatorial positions, jobs are not available now and probably will not be available for some time to come.

2
Avoiding unnecessary repetition

Deliberately repeating words for parallelism or emphasis may clarify meaning and enhance coherence (see 17b and 18b). But unnecessary repetition weakens sentences. Avoid the kind of flabby repetition illustrated in the following examples.

con
31c

WORDY	When he died, Fitzgerald was writing a book that promised to be his best book.
CONCISE	When he died, Fitzgerald was writing what promised to be his best book.
WORDY	The plane was flying directly in the direction of Dallas when it crashed.
CONCISE	The plane was flying toward Dallas when it crashed.

WORDY	The machine crushes the ore into fine bits and dumps the crushed ore into a bin.
CONCISE	The machine pulverizes the ore and then dumps it into a bin.

Notice that using one word two different ways within a sentence is especially confusing.

CONFUSING	In grade school and high school I always had good grades.
CLEAR	In both grammar and high school I always had good grades.

The simplest kind of useless repetition is the **redundant phrase,** a phrase that says the same thing twice, such as *few in number* and *large in size.* Some of the most common redundant phrases are listed below. (The unneeded words are italicized.)

biography *of his life*	large (small) *in size*
consensus *of opinion*	puzzling *in nature*
cooperate *together*	repeat *again*
final completion	return *again*
habitual custom	square (round, oblong) *in shape*
important (*basic*) essentials	*surrounding* circumstances

A related form of redundancy is repetition of the same idea in slightly different words. In the sentences below the unneeded phrases are italicized.

WORDY	We planned to meet just before sunrise *very early in the morning.*
WORDY	Many unskilled workers *without training in a particular job* are unemployed *and don't have any work.*

con

31c

EXERCISE 10

Revise the following sentences to achieve conciseness. Concentrate on eliminating unnecessary or confusing repetition and redundancy.

Example:

In today's world in the last quarter of the twentieth century, security is a more compelling goal than social reform.

In today's world (or *In the last quarter of the twentieth century*), security is a more compelling goal than social reform.

1. The circumstances that surround the cancellation of classes are murky and unclear, but the vice-provost showed some class by telling us what he knew.

2. Deadly nightshade is aptly named. It has small white flowers and deep black fruit. The fruit looks like night, and it also looks like death. The fruit does happen to be poisonous, too.
3. The fire that destroyed my apartment also destroyed my books and papers. Now, with the research for my thesis destroyed, I'll have to start it all over again from the beginning.
4. The disastrous drought was devastating to crops, but the farmers cooperated together to help each other out.
5. In his autobiography of his life, and particularly in his version of the Watergate scandal, Richard Nixon rehashed old claims and did not reveal anything new.

3
Simplifying word groups and sentences

Choose the simplest and most direct grammatical construction that fits your meaning. Don't use a clause if a phrase will do; don't use a phrase if a word will do. *The strength that the panther has, the strength of the panther,* and *the panther's strength* mean the same thing. But the first takes six words, the last only three.

WORDY	The figurine, which was carved and made of ivory, measured three inches.
REVISED	The figurine, carved of ivory, measured three inches.
CONCISE	The carved ivory figurine measured three inches.
WORDY	On a corner of Main Street a man was selling mice that were mechanical.
CONCISE	On a Main Street corner a man was selling mechanical mice.

(See 16b for advice on the ways to subordinate information.)

You can streamline and strengthen sentences by choosing strong verbs that advance the action rather than weak verbs that mark time. Weak verbs, along with their usual baggage of inflated nouns and unnecessary adjectives and prepositional phrases, weaken a sentence just where it should be strongest and pad it with useless words. The sentence below conveys its simple meaning with minimum words.

con
31c

CONCISE	The painting *glorifies* Queen Victoria.

The following sentence adds no information but takes on three more words and sacrifices its power.

WORDY	The painting *is a glorification of* Queen Victoria.

In the second sentence the direct, evocative verb *glorifies* changes to the long noun *glorification* (which then requires a prepositional phrase), and the colorless linking verb *is* takes its place. Wordy constructions of a weak verb like *is, has,* or *make* plus an adjective or noun commonly clutter writing.

WORDY	I *am desirous* of teaching music to children.
CONCISE	I *want* to teach music to children.
WORDY	He *had the sense* that she would die.
CONCISE	He *sensed* that she would die.
WORDY	Though they *made some advancement* over the next hours, they still failed to reach camp.
CONCISE	Though they *advanced* over the next hours, they still failed to reach camp.

Passive constructions usually contain more words (and much more indirectness) than active constructions. Revise passive constructions by shifting their verbs to the active voice and positioning the actor as the subject.

WORDY	*The building had been designed by architects* six years earlier, and *the plans had been reviewed by no one* before *construction was begun.*
CONCISE	*Architects had designed the building* six years earlier, and *no one had reviewed the plans* before *construction began.*

Whenever possible, avoid sentences beginning with the expletive constructions *there is* and *there are.* Revise expletive constructions by removing *there,* moving the subject to the beginning of the sentence, and substituting the strong verb for *is* or *are.*

WORDY	*There are several different plots that occur* repeatedly in television drama.
CONCISE	*Several different plots occur* repeatedly in television drama.

con
31c

EXERCISE 11

Make the following sentences concise. Simplify grammatical structures, replace weak verbs with strong ones, and eliminate passive and expletive constructions.

Example:

He was taking some exercise in the park when several thugs were suddenly ahead in his path.

He was *exercising* (or *jogging* or *strolling* or *doing calisthenics*) in the park when several thugs suddenly *loomed* in his path.

1. The new goalposts were torn down by vandals before the first game, and the science building windows were broken.
2. The house on Hedron Street that is brightly lit belongs to a woman who was once a madam.
3. I am aware that most people of about my age are bored by politics, but I myself am becoming more and more interested in the subject.
4. When a social or economic reform takes root, such as affirmative action in education and business, it is followed shortly by backlash from those whom the reform has not directly benefited.
5. The attendance at the conference was lower than we expected, but there is evidence that the results of the meeting have been spread by word of mouth.

4

Avoiding jargon

Jargon is the special vocabulary of any group; medical and economic terms are examples. (See 31a-6.) But *jargon* is also commonly used to describe any vague, inflated language that states relatively simple ideas in unnecessarily complicated ways. The directions for using a shower head tell us that *the nozzles with which this spray system is equipped will allow the user to reduce the mean diameter of the spray spectrum* instead of simply saying that *this nozzle will concentrate the spray.* Jargon often sounds as if the writer had studied all guidelines for being exact and concise and then had set out to violate every one.

JARGON	The necessity for the individual to become a separate entity in his own right may impel a child to engage in open rebelliousness against parental authority or against sibling influence, with resultant confusion on the part of those being rebelled against.
TRANSLATION	A child's natural desire to become himself may make him rebel against bewildered parents or siblings.
JARGON	Please interface with employees by spending time on the floor for information getting and listening to employees' inputs and feedbacks as they offer same.
TRANSLATION	Spend time with employees and listen to their complaints and suggestions.

con

31c

EXERCISE 12

Make the following passage concise. Eliminate jargon by cutting
unneeded or repeated words and by simplifying both words and
grammatical structures. Consult a dictionary as needed. Be
merciless.

Example:

The nursery school teacher education training sessions involve active interfacing with preschool children of the appropriate age as well as intensive peer interaction in the form of
role plays.

Training for nursery school teachers involves *interaction* with
preschoolers and *role playing with peers.*

At the end of a lengthy line of reasoning, he came to the conclusion that the situation with carcinogens [cancer-causing
substances] should be regarded as analogous to the situation
with the automobile. Rather than giving in to an irrational fear
of cancer, we should consider all aspects of the problem in a
balanced and dispassionate frame of mind, making a total of
the benefits received from potential carcinogens (plastic, pesticides, and other similar products) and measuring said total
against the damage done by such products. This is the nature
of most discussions about the automobile. Rather than responding irrationally to the visual, aural, and oral pollution
caused by automobiles, we have decided to live with them
(while simultaneously working to improve on them) for the
benefits brought to society as a whole by their use.

32

Using the Dictionary

Using a dictionary can strengthen your use of words. It can tell you what words fit your needs (see Chapter 31); it can help you build your vocabulary (see Chapter 33); and it can tell you how to spell words (see Chapter 34). It can answer most of the questions about words you may ask. In addition, it is a comprehensive source of general information. This chapter will show you how to choose a dictionary that suits your purpose, how to read a dictionary without difficulty, and how to work with a dictionary as a flexible, compact, and thorough word reference.

An ordinary dictionary records in an alphabetical list the current usage and meaning of the words of a language. To do this, it includes a word's spelling, syllables, pronunciation, origin, meanings, grammatical functions, and grammatical forms. For some words the dictionary may provide a label indicating the status of the word according to geography, time, style, or subject matter. It may also list other words closely related in meaning and explain the distinctions among them. Some dictionaries include quotations illustrating a word's history or special uses. Many dictionaries include additional reference information, such as an essay on the history of English, rules for punctuation and spelling, a vocabulary of rhymes, names and locations of colleges, and tables of weights and measures.

32a

Choosing a dictionary

1

Abridged dictionaries

Abridged dictionaries are the most practical for everyday use. Often called desk dictionaries because of their convenient size, they are economical. They usually list 100,000 to 150,000 words and concentrate on fairly common words and meanings. Though you may sometimes need to consult an unabridged or a more specialized dictionary, a good abridged dictionary will serve most reference needs for writing and reading. Any of the following abridged dictionaries, listed alphabetically, will be useful.

> *The American Heritage Dictionary of the English Language.* New college ed. Boston: Houghton Mifflin, 1978.

This dictionary's most obvious feature is its wealth of illustrations—more than 4000 photographs, drawings, and maps. The dictionary includes foreign words, abbreviations, and geographical and biographical names among the main entries. The definitions are arranged so the most central meaning comes first. Usage labels (*slang, informal,* and so on) are applied liberally. Many words are followed by usage notes, which reflect the consensus of a panel of one hundred writers, editors, and teachers. The dictionary uses as few abbreviations and symbols as practicable. It includes guides to usage, grammar, spelling, and punctuation, and an appendix on Indo-European roots.

> *Funk & Wagnalls Standard College Dictionary.* New York: Funk & Wagnalls, 1974.

This dictionary includes foreign words, abbreviations, and geographical and biographical names in the main alphabetical listing. Usage labels (*slang, informal,* and so on) are often applied, and definitions of words are usually arranged according to the frequency of their use. Appendixes deal with vocabulary building, reference works, punctuation, and manuscript preparation.

> *The Random House Dictionary of the English Language.* College ed. New York: Random House, 1975.

Based on the unabridged *Random House Dictionary* (see below), this dictionary includes abbreviations and biographical and geographical names in the main alphabetical listing. Its list of words is particularly up to date. Appendixes include a manual of style.

32a

> *Webster's New Collegiate Dictionary.* 8th ed. Springfield, Mass.: G. & C. Merriam, 1976.

This dictionary, based on the unabridged *Webster's Third New International Dictionary* (see below), concentrates on standard English and applies usage labels (such as *slang*) less frequently than do other dictionaries. Word definitions are listed in chronological order rather than in order of preferred meaning. The main alphabetical listing includes abbreviations, but geographical and biographical names and foreign words and phrases appear in appendixes, as does a manual of style.

> *Webster's New World Dictionary of the American Language.* 2nd coll. ed. Cleveland: William Collins + World, 1978.

This dictionary includes foreign words, abbreviations, and geographical and biographical names in the main alphabetical listing. The definitions of words are arranged in chronological order. Usage labels (*colloquial, slang,* and so on) are applied liberally, and words and phrases of American origin are starred. Appendixes dealing with punctuation and mechanics and with manuscript form are included.

2
Unabridged dictionaries

Unabridged dictionaries are the most scholarly and comprehensive of all dictionaries, sometimes consisting of several volumes. They emphasize the history of words and the variety of their uses. An unabridged dictionary is useful when you are making an in-depth study of a word, reading or writing about the literature of another century, or looking for a quotation containing a particular word. The following unabridged dictionaries are available at most libraries.

> *The Oxford English Dictionary.* 13 volumes plus 4 supplements (in progress). New York: Oxford Univ. Press, 1933, 1972, 1976. Also available in a compact, photographically reduced, two-volume edition, 1971.

This is the greatest dictionary of our language. Its purpose is to show the histories and current uses of all words. Its entries illustrate the changes in a word's spelling, pronunciation, and meaning with quotations from writers of every century. Some entries span pages. The main dictionary focuses primarily on British words and word uses, but the supplements include American words and uses.

32a

> *The Random House Dictionary of the English Language.* New York: Random House, 1973.

This dictionary is smaller (and less expensive) than many unabridged dictionaries (it has 260,000 entries compared to 450,000 in *Webster's Third New International*). Its entries and definitions are especially up to date. Its appendixes include a brief atlas with color maps and a list of reference books.

> *Webster's Third New International Dictionary of the English Language.* Springfield, Mass.: G. & C. Merriam, 1976.

This dictionary attempts to record our language more as it *is* used than as it *should* be used. Therefore, usage labels (such as *slang*) are minimal. Definitions are given in order of appearance in the language. Most acceptable spellings and pronunciations are provided. Plentiful illustrative quotations show variations in uses of words. The dictionary is unusually strong in new scientific and technical terms.

3
Special dictionaries

Special dictionaries limit their attention to a single kind of word (for example, slang, engineering terms, abbreviations), to a single kind of problem (synonyms, usage, word origins), or to a specific field (black culture, biography, history). Thus special dictionaries provide more extensive and complete information about their topics than general dictionaries do.

Special dictionaries on slang or word origins not only can help you track down uncommon information but also can give you a sense of the great richness and variety of language.

FOR INFORMATION ON SLANG

Partridge, Eric. *Dictionary of Slang and Unconventional English.* 7th ed. New York: Macmillan, 1970.

Wentworth, Harold, and Stuart Berg Flexner. *Dictionary of American Slang.* 2nd supp. ed. New York: Thomas Y. Crowell, 1975.

FOR THE ORIGINS OF WORDS

Morris, William, and Mary Morris. *Dictionary of Word and Phrase Origins.* 3 vols. New York: Harper & Row, 1971.

Partridge, Eric. *Origins: A Short Etymological Dictionary of Modern English.* 4th ed. New York: Macmillan, 1966.

32a

Two kinds of special dictionaries—a usage dictionary and a dictionary of synonyms—are such useful references for everyday writing that it is worthwhile to have one of each on your reference shelf. A dictionary of usage gives extensive discussions of the words, phrases, and constructions that cause frequent problems and controversy in writing.

FOR DISCUSSIONS OF ENGLISH USAGE

Follett, Wilson. *Modern American Usage.* Ed. Jacques Barzun. New York: Hill and Wang, 1966.

Fowler, H. W. *A Dictionary of Modern English Usage.* 2nd ed. Rev. and ed. Sir Ernest Gowers. Oxford Univ. Press, 1965.

A dictionary of synonyms provides lists of words closely related in meaning that are much more extensive than such lists in a general dictionary. Some dictionaries of synonyms contain extended discussions and illustrations of various shades of meaning.

FOR INFORMATION ABOUT SYNONYMS

Lewis, Norman. *The New Roget's Thesaurus of the English Language in Dictionary Form.* New York: G. P. Putnam's Sons, 1964.

Webster's New Dictionary of Synonyms. Springfield, Mass.: G. & C. Merriam, 1973.

See 35b for an extensive list of special dictionaries in fields such as literature, business, history, psychology, and science.

32b

Reading a dictionary's abbreviations and symbols

Dictionaries use abbreviations and symbols to get a lot of information into a relatively small book. This system of condensed information may at first seem difficult to read. But all dictionaries include in their opening pages detailed information on the arrangement of entries, pronunciation symbols, and abbreviations. And the format is quite similar from dictionary to dictionary, so becoming familiar with the abbreviations and symbols in one dictionary makes reading any dictionary an easy routine.

The following entry for the word *mistake*—from the unabridged *Webster's Third New International Dictionary*—shows the basic arrangement of material in a dictionary and one system of abbreviations and symbols. (A more detailed discussion of a dictionary's contents follows in the next section.)

32b

¹mis·take \mə'stāk\ *vb* mis·took \mə'stůk\, (')mi's-\ mis-tak·en \mə'stākən\ mistaking; mistakes [ME *mistaken,* fr. ON *mistaka* to take by mistake, make a slip, fr. *mis-* ¹mis- + *taka* to take — more at TAKE] *vt* 1 : to choose wrongly : blunder in the choice of ⟨ambition quite ~*s* her road —Edward Young⟩ ⟨*mistook* the track across the moors, and led the army into boggy ground —T.B.Macaulay⟩ 2 a : to take in a wrong sense : misunderstand the meaning or intention of ⟨don't ~ me; I will do exactly as I say⟩ ⟨had *mistaken* the meaning of her question —Carson McCullers⟩ b : to be wrong in the estimation or understanding of : MISINTERPRET ⟨*mistook* the class structure and ownership distribution of developed capitalism —Peter Wiles⟩ c : to make a wrong judgment of the character or ability of : UNDERESTIMATE ⟨they ~ their man if they think they can frighten me⟩ 3 a : to fail to recognize or to identify wrongly ⟨there's no *mistaking* him⟩ ⟨there's no *mistaking* that house⟩ b : to substitute incorrectly in thought or perception : take wrongly for someone or something else ⟨~ gush for vigor and substitute rhetoric for imagination —C.D.Lewis⟩ ⟨could be and often was *mistaken* for a farmer —H.S.Canby⟩ 4 : to be wrong in regard to (time) ⟨somehow *mistook* the hour . . . I had told her nine o'clock,

and she came at ten —Mary R. Rinehart⟩ ∼ *vi* **:** to be wrong **:** be under a misapprehension ⟨you *mistook* when you thought I laughed at you —Thomas Hardy⟩ ⟨if I ∼ not . . . the entire import of the illustration changes —John Dewey⟩ — **mis‧tak‧er** \-kə(r)\ *n*
²mistake \"\ *n* **1 :** a misunderstanding of the meaning or implication of something ⟨it is a ∼ to think that the supreme or legislative power of a commonwealth can do what it will —John Locke⟩ ⟨it is a great ∼ to think that the bare scientific idea is the required invention —A.N.Whitehead⟩ **2 :** a wrong action or statement proceeding from faulty judgment, inadequate knowledge, or inattention **:** an unintentional error ⟨it would be a ∼, however, to drain all bogs —*Boy Scout Handbook*⟩ ⟨gave him a ten-dollar bill in ∼ for a one⟩ **3** *law* **:** an erroneous belief **:** a state of mind not in accordance with the facts **syn** see ERROR — **and no mistake :** SURELY, UN-DOUBTEDLY ⟨he's the one I saw, *and no mistake*⟩

The dictionary gives two different entries for *mistake,* one for *mistake* as a verb, the other for *mistake* as a noun. Both entries are in **boldface** type, preceded by a small, raised number. The division between syllables is shown by a centered period in the entry (**mis‧take**). The pronunciation appears between reverse slashes (\ \ ). The symbols used in the pronunciation (such as ə) are explained in the front of the dictionary. The accented syllable is preceded by an accent mark ('). In the first entry, after the pronunciation, the abbreviation *vb* signals that *mistake* is a verb. Its principal parts and their pronunciations follow: past tense, past participle, present participle, and third-person singular present tense. Immediately after the principal parts comes the word's **etymology—** its history—in square brackets. Here we learn that *mistake* comes from a Middle English (ME) word, which comes from an Old Norse (ON) word made up of two parts. "More at TAKE" uses small capital letters to signal a cross-reference, indicating that more on the word's etymology may be found under the word *take.* After the etymology comes *mistake* as *vt,* transitive verb. Here four main meanings are provided, each with at least one illustrative quotation in angled brackets (⟨ ⟩). In the quotations and elsewhere in the entry, a swung dash (∼) substitutes for the word as it is entered: *mistake.* The main meanings **2** and **3** have three and two closely related submeanings, respectively, indicated by the boldface letters **a, b,** and **c.** In **2b** and **2c,** MISINTERPRET and UNDERESTIMATE in small capital letters indicate synonyms of these submeanings that are defined elsewhere in the dictionary. After the fourth meaning of the transitive verb *mistake,* the abbreviation *vi* indicates that it is also an intransitive verb. Its meaning and two illustrative quotations follow. The first entry ends with a noun (*n*), *mistaker,* that is derived from the verb *mistake.*

The second entry for *mistake* is simpler because the pronunciation is the same (shown by \" \ ), the etymology is the same, and the noun (*n*) has fewer forms and meanings than the verb. The word *law* just before the third meaning is a subject label indicating that the noun *mistake* has this special meaning in the area of the law. After the last meaning the boldface abbreviation **syn** indicates

32b

a **synonymy,** a discussion of synonyms. In this case "see ERROR" indicates that the full synonymy is presented under the entry for *error.* The final item in the entry is an idiomatic phrase employing *mistake: and no mistake.* Two cross-references serve to define the idiom, and a quotation illustrates its use.

EXERCISE 1

Look up the following words in a dictionary. Consult the dictionary's own explanations of its entries until you are sure you can explain what all the abbreviations and symbols mean.

1. silly   3. hard   5. aggravate
2. tuxedo   4. dictionary   6. evaluate

32c
Working with a dictionary's contents

1
Finding general information

The dictionary is a convenient reference for information of every sort. Most abridged dictionaries will tell you the atomic weight of oxygen, Napoleon's birth and death dates, the location of Fort Knox, the population of Gambia, what the Conestoga wagon of the Old West looked like, the origin and nature of surrealism, or the number of cups in a quart. Finding such information may require a little work—for instance, checking the entry *periodic table* or *element* as well as *oxygen;* or consulting an appendix of biographical names for Napoleon. But a dictionary is often the quickest and most accessible reference for general information when an encyclopedia, textbook, or other reference book is unavailable or inconvenient to refer to.

2
Answering specific questions

As we have seen in examining the entries for *mistake* in *Webster's Third New International* (see 32b), a dictionary provides specific information on a word's spelling, pronunciation, etymology, meanings, uses, synonyms, and so on. Now we will go into these a little more deeply and also touch on other information contained in a dictionary entry. The labeled parts of the two entries below— *conjecture* from the *American Heritage Dictionary* (referred to from now on as *AHD*) and *reckon* from *Webster's New Collegiate Dictionary*— are discussed in the sections below.

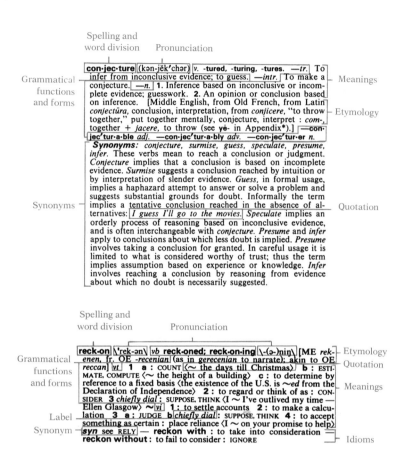

Spelling and word division — Pronunciation

Grammatical functions and forms — **con·jec·ture** (kən-jĕk′chər) *v.* -tured, -turing, -tures. —*tr.* To infer from inconclusive evidence; to guess. —*intr.* To make a conjecture. —*n.* **1.** Inference based on inconclusive or incomplete evidence; guesswork. **2.** An opinion or conclusion based on inference. [Middle English, from Old French, from Latin *conjectūra*, conclusion, interpretation, from *conjicere*, "to throw together," put together mentally, conjecture, interpret : *com-*, together + *jacere*, to throw (see **yē-** in Appendix*).] —**con·jec′tur·a·ble** *adj.* —**con·jec′tur·a·bly** *adv.* —**con·jec′tur·er** *n.*

— Meanings

— Etymology

Synonyms — **Synonyms:** *conjecture, surmise, guess, speculate, presume, infer.* These verbs mean to reach a conclusion or judgment. *Conjecture* implies that a conclusion is based on incomplete evidence. *Surmise* suggests a conclusion reached by intuition or by interpretation of slender evidence. *Guess,* in formal usage, implies a haphazard attempt to answer or solve a problem and suggests substantial grounds for doubt. Informally the term implies a tentative conclusion reached in the absence of alternatives: *I guess I'll go to the movies. Speculate* implies an orderly process of reasoning based on inconclusive evidence, and is often interchangeable with *conjecture. Presume* and *infer* apply to conclusions about which less doubt is implied. *Presume* involves taking a conclusion for granted. In careful usage it is limited to what is considered worthy of trust; thus the term implies assumption based on experience or knowledge. *Infer* involves reaching a conclusion by reasoning from evidence about which no doubt is necessarily suggested.

— Quotation

Spelling and word division — Pronunciation

Grammatical functions and forms — **reck·on** \′rek-ən\ *vb* **reck·oned; reck·on·ing** \-(ə-)niŋ\ [ME *rek-enen,* fr. OE *-recenian* (as in *gerecenian* to narrate); akin to OE *reccan*] *vt* **1 a :** COUNT ⟨~ the days till Christmas⟩ **b :** ESTIMATE, COMPUTE ⟨~ the height of a building⟩ **c :** to determine by reference to a fixed basis ⟨the existence of the U.S. is ~ed from the Declaration of Independence⟩ **2 :** to regard or think of as : CONSIDER **3** *chiefly dial* **:** SUPPOSE, THINK ⟨I ~ I've outlived my time — Ellen Glasgow⟩ ~*vi* **1 :** to settle accounts **2 :** to make a calculation **3 a :** JUDGE **b** *chiefly dial***:** SUPPOSE, THINK **4 :** to accept something as certain : place reliance ⟨I ~ on your promise to help⟩ **syn** see RELY — **reckon with :** to take into consideration — **reckon without:** to fail to consider : IGNORE

— Etymology

— Quotation

— Meanings

Label — Synonym

— Idioms

Spelling and word division

The lower case initial letters for both *conjecture* and *reckon* indicate that these words are not normally capitalized. (On the other hand, *Franklin stove* is capitalized in both the *AHD* and *Webster's Collegiate.*)

The centered periods in **con·jec·ture** and **reck·on** show the divisions of these words into syllables. If you are writing or typing a word of more than one syllable and need to break it at the end of a line, follow the dictionary's division of the word into syllables. (See also Chapter 30 for general rules about word division.)

If a word is a hyphenated compound word, such as *cross-reference*, a dictionary shows the hyphen as part of the spelling: **cross-ref·er·ence.** The treatment of foreign words such as *joie de vivre* or *ex post facto,* which are normally italicized (or underlined) in writing, is more varied. *Webster's New World Dictionary* places a special symbol (‡) before each one. The *AHD* simply designates them as *French* and *Latin*, respectively, thereby indicating they should be italicized.

Dictionaries provide any variant spellings of a word at the beginning of an entry. For the word *dexterous, Webster's Collegiate* has "**dex•ter•ous** *or* **dex•trous**"; whereas both the *AHD* and the abridged *Random House Dictionary* list "**dex•ter•ous. . . .** Also **dex•trous.**" *Webster's New World Dictionary* has a separate entry **dex•trous** but there says only "same as DEXTEROUS." In every case these dictionaries are indicating that the more common spelling is *dexterous,* although *dextrous* is acceptable.

EXERCISE 2

Check the spelling of the following words in a dictionary. Correct any incorrect spellings, and divide all the words into syllables.

1. England	5. inheritence	9. grievance
2. innoculate	6. over-estimate	10. secretery
3. recommend	7. depreciation	11. trans-Atlantic
4. methodical	8. excruciating	12. crosscultural

Pronunciation

The entries for *conjecture* and *reckon* show two slightly different systems for illustrating how to pronounce a word. In the *AHD*'s *conjecture* the pronunciation appears in parentheses; in *Webster's Collegiate* it appears in reversed slashes. In both entries the stressed syllable is indicated by an accent mark (ʹ and ˈ); but in *AHD* the mark follows the stressed syllable (kən-jĕkʹchər), whereas in *Webster's Collegiate* it precedes the stressed syllable (ˈrek-ən).

As these examples show, dictionaries also use symbols to indicate pronunciation of combinations of letters in a word, because the alphabet itself does not record all the sounds in the language (listen to the different sounds of *a* in only three words: *far, make,* and *answer*). Most dictionaries provide a key to their pronunciation symbols in their opening pages and at the foot of each page or every two facing pages. The key provides common words with sounds like the ones symbolized.

Most unabridged and some abridged dictionaries provide variant pronunciations, including major regional differences. *Webster's Collegiate,* for example, gives this Southern variation of the pronunciation of *great:* ˈgrāt, *South also* ˈgre(ə)t. And *AHD* provides two pronunciations for *licorice,* indicating that the last syllable may be pronounced either of two ways: lĭkʹər-ĭs, -ĭsh.

32c

EXERCISE 3

Consult a dictionary for the correct pronunciation of the following words. Write out the pronunciation as given, using the dictionary's symbols. (If more than one pronunciation is given, write them all out.)

1. crucifixion	5. generosity	9. theory
2. mnemonics	6. intellectual	10. yacht
3. timorous	7. miserable	11. promenade
4. exculpate	8. personable	12. stereophonic

Grammatical functions and forms

Dictionaries say a great deal about a word's function and forms. The *Webster's Collegiate* entry for *reckon* shows the word to be a verb (*vb*), with the past tense and past participle *reckoned* and the present participle *reckoning,* and with both transitive (*vt*) and intransitive (*vi*) meanings. The *AHD* entry for *conjecture* shows it to be an even more versatile word. It is a verb (*v.*): past tense and past participle *conjectured,* present participle *conjecturing,* and third-person singular present tense *conjectures.* The verb has both transitive (*tr.*) and intransitive (*intr.*) meanings. And *conjecture* is also a noun (*n.*), with separate meanings in that function.

Most dictionaries provide the principal forms of irregular nouns and verbs and the comparative and superlative forms of adjectives and adverbs that commonly show degree with *-er* and *-est.* The *AHD, Webster's Collegiate, Webster's New World,* and *Random House* all give the comparative and superlative forms of *happy* (*happier, happiest*). The lack of similar forms for *beautiful* in all these dictionaries indicates that its comparative and superlative are formed only with the words *more* and *most.*

When other parts of speech are formed from the word being defined and have the same basic meaning, those words are grouped at the end of the entry, where they are spelled, divided, accented, and identified by part of speech but not defined. The *Webster's Third New International* entry for *mistake* (pp. 369–70) included one of these so-called derivative forms (*mistaker*). Several are provided at the end of the *AHD* entry for *conjecture: conjecturable* (*adj.*), *conjecturably* (*adv.*), and *conjecturer* (*n.*).

The *Webster's Collegiate* entry for *reckon* ends with two uses of the word in idiomatic expressions (*reckon with* and *reckon without*). These phrases are defined (unlike the related parts of speech of *conjecture*) because, like all idioms, their meanings cannot be determined simply from the words they consist of (see 31b-3).

32c

EXERCISE 4

Consult a dictionary to determine the part of speech of each of the following words. If the word functions as more than one part of speech, list them all. If the word is a verb, list its principal parts; if a noun, its plural form; if an adjective or adverb, its comparative and superlative.

1. little	5. machine	9. upset
2. that	6. orient	10. steal
3. study	7. roof	11. manifest
4. happen	8. ring	12. firm

Etymology

Dictionaries provide the **etymology** of a word—its history—to indicate its origin and the evolution of its meanings and forms. The dictionary can compress a great deal of information about a word into a small space by using symbols, abbreviations, and different typefaces. These systems are explained in the dictionary's opening pages. The *AHD* traces *conjecture* first to Middle English (twelfth to fifteenth centuries), back through Old French (ninth to sixteenth centuries), and then to Latin. The final parenthetical reference to the Appendix directs us to a list of roots in Indo-European, the un-written parent language of most modern languages of India, Europe, and the Americas. Indo-European is thought to date back as far as 5000 B.C. (See 33a for a brief history of the English language.) As the entry in *Webster's Collegiate* shows, *reckon* came to English by a different route, arriving from Old English (OE) by way of Middle English (ME).

Sometimes dictionaries will not give the etymology for a word. Their practices differ (and are explained in their opening pages), but in general they omit etymology when it is obvious, available elsewhere, or unknown.

32c

EXERCISE 5

Consult a dictionary for the etymologies of the following words. Use the dictionary's own explanations of abbreviations and symbols to get the fullest history of the word, and write out that history in your own words.

1. mother	5. penetrate	9. calico
2. engage	6. promote	10. chauvinism
3. leaf	7. retrieve	11. assassin
4. moon	8. toxic	12. water

Meanings

Dictionaries divide the general meaning of a word into particular meanings on the basis of context, the sense of a word as it is actually used. They arrange a word's meanings differently, however, explaining the basis of their arrangement in their opening pages. *Webster's Collegiate* and *Webster's New World* list meanings in order of their appearance in the language, earliest first. The *AHD* and the abridged *Random House,* on the other hand, place the word's central or most common meaning first and follow it with the other meanings. When the oldest meaning of a word is also the most common, these different policies will result in roughly the same arrangement of meanings. Thus the first two meanings of *reckon* in *Webster's Collegiate*—COUNT and COMPUTE—are roughly the same as the first meaning in the *AHD*—"To count or compute." However, the different policies will also result in quite different arrangements. Whereas the *AHD*'s first meaning of the noun *conjecture* is "Inference based on inconclusive or incomplete evidence; guesswork," *Webster's Collegiate* begins with an obsolete meaning, "interpretation of omens," and doesn't get to the main current meaning until the end of the entry.

Most dictionaries provide any special technical and scientific meanings of a word in separately numbered entries that are usually labeled. We saw one such technical meaning for *mistake,* labeled *law,* in the *Webster's Third New International* entry reproduced earlier (p. 370). *Webster's New World* and the *AHD* both provide and label special grammatical, legal, and ecclesiastical meanings for the word *common. Webster's Collegiate* provides the same meanings separately but does not label them. (Labels are discussed in more detail below.)

When you consult a dictionary for the meaning of a word, be sure you know the system of arrangement used by the dictionary. Then read through the entire entry before settling on the meaning that most closely fits the context of what you're reading or writing.

32c

EXERCISE 6

Consult a dictionary for the meanings of the following words. How many different meanings does each word have? How does the dictionary list meanings—chronologically or in order of importance? If chronologically, is the oldest meaning also the most central? What changes have occurred in each word's use over time?

1. weight	5. order	9. prefer
2. recipe	6. apt	10. quit
3. color	7. astrology	11. rugged
4. condition	8. offered	12. sue

Synonyms and antonyms

Synonyms are words whose meanings are approximately the same, such as *small* and *little*. **Antonyms** are words whose meanings are approximately opposite, such as *small* and *big*. Dictionaries deal with synonyms and antonyms in varied ways. Most unabridged dictionaries devote considerable space to such related words; abridged dictionaries are usually more selective. When there are many closely related synonyms that are hard to distinguish, abridged dictionaries may devote a separate paragraph to synonyms. In its entry for *conjecture* the *AHD* uses a paragraph to distinguish the verb *conjecture* from the other verbs *surmise, guess, speculate, presume,* and *infer,* each of which can also be looked up in its alphabetical place. *Webster's Collegiate* uses synonyms to provide some of the meanings for *reckon.* The words in small capital letters (COUNT, ESTIMATE, COMPUTE, CONSIDER, SUPPOSE, THINK, JUDGE) are both synonyms and cross-references, in that each word may be looked up in its alphabetical place. At the boldface **syn** at the end of the entry, the phrase "see RELY" directs us to a brief treatment of synonyms at the entry for *rely.*

Antonyms are provided less often than synonyms but are identified in the same way, usually with a boldface **ant** at the end of the entry. *Webster's New World,* for instance, identifies the antonyms of *hard,* meaning "difficult," as *easy* or *simple.* Reading through the lists and discussions of synonyms and antonyms for a word can help you locate its meaning in a given context more exactly. (See 33c-2 for a discussion of how to use the synonyms provided by a dictionary to increase your vocabulary.)

EXERCISE 7

Consult a dictionary for the synonyms and antonyms of the following words. Use the word itself and each synonym or antonym appropriately in a sentence of your own.

1. suggest	4. discover	7. kind (*adj.*)
2. plain (*adj.*)	5. change (*v.*)	8. memory
3. high (*adj.*)	6. beautiful	9. serious

32c

Labels

Dictionaries use labels to indicate that a word or one or more of its meanings have a certain status or a special use. Generally, words considered appropriate for standard, educated English usage in all regions, such as *conjecture,* are not labeled by any dictionary. *Webster's Collegiate* uses fewer labels than other abridged dictionaries. The *AHD* and *Webster's New World* use slightly more labels. The labels are usually of four kinds: subject, style, region, and time.

Subject labels, like the label *law* in the *Webster's Third New International* definition of *mistake,* tell us that a word or one of its meanings has special use in a field of knowledge or a profession. In its entry for *relaxation,* for instance, the *AHD* provides general meanings such as "the act of relaxing" and "refreshment of body or mind." But it also provides special meanings with the subject labels *physiology* ("the lengthening of inactive muscle or muscle fibers"), *physics* ("the return or adjustment of a system to equilibrium"), and *mathematics* ("a numerical method in which the errors . . . resulting from an initial approximation are reduced").

Style labels restrict a word or one of its meanings to a particular level of usage, such as *slang, colloquial* or *informal, nonstandard* and *substandard, vulgar,* or *poetic* and *literary. Slang* indicates that a word should be used in writing only for a special effect. All the abridged dictionaries label *crumb* as slang when it is used to mean "a worthless or despicable person." The labels *informal* or *colloquial* are applied to words that are appropriate for conversation and informal writing but not for formal writing. For instance, the *AHD* labels as informal the use of *sure* in the sentence *We sure need that money* but not in *Sure of victory, the army camped for the night.* The labels *nonstandard* and *substandard* are applied to words or their meanings that are considered inappropriate for educated speech and writing. The *AHD* labels all uses of *ain't* as nonstandard. *Webster's New World* labels *I ain't* only as colloquial but labels other expressions such as *he ain't* and *we ain't* as nonstandard. *Webster's Collegiate* remarks that *ain't* is "disapproved by many" but labels expressions like *I ain't got* as substandard. The label *vulgar,* or sometimes *vulgar slang,* is applied to words or their meanings that are considered offensive in speech and writing. The labels *poetic* and *literary* designate words or their meanings used only in poetry or the most formal writing. The *AHD, Webster's New World,* and *Random House* all label as poetic the words *eve* for *evening* and *o'er* for *over.*

Region labels indicate that the particular spelling, pronunciation, or meaning of a word is not national but limited to some area. A regional difference may be indicated by the label *dialect.* In the *Webster's Collegiate* entry for *reckon* (p. 372), the uses of the word to mean "suppose" or "think" (as in *I reckon I'll do that*) are labeled as dialect (*dial*). More specific region labels may be applied to areas of the United States or to other countries. The word *bloke* (meaning "fellow") is labeled as British by most dictionaries. *Webster's New World* labels as Southern dialect the use of *carry* to mean "accompany." And the *AHD* labels *arroyo,* "a deep gully" or "a dry gulch," as Southwestern U.S.

32c

Time labels indicate words or their meanings that the language, in evolving, has discarded. These words and meanings are included in the dictionary primarily to help readers of some older texts that used them. The label *obsolete* designates words or specific meanings that are no longer used. As we saw above, *Webster's Collegiate* applies this label to the first and oldest definition of conjecture, "interpretation of omens." The label *archaic* designates words or specific meanings that are out of date though still in occasional use. The *AHD* applies this label for the word *affright*, a verb meaning "to arouse fear in" and a noun meaning "terror."

See 31a for further discussion of levels of usage and their appropriateness in your writing.

EXERCISE 8

Consult at least two dictionaries to determine the status of each of the following words or any one of their meanings according to subject, style, region, or time.

1. impulse	5. goof	9. mad
2. OK	6. goober	10. sing
3. irregardless	7. lift	11. brief (*n.*)
4. neath	8. potlatch	12. joint

Illustrative quotations

Dictionaries are made by collecting quotations showing actual uses of words in all kinds of speech and writing. Some of these quotations, or others that the dictionary makers invent, may be used in the dictionary's entries as illustrations of how a word may be used. Unabridged dictionaries tend to give many such examples, not only to illustrate a word's current uses but also to show the changes in its meanings over time. Abridged dictionaries use quotations more selectively—to illustrate an unusual use of the word, to help distinguish between two closely related meanings of the same word, or to show the differences between synonyms. The *AHD* entry for *conjecture* and the *Webster's Collegiate* entry for *reckon* (p. 372) both employ quotation.

32c

EXERCISE 9

Consult a dictionary to find a quotation illustrating at least one meaning of each word below. Then write an illustrative sentence of your own for each word.

1. jolt	4. ceremonial	7. legitimate
2. inarticulate	5. sensuous	8. inquire
3. discreet	6. tremble	9. nether

33

Improving Your Vocabulary

A precise and versatile vocabulary—the exact use of a variety of words—is essential to effective communication. As you gain experience with writing, you will want to strengthen the way you use familiar words (see Chapter 31) and increase the number of words you can use appropriately.

This chapter briefly describes the development of English and explains how words are formed. Then it offers some advice for learning to use new words. The chapter has a twofold purpose: to provide a sense of the potential of English by acquainting you with its history and range of words; and to help you increase the range, versatility, and precision of your own vocabulary.

33a
Understanding the sources of English

People change their language as they and their surroundings change. They revise spellings, pronunciation, and syntax, alter meanings, and even add or drop words to keep the language useful. English is continuously changing, but its subtle and complex character stays the same.

English has over 500,000 words, more than any other language. This exceptional vocabulary and the great power and range of expression that accompany it derive from its special mix of word sources. For English, unlike many other languages, has borrowed a large number of words.

How English drew on its several sources and acquired its large vocabulary is the story of historical changes. The ancestor of English, Indo-European, was spoken (but not written) perhaps as far back as 5000 B.C., and it eventually spread to cover the area from India west to the British Isles. In what is now England, an Indo-

European offshoot called Celtic was spoken extensively until the fifth century A.D. But over the next few centuries invaders from the European continent, speaking a dialect of another Indo-European language, Germanic, overran the native Britons. The Germanic dialect became the source of English.

Old English, spoken from the eighth to the twelfth centuries, was a rugged, guttural language, as the passage at the end of this paragraph illustrates. Old English used a slightly different alphabet from ours (including the characters ð and þ for *th*), which has been transcribed in the sample below. The sample shows the opening lines of the Lord's Prayer, which we know as "Our father, who art in heaven, hallowed be thy name. Thy kingdom come. Thy will be done on earth as it is in heaven."

> Fæder ure thu the eart on heofonum, si thin nama gehalgod. Tobecume thin rice. Gewurthe thin willa on eorthan swa swa on heofonum.

Many of our nouns, such as *stone, word, gift,* and *foot,* come from Old English. So do most of our pronouns, prepositions, and conjunctions, some—such as *he, under,* and *to*—without any change in spelling. Other Germanic tribes, using a similar dialect but settling on the European continent instead of in England, fostered two other languages, Dutch and German. As a result Dutch, German, and English are related languages with similar traits.

In 1066 the Normans, under William the Conqueror, conquered England. The Normans were originally Vikings who had settled in northern France and had given up speaking Old Norse for their own dialect of Old French. They made Norman French the language of law, literature, and the ruling class in England. As a result English acquired many French words, including many military and governmental words like *authority, mayor, crime, army,* and *guard.* The common English people kept English alive during the French Norman occupation, but they adopted many French words intact (*air, point, place, age*), and eventually the French influence caused the language to shift from Old to Middle English, which lasted from the twelfth through the fifteenth centuries. During this time a great many Latin words also entered English, for Latin formed the background of Norman French, and it was the language of the Church and of scholars. English words that entered Middle English directly from Latin or from Latin through French include *language, luminous, memory, liberal,* and *sober.*

Middle English, as the following passage from Geoffrey Chaucer's *Canterbury Tales* shows, was much closer to our own language than to Old English.

33a

> A clerk there was of Oxenford also,
> That unto logyk hadde longe ygo.
> As leene was his hors as is a rake,
> And he nas nat right fat, I undertake,
> But looked holwe, and therto sobrely.

Modern English began in the fourteenth and fifteenth centuries as the language's sound and spellings changed. This was the time of the Renaissance in Europe. Ancient Latin and Greek art, learning, and literature were revived, first in Italy and then throughout the continent. English vocabulary expanded tremendously, not only with more Latin and many Greek words (such as *democracy* and *physics*) but also with words from Italy and France. Advances in printing, beginning in the fifteenth century, made printed materials widely available to an increasingly literate audience. The Modern English of twentieth-century America is four centuries and an ocean removed from the Modern English of sixteenth-century England, but the two are fundamentally the same. The differences and the similarities are evident in this passage from the King James Bible, published in 1611:

> And the Lord God commanded the man, saying, Of euery tree of the garden thou mayest freely eate. But of the tree of the knowledge of good and euill, thou shalt not eate of it: for in the day that thou eatest thereof, thou shalt surely die.

33b
Learning the make-up of words

Words can often be broken down into meaningful parts. A *handbook*, for instance, is a book you keep at hand (for reference). A *shepherd* herds sheep (or other animals). Knowing what the parts of a word mean by themselves, as you do here, can often help you see approximately what they mean together.

The following explanations of roots, prefixes, and suffixes provide information that can open up the meanings and uses of words whose parts may not be so familiar or so easy to see. For more information, refer to a dictionary's etymologies, which provide the histories of words (see 32c).

33b

1
Learning roots

A **root** is the unchanging component of words related in origin and meaning. Both *illiterate* ("unable to read and write") and *literal* ("sticking to the facts or to the first and most obvious meaning of an idea") share the root *liter*, derived from *littera*, a Latin word meaning "letter." A person who can't understand the letters that make up writing is *illiterate*. A person who wants to understand the primary meaning of the letters (the words) in a contract is seeking the *literal* meaning of that contract.

At least half our words came from Latin and Greek. The list below gives examples of Latin and Greek roots, their meanings, and examples of English words that contain the root. (Many of the English words are made up of the root and a prefix or suffix. Other English words have two roots, in which case the second root is also listed and the English word is repeated.)

ROOT (SOURCE)	MEANING	ENGLISH WORDS
anthrop (G)	human being	anthropology
aster, astr (G)	star	astronomy, astrology
audi (L)	to hear	audible, audience
bene (L)	good, well	benefactor, benevolent
bio (G)	life	biology, autobiography
ceed, ced, cede (L)	to go	proceed, antecedent
chron (G)	time	chronological
crac, crat (G)	strength, power	democracy
dem (G)	people	democracy
dic, dict (L)	to speak	dictator, dictionary
fac, fic, fit, fy (L)	to do, to make	benefactor, magnificent
fer (L)	to carry	transfer, referral
fix (L)	to fasten	fix, suffix, prefix
geo (G)	earth	geography, geology
graph (G)	to write	geography, photography, telegraph
jur, jus (L)	law	jury, justice
log, logue (G)	word, thought, speech	anthropology, astrology, biology, chronological, geology, neologism, psychology
luc (L)	light	lucid, translucent
manu (L)	hand	manual, manuscript
mater, matr (L)	mother	maternal, matron
meter, metr (G)	measure	metric, thermometer
neo (G)	new	neologism, neoclassical
nom (G)	law	astronomy
op, oper (L)	work	operation, operator
pater, patr (L)	father	paternal, patron
path (G)	feeling	pathetic, sympathy
ped (G)	child	pediatrics
phil (G)	love	philosophy, Anglophile
phys (G)	body, nature	physical, physics
phos, phot (G)	light	photography

33b

Root (source)	Meaning	English words
psych (G)	soul	psychic, psychology
quer, ques (L)	to seek, to ask	query, question
scrib, script (L)	to write	scribble, manuscript
soph (G)	wisdom	sophisticated, philosophy
tele (G)	far off	telegraph, telephone, television
tempor (L)	time	temporal, contemporary
ter, terr (L)	earth	territory, extraterrestrial
therm (G)	heat	thermometer
uni (L)	one	unit, unify, universal
vac (L)	empty	vacant, vacuum, evacuate
verb (L)	word	verbal, verbose
vers (L)	to turn	reverse, universal
vid, vis (L)	to see	video, vision, television
vol (L)	to wish, to will	volunteer, benevolent
vol(v), volv (L)	to roll	evolution, involve

EXERCISE 1

Provide meanings for the following italicized words, using the list of roots and any clues given by the rest of the sentence. Check the accuracy of your meanings in a dictionary.

1. The plot of the soap opera was so *involuted* that it could not be summarized.
2. Always afraid of leading a *vacuous* life, the heiress immersed herself in volunteer work.
3. The posters *affixed* to the construction wall advertised a pornographic movie.
4. After his *auditory* nerve was damaged, he had trouble catching people's words.
5. The child *empathized* so completely with his mother that he felt pain when she broke her arm.

33b

2
Learning prefixes

Prefixes are standard syllables fastened to the front of a word to modify its meaning. For example, the word *prehistorical* is a combination of the word *history*, meaning "based on a written record explaining past events," and the prefix *pre-*, meaning "before." Together, prefix and word mean "before a written record explaining past events," or before events were recorded. Learning standard prefixes—many of them derived from Latin and Greek prepositions—can help you improve vocabulary and spelling just as learning word roots can. The following lists group prefixes according to sense so that they are easier to remember. (The same prefix may appear in more than one list because it may have more than one meaning, just as the English preposition *before* can mean either "earlier than" or "in front of.")

Prefixes showing quantity

MEANING	PREFIX (SOURCE)	ENGLISH WORDS
half	semi- (L)	semiannual
	hemi- (G)	hemisphere
one	uni- (L)	unicycle
	mon-, mono- (G)	monarch, monorail
two	bi- (L)	binary, bimonthly
	di-, dicho- (G)	dilemma, dichotomy
three	tri- (L,G)	triangle, trilogy
four	quadr-, quart- (L)	quadrangle, quart
	tetra- (G)	tetrachloride
five	quint- (L)	quintet
	penta- (G)	pentagon
six	sex- (L)	sextuplets
	hexa- (G)	hexameter
seven	sept- (L)	septuagenarian
	hept- (G)	heptarchy
eight	oct-, octo- (L,G)	octave, octopus
nine	nona- (L)	nonagenerian
ten	dec- (L)	decade
	deca- (G)	decathlon
hundred	cent- (L)	century, percentage
	hecto- (G)	hectoliter
thousand	milli- (L)	millimeter
	kilo- (G)	kilocycle

Prefixes showing negation

MEANING	PREFIX (SOURCE)	ENGLISH WORDS
without, no, not	a-, an- (L,G)	asexual, amoral
not	il-, im-, in-, ir- (L)	illegal, immoral, invalid, irreverent
	un- (OE)	unskilled, unknown
not, absence of,	non- (L)	nonbreakable, nonbeliever
opposing, against	ant-, anti- (L,G)	antacid, antipathetic
	contra- (L)	contrary, contradict
opposite to, complement to	counter- (F,L)	counterclockwise, counterweight
do the opposite of, remove, reduce	de- (L)	devitalize, dehorn, devalue

33b

MEANING	PREFIX (SOURCE)	ENGLISH WORDS
do the opposite of, deprive of, exclude	dis- (F,L)	disestablish, disarm, disbar
wrongly, bad	mis- (OE,OF)	misjudge, misdeed

Prefixes showing time

MEANING	PREFIX (SOURCE)	ENGLISH WORDS
before	ante- (L)	antecedent
	fore- (OE)	forecast, foretell
	pre- (L)	prenatal, precede
	pro- (L,G)	provide, prologue
occurring later	met-, meta- (G)	metazoan
after	post- (L)	postwar, postoperative
again	re- (L)	redo

Prefixes showing direction or position

MEANING	PREFIX (SOURCE)	ENGLISH WORDS
above, over	super- (L)	superior, supervise
below, under	infra-, sub- (L)	infrasonic, subterranean
	hypo- (G)	hypodermic, hypothesis
in front of	pro-, pre- (L)	proceed, prefix
	pro- (G)	proscenium
behind	re- (L)	recede, refer
out of	e-, ex- (L)	erupt, explicit
	ec- (G)	ecstasy
into	in-, im- (L)	injection, immerse
	en-, em- (OF)	encourage, empower
around	circum- (L)	circumference
	peri- (G)	perimeter, periphery
with	co-, col-, com-, con-, cor- (L)	coexist, colloquial, communicate, consequential, correspond
	sym-, syn- (G)	sympathy, synchronize

33b

EXERCISE 2

Provide meanings for the following italicized words, using the lists of prefixes and any clues given by the rest of the sentence. Check the accuracy of your meanings in a dictionary.

1. In the twenty-first century some of our major cities will celebrate their *quadricentennials.*
2. Most poems called sonnets consist of fourteen lines divided into an *octave* and a *sestet.*

3. When the Congress seemed ready to cut Social Security benefits, some representatives proposed the *countermeasure* of increasing Medicare payments.
4. By increasing Medicare payments, the representatives hoped to *forestall* the inevitable financial squeeze on the elderly.
5. Ferdinand Magellan was a Portuguese sailor who commanded the first expedition to *circumnavigate* the globe.

3
Learning suffixes

Suffixes are standard syllables fastened to the end of a word to modify its meaning and usually its function. The word *popular* is an adjective. It becomes a different adjective, an adverb, a noun, and two different verbs by changing suffixes.

ADJECTIVE	popul*ar*
	popul*ous*
ADVERB	popul*arly*
NOUN	popul*ation*
VERB	popul*ate*
	popul*arize*

Many words change suffixes in the same way. In fact, we easily recognize the functions of many words by their suffixes, as the following examples show.

NOUN SUFFIXES

mis*ery*	base*ment*	discus*sion*
refer*ence*	national*ist*	agita*tion*
relev*ance*	national*ism*	random*ness*
operat*or*	intern*ship*	brother*hood*
min*er*	presid*ency*	king*dom*

VERB SUFFIXES

hard*en*	pur*ify*
national*ize*	agit*ate*

ADJECTIVE SUFFIXES

miser*able*	gigan*tic*	adopt*ive*
edi*ble*	friend*ly*	use*less*
nation*al*	wonder*ful*	self*ish*
presiden*tial*	fibr*ous*	flatul*ent*

33b

The only suffix regularly applied to adverbs is *-ly*: openly, selfishly.

NOTE: Inflectional endings, such as the plural *-s*, the possessive *-'s*, the past tense *-ed*, and the comparative *-er* or *-est*, appear at the ends of words but do not change a word's grammatical function.

EXERCISE 3

Identify the part of speech of each word below, and then change it to the part or parts of speech in parentheses by deleting, adding, or changing a suffix. Use the given word and each created word in a sentence. Check a dictionary if necessary to be sure suffixes and spellings are correct.

1. magic (*adjective*)
2. durable (*noun; adverb*)
3. refrigerator (*verb*)
4. self-critical (*noun*)
5. differ (*noun; adjective*)
6. equal (*noun; adverb*)
7. conversion (*verb; adjective*)
8. strictly (*adjective; noun*)
9. assist (*noun*)
10. qualification (*verb; adjective*)

33c
Learning to use new words

New words are usually learned in stages. Looking at a new word's root, prefix, or suffix may give a sense of its meaning; reading or hearing the word more than once aids memory; and seeing the same word in various contexts gradually makes its meaning clear. You can learn a new word not only by understanding its make-up but also by examining the context in which it appears for hints about its meaning and by looking it up in a dictionary—both ways to increase your vocabulary by multiplying and varying your experience with language.

1
Examining context

Most people guess the meaning of an unfamiliar word by looking at familiar words around it. Imagine, for example, that you overheard someone saying the following:

> I was so tired I didn't bother with a real bed. I just lay down on the liclac in the living room. As soon as my feet rested at one end and my head at the other, I fell asleep. In the morning I was cramped from pushing against the back of the liclac.

To guess what *liclac* means, you could examine all the familiar words and learn that (1) a liclac isn't a bed, but you can lie on it; (2) it's part of a living room; (3) it's the length of a person; (4) it's narrow and has a back. From these clues you might guess that the nonsense word *liclac* represents a piece of living room furniture similar to a couch or sofa.

If you didn't know the word *provocative*, you could probably guess its meaning from the words around it in the sentence below.

To encourage creativity in your children, introduce them to inspiring people, *provocative* books, and stimulating environments.

People, books, and *environments* are parallel in the sentence, and if you knew that *inspiring* and *stimulating* are both words having to do with "causing excitement," then you might safely assume that *provocative* is like its two partners and means "causing excitement" in a general sense.

Parallelism shows you which ideas line up or go together and can often suggest the meaning of a new word. Watch for parallel ideas in the following sentence.

The kittens see their mother hunt and kill, and they in turn take up *predatory* behavior.

If you did not know the word *predatory*, you could put together clues from the context: parallel construction (*kittens see . . . and they . . . take up*); the tip-off phrase *in turn*; and the suggested idea of imitation (kittens watching their mother and taking up her behavior). These clues produce the correct assumption that predatory behavior consists of hunting and killing.

The phrase *is called* or the word *is* often points out that a definition providing meaning is near an unfamiliar word.

The point where the light rays come together is called the *focus* of the lens.

Sometimes definitions are set in parentheses or set off by commas or dashes.

In early childhood these tendencies lead to the development of *schemes* (organized patterns of behavior).

Many Chinese practice *Tai Chi,* an ancient method of self-defense performed as exercise in slow, graceful motions.

At *burnout*—the instant a rocket stops firing—the satellite's path is fixed.

Noticing the use of examples can also help you figure out the meaning of a word. The phrases *such as, for example, for instance, to illustrate,* and *including* often precede examples.

Society often has difficulty understanding nonconformists *such as* criminals, inventors, artists, saints, and political protesters.

The parallel examples help explain *nonconformist* because they all seem to be exceptions, people who go beyond the average or beyond

33c

the rules. This is close to an understanding of *nonconformists* as people who do not adapt themselves to the usual standards and customs of society.

Sometimes an example that reveals the meaning of an unfamiliar word is spread through the sentence and is not announced by a phrase.

> During the first weeks of *rehabilitation,* Brian exercised as best he could, took his medicine daily, and thought constantly about the physical condition he once possessed.

Guessing the meaning of *rehabilitation* requires thinking about the examples of what occurred during it: (1) exercising "as best he could"—as if Brian had some kind of handicap; (2) taking medicine—as if he were ill; and (3) thinking about his past physical condition—as if he were wishing for the good shape he used to be in. Putting these examples together suggests that *rehabilitation* is getting back to a healthy condition, which is one of its meanings. (The more precise definition is "restoring a former capacity"; and that idea can include reviving a skill as well as recuperating from a sickness.)

EXERCISE 4

Use context to determine the meanings of the words italicized below (not including titles). Check the accuracy of your guess by consulting a dictionary.

1. Anything that is *theoretically* possible will be achieved in practice, no matter what the technical difficulties, if it is desired enough.
   —Arthur C. Clarke
2. Although never as popular or as controversial as *The Birth of a Nation, Intolerance* has gradually attained the *eminence* of that earlier Griffith masterpiece.
   —Stanley J. Solomon
3. Like America, Michael [Corleone, in *The Godfather*] began as a clean, brilliant young man *endowed* with incredible resources and believing in a humanistic idealism. Like America, Michael was an innocent who had tried to correct the ills and injustices of his *progenitors.*
   —Francis Ford Coppola
4. Human evolution proceeded in a period of *unprecedented* unrest. The climate became cooler and drier, a change marked by the *dwindling* of seas and the spread of savannas, deserts, and semi-deserts. The vast sea that stretched from Spain to Malaya 70 million years ago . . . continued to shrink toward its present-day dimensions.
   —John E. Pfeiffer

33c

5. Everything about man is a *paradox*. The *magnanimous* man grown rich becomes mean. The creative artist for whom everything is made easy nods. Every doctrine swears that it will breed men, but none can tell us in advance what sort of men it will breed.

—Antoine de Saint Exupéry

2
Using the dictionary

The dictionary is a quick reference for the meaning of words (see 32c). It can give the precise meaning of a word whose general meaning you have guessed by examining the word's context. It can also help you fix the word in your memory by showing its spelling, pronunciation, grammatical functions and forms, etymology, and synonyms and antonyms.

For example, suppose you did not understand the word *homogeneous* in the following sentence:

Its homogeneous population makes the town stable but dull.

The dictionary gives the meanings of the word—"of the same kind," "of similar composition throughout." Thus the town's population is made up of similar kinds of people. *Homogeneous* comes from the Greek words *hom*, meaning "same," and *genos*, meaning "kind, type." Obviously the make-up of the word reinforces its definitions. Looking down the dictionary's column under *homogeneous*, you would find a related word, *homogenize*, which might be more familiar because of the common phrase *homogenized milk*. To *homogenize* means "to blend into a smooth mixture" and "to break up the fat globules of milk by forcing them through minute openings." The relation between this familiar word and the other, less familiar one gives added meaning to both words. A similar expansion of meaning could come from examining an antonym of *homogeneous*, such as *heterogeneous*, meaning "consisting of dissimilar ingredients." Thinking of the two exactly opposite words together might fix them both in your memory.

Studying a dictionary's discussion of a word's synonyms is a good way to learn the precise meanings of similar words. A dictionary of synonyms is the best source (see 32a-3). But even an abridged general dictionary will supply quite a bit of information on synonyms (see 32a-1). Most abridged dictionaries list a word's common synonyms and either direct you to the entries for the synonyms or distinguish among them in one place. An example of the latter format is the following passage of the *American Heritage Dictionary of the English Language*, in which a paragraph on the synonyms for

33c

real follows the main entry. Applying the information provided in this paragraph, you can avoid overreliance on the word *real* when a more precise word is appropriate.

re·al[1] (rē′əl, rēl) *adj.* **1.** Being or occurring in fact or actuality; having verifiable existence: *The child shows real intelligence.* **2.** True and actual; not illusory or fictitious: *real people.* **3.** Genuine and authentic; not artificial or spurious: *real mink; real humility.* **4.** *Philosophy.* Existing actually and objectively. **5.** *Optics.* Of, pertaining to, or designating an image formed by light rays that converge in space. **6.** *Mathematics.* Of, pertaining to, or designating the nonimaginary part of a complex quantity. **7.** *Law.* Of or pertaining to stationary or fixed property, as buildings or land. Compare **personal.** —*adv. Informal.* Very: *real sorry.* [Middle English, of real property or things, from Norman French, of real property or things, from Late Latin *reālis,* actual, real, from Latin *rēs,* thing. See **rei-**[3] in Appendix.*] —**real′ness** *n.*
  Synonyms: *real, actual, true, authentic, concrete, existent, genuine, tangible, veritable. Real,* although frequently used interchangeably with the terms that follow, pertains basically to that which is not imaginary but is existent and identifiable as a thing, state, or quality. *Actual* connotes that which is demonstrable. *True* implies belief in that which conforms to fact. *Authentic* implies acceptance of historical or attributable reliability rather than visible proof. *Concrete* implies the reality of actual things. *Existent* applies to concepts or objects existing either in time or space: *existent tensions. Genuine* presupposes evidence or belief that a thing or object is what it is claimed to be. *Tangible* stresses the mind's acceptance of that which can be touched or seen. *Veritable,* which should be used sparingly, applies to persons and things having all the qualities claimed for them.

EXERCISE 5

The dictionary entry in the previous section lists the following words as synonyms for *real: actual, true, authentic, concrete, existent, genuine, tangible,* and *veritable.* Using the dictionary entry and consulting a dictionary of synonyms if necessary, write nine sentences that make precise use of *real* and each of its eight synonyms.

33c

34

Spelling

Because of the history and complexity of English, spelling English words according to standard usage requires consistent attention. Learning to spell well, however, is worth the effort, because misspelling can make writing seem incompetent or lazy. This chapter will show you how to recognize typical spelling problems, how to use a handful of rules as a guide to spelling, and how to develop spelling skills through conscious effort.

34a
Avoiding typical spelling problems

Spelling well involves recognizing situations that commonly lead to misspelling. Pronunciation can mislead you in several ways; different forms of the same word may have different spellings; and some words have more than one acceptable spelling. Watching for the errors these situations encourage will prevent many spelling mistakes.

1
Avoiding excessive reliance on pronunciation

In English, pronunciation of words is an unreliable guide to their spelling. The same letter or combination of letters may be given different sounds in the pronunciation of different words. For an example, say aloud these different ways of pronouncing the letters *ough: tough, dough, cough, through, bough.* And say aloud these ways of pronouncing *ea: beat, tread, pear, search, fear.* Another problem is that some words contain letters that aren't pronounced clearly or at all, such as the *ed* in *asked,* the silent *e* in *swipe,* or the unpronounced *gh* in *tight.*

Pronunciation is a particularly unreliable guide to the spelling of **homonyms,** which are words pronounced the same though they have different spellings and meanings: for example, *great/grate, to/ too/two, threw/through, horse/hoarse, board/bored, break/brake.* Homonyms and words with very similar pronunciations, such as *gorilla/guerilla* and *accept/except,* are common sources of spelling errors. Studying the following list of homonyms and similar-sounding words will help you avoid spelling errors caused by how words sound. (See 34c-4 for some tips on how to use spelling lists.)

accept (to receive)
except (other than)

affect (to have an influence on)
effect (result)

all ready (prepared)
already (by this time)

allude (to refer to indirectly)
elude (to avoid)

allusion (indirect reference)
illusion (erroneous belief or
    perception)

ascent (a rise)
assent (agreement)

bare (unclothed)
bear (to carry, or an animal)

board (a plank of wood)
bored (uninterested)

born (brought into life)
borne (carried)

brake (stop)
break (smash)

buy (purchase)
by (next to)

capital (the seat of a govern-
    ment)
capitol (the building where a
    legislature meets)

cite (to quote an authority)
sight (the ability to see)
site (a place)

descent (a movement down)
dissent (disagreement)

desert (to abandon)
dessert (the course after din-
    ner)

discreet (reserved, respectful)
discrete (individual or distinct)

elicit (to bring out)
illicit (illegal)

fair (average, or lovely)
fare (a charge for transporta-
    tion)

formally (conventionally)
formerly (in the past)

forth (forward)
fourth (after *third*)

gorilla (a large primate)
guerilla (a kind of soldier)

hear (to perceive by ear)
here (in this place)

heard (past tense of *hear*)
herd (a group of animals)

hole (an opening)
whole (complete)

its (belonging to *it*)
it's (contraction of *it is*)

lead (heavy metal)
led (past tense of *lead*)

lessen (to make less)
lesson (something learned)

meat (flesh)
meet (encounter)

no (the opposite of *yes*)
know (to be certain)

passed (past tense of *pass*)
past (after, or a time gone by)

patience (forbearance)
patients (persons under medical care)

peace (the absence of war)
piece (a portion of something)

plain (clear)
plane (a carpenter's tool, or an airborne vehicle)

presence (the state of being at hand)
presents (gifts)

principal (most important, or the head of a school)
principle (a basic truth or law)

rain (precipitation)
reign (to rule)
rein (a strap for controlling an animal)

raise (to build up)
raze (to tear down)

right (correct)
rite (a religious ceremony)
write (to make letters)

road (a surface for driving)
rode (past tense of *ride*)

scene (where an action occurs)
seen (past participle of *see*)

stationary (unmoving)
stationery (writing paper)

straight (unbending)
strait (a water passageway)

their (belonging to *them*)
there (the opposite of *here*)
they're (the contraction of *they are*)

to (toward)
too (also)
two (following *one*)

waist (the narrow middle of the body)
waste (discarded material)

weak (not strong)
week (Sunday through Saturday)

which (one of a group)
witch (a sorcerer)

who's (the contraction of *who is*)
whose (belonging to *who*)

your (belonging to *you*)
you're (the contraction of *you are*)

2

Distinguishing between different forms of the same word

Other spelling problems occur because the noun form and the verb form of the same word are spelled quite differently. For example:

sp
34a

VERB	NOUN
advise	advice
argue	argument
describe	description
enter	entrance
marry	marriage
omit	omission

Sometimes there is a difference between the noun and the adjective forms of the same word.

Noun	Adjective
comedy	comic
courtesy	courteous
generosity	generous
height	high
Britain	British

The different principal parts of irregular verbs are usually spelled differently.

begin, began, begun	know, knew, known
break, broke, broken	ride, rode, ridden
do, did, done	ring, rang, rung

Irregular nouns also change spelling from singular to plural.

child, children	shelf, shelves
goose, geese	tooth, teeth
mouse, mice	woman, women

Notice, too, that the stem of a word may change its spelling in different forms.

four, forty
thief, theft

3
Using preferred spellings

Many words have variant spellings as well as preferred spellings (see 32c-2). Since the variant spellings listed in the dictionary are often British spellings, it is useful to know the main differences between American and British spellings. Where Americans use *e* (encyclop*e*dia, an*e*mia), the British sometimes use *ae* (encyclop*ae*dia, an*ae*mia). Americans use *or* (col*or*, hum*or*) where the British use *our* (col*our*, hum*our*). Americans use *er* in words like theat*er* and cent*er*; the British use *re:* theat*re*, cent*re*. Americans often use a single *l* where the British use a double *l: canceled, traveled* versus *cancelled, travelled.* Americans have come to eliminate the *e* in *judgment* and *acknowledgment* that the British retain: *judgement* and *acknowledgement.* And Americans often use a *z* where the British use an *s: realize* is American, *realise* is British.

sp
34b

34b
Following spelling rules

Misspelling is often a matter of misspelling a syllable rather than the whole word. The following general rules focus on troublesome syllables, with notes for the occasional exceptions.

1
Distinguishing between *ie* and *ei*

Words like *believe* and *receive* sound alike in the second syllable, but the syllable is spelled differently. How do you know which word should have *ie* and which one *ei?* The answer is in the familiar jingle:

> *I* before *e*, except after *c*, or when pronounced "ay" as in *neighbor* and *weigh.*

I BEFORE *e*	believe	thief
	grief	fiend
	chief	hygiene
	bier	friend
Ei AFTER *c*	ceiling	deceit
	receive	perceive
	conceive	conceit
Ei SOUNDED AS "ay"	neighbor	eight
	sleigh	vein
	weigh	beige
	freight	heinous

EXCEPTIONS: Some words are spelled with an *ei* combination even though it doesn't follow a *c* and isn't pronounced "ay." These words include *either, neither, foreign, forfeit, height, leisure, weird, seize, seizure,* and *sheik.* The most common of these are contained in this sentence that might help you remember them:

> The weird foreigner seizes neither leisure nor sport at its height.

EXERCISE 1

Insert *ie* or *ei* in the words below. Check doubtful spellings in a dictionary.

1. br__f
2. dec__ve
3. rec__pt
4. s__ze
5. for__gn
6. pr__st
7. gr__vance
8. f__nd
9. L__surely
10. ach__ve
11. pat__nce
12. p__rce
13. h__ght
14. fr__ght
15. f__nt

sp
34b

2
Keeping or dropping a final *e*

Many words end with an unpronounced or silent *e:* for instance, *move, brave, late, rinse.* When adding endings like *-ing* or *-ly* to these words, do you keep the final *e* or drop it? You drop it if the ending begins with a vowel.

advise + able = advisable
force + ible = forcible
surprise + ing = surprising

You keep the final, silent *e* if the ending begins with a consonant.

advance + ment = advancement
accurate + ly = accurately
care + ful = careful

EXCEPTIONS: The silent *e* is sometimes retained before an ending beginning with a vowel. It is kept when *dye* becomes *dyeing*, to avoid confusion with *dying*. It is kept to prevent mispronunciation of words like *shoeing* (not *shoing*) and *mileage* (not *milage*). And the final *e* is often retained after a soft *c* or *g*, to keep the sound of the consonant soft rather than hard.

courageous   noticeable
outrageous   embraceable
changeable

The silent *e* is also sometimes *dropped* before an ending beginning with a consonant, when the *e* is preceded by another vowel.

argue + ment = argument
true + ly = truly
due + ly = duly

EXERCISE 2

Combine the following words and endings, dropping final *e*'s as necessary to make correctly spelled words. Check doubtful spellings in a dictionary.

1. malice + ious   5. sue + ing   9. suspense + ion
2. love + able   6. virtue + ous   10. astute + ness
3. change + able   7. mile + age
4. retire + ment   8. battle + ing

sp
34b

3
Keeping or dropping a final *y*

Words ending in *y*, such as *party* or *cry*, often change their spelling when an ending is added to them. Adding an ending to make *party* plural produces *parties*. Adding endings to make *cry* third-person singular or past tense produces *cries* or *cried*. But the plural of *valley* is *valleys*, and the third-person singular of *delay* is *delays.* The basic rule is to change the *y* to *i* when it follows a consonant, such as the *r* in *cry* or the *t* in *party.*

beauty, beauties	merry, merrier
folly, follies	supply, supplier
worry, worried	deputy, deputize

Keep the *y* when it follows a vowel, as it does in *valley* and *delay,* when the ending is *-ing,* or when it ends a proper name.

day, days	cry, crying	O'Malley, O'Malleys
obey, obeyed	study, studying	Minsky, Minskys
key, keyed	beautify, beautifying	

EXERCISE 3

Combine the following words and endings, dropping final *y*'s as necessary to make correctly spelled words. Check doubtful spellings in a dictionary.

1. imply + s
2. messy + er
3. apply + ing
4. delay + ing
5. defy + ance
6. say + s
7. solidify + s
8. Murphy + s
9. misty + er
10. supply + ed

4
Doubling consonants

Sometimes words ending in a consonant double the last consonant when adding an ending: *plot* becomes *plotted; refer* becomes *referring.* But sometimes they do not: *develop* becomes *developing; work, working;* and *despair, despairing.* Whether to double the final consonant depends on the word's number of syllables, on the letters preceding the final consonant, and on which syllable is stressed in pronunciation.

In one-syllable words double the final consonant when a single vowel precedes the final consonant.

slap, slapping
tip, tipped
flat, flatter

However, *don't* double the final consonant when two vowels or a vowel and another consonant precede the final consonant.

pair, paired
real, realize
park, parking

In words of more than one syllable, double the final consonant when a single vowel precedes the final consonant and the stress falls on the last syllable of the stem once the ending is added.

> submit, submitted
> occur, occurred
> refer, referring

But *don't* double the final consonant when it is preceded by two vowels or a vowel and another consonant, or when the stress falls on other than the stem's last syllable once the ending is added.

> refer, reference   despair, despairing
> relent, relented   beckon, beckoned

EXERCISE 4

Combine the following words and endings, doubling final consonants as necessary to make correctly spelled words. Check doubtful spellings in a dictionary.

1. repair + ing
2. admit + ance
3. act + ion
4. brew + er
5. shop + ed
6. fear + ing
7. conceal + ed
8. allot + ment
9. drip + ing
10. declaim + ed

5
Attaching prefixes

Adding prefixes such as *dis-*, *mis-*, and *un-* does not change the spelling of the word. *Appear* becomes *disappear*. *Spell* becomes *misspell*. *Necessary* becomes *unnecessary*. This rule can be stated another way. When adding a prefix, do not drop a letter from or add a letter to the original word.

> uneasy   disappoint   misinform
> unneeded   dissatisfied   misstate
> antifreeze   defuse
> anti-intellectual de-emphasize

6
Forming plurals

Nouns

Most nouns form plurals by adding *-s* to the singular form.

> boy, boys
> table, tables
> carnival, carnivals

Some nouns ending in *f* or *fe* form the plural by changing the ending to *ve* before adding -*s*.

leaf, leaves
life, lives
yourself, yourselves

Singular nouns ending in -*s*, -*sh*, -*ch*, or -*x* form the plural by adding -*es*.

kiss, kisses   church, churches
wish, wishes   fox, foxes

(Notice that verbs ending in -*s*, -*sh*, -*ch*, or -*x* form the third-person singular in the same way. *Taxes* and *lurches* are examples.)

Nouns ending in *o* preceded by a vowel usually form the plural by adding -*s*.

ratio, ratios
zoo, zoos

Nouns ending in *o* preceded by a consonant usually form the plural by adding -*es*.

hero, heroes
zero, zeroes
tomato, tomatoes

Some English nouns that were originally Italian, Greek, Latin, or French form the plural according to their original language: *piano, pianos*; *medium, media*.

Compound nouns

Compound nouns form plurals in two ways. An -*s* is added to the last word when two or more main words (usually nouns and verbs) make up the compound word, whether or not they are hyphenated.

city-states   booby traps
painter-sculptors   breakthroughs
bucket seats

sp
34b

When the parts of the compound word are not equal—when a noun is combined with other parts of speech—then *s* is added to the noun.

fathers-in-law
spoonsful
passersby

NOTE: In informal usage *father-in-laws, spoonfuls,* and *passerbys* are usually acceptable.

EXERCISE 5

Make correct plurals of the following words. Check doubtful spellings in a dictionary.

1. pile	6. box	11. libretto
2. donkey	7. switch	12. sister-in-law
3. beach	8. rodeo	13. mile-per-hour
4. summary	9. criterion	14. cargo
5. thief	10. cupful	15. hiss

34c
Developing spelling skills

There are several ways to improve spelling besides recognizing common spelling problems and following spelling rules. You can also draw on knowledge of roots, prefixes, and suffixes to guide your spelling (see Chapter 33). And you can use the dictionary regularly to check words you are unsure of (see Chapter 32). Start by looking up the word as you think it is spelled. Then try different variations based on the pronunciation of the word. Once you think you have found the correct spelling, check the definition to make sure you have the word you want.

1
Pronouncing carefully

Pronunciation will not always work to tell you how to spell because, as we observed in 34a, accurate pronunciation may not give you all the information you need. Nevertheless, careful pronunciation can help you spell many words in which sounds are frequently added, omitted, or reversed in pronunciation.

athletics (not ath*e*letics)	laboratory (not labratory)
disastrous (not disas*te*rous)	lib*r*ary (not libary)
mischievous (not mischiev*i*ous)	recognize (not reconize)
lightning (not light*e*ning)	stric*t*ly (not stricly)
height (not height*h*)	gover*n*ment (not goverment)
ir*r*elevant (not ir*re*v*e*lant)	hist*o*ry (not histry)
perform (not p*r*eform)	temper*a*ment (not temperment)
nuclear (not nuc*u*lar)	represent*a*tive (not representive)

2
Using mnemonics

Mnemonics are techniques for assisting your memory. To remember that secretary ends in *-ary*, not *-ery*, think of the mnemonic sentence "A good secretary is able." The *a* in *able* will remind you to spell *secretary* with an *a*. The *er* in *letter* and *paper* can remind you that *stationery* (meaning "writing paper") has an *er* near the end; *stationary* with an *a* means "standing in place." Or the word *dome* with its long *o* sound can remind you that the building in which the legislature meets is spelled *capitol,* with an *o.* The *capital* city is spelled with *al* like *Albany,* the capital of New York. If you identify the words you have trouble spelling, you can take a few minutes to think of your own mnemonics, which may work better for you than someone else's.

3
Studying spelling lists

Learning to spell commonly misspelled words will reduce your spelling errors. As you work with the following list, study only a small group of words at a time. (Learning tests have demonstrated that seven items is a good number to work with.) Be sure you understand the meaning of the word before you try to memorize its spelling. Look it up in a dictionary if you are uncertain, and try using it in a sentence. Pronounce the word out loud, syllable by syllable, and write the word out. (For additional words that are commonly misspelled, see the list of similar-sounding words on pp. 394–95.)

absence	Britain	fascinate	occurrence
abundance	calendar	February	omission
academic	category	foreign	parallel
accommodate	cemetery	forty	perform
achieve	certain	fourth	perhaps
acknowledge	coming	friend	possess
across	column	government	precede
acquaintance	conceit	grammar	prejudice
address	condemn	harass	prevalent
aggravate	definite	height	primitive
aggressive	descendant	illiterate	privilege
all right	describe	indefinite	procedure
all together	develop	independent	proceed
already	dictionary	infinite	quizzes
altogether	dining	license	receive
appearance	embarrass	luxury	recommend
argument	emphasize	marriage	reference
athlete	entirely	mathematics	referring
attendance	entrance	medicine	reminisce
audience	environment	necessary	renown
basically	etc.	neither	rhythm
believe	exaggerate	occasion	roommate
benefited	existence	occur	safety

sp
34c

seize	sincerely	than	usually
separate	sophomore	then	vacuum
sergeant	sponsor	tragedy	villain
several	succeed	truly	weird
similar	supersede	until	writing

34d
Using the hyphen to form compound words

The hyphen (-) is a mark of punctuation used either to divide a word or to form a compound word. Use a hyphen to divide a word at the end of a line and continue it on the next line as explained in Chapter 30 on word division. Whether to use a hyphen to form compound words depends first on a general understanding of compound words.

Compound words express a combination of ideas. They may be written as a single word, like the noun *breakthrough;* as two words, like the noun *decision making;* or as a hyphenated word, like the noun *cave-in. Breakthrough* was originally spelled as two words, then as a hyphenated word, before it became a single word. This typical historical pattern of spelling compound words influences the correct use of the hyphen. So does the function a particular compound word performs. As a noun, *decision making* is spelled as two words. As a compound adjective, it is hyphenated, as in *decision-making process,* so there can be no confusion over whether *making* belongs with *decision* or with *process.* But historical pattern and function cannot account for all variations in the spelling of compound words. Sometimes compound words using the same element and performing the same function still are spelled differently. For instance, the nouns *cross-reference, crosswalk,* and *cross section* have all been in use for some time.

Because of the variations in spelling compound words, check a recent edition of a dictionary for their current standard spelling. However, several reliable generalizations can be made about using the hyphen for compound adjectives, for fractions and compound numbers, for coined compounds, for certain prefixes and suffixes, and to avoid confusion.

1
Forming compound adjectives

When two or more words serve together as a single modifier before a noun, the hyphen forms the words into a unit.

well-known actor
up-to-date statistics
English-speaking people

When the same compound adjectives follow the noun, hyphens are unnecessary and are usually left out.

The actor is *well known.*
The statistics are *up to date.*
Those people are *English speaking.*

When the main part of a compound adjective is used only once in a series, hyphens indicate which words the reader should mentally join with the main part.

He sawed off 2- and 3-foot lengths of board.
School-age children should have eight- or nine-o'clock bedtimes.

2
Writing fractions and compound numbers

Hyphens join the numerator and denominator of fractions.

three-fourths
one-half

The whole numbers twenty-one to ninety-nine are always hyphenated regardless of their function or of their position in relation to the noun or verb.

Eighteen girls and twenty-four boys took the bus.
The total is eighty-seven.

3
Forming coined compounds

Writers sometimes create (coin) temporary compounds to express a series of ideas as one.

Mohammed Ali gave his opponent a classic come-on-over-here-and-get-me look.

4
Attaching some prefixes and suffixes

Prefixes are usually attached to word stems without hyphens: *predetermine, unnatural, disengage.* However, when the prefix precedes a capitalized word, or when a capital letter is combined with a word, a hyphen usually separates the two: *un-American, pre-Eisenhower, non-European, X-ray, A-frame.* And some prefixes—such as *self-*, *all-*, *co-*, and *ex-* (meaning "formerly")—usually require hyphens whether or not they precede capitalized words: *self-control, all-inclusive, co-chairman, ex-student.*

The only suffix that regularly requires a hyphen is *-elect,* as in *president-elect.*

5
Avoiding confusion

If you wrote the sentence *Doonesbury is a comic strip character,* the reader might stumble briefly over your meaning. Is Doonesbury a character in a comic strip or a comic (funny) character who strips? Presumably you would mean the former, but a hyphen would prevent any possible confusion: *Doonesbury is a comic-strip character.*

Adding prefixes to words can sometimes create ambiguity. *Recreation* (*creation* with the prefix *re-*) could mean either "a new creation" or "diverting, pleasurable activity." Using a hyphen, *re-creation,* limits the word to the first meaning. Without a hyphen the word suggests the second meaning.

Combinations of prefixes and stems that place two vowels or the same three consonants together are often more readable when a hyphen separates them.

> preeminent, pre-eminent
> trilllike, trill-like
> reevaluate, re-evaluate

Check a dictionary for the standard form, particularly for words that join two *e*'s.

EXERCISE 6

Insert hyphens as needed in the following compounds. Circle all compounds that are correct as given. Consult a dictionary as needed.

1. reimburse
2. deemphasize
3. forty odd soldiers
4. little known bar
5. seven eighths
6. seventy eight
7. happy go lucky
8. preexisting
9. senator elect
10. postman
11. two and six person cars
12. ex songwriter
13. V shaped
14. reeducate

VIII
Special Writing Assignments

35

Writing
a Research Paper

A **research paper** is a composition for which you assemble information from sources usually found in a library, arrange the information to support a thesis or answer a question, and document your sources using footnotes and a bibliography. Your purpose is to arrive at a thoughtful conclusion about some question or issue after examining several sources. In the process, you learn how to find comprehensive and up-to-date information on a topic and how to analyze, interpret, judge, and acknowledge other people's ideas and reasoning.

This chapter shows the steps in planning and writing a research paper. Many of them—such as limiting your subject and developing a thesis—are the same as those you use to write other kinds of essays (see Chapter 1). But library research leads you to read, analyze, and organize the ideas of others. These three processes—reading, analyzing, and organizing—underlie the following steps.

1. Find and limit a researchable topic.
2. Find information on the topic and read to refine the topic further.
3. Record where the information is located.
4. Read to strengthen your overview of the topic and work up a tentative thesis and outline.
5. Take detailed notes.
6. Revise the thesis and write a formal outline.
7. Write and revise the paper.
8. Prepare the footnotes.
9. Prepare the bibliography.

As this list shows, a research paper, like an essay, evolves gradually. While you do research, your reading leads you to organize ideas. And while you organize ideas, you discover where you need to do more research. You begin to limit your topic as soon as you have chosen it, and you continue to limit it as you progress. The working thesis and outline you develop must later be refined. Anticipating changes like these as you read, analyze, and organize will help make writing a research paper a straightforward and satisfying project.

35a

Finding and limiting a researchable topic

Before reading this section, you may want to review the suggestions for finding and limiting an essay topic described in Chapter 1. Generally, the same procedure applies to writing a research paper: take a subject assigned to you or think of one that interests you, and narrow it to manageable dimensions by making it specific.

If you don't see how your interest in something like sports, for example, could become a research topic, start with the general idea and gradually make it more specific by asking yourself questions. What about sports particularly interests you? Are you most interested in playing, watching, or coaching sports? If you are most interested in coaching, what do you know about it, and what do you want to learn? You may know about methods of physical conditioning, but you may want to know more about how players' attitudes affect their conditioning. At this point you have a topic—"how psychological attitude affects physical conditioning of athletes"—that could become the subject of a research paper.

One student, Paul Fuller, wants to write about marketing. He lists topics he associates with marketing and then makes another list of his associations for advertising, the subtopic he is most interested in. From there, he moves to three questions, three paths his investigation can take. In the end, he selects "How do advertisers persuade consumers?" as the topic with which to begin his research.

To narrow his topic still further, Fuller has to begin research-ing the ways advertising influences consumers. But his topic does seem to satisfy two main requirements of a subject for a research paper. First, the topic needs to be researched in several sources, so Fuller can present a range of opinion and fact. A topic that requires only personal opinion and experience, such as "how I see house-wives being depicted in detergent commercials," might be suitable for an essay but not for a research paper. Nor would a topic be suit-able if it required research in only one source. For this reason how-to topics like "operating a television camera" or "making lenses for eyeglasses" are generally poor research subjects.

The second requirement satisfied by Fuller's topic is that it is suited to the length of paper he's been assigned (1500 to 2000 words, or about seven to ten pages) and the amount of time he's been given to prepare the paper (four weeks). In seven to ten pages, Fuller could not cover one of his broader topics like "advertising and con-sumers" because he would need to deal with so many aspects of the relation (as suggested by the three questions he came up with) that no one aspect could be explored fully. Such a broad topic would also require research in so many sources (including the writings not only of advertising specialists and psychologists but also of con-sumers and consumer representatives) that Fuller might need months, not weeks, to complete his research. The same would be true of a topic like "infant perception," which requires delving into complex biology, chemistry, and psychology. On the other hand, "what a three-month-old infant can see" might be more appropriate for a ten-page paper that takes four weeks to prepare.

EXERCISE 1

Choose three of the following subjects and limit each one to at least one topic suitable for beginning library work on a research paper. Or list and then limit three subjects of your own that you would enjoy investigating. (This exercise can be the first step in a research paper project that continues through Exercises 2, 5, 6, 9, 11, 12, 14, and 15.)

1. the United States in world affairs
2. the Opium War
3. dance in America
4. the history of women's suffrage
5. food additives
6. illegal aliens in the United States
7. exploration of the moon (or Mars)
8. energy sources other than oil and coal
9. the impact of television on professional sports
10. religious cults in America

11. the modern automobile engine
12. recent developments in cancer research
13. the European exploration of North America before Columbus
14. the Sacco and Vanzetti trial
15. Social Security
16. microwaves
17. Native American tribal rights today
18. science fiction
19. irrigation rights
20. water pollution
21. women writers
22. the history of child labor practices
23. the novels of Kurt Vonnegut
24. comic film actors
25. genetic engineering

35b

Finding information on the topic and reading to refine the topic further

When you go to the library with a topic to investigate, you can find information in at least three different sources: reference books, periodicals, and general books. Reference books are a good place to start because they provide either a summary of a topic or comprehensive information on where to find out about the topic. Periodicals (magazines, journals, and newspapers) usually contain detailed and current information on the topic. General books, which constitute the bulk of a library's collection and contain almost every kind of information, are those available for circulation.

Most information for a brief research paper will be in **secondary sources,** works that report and analyze information drawn from other sources. If possible, however, you should use **primary sources,** which include works of literature and historical documents (letters, diaries, speeches, and the like) as well as your own interviews, experiments, observations, or correspondence. (Paul Fuller uses a primary source—his own survey of magazine advertisements—in his research paper. See p. 460.)

1
Using reference books

Reference books available in the library include encyclopedias, dictionaries, digests, bibliographies, indexes, atlases, almanacs, and handbooks. The overviews these sources provide can help you decide whether your topic really interests you and whether it

35b

meets the requirements of a research paper (Do you need to consult several sources? Is the topic appropriately complex?). Preliminary research in reference books will also direct you to more detailed information on your topic.

The following list gives the types of reference works and suggests when each may be used profitably. Once you have a topic, you can scan this list for a reference book with which to start. If you want a more comprehensive catalog and explanation of reference works than this list provides, consult Eugene P. Sheehy, *Guide to Reference Books*, 9th ed. (Chicago: American Library Association, 1976).

General encyclopedias

General encyclopedias give brief overviews and brief bibliographies. Because they try to cover all fields, they are a convenient, but limited, starting point. Look for the most recent edition.

> *Collier's Encyclopedia.* 24 vols. New York: Macmillan Educational Corporation, 1977.
> *Encyclopedia Americana.* 30 vols. New York: Americana Corporation, 1977.
> *Encyclopedia International.* 20 vols. New York: Grolier, 1963–64.
> *The New Columbia Encyclopedia.* 1 vol. New York: Columbia Univ. Press, 1975.
> *The New Encyclopaedia Britannica.* 30 vols. Chicago: Encyclopaedia Britannica, 1974.
> *Random House Encyclopedia.* 1 vol. New York: Random House, 1977.

Special encyclopedias, dictionaries, bibliographies

These reference works specialize, trying to cover one field completely. They can give you more detailed and technical information than a general reference book can.

THE ARTS

> Boger, Louise Ade, and H. B. Boger. *The Dictionary of Antiques and the Decorative Arts.* New York: Charles Scribner's Sons, 1967.
> *Encyclopedia of World Art.* 15 vols. New York: McGraw-Hill, 1959–68.
> Lucas, Edna Louise. *Art Books: A Basic Bibliography on the Fine Arts.* Greenwich, Conn.: New York Graphic Society, 1968.
> Maillard, Robert, ed. *New Dictionary of Modern Sculpture.* Trans. Bettina Wadia. New York: Tudor, 1971.
> Myers, Bernard S. *Encyclopedia of Painting.* New York: Crown, 1955.

35b

BUSINESS AND ECONOMICS

Buell, Victor P., ed. *Handbook of Modern Marketing.* New York: McGraw-Hill, 1970.

Graham, Irwin. *Encyclopedia of Advertising.* 2nd ed. New York: Fairchild, 1969.

Heyel, Carl. *The Encyclopedia of Management.* 2nd ed. New York: Van Nostrand Reinhold, 1973.

Lazarus, Harold. *American Business Dictionary.* New York: Philosophical Library, 1957.

Munn, Glenn G. *Encyclopedia of Banking and Finance.* 7th ed. Ed. Ferdinand L. Garcia. Boston: Bankers, 1973.

Shapiro, Irving J. *Marketing Terms: Definitions, Explanations, and/or Aspects.* 3rd ed. West Long Branch. N.J.: S-M-C Publishing, 1973.

Sloan, Harold S., and Arnold Zurcher. *A Dictionary of Economics.* 5th ed. New York: Barnes & Noble, 1970.

Wyckham, Robert G. *Images and Marketing: A Selected and Annotated Bibliography.* Chicago: American Marketing Association, 1971.

HISTORY

Adams, James T. *Dictionary of American History.* 6 vols. New York: Charles Scribner's Sons, 1940–63.

American Historical Association: Guide to Historical Literature. New York: Macmillan, 1961.

Cambridge Ancient History. 12 vols. London: Cambridge Univ. Press, 1923–39. Revision in progress.

Cambridge Mediaeval History. 8 vols. London: Cambridge Univ. Press, 1911–36. Revision in progress.

Cambridge Modern History. 14 vols. London: Cambridge Univ. Press, 1902–26. Revision in progress.

Commager, Henry Steele. *Documents of American History.* 9th ed. 2 vols. New York: Appleton-Century-Crofts, 1973.

Friedl, Frank, ed. *Harvard Guide to American History.* Cambridge: Belknap Press of Harvard Univ. Press, 1974.

Hammond, N. G. L., and H. H. Scullard. *Oxford Classical Dictionary.* 2nd ed. Oxford: Clarendon Press, 1970.

Hodge, Frederick W. *Handbook of American Indians North of Mexico.* 2 vols. Washington, D.C.: GPO, 1907–10.

Langer, William Leonard. *An Encyclopedia of World History.* 5th ed., rev. Boston: Houghton Mifflin, 1972.

Martin, Michael R., et al. *An Encyclopedia of Latin-American History.* Indianapolis: Bobbs-Merrill, 1968.

Miller, Elizabeth. *The Negro in America: A Bibliography.* Cambridge: Harvard Univ. Press, 1970.

35b

LITERATURE, THEATER, FILM, AND TELEVISION

Aaronson, C. S., ed. *International Television Almanac.* New York: Quigley Publications, published annually since 1956.

Adelman, Irving, and R. Dworkin. *Modern Drama: A Checklist of Critical Literature on Twentieth Century Plays.* Metuchen, N.J.: Scarecrow, 1967.

Bateson, F. W., ed. *Cambridge Bibliography of English Literature.* 5 vols. New York: Macmillan, 1941–57.

Baugh, Albert C., et al., eds. *Literary History of England.* 2nd ed. 4 vols. New York: Appleton-Century-Crofts, 1967.

Blanck, Jacob N. *Bibliography of American Literature.* 6 vols. New Haven: Yale Univ. Press, 1955–73.

Bond, Donald F. *A Reference Guide to English Studies.* 2nd ed. Chicago: Univ. of Chicago Press, 1971.

Hartnoll, Phyllis. *The Oxford Companion to the Theatre.* 3rd ed. London: Oxford Univ. Press, 1967.

Harvey, Paul. *The Oxford Companion to English Literature.* Oxford: Clarendon Press, 1937.

Manvel, Roger, gen. ed. *The International Encyclopedia of Film.* New York: Crown, 1972.

MLA International Bibliography of Books and Articles on the Modern Languages and Literatures. New York: Modern Language Association, published annually since 1922.

Spiller, Robert, et al. *Literary History of the United States.* 4th ed. 2 vols. New York: Macmillan, 1974.

Ward, A. W., and A. R. Waller, eds. *The Cambridge History of English Literature.* 15 vols. New York: G. P. Putnam's Sons, 1907–33.

Music and dance

Apel, Willi, *The Harvard Dictionary of Music.* 2nd rev. ed. Cambridge: Harvard Univ. Press, 1969.

Blom, Eric. *Everyman's Dictionary of Music.* New York: New American Library, 1973.

Chujoy, Anatole, and P. W. Manchester. *The Dance Encyclopedia.* New York: Simon and Schuster, 1967.

Moore, Frank L., comp. *Crowell's Handbook of World Opera.* Westport, Conn.: Greenwood Press, 1974.

Stambler, Irwin. *Encyclopedia of Pop, Rock, and Soul.* New York: St. Martin's, 1975.

Thompson, Oscar. *International Cyclopedia of Music and Musicians.* 10th ed. New York: Dodd, Mead, 1975.

Philosophy and religion

Buttrick, George Arthur, ed. *The Interpreter's Dictionary of the Bible.* 4 vols. Nashville: Abingdon, 1962.

The Catholic Encyclopedia. 18 vols. New York: Thomas Nelson, 1976.

Cross, F. L., and Elizabeth A. Livingston. *The Oxford Dictionary of the Christian Church.* New York: Oxford Univ. Press, 1974.

Edwards, Paul, ed. *The Encyclopedia of Philosophy.* 8 vols. New York: Macmillan, 1967.

35b

Fern, Vergilius, ed. *An Encyclopedia of Religion.* Westport, Conn.: Greenwood Press, 1976.

Roth, Cecil, ed. *The New Standard Jewish Encyclopedia.* 5th ed. New rev. ed. edited by Geoffrey Wigoder. Garden City, N.Y.: Doubleday, 1977.

Urmson, J. O., ed. *The Concise Encyclopedia of Western Philosophy and Philosophers.* New York: Hawthorn, 1960.

SOCIAL SCIENCES

Beigel, Hugo G. *A Dictionary of Psychology and Related Fields.* New York: Frederick Ungar, 1974.

Brock, Clifton. *The Literature of Political Science.* New York: R. R. Bowker, 1969.

Ebel, R. L. *Encyclopedia of Educational Research.* 4th ed. New York: Macmillan, 1969.

Kreslins, Janis A., ed. *Foreign Affairs Bibliography 1962–1972.* New York: R. R. Bowker, 1976.

Mitchell, G. Duncan, ed. *A Dictionary of Sociology.* Chicago: Aldine, 1967.

Sills, David L., ed. *International Encyclopedia of the Social Sciences.* 8 vols. New York: Free Press, 1977.

UNESCO International Committee for Social Science Documentation, ed. *International Bibliography of the Social Sciences.* Chicago: Aldine, 1960–76.

White, Carl M., et al. *Sources of Information in the Social Sciences: A Guide to the Literature.* 2nd ed. Chicago: American Library Association, 1973.

SCIENCES

Collocott, Thomas C. *Chambers Dictionary of Science and Technology.* New. ed. New York: Barnes & Noble, 1972.

Fairbridge, Rhodes W., ed. *The Encyclopedia of Oceanography.* New York: Van Nostrand Reinhold, 1966.

Gray, Peter. *The Encyclopedia of Biological Sciences.* 2nd ed. New York: Van Nostrand Reinhold, 1970.

Hampel, Clifford A., and Gessner G. Hawley, eds. *The Encyclopedia of Chemistry.* 3rd ed. New York: Van Nostrand Reinhold, 1973.

The International Dictionary of Physics and Electronics. 2nd ed. Princeton, N.J.: Van Nostrand Reinhold, 1961.

Jobes, Gertrude, and James Jobes. *Outer Space: Myths, Names, Meanings, Calendars.* Metuchen, N.J.: Scarecrow, 1965.

Lapedes, Daniel N., ed. *The McGraw-Hill Encyclopedia of Science and Technology.* New York: McGraw-Hill, 1977.

The Larousse Encyclopedia of Animal Life. London: Hamlyn, 1967.

Sarton, George. *An Introduction to the History of Science.* 3 vols. Baltimore: Williams & Wilkins, 1968.

Thewlis, J., ed. *Encyclopaedic Dictionary of Physics.* 9 vols. plus supplements. Elmsford, N.Y.: Pergamon, 1965–71.

35b

Unabridged dictionaries and special dictionaries on language

Unabridged dictionaries are more comprehensive than abridged or college dictionaries. Special dictionaries give authoritative information on individual aspects of language. (See Chapter 32 for further explanation of the kinds of dictionaries and how to use them.)

UNABRIDGED DICTIONARIES

Alexander, Sir William, and James R. Hulbert. *A Dictionary of American English on Historical Principles.* 4 vols. Chicago: Univ. of Chicago Press, 1936–44.

The Oxford English Dictionary. 13 vols. plus supplements. New York: Oxford Univ. Press, 1933–76. *The Compact Edition,* 2 vols., was issued in 1971.

The Random House Dictionary of the English Language. New York: Random House, 1973.

Webster's Third New International Dictionary of the English Language. Springfield, Mass.: G. & C. Merriam, 1976.

SPECIAL DICTIONARIES

Follett, Wilson. *Modern American Usage.* Ed. Jacques Barzun. New York: Hill and Wang, 1966.

Fowler, H. W. *Dictionary of Modern English Usage.* 2nd ed. Rev. and ed. Sir Ernest Gowers. New York: Oxford Univ. Press, 1965.

Lewis, Norman. *The New Roget's Thesaurus of the English Language in Dictionary Form.* New York: G. P. Putnam's Sons, 1964.

Morris, William, and Mary Morris. *Dictionary of Word and Phrase Origins.* 3 vols. New York: Harper & Row, 1971.

Partridge, Eric. *Dictionary of Slang and Unconventional English.* 7th ed. New York: Macmillan, 1970.

Partridge, Eric. *Origins: A Short Etymological Dictionary of Modern English.* 4th ed. New York: Macmillan, 1966.

Webster's New Dictionary of Synonyms. Springfield, Mass.: G. & C. Merriam, 1973.

Wentworth, Harold, and Stuart Berg Flexner. *Dictionary of American Slang.* 2nd supp. ed. New York: Thomas Y. Crowell, 1975.

Biographical reference works

35b

If you want to learn about someone's life, achievements, credentials, or position, or if you want to learn the significance of a name you've come across, consult one of these reference works.

American Men and Women of Science. 12th ed. 8 vols. New York: R. R. Bowker, 1971.

Chambers Biographical Dictionary. Rev. ed. New York: St. Martin's, 1969.

Contemporary Authors. 44 vols. Detroit: Gale, 1965–73.

Current Biography. New York: H. W. Wilson, published annually since 1940.

Dictionary of American Biography. 20 vols. plus supplements. New York: Charles Scribner's Sons, 1928–50.

Dictionary of National Biography (British). 22 vols. plus supplements. London: Smith, Elder, published annually since 1908.

Webster's Biographical Dictionary. Springfield, Mass.: G. & C. Merriam, 1972.

Who's Who in America. 2 vols. Chicago: Marquis Who's Who, published biennially since 1899.

Who's Who of American Women. Chicago: Marquis Who's Who, published biennially since 1958.

Atlases and gazetteers

Atlases are bound collections of maps; gazetteers are geographical dictionaries.

Columbia Lippincott Gazetteer of the World. New York: Columbia Univ. Press, 1962.

Encyclopaedia Britannica World Atlas International. Chicago: Encyclopaedia Britannica, 1969.

National Geographic Atlas of the World. 4th ed. Washington, D.C.: National Geographic Society, 1975.

Rand-McNally Cosmopolitan World Atlas. Rev. ed. Chicago: Rand McNally, 1971.

The Times Atlas of the World. Boston: Houghton Mifflin, 1975.

Almanacs and yearbooks

Both almanacs and yearbooks are annual compilations of facts. Yearbooks record information about the previous year as a history of that year. Almanacs provide lists, charts, and tables to give facts and statistics about a variety of fields.

American Annual. New York: Americana Corporation, published annually since 1923.

Britannica Book of the Year. Chicago: Encyclopaedia Britannica, published annually since 1938.

Facts on File Yearbook. New York: Facts on File, published annually since 1940.

Information Please Almanac. New York: Viking Press, published annually since 1947.

U.S. Bureau of the Census. *Statistical Abstract of the United States.* Washington, D.C.: GPO, published annually since 1878.

World Almanac and Book of Facts. New York: World-Telegram, published annually since 1868.

35b

As a starting point for his topic on "how advertising persuades consumers," Paul Fuller goes first to a general encyclopedia and skims the article on advertising. He learns that most advertisements are meant not so much to persuade consumers to buy as to make them aware that the product exists. The article also mentions that consumers often buy for irrational reasons and that advertisers' research into motivation has taught them to include in their ads scientific-sounding claims and symbols of comfort, sex, love of family, and so on. Fuller decides he can narrow his topic to the use of such nonrational, emotional appeals in advertising. He then consults the *Encyclopedia of Advertising,* where he finds references to several books—including *The Hidden Persuaders* and *Motivation in Advertising*—whose titles make them seem promising sources for his topic.

2
Using indexes to periodicals

Several guides provide information on the contents of journals, magazines, newspapers, and other periodicals. A typical and general guide is the *Readers' Guide to Periodical Literature,* published since 1900, which lists, by author, title, and subject, articles in more than one hundred popular magazines. About a quarter of its entries under the heading "Advertising" for a one-year period (March 1977–February 1978) are shown below.

By looking in the *Readers' Guide,* Fuller finds two pertinent articles, both under the subheading "Psychological aspects," both from *Psychology Today.*

ADVERTISING
Art director who has a way with words also has a book coming from Abrams; publication of The art of advertising; interview, ed by R. Dahlin. G. Lois. Pub W 211:55+ Ja 17 '77
Giving impact to ideas; address, October 11, 1977. L. T. Hagopian. Vital Speeches 44:154-7 D 15 '77
News behind the ads. See alternate issues of Changing times
Preaching in the marketplace. America 136:457 My 21 '77
Selling it. Consumer Rep 42:385, 458, 635 Jl-Ag, N '77
    See also
Photography in advertising
Religious advertising
Television advertising
Women in advertising
    also subhead Advertising under various subjects, e.g. Books—Advertising

Awards, prizes, etc.
Saturday review's 23rd annual Advertising Awards. C. Tucker. il Sat R 4:34-5 Jl 23 '77

Laws and regulations
Crackdown ahead on advertising: what the government plans next; interview. M. Pertschuk. pors U.S. News 83:70-2 O 17 '77
FTC broadens its attack on ads. Bus W p27-8 Je 20 '77

Moral aspects
See Advertising ethics

Psychological aspects
Art of implying more than you say; work of Richard Harris. S. Bush. Psychol Today 10: 36+ My '77
Genderisms; reinforcement of sex role stereotypes. E. Goffman. il Psychol Today 11:60-3 Ag '77

Rates
Challenge to ad discounts; effect on small retailers of rate structure used in newspaper and magazine advertising. il Bus W p 146 S 19 '77
Drop in TV viewing, but not in ad pricing. il Bus W p33-4 Ja 16 '78

Other general indexes to periodicals include the following.

Humanities Index. New York: H. W. Wilson, published quarterly since 1974.

The New York Times Index. New York: The New York Times Company/R. R. Bowker, published annually since 1913.

Poole's Index to Periodical Literature. Boston: Houghton Mifflin, 1802–1907. An index by subject to British and American periodicals of the nineteenth century.

Popular Periodicals Index. Camden, N.J.: Popular Periodicals, published annually since 1973. An index to about twenty-five contemporary, popular periodicals not listed in major indexes.

Many special indexes and indexes to scholarly articles are available in most libraries. The following is a partial list.

Applied Science and Technology Index. New York: H. W. Wilson, published monthly since 1958. From 1913 to 1957 this work was combined with the *Business Periodicals Index* in the *Industrial Arts Index.*

Art Index. New York: H. W. Wilson, published quarterly since 1929.

Biological Abstracts. Philadelphia: Biological Abstracts, published semimonthly since 1926.

Biological and Agricultural Index. New York: H. W. Wilson, published monthly since 1964. From 1916 to 1963 this work was called the *Agricultural Index.*

Business Periodicals Index. New York: H. W. Wilson, published annually since 1958. From 1913 to 1957 this work was combined with the *Applied Science and Technology Index* in the *Industrial Arts Index.*

The Education Index. New York: H. W. Wilson, published monthly since 1929.

Index Medicus. Washington, D.C.: National Library of Medicine, published monthly since 1960. From 1927 to 1959 this work was called *Quarterly Cumulative Index Medicus.* From 1899 to 1926 it was *Index Medicus.*

MLA Abstracts of Articles in Scholarly Journals. New York: Modern Language Association, published three times a year since 1971.

35b

Psychological Abstracts. Washington, D.C.: American Psychological Association, published monthly since 1927.

Science Citation Index. Philadelphia: Institute for Scientific Information, published quarterly since 1961.

Social Sciences Index. New York: H. W. Wilson, published quarterly since 1974. From 1965 to 1974 these author and subject indexes were combined in the *Social Sciences and Humanities Index.* From 1907 to 1965 the combined volume was called the *International Index.*

3
Using guides to general books

The library's card catalog lists general books alphabetically by names of authors, titles of books, and subjects. (Many libraries are converting their card catalogs to computer printouts that are organized the same way.) If you are starting research on a subject you don't know very well, begin by looking for subject cards. If you know of an expert in the field and you want to find his or her books, use the author cards. If you know the title of a relevant book, but not the author's name, use the title cards. Here are samples of each type of card.

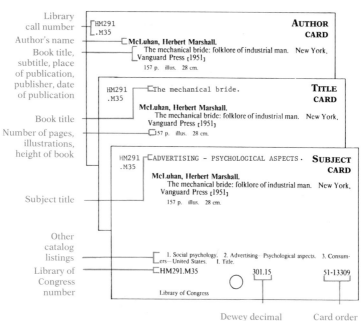

Library call number — HM291 .M35

Author's name — McLuhan, Herbert Marshall.

Book title, subtitle, place of publication, publisher, date of publication — The mechanical bride: folklore of industrial man. New York, Vanguard Press [1951]

157 p. illus. 28 cm.

AUTHOR CARD

HM291 .M35 — The mechanical bride.

TITLE CARD

McLuhan, Herbert Marshall.
The mechanical bride: folklore of industrial man. New York, Vanguard Press [1951]

Book title

Number of pages, illustrations, height of book — 157 p. illus. 28 cm.

HM291 .M35 — ADVERTISING – PSYCHOLOGICAL ASPECTS.

SUBJECT CARD

McLuhan, Herbert Marshall.
The mechanical bride: folklore of industrial man. New York, Vanguard Press [1951]

157 p. illus. 28 cm.

Subject title

Other catalog listings — 1. Social psychology. 2. Advertising– Psychological aspects. 3. Consumers– United States. I. Title.

Library of Congress number — HM291.M35

Library of Congress

Dewey decimal number — 301.15

Card order number — 51-13309

35b

Two types of reference books can help you to identify general books that have information about your topic: publishing bibliographies and digests. Publishing bibliographies tell whether a book is still in print, whether a paperback edition is available, what books were published on a certain topic in a certain year, and so on. These bibliographies include:

> *Books in Print.* New York: R. R. Bowker, published and supplemented annually since 1873. Books indexed by author, title, and subject.
>
> *Cumulative Book Index.* New York: H. W. Wilson, published monthly since 1898.
>
> *Paperbound Books in Print.* New York: R. R. Bowker, published semiannually since 1955.

You might, for example, want to know if the author of an encyclopedia article has published any relevant books since the date of the encyclopedia. You could look up the author's name in the latest *Books in Print* to find out.

If you want to evaluate a book's relevance to your topic without actually skimming it yourself, you can use the *Book Review Digest* (New York: H. W. Wilson, published annually since 1905). This digest tells you where to find reviews of current books and summarizes reviews. Another general digest is *Book Review Index* (Detroit: Gale, published annually since 1965). There are also digests for separate subjects such as *Recent Publications in the Social and Behavioral Sciences* (New York: American Behavioral Scientist, published annually).

EXERCISE 2

List at least five sources you can consult for further leads on each of the three topics you came up with in Exercise 1 (p. 410), or for three other topics. Use the information provided in the preceding section and additional information at your library.

35c
Making a working bibliography

If you tried to pursue every lead as you came across it in an encyclopedia or index or in the card catalog, your search for sources of information—and thus the information you found—would not be very well organized. Instead, you'll want to find out what is available before deciding which leads to follow, and that requires systematically keeping track of where information is and what it is. You can do this by making a working bibliography—a file on cards of the books, articles, and other sources you want to look up. When you have a substantial card file of material, you can decide what looks most promising and look it up first.

A working bibliography records all the information you need to find the source. Putting each source on an individual 3″ x 5″ card will allow you to arrange your sources alphabetically by author, to discard irrelevant sources without disrupting your list, and later to transfer the information easily to your final bibliography.

Make a bibliography card for each source you think may be useful—whether you find it in the card catalog, in a reference book, or in an index to periodicals. Include, in standard bibliographical form (see the models below), all the information you will need for your final bibliography. For sources you find in the card catalog, list the call number on the bibliography card to save time later. (However, the call number will not be transferred to the final bibliography.) Here are two examples of bibliography cards, the first for a book and the second for a periodical.

HF
5813
V6655   Glatzer, Robert. _The New Advertising:_

The Great Campaigns. New York:

Citadel Press, 1970.

Gregg, Gary. "To Sell Your Product,

Admit It's Not Perfect." _Psychology_

Today, Oct. 1974, p. 35.

35c

The following models show you how to record bibliographic information for different sources. These models are based on the *MLA Handbook,* a publication of the Modern Language Association (New York, 1977). Other guides may give slightly different formats. Your instructor will assign the bibliographic format you should use.

Books

BOOK WITH ONE AUTHOR

Kael, Pauline. <u>Going Steady</u>. Boston: Atlantic-Little,

    Brown, 1970.

BOOK WITH TWO OR THREE AUTHORS

Wimsatt, William K., and Cleanth Brooks. <u>Literary</u>

    <u>Criticism: A Short History</u>. Chicago: Univ. of

    Chicago Press, 1978.

BOOK WITH MORE THAN THREE AUTHORS

Mussen, Paul, et al. <u>Psychology: An Introduction</u>.

    Lexington, Mass.: D. C. Heath, 1973.

BOOK WITH CORPORATE AUTHORSHIP

Editors of <u>The Progressive</u>. <u>The Crisis of Survival</u>.

    Glenview, Ill.: Scott, Foresman, 1970.

A LATER EDITION

Kennedy, X. J. <u>An Introduction to Poetry</u>. 4th ed. Boston:

    Little, Brown, 1978.

A WORK IN MORE THAN ONE VOLUME

Blotner, Joseph. <u>Faulkner: A Biography</u>. 2 vols. New

    York: Random House, 1974.

A TRANSLATION

Alighieri, Dante. <u>The Inferno</u>. Trans. **John Ciardi.** New

    York: New American Library, 1971.

A WORK IN A SERIES

Bergman, Ingmar. <u>The Seventh Seal</u>. Modern Film Scripts

    Series. New York: Simon and Schuster, 1968.

A BOOK WITH AN EDITOR

Spradley, James P., and David W. McCurdy, eds. <u>Conformity</u>

    <u>and Conflict</u>. 4th ed. Boston: Little, Brown, 1980.

35c

A BOOK WITH AN AUTHOR AND AN EDITOR

Melville, Herman. The Confidence Man: His Masquerade. Ed.

    Hershel Parker. New York: W. W. Norton, 1971.

A SELECTION FROM AN EDITED ANTHOLOGY OR COLLECTION

Gerald, Carolyn F. "The Black Writer and His Role." In

    The Black Aesthetic. Ed. Addison Gayle, Jr. Garden

    City, N.Y.: Anchor-Doubleday, 1972.

A REPRINT

Tennyson, Alfred. Poems, Chiefly Lyrical. London, 1832;

    rpt. Guilford, Pa.: AME Press, 1971.

Magazines, periodicals, and newspapers

A SIGNED ARTICLE IN A PERIODICAL

Franklin, Rosemary. "The Early History of Anti-

    Contraceptive Laws." American Quarterly, 18 (Spring

    1966), 3-23.

A SIGNED ARTICLE IN A MAGAZINE

Katz, Donald R. "Drawing Fire: Cartoonist Bill Mauldin

    and His 35-Year Fight for Truth, Justice, and the

    American Way." Rolling Stone, 4 Nov. 1976, pp. 52-54,

    56, 58, 60, 89.

AN UNSIGNED ARTICLE IN A MAGAZINE

"The Right to Die." Time, 11 Oct. 1976, p. 101.

A SIGNED ARTICLE FROM A NEWSPAPER

Bowman, David. "Wrath: My Cow O'Leary's Plan for a

    Greater Memphis." Center City, 11 Nov. 1976, pp. 1-2,

    col. 1.

AN UNSIGNED ARTICLE FROM A NEWSPAPER

"500 March Against Death Penalty." Boston Sunday Globe,

    13 May 1979, Sec. 1, p. 21, col. 4.

35c

Encyclopedias and almanacs

AN UNSIGNED ARTICLE FROM AN ENCYCLOPEDIA

"Mammoth." The New Columbia Encyclopedia. 1975 ed.

A SIGNED ARTICLE FROM AN ENCYCLOPEDIA

Hutton, J. E. "Moravian Brethren." Encyclopaedia

    Brittanica. 1911 ed.

Bulletins, pamphlets, and government documents

Resource Notebook. Washington, D.C.: Project on

    Institutional Renewal through the Improvement of

    Teaching, 1976.

National Endowment for the Humanities. "National

    Endowment for the Humanities Education Program

    Guidelines, 1978-1979." Washington, D.C.: GPO, 1978.

Unpublished dissertations and theses

Wilson, Stuart M. "John Stuart Mill as a Literary Critic."

    Diss. Univ. of Michigan 1970.

Films and television programs

Allen, Woody, dir. Manhattan. With Woody Allen, Diane

    Keaton, Michael Murphy, Meryl Streep, and Anne Byrne.

    United Artists, 1979.

Hollow Image. Writ. Lee Hunkins. Dir. Marvin Chomsky.

    ABC Theatre. 24 June 1979.

Plays and concerts

Wheeler, David, dir. Richard III. By William Shakespeare.

    With Al Pacino. Cort Theatre, New York. 28 June 1979.

Ozawa, Seiji, cond. Boston Symphony Orchestra Concert.

    Symphony Hall, Boston. 31 March 1979.

Records

Mitchell, Joni. For the Roses. Asylum, SD 5057, 1972.

Interviews

Galbraith, John Kenneth. Telephone interview. 2 July 1979.

35c

EXERCISE 3

Prepare bibliography entries from the following information. Follow the models of the *MLA Handbook,* given in the preceding section, or use the format suggested by your instructor.

1. A book called *Black Voices: An Anthology of Afro-American Literature,* published in 1968 by The New American Library in New York, edited by Abraham Clapham.

2. An article in *Southern Folklore Quarterly,* volume 24, published in 1960. The article is "The New Orleans Voodoo Ritual Dance and Its Twentieth-Century Survivals," written by John Q. Anderson, on pages 135–43.

3. The fifth volume of *The History of Technology,* published in 1958 in London by Oxford Unversity Press, written by Charles Singer, E. J. Holmroyd, A. R. Hall, and Trevor I. Williams.

4. A pamphlet entitled *George Segal,* published in 1979 by the Whitney Museum of American Art in New York.

5. A book by John Bartlett called *Familiar Quotations,* in its fourteenth edition which was edited by Emily Morison Beck, published in 1968 by Little, Brown and Company in Boston, Massachusetts.

EXERCISE 4

Prepare a working bibliography of at least ten sources for a research paper on one of the following people or on someone of your own choosing. Begin by limiting the subject to a manageable size. Then consult reference books, periodical indexes, and the library card catalog. Record bibliographic information on note cards using the models given in the preceding section or a format suggested by your instructor.

1. Menachem Begin
2. Helen Keller
3. John Wayne
4. Kareem Abdul-Jabbar
5. Joan Baez
6. Emily Dickinson

EXERCISE 5

35c

Using one of the topics and the possible references for it from Exercise 2 (p. 421), or starting with a different topic and references, prepare a working bibliography of at least ten sources for a research paper. List on 3″ x 5″ cards the complete bibliographic information for each source. Use the format of the models given in the preceding section or the format chosen by your instructor.

35d

Reading to strengthen your overview and working up a
tentative thesis and outline

When to stop looking for sources and start reading depends,
of course, on the length of your paper and on the complexity of your
subject. You are probably ready to begin reading when your working bibliography suggests that you have explored most aspects of
your topic and at least some sources that deal directly with your
central concern. For a paper of fifteen hundred to two thousand
words, ten to fifteen promising titles should give you a good base.

Once you have a satisfactory working bibliography, scan the
cards for the titles that are most likely to help you work up a tentative outline and thesis. For his topic, "the use of emotional appeals
in advertising," Paul Fuller begins by looking at sources on research
into motivation as well as more general sources on advertising.

As you read quickly through your sources, your purpose is to
shape your thinking, not to collect information. You need this preliminary reading to obtain an overview of your topic so that your
thesis encompasses the range of available information and represents your informed interpretation. Don't allow yourself to get
bogged down in taking very detailed notes at this stage. Without a
sense of what information is pertinent, you may not leave time to
cover all the sources you have selected as possibly relevant to your
topic.

While reading and learning about your topic, do write down
general ideas that seem fundamental to your topic. Be especially
careful to record ideas of your own—such as a connection between
statements by two different writers—because these may not occur to
you later. When you've consulted the sources in your working bibliography, think of how you can arrange your list of ideas into groups
of related thoughts. These rough groups—similar to the groups of
ideas you use in writing an essay (see 1c)—will give you a view of
your topic that should help you write a thesis for your paper.

Your thesis should state, in one or two sentences, your general
idea and the perspective you take. (See 1d.) The thesis not only tells
readers what to expect from your paper but also helps keep you on
track while you do further research and write the first draft. For his
paper on advertising, Fuller writes the following tentative thesis:

> Advertisers appeal to consumers' emotions, rather than to their
> reason, because they want to manipulate consumers.

This thesis states Fuller's central idea (that advertisers appeal to
consumers' emotions) and also his view that advertisers use emo-

35d

tional appeals because they want to manipulate consumers. After further research, Fuller may have to revise his thesis, but for the moment it gives him a way to organize his work.

Having written a tentative thesis for your paper, you will be ready to prepare a working outline that will guide your subsequent research. Like the working outline for an essay (see 1f), the outline should show your main points, in the order you think you will cover them, and it should include the important supporting ideas for each main point. Fuller's working outline, below, is fairly complete. Notice that the organization corresponds to the arrangement of ideas in the thesis sentence: Fuller's central idea comes first, followed by his perspective on it. Notice also that Fuller questions some ideas he hasn't found evidence for and must research further.

> Advertisers appeal to consumers' emotions
> > Shows in the ads
> > > —full of adventure, humor, sex, status, and other emotional subjects
> > > —little information on quality and performance of product or sound reasons to buy
> > Advertisers admit they emphasize emotional appeals
> > > —they say advertising is communication and therefore emotional
> > > —they say consumers choose irrationally
> > > —they say sales increase when ads stress emotion
> Advertisers appeal to emotions because they want to manipulate consumers
> > So say critics: McLuhan, Packard
> > Research proves that advertisers use emotional appeals to manipulate (?)
> > > —consumers are manipulated by emotional appeals (?)
> > > —consumers would respond to rational appeals if they were provided (?)

If at this point you feel you don't have enough information to complete a working outline, or that one of your points lacks support (as Fuller's last point about research seems to), consult sources on your working bibliography that you skipped before, or reexamine the ones you skimmed. But don't try to construct a detailed, final outline now. It and the thesis will undoubtedly change as you do more research.

35d

EXERCISE 6

Read through the sources in the working bibliography you made in Exercise 5 (p. 426). Jot down the main ideas related to your topic. Draft a thesis based on those ideas that states both the topic and your perspective on it. Finally, construct a working outline that contains your main points and several supporting points for each, returning to your sources as needed.

35e
Taking detailed notes

After you have written a thesis statement and prepared a working outline, you are ready to gather, interpret, and analyze information. To begin this stage, take detailed notes from your sources to help verify and expand your ideas as well as collect evidence to support them.

Keep a copy of your working outline with you in the library as a guide to give order to your search. Try to research the headings and subheadings of your working outline one at a time. But don't let the outline dominate your thinking. As you learn more about your topic, you will probably revise your outline by changing a heading, by dropping or adding one, or by rearranging headings. Revising is an inevitable part of research writing.

The most efficient method of reading during research is skimming, reading quickly to look for pertinent information. Skimming is not reading randomly in hopes of hitting what you want. Rather, you read with a specific question in mind. Use the table of contents or index to find what you want, and concentrate on headings and main ideas, skipping material unrelated to the specific question you are researching. When you find something useful, read slowly and thoroughly to evaluate and interpret the material and to decide what information to write down.

Taking notes is not a mechanical process of copying from books and magazines. Your notes are your thinking. As you read and take notes, you decide what information supports your thesis, and you interpret and organize that information according to your thesis and outline.

Using a system for taking notes helps simplify the process and later makes writing the paper easier. The most common method involves note cards (4″ x 6″ cards allow more room than 3″ x 5″). Write only one idea on a card, so you can rearrange information when you want to. If the same source gives you more than one idea, make more than one card. At the top of every card, write the author, title, and pages of your source and also the heading from your working outline that this note belongs under. Then you will always know where the idea came from and what you intended to do with it. One of Paul Fuller's note cards, showing this format, follows.

35e

Advertising as communication
Martineau, Motivation in Advertising
p. 139.

Because advertising is a form of
human communication, emotional
and rational meanings are
communicated at the same time.

You can use four different kinds of notes: (1) summary, (2) paraphrase, (3) direct quotation, and (4) a combination of summary or paraphrase and direct quotation. When you **summarize,** you use your own words to condense an extended idea or argument to a sentence or two. When you **paraphrase,** you follow much more closely the author's original presentation, but you still restate it in your own words. Paraphrase is most useful when you want to use an author's line of reasoning but don't feel the original words merit direct quotation. As you summarize and paraphrase, be careful not to distort the author's meaning, but don't feel you have to put down in new words the whole passage or all the details. Select what is pertinent and restate only that. In this way you will be developing your thoughts about the topic as you read and take notes. The sample note given above is a paraphrase. You can compare this note to the original statement by Pierre Martineau from *Motivation in Advertising* (New York: McGraw-Hill, 1957), p. 139:

> Advertising combines forces of both logical thought and emotive, aesthetic thought. Because it is communication from one set of humans to another set of humans, part of the meaning will be rational; but also there will be much meaning conveyed by nonrational symbols.

(For more information on paraphrasing, see Appendix A on avoiding plagiarism.)

Summary and paraphrase are the methods of making notes you will use most often. Use **direct quotation** only when you feel the source's words give a special effect you want to include, when you are discussing an author's writing, when you want to give impact to an authority's opinion, or when you plan to use a graph, table, or diagram from the source. When you quote directly, keep in mind that you can use brackets to show the additional words needed for

35e

understanding (see 25d) and ellipses to show omissions of irrelevant words or sentences (see 25e). The following note card shows how Fuller might have quoted rather than paraphrased Martineau, using both ellipses and brackets to make the quotation more concise without changing its meaning.

Advertising as communication

Martineau, Motivation in Advertising
p. 139.

"Advertising combines... logical thought and emotive, aesthetic thought. Because it is [human] communication..., part of the meaning will be rational; but also there will be much meaning conveyed by non-rational symbols."

Be sure to proofread any direct quotation at least twice to ensure complete accuracy, and be sure you have supplied the quotation marks so that later you won't confuse the direct quotation card with a paraphrase or summary card.

Using quotation in combination with paraphrase helps you shape the material to suit your purposes (although you must be careful not to distort the author's meaning). The following card shows how Fuller might have used a combination of quotation and paraphrase for the statement by Martineau. Notice that the quotation marks are clearly visible.

Advertising as communication

Martineau, Motivation in Advertising
p. 139.

Advertisers themselves say that "advertising combines forces of both logical thought and emotive, aesthetic thought" because of its nature as "communication from one set of humans to another."

35e

If the material you are quoting, summarizing, or paraphrasing runs from one page to the next in the source, make a mark (such as a check mark or a slash) at the exact spot where one page ends and the next begins. When writing your paper, you may want to use only a part of the material (say, the first or second half). The mark will save you from having to go back to your source to find which page the material actually occurred on.

When you have enough note cards to back up or explain all the points on your working outline, you can move to the next step of revising your thesis and writing a formal outline.

EXERCISE 7

Prepare two note cards, one containing a paraphrase of the paragraph below and the other containing a summary of the paragraph. Use the format for a note card provided in the preceding section, omitting only the outline heading.

> Federal organization has made it possible for the different states to deal with the same problems in many different ways. One consequence of federalism, then, has been that people are treated differently, by law, from state to state. The great strength of this system is that differences from state to state in cultural preferences, moral standards, and levels of wealth can be accommodated. In contrast to a unitary system in which the central government makes all important decisions (as in France), federalism is a powerful arrangement for maximizing regional freedom and autonomy. The great weakness of our federal system, however, is that people in some states receive less than the best or the most advanced or the least expensive services and policies that government can offer. The federal dilemma does not invite easy solutions, for the costs and benefits of the arrangement have tended to balance out.
>
> —Peter K. Eisinger et al., *American Politics*, p. 44

EXERCISE 8

Prepare a note card containing a combination of paraphrase or summary and direct quotation that states the major idea of the passage below. Use the format for a note card provided in the preceding section, omitting only the outline heading.

> Most speakers unconsciously duel even during seemingly casual conversations, as can often be observed at social gatherings where they show less concern for exchanging information with other guests than for asserting their own dominance. Their verbal dueling often employs very subtle weapons like mumbling, a hostile act which defeats the listener's desire to understand what the speaker claims he is trying to say (but is

really not saying because he is mumbling!). Or the verbal dueler may keep talking after someone has passed out of hearing range—which is often an aggressive challenge to the listener to return and acknowledge the dominance of the speaker.   —Peter Farb, *Word Play*, p. 107

EXERCISE 9

Continuing from Exercise 5 (p. 426), as the next step in preparing a research paper, make notes of specific information from your sources. As much as practicable, adhere to your thesis and follow your working outline. Use paraphrase, direct quotation, and a combination of the two. Mark each card with the author's name, title, and page number as well as your outline heading.

35f
Revising the thesis and writing a formal outline

As you took notes, you began to revise your thesis and outline in your mind and perhaps in your writing. These revisions occupy most of the next step in writing a research paper. After investigating your topic thoroughly through reading and note taking, you will want to evaluate your thesis sentence in light of what you now know. At this point, the thesis should be close to final in its wording and in its description of your topic and what you have to say about it. In his research, for example, Paul Fuller could not find evidence to support his belief that consumers would make rational choices if they were given advertisements that appealed to reason. (See his working outline on p. 428.) Instead, he found the opposite: consumers choose products emotionally and do not use reason even when they are given the chance. Consequently, he revises his working outline and his thesis.

TENTATIVE THESIS

Advertisers appeal to consumers' emotions, rather than to their reason, because they want to manipulate consumers.

REVISED THESIS

Advertisers appeal to consumers' emotions, rather than to their reason, because consumers choose products irrationally.

After revising your thesis sentence, prepare a detailed outline from which to write your paper. This **formal outline** is more complete than a working outline and arranges ideas in a logical way. Inadequate coverage of the thesis, overlapping ideas, ideas that are

35f

not parallel yet are in parallel positions, and imprecise phrasing—all of these are corrected in the process of writing a formal outline. The goal is to produce an outline that presents your ideas in a sensible and persuasive sequence and that supports ideas at each level with enough explanation and evidence.

Before actually beginning work on your formal outline, you should group your note cards according to their headings, which are the headings of your working outline. You can begin revising your outline by rearranging and retitling cards to reflect your changed ideas and the sense of your revised thesis sentence. Gradually you will begin to see a complete outline of your thinking.

The format for a formal outline looks like this.

```
  I. _____
     A. _____
        1. _____
           a. _____
              (1) _____
              (2) _____
           b. _____
        2. _____
     B. _____
 II. _____
```

Main topics are numbered with Roman numerals, the first sublevel with capital letters, the second with Arabic numerals, the third with lowercase letters, and the fourth with Arabic numerals enclosed by parentheses. Use only as many levels of ideas as you need.

A formal outline may be written in phrases—a **topic outline**—or in sentences—a **sentence outline.** Either is suitable for a research paper, though a sentence outline, because it requires complete statements, conveys more information. Ideas at the same numbered or lettered level should be parallel in importance and expression. Be sure that sublevels fit logically under the levels above them. And be sure to avoid single sublevels, which illogically imply that something is divided into only one part. The following excerpt from an outline is an example of such illogical subdivision.

> 1. Public television should be funded only by local donors.
>   a. It is intended to serve only local audiences.

The two levels here are really two parts of the same idea and should be treated as such:

> 1. Public television should be funded only by local donors because it is intended to serve only local audiences.

Paul Fuller's formal sentence outline is on pages 448–449, pre-

35f

ceding his research paper at the end of this chapter. Comparing it with his working outline on page 428, you can see the formal outline's much greater quantity of information and more logical arrangement of ideas.

EXERCISE 10

Identify the flaws in the following partial outline for a research paper. Check especially for incorrect use of formal outline form, including illogical subdivision of topics, inconsistent wording of items, and nonparallel placement for ideas parallel in importance.

THESIS SENTENCE

Food additives, which are used to process foods and to preserve them or improve their appearance, are more useful to us than they are dangerous.

FORMAL OUTLINE

I. Processing, preservation, appearance
    A. Processing
        1. Leavening agents
        2. Anti-foaming agents
        3. Emulsifiers
            a. Bind ingredients together
    B. Preservation
        1. Protect from internal destruction
            a. Natural enzymes can cause discoloration or overripening
            b. Must remove or disable enzymes
        2. External destruction
            a. Bacteria
            b. Fungus
        3. Environment
            a. Heat, moisture, humidity
            b. Humectants protect foods from excess moisture
    C. Appearance
        1. Glazing agents
        2. Foaming agents cause bubbles to appear in hot chocolate
        3. Firming agents
            a. Keep fruits and vegetables firm in cans
            b. Thickeners
                1. Prevent ice crystal formation, as in ice cream
                2. Improve texture
        4. Sequestrants prevent discoloration

35f

EXERCISE 11

Using the note cards you prepared in Exercise 9 (p. 433), revise the thesis statement from Exercise 6 (p. 428) and construct a formal sentence or topic outline from which to write a paper.

35g
Writing and revising the paper

After you have taken notes from your sources, have revised your thesis as necessary, and have written a formal outline for your paper, you're ready to begin writing the first draft. Take time to organize your notes carefully according to your formal outline. Once the notes are arranged, go through them slowly, considering how you will link ideas or facts to each other, how you will emphasize an idea or de-emphasize it, where you can use direct quotation most effectively, and so on. With this kind of preparation, the actual writing of the first draft should be relatively effortless.

Your outline, note cards, and working bibliography are the resources on which you base the first and subsequent drafts. They are crucial, but you needn't feel enslaved by them. Though you could produce a first draft by adhering to the outline and simply stitching notes together, your draft will be better, and you will need less revision later, if you remain open to new interpretations or new arrangements of information that occur to you and incorporate the sensible ones in your paper.

In writing, think of the audience for your research paper as general college-level readers—serious and thoughtful, appreciating specificity and clarity while expecting assertions to be supported with evidence (see 1e). Adopt a rational, straightforward tone by remaining moderate in your expression and by using standard diction and a full range of sentence structures.

When you have written a first draft, take a break—for a day or so if possible—so that you can read the draft with a critical eye when you begin to revise. Then use the advice and revision checklist in 2b (p. 33) to evaluate your first draft. Proofread, of course, to catch simple mistakes. But, more importantly, rethink the content and effectiveness of every sentence. Start with your thesis sentence (Does it accurately describe your topic and your perspective? Is the paper unified around it?), and proceed through each paragraph. Check for the irrelevant idea that crept in just because you had a note card on it. Look for omissions of supporting evidence, for points that once seemed strong but are now unclear. Examine the paper for a balance between the views of others (support) and your own views (interpretation). Try to read the paper from the point of view of someone who has not spent hours planning and researching, but instead has come fresh to the paper—skeptical perhaps, but capable of being informed and convinced.

EXERCISE 12

Write the research paper you have been preparing in Exercises 1, 2, 5, 6, 9, and 11. Before beginning the first draft, study your notes. While writing, follow your note cards (Exercise 9) and formal outline (Exercise 11), but stay open to new ideas, associations, and arrangements. Then revise thoroughly, working to improve not only your presentation of ideas but also the ideas themselves, if necessary.

35h
Preparing the footnotes

The primary purpose of footnotes is to acknowledge sources of information and quotation used in the text of the paper. (You may also use footnotes to provide parenthetical explanation or comment, as Paul Fuller does twice in his final draft; see pages 466 and 468. But such notes should contain information that is clearly parenthetical, not a digression or a necessary extension of the paper's topic.) You must acknowledge sources of direct quotation as well as of tables and diagrams. You must also acknowledge sources of ideas, facts, or associations between them that you paraphrase or summarize from books, magazines, newspapers, movies, television programs, interviews, letters, and the like. Acknowledge all quotations and paraphrases no matter what their length or how often you have already cited the source. You do not need to acknowledge your own ideas or ideas that are considered common knowledge, such as well-known historical and scientific facts, when these are expressed in your own words. (For a detailed discussion of what to acknowledge and when, see Appendix A on avoiding plagiarism.)

As you read through your paper, check the note cards you have used. Identify each paraphrase and quotation in the text, proofread every quotation a final time, then locate the corresponding bibliography card. The page numbers on your note cards and the information on your bibliography cards give you everything you need to write your footnotes.

35h

Footnotes may be written in a variety of ways. The style of the Modern Language Association (available in the *MLA Handbook* cited earlier) is the one described here. Your instructor may want you to use this one or a slightly different one. Whatever style you use, be consistent. Number the footnotes consecutively throughout your paper. Place them at the bottoms of appropriate text pages or on a separate group of pages at the end of your paper as your instructor requires. (Footnotes collected at the end of a paper are often called *endnotes* or simply *notes*.) In the text use a raised numeral (¹) at the end of the material you are acknowledging, then use the same raised numeral at the start of the note. (See Paul Fuller's research paper beginning on p. 446.) For graphs, tables, and diagrams, place the word *Source* under the illustration, follow it with a colon, and then give the note. Double-space footnotes and notes, and start each one on a new line, indenting the first line five spaces from the left margin.

Notice that the following models for footnotes and notes differ from the models for bibliography entries (pp. 423–425) in some details, although the information presented is essentially the same. Be sure to use footnote models for your footnotes and bibliography models for your bibliography. (The footnote models following are those for first references. When the same source is acknowledged more than once in the same paper, a shortened form of reference should be used according to the guidelines that are provided on pp. 441–443.)

Books

BOOK WITH ONE AUTHOR

[1]Pauline Kael, <u>Going Steady</u> (Boston: Atlantic–Little, Brown, 1970), p. 87.

BOOK WITH TWO OR THREE AUTHORS

[2]William K. Wimsatt and Cleanth Brooks, <u>Literary Criticism: A Short History</u> (Chicago: Univ. of Chicago Press, 1978), p. 312.

BOOK WITH MORE THAN THREE AUTHORS

[3]Paul Mussen et al., <u>Psychology: An Introduction</u> (Lexington, Mass.: D. C. Heath, 1973), p. 183.

BOOK WITH CORPORATE AUTHORSHIP

[4]Editors of The Progressive, The Crisis of Survival (Glenview, Ill.: Scott, Foresman, 1970), p. 61.

A LATER EDITION

[5]X. J. Kennedy, An Introduction to Poetry, 4th ed. (Boston: Little, Brown, 1978), pp. 103-12.

A WORK IN MORE THAN ONE VOLUME

[6]Joseph Blotner, Faulkner: A Biography (New York: Random House, 1974), II, 117.

A TRANSLATION

[7]Dante Alighieri, The Inferno, trans. John Ciardi (New York: New American Library, 1971), pp. 73-74.

A WORK IN A SERIES

[8]Ingmar Bergman, The Seventh Seal, Modern Film Scripts Series (New York: Simon and Schuster, 1968), p. 6.

A BOOK WITH AN EDITOR

[9]James P. Spradley and David W. McCurdy, eds., Conformity and Conflict, 4th ed. (Boston: Little, Brown, 1980), p. 4.

A BOOK WITH AN AUTHOR AND AN EDITOR

[10]Herman Melville, The Confidence Man: His Masquerade, ed. Hershel Parker (New York: W. W. Norton, 1971), p. 49.

A SELECTION FROM AN EDITED ANTHOLOGY OR COLLECTION

[11]Carolyn F. Gerald, "The Black Writer and His Role," in The Black Aesthetic, ed. Addison Gayle, Jr. (Garden City, N.Y.: Anchor-Doubleday, 1972), pp. 197-98.

A REPRINT

[12]Alfred Tennyson, Poems, Chiefly Lyrical (London, 1832; rpt. Guilford, Pa.: AME Press, 1971), p. 31.

35h

Magazines, periodicals, and newspapers

A SIGNED ARTICLE IN A PERIODICAL

[13]Rosemary Franklin, "The Early History of Anti-Contraceptive Laws," <u>American Quarterly</u>, 18 (Spring 1966), 14.

A SIGNED ARTICLE IN A MAGAZINE

[14]Donald R. Katz, "Drawing Fire: Cartoonist Bill Mauldin and His 35-Year Fight for Truth, Justice, and the American Way," <u>Rolling Stone</u>, 4 Nov. 1976, p. 56.

AN UNSIGNED ARTICLE IN A MAGAZINE

[15]"The Right to Die," <u>Time</u>, 11 Oct. 1976, p. 101.

A SIGNED ARTICLE FROM A NEWSPAPER

[16]David Bowman, "Wrath: My Cow O'Leary's Plan for a Greater Memphis," <u>Center City</u>, 11 Nov. 1976, p. 2, col. 1.

AN UNSIGNED ARTICLE FROM A NEWSPAPER

[17]"500 March Against Death Penalty," <u>Boston Sunday Globe</u>, 13 May 1979, Sec. 1, p. 21, col. 4.

Encyclopedias and almanacs

AN UNSIGNED ARTICLE FROM AN ENCYCLOPEDIA

[18]"Mammoth," <u>The New Columbia Encyclopedia</u>, 1975 ed.

A SIGNED ARTICLE FROM AN ENCYCLOPEDIA

[19]J. E. Hutton, "Moravian Brethren," <u>Encyclopaedia Brittanica</u>, 1911 ed.

Bulletins, pamphlets, and government documents

35h

[20]<u>Resource Notebook</u> (Washington, D.C.: Project on Institutional Renewal through the Improvement of Teaching, 1976), p. 17.

[21]National Endowment for the Humanities, "National Endowment for the Humanities Education Program Guidelines, 1978-1979" (Washington, D.C.: GPO, 1978), p. 8.

Unpublished dissertations and theses

[22]Stuart M. Wilson, "John Stuart Mill as a Literary Critic," Diss. Univ. of Michigan 1970, p. 7.

Films and television programs

[23]Woody Allen, dir., *Manhattan*, with Woody Allen, Diane Keaton, Michael Murphy, Meryl Streep, and Anne Byrne, United Artists, 1979.

[24]*Hollow Image*, writ. Lee Hunkins, dir. Marvin Chomsky, ABC Theatre, 24 June 1979.

Plays and concerts

[25]David Wheeler, dir., *Richard III*, by William Shakespeare, with Al Pacino, Cort Theatre, New York, 28 June 1979.

[26]Seiji Ozawa, cond., Boston Symphony Orchestra Concert, Symphony Hall, Boston, 31 March 1979.

Records

[27]Joni Mitchell, *For the Roses*, Asylum, SD 5057, 1972.

Interviews

[28]Telephone interview with John Kenneth Galbraith, 2 July 1979.

Subsequent references to the same source

35h

To minimize clutter in your footnotes or notes, and to give readers a quick sense of how often you acknowledge a source, you should use a shortened form for subsequent references to a source already cited fully. When you are using only one source by the author cited or bearing the title cited if there is no author, the *MLA Handbook* recommends that subsequent references carry only the author's name or the title and the page reference appropriate for the later citation. Here are three examples, both preceded by the full citations.

> [1]Pauline Kael, <u>Going Steady</u> (Boston: Atlantic–Little,
> Brown, 1970), p. 87.
> [29]Kael, p. 96.

> [10]Herman Melville, <u>The Confidence Man: His Masquerade</u>,
> ed. Hershel Parker (New York: W. W. Norton, 1971), p. 49.
> [30]Melville, p. 62.

> [15]"The Right to Die," <u>Time</u>, 11 Oct. 1976, p. 101.
> [31]"The Right to Die," p. 101.

However, if two of your sources are by the same author or bear the same title, give the title or the name of the source so there can be no confusion about the work you are citing. The title or source may be shortened. For example:

> [1]Pauline Kael, <u>Going Steady</u> (Boston: Atlantic–Little,
> Brown, 1970), p. 87.
> [32]Pauline Kael, <u>Kiss Kiss Bang Bang</u> (Boston: Little,
> Brown, 1968), p. 263.
> [33]Kael, <u>Kiss Kiss</u>, p. 266.

> [18]"Mammoth," <u>The New Columbia Encyclopedia</u>, 1975 ed.
> [34]"Mammoth," <u>Encyclopaedia Brittanica</u>, 1911 ed.
> [35]"Mammoth," <u>Columbia Encyclopedia</u>.

35h

If you have previously cited one volume of a multi-volume work, be sure to note the volume number in the new, shortened citation, even if it is the same.

> [6]Joseph Blotner, <u>Faulkner: A Biography</u> (New York:
> Random House, 1974), II, 117.
> [36]Blotner, II, 127.

NOTE: Although the *MLA Handbook* does not recommend it, the Latin abbreviation *ibid.*, for *ibidem* ("in the same place"), is still a common means of indicating that a citation refers to the source in the preceding note, though perhaps to a different page of the source:

> ³Paul Mussen et al., Psychology: An Introduction
>
> (Lexington, Mass.: D. C. Heath, 1973), p. 183.
>
> ⁴Ibid., p. 184.

Abbreviations

The *MLA Handbook* style for footnotes and notes eliminates many abbreviations. However, the guide still uses several abbreviations, and other styles of documentation use even more. Some of the most common abbreviations are listed below.

anon.	anonymous
bk., bks.	book(s)
c., ca.	*circa* ("about"), used with approximate dates
cf.	compare
ch., chs.	chapter(s)
col., cols.	column(s)
comp., comps.	compiled by, compiler(s)
diss.	dissertation
ed., eds.	edition(s), editor(s)
et al.	*et alii* ("and others")
ff.	and the following pages, as in pp. 17 ff.
ibid.	*ibidem* ("in the same place")
illus.	illustrated by, illustrator, illustration(s)
l., ll.	line(s)
loc. cit.	*loco citato* ("in the place cited")
ms, mss	manuscript(s)
n., nn.	note(s), as in p. 24, n. 2
n.d.	no date (of publication)
no., nos.	number(s)
n. pag.	no pagination
n.p.	no place (of publication), no publisher
op. cit.	*opere citato* ("in the work cited")
p., pp.	page(s)
passim	throughout
q.v.	*quod vide* ("which see")
rev.	revision, revised by
rpt.	reprint, reprinted
supp., supps.	supplement(s)
trans.	translator, translated by
univ.	university
vol., vols.	volume(s)

35h

EXERCISE 13

Prepare footnotes from the following information. Follow the models of the *MLA Handbook* given in the preceding section, or use the style suggested by your instructor.

1. In the first note, cite page 95 in a book called *The Old Stone Age*, which was written by François Bordes and translated by J. E. Anderson. The translation was published in 1973 by McGraw-Hill in New York.
2. In the second note, cite page 121 in the book above.
3. In the third note, cite Abraham Maslow's article entitled "Self-Actualizing People," which appeared in 1950 on page 26 of volume 1 of *Personality Symposia*.
4. In the fourth note, cite page 34 in a book by Abraham Maslow called *Motivation and Personality*, published in 1954 by Harper & Row in New York.
5. In the fifth note, cite page 164 in Maslow's book above.

EXERCISE 14

Prepare the footnotes or notes, as specified by your instructor, for the research paper you wrote and revised in Exercise 12 (p. 437). Use the models given in the preceding section, or follow the style suggested by your instructor.

35i
Preparing the final bibliography

When your paper is completed, prepare a final bibliography from the working bibliography you used throughout your research and writing. Include in the bibliography all sources from which you quoted, paraphrased, or summarized. Unless your instructor requests it, don't include sources you examined but did not acknowledge in notes.

Place the bibliography at the end of your paper after the footnotes. List your sources in alphabetical order. Double-space all the entries, indenting the second and subsequent lines of each one five spaces. Use the form given on pages 423–425 (from the *MLA Handbook*) or a style recommended by your instructor.

35i

EXERCISE 15

Prepare the final bibliography for the research paper you wrote and revised in Exercise 12 (p. 437). Use the models given on pages 423–425, or follow the style suggested by your instructor.

35j

Examining a sample research paper

Paul Fuller's research paper, presented on the following pages, illustrates the advice explained in this chapter. Fuller uses the style for footnotes and bibliography described in the *MLA Handbook*. He types the paper following advice on manuscript preparation such as that given in Appendix B. The comments on pages facing the research paper, keyed by number, describe some of the decisions Fuller makes and mention other acceptable options.

How Advertisers Make Us Buy   1

By

Paul Fuller

English 101, Section A

Mr. R. Macek

March 12, 1979

35j

1. On his title page, Fuller includes the title of his paper about a third of the way down the page, his own name (preceded by *By*) about an inch below the title, and, starting about an inch below his name, some identifying information requested by his instructor (course number, section label, and instructor's name) and the date. All lines are centered in the width of the page and separated by at least one line of space.

   NEXT TWO PAGES

2. If your instructor asks you to include your final outline, place it between the title page and the text, as Fuller does on the following pages. You may leave its pages unnumbered, or you may number them with lowercase Roman numerals, as Fuller does. If you number the outline pages, leave the number off the first page and begin numbering with *ii* on the second page. Place the heading "Outline" at the top of the first page.

3. Fuller includes his final thesis sentence as part of his outline, so his instructor can see how the parts relate to the whole.

4. Fuller's final outline is in full sentences. Some instructors request topic outlines, in which ideas are stated in phrases instead of in sentences and are not followed by periods.

5. Notice that each main point (numbered with Roman numerals) refers directly to a portion of the thesis sentence and that all the subdivisions relate directly to their main idea. Notice, too, the use of parallel phrasing for parallel levels. You need not repeat words such as *advertisers say,* but in this case they help Fuller relate his ideas clearly.

35j

Outline

2

<u>Thesis</u>: Advertisers appeal to consumers' emotions, rather than to their reason, because consumers choose products irrationally.

3

I. Critics of advertising say advertisers deliberately use strong emotional and irrational appeals.

4

    A. Marshall McLuhan says the appeals of advertising are directed to the unconscious.

    B. Vance Packard says the methods of advertisers represent regression for the rational nature of human beings.

    C. David Ogilvy says that most advertising treats consumers as if they were idiots, unable to reason.

II. Advertisers say they appeal to emotion because consumers choose products irrationally.

5

    A. Advertisers say that advertising by its nature as human communication expresses both emotional and rational messages.

    B. Advertisers say human beings choose irrationally.

    C. Advertisers say that appealing to emotion increases sales.

        1. Adding color to products or their ads increases sales.

35j

ii

2. Adding cartoon characters to products or
    their packages increases sales.

3. Adding emotional symbols to ads increases
    sales.

III. Studies of advertising indicate that advertisers do
     appeal to emotions, as both critics and advertisers
     claim, and that consumers seem to choose products
     emotionally, as advertisers claim.

A. An informal survey of ads indicates that the
    average ad uses much more emotional appeal than
    rational appeal.

B. Experiments by independent researchers suggest
    that consumers respond to emotional appeals in
    advertising and that they do not examine ads
    rationally.

    1. One study showed that consumers make an
        emotional choice in favor of ads that merely
        sound truthful.

    2. Another study showed that consumers do not
        examine ads rationally, but do respond
        emotionally to a claim that merely sounds
        rational.

35j

How Advertisers Make Us Buy

6

7

The deep voice speaking in a proud marching stride
about "winning the world" and the rolling background music
call to mind a theater newsreel of World War II. The
camera's steep view of a mast shows a woman descending from
a swirl of sailcloth and clouds. The camera leaves this
close-up shot of strength and urgency to view the whole
scene--ship, ocean, sky--in a panorama that seems cosmic.
What is the purpose of this drama? To make a television
audience buy some coffee.

This advertisement's outsized play for emotional

8

attention and response is typical of contemporary advertising.
To persuade consumers to buy, advertisers seem to appeal to
their emotions about humor, sex, status, and adventure and
to their unquestioning faith in science. In doing so,
advertisers seem to ignore opportunities to appeal to the
human capacity for reason, for choosing a product by
considering the pros and cons of its performance and
quality. Advertisers' apparent emphasis on emotion
indicates that they believe consumers make decisions based
on irrelevant or momentary feelings about a product rather
than on objective and logical appraisals of it. Is it
true that advertisers emphasize appeals to emotion and that
they believe consumers are irrational? Do customers
actually make choices emotionally?

35j

6. Although a title such as "Appeals to Emotion in Advertising" would reflect Fuller's thesis more accurately, it would also be less vivid. The title is typed two inches from the top of the page and is separated from the text by four lines of space. The text is double-spaced. The first page of the paper is not numbered, so the first numbered page is page 2.

7. Fuller's first paragraph summarizes a television commercial to demonstrate how illogical advertising can be and to introduce readers to the issues of the thesis. The opening is concrete and effective. However, Fuller could have begun his paper with the second paragraph by phrasing the first sentence a little differently ("Outsized plays for emotional attention and response seem typical of contemporary advertising").

8. In his second paragraph, Fuller uses words such as *seem, apparent,* and *indicates* to describe the issues of his thesis without yet taking a stand. He presents his thesis at the end of the paragraph in the form of two questions. (In the last paragraph of the paper, after presenting his evidence, he states his thesis declaratively.) Fuller thus presents his ideas as questions he will answer by going over the appropriate evidence. In the second paragraph, Fuller also clarifies what he means by two central terms he will use throughout the paper: *appeal to emotion* and *appeal to reason*.

35j

2

Marshall McLuhan, the philosopher of mass-media culture, says the appeals of advertising are directed to the unconscious:

> Ours is the first age in which many thousands of the best-trained individual minds have made it a full-time business to get inside the collective public mind . . . to manipulate, exploit, control. . . . Why not assist the public to observe consciously the drama intended to operate unconsciously?[1]

Vance Packard, who brought national attention to the manipulative method of advertisers in his best-selling <u>The Hidden Persuaders</u>, says that the methods of advertisers "represent regress rather than progress for man in his long struggle to become a rational and self-guiding being."[2] David Ogilvy, one of advertising's most famous successes, says that most advertising treats consumers as if they were unable to reason:

> When I first began making advertisements . . . , I looked at the so-called mass magazines and I was impressed by the extraordinary gap between editorial content and advertising content. I saw that the editors were writing with taste to an intelligent audience, and the advertising writers were writing to idiots.[3]

Advertisers themselves say that ads are a mixture of rational and emotional appeals.[4] This they claim comes from advertising's nature as another form of human communication. Regular conversation illustrates how all human communication, including advertising, works. In regular conversation <u>how</u> something is said is as important as <u>what</u> is said. The speaker's voice, gestures, and facial expression carry emotional messages just as important as the rational content of what the speaker says. In print advertising, art, layout,

9

10

11

12

13

14

35j

9. The first paragraph on this page corresponds to Part I of Fuller's outline. The paragraphs from the bottom of this page to the bottom of page 4 correspond to Part II of the outline.

10. Fuller uses three direct quotations from his sources on this page. He introduces his quotations smoothly by establishing the credentials of each author in an identifying phrase. Two of the quotations (McLuhan's and Ogilvy's) are longer than four typed lines, so Fuller sets these off from the text. (The block quotations are indented from the left and single-spaced. If he were submitting his paper for publication, Fuller would double-space these long quotations to allow them to be marked for a typesetter.)

11. Fuller uses ellipses in the two long quotations to eliminate material irrelevant to his points (see 25e). But he is not entirely successful in editing the first quotation. The point Fuller wants to make is that McLuhan says advertising appeals are directed to the unconscious. But he leaves in a sentence (the last) that strays from this idea: "Why not assist the public to observe consciously the drama intended to operate unconsciously?" These words should also be deleted, and the quotation, shortened to four lines, should be run into the text.

12. Fuller raises footnote numbers above the line of type and makes sure that the number always follows punctuation after the idea or quotation being acknowledged. The numbers will run consecutively through the text, a new number for each citation, even when the source was acknowledged earlier.

13. Fuller does not begin a new paragraph after the McLuhan quotation because the material following (the Packard and Ogilvy quotations) is directly related. After the Ogilvy quotation, Fuller does begin a new paragraph because he's embarking on a new thought.

14. Here Fuller is paraphrasing from a source, so he cites the source as he would the source of a quotation.

35j

3

and typeface carry the emotional messages. In television advertising, the personalities of announcers and actors, the music, and the visual imagery become symbols of emotional meaning.[5]

15

Advertisers emphasize emotional appeals in advertising[6] because they say that human beings are essentially irrational. Car salespeople have noticed that customers on the verge of buying an expensive car for an emotional motive, such as a desire for status, like to talk at the last minute about superior mechanical performance in order to justify their emotional decision with a rational motive.[7] In Motivation in Advertising: Motives That Make People Buy, Pierre Martineau explained this idea more formally and more forcefully:

> The entire personality of every individual
> is built around basic emotional needs, and
> the whole system of his thinking is determined
> by these needs, even though superficially the
> individual defends his point of view on purely
> rational grounds. Experiments repeatedly show
> that his rationality is highly selective
> rationality (or in other words, not rational
> at all). [Emphasis added.][8]

16

Other recent studies confirm the same view of consumers by advertisers.[9]

17

18

Advertisers claim many sales successes through appeals to emotion. One technique for increasing the emotional appeal of products is "color engineering." Adding color to an ad or to a product in which color has no practical function increases sales. For example, until the 1920s fountain pens were made of hard black rubber. When colored plastic pens were introduced, sales improved "astronomically."[10] Using aluminum paint instead of black on bedsprings improved

35j

15. Note 5 refers to the source for all preceding sentences concerned with advertising as a form of human communication. Note 6, following, documents only the part of the sentence preceding the number.

16. Fuller underlines certain words in the quotation to emphasize them. He explains this change in brackets at the end of the quotation, before the footnote number. The brackets indicate clearly that the added emphasis was not part of the original citation.

17. Rather than continuing to quote and paraphrase the same view of consumers, Fuller lets readers know that further support is available, and his note tells where to find it. This kind of summary sentence, with added documentation, can help prevent a long-winded discussion.

18. In these paragraphs listing sales successes that resulted from appeals to emotion, Fuller has selected from his sources the most dramatic and vivid success stories he found. He provides concrete evidence that makes his point convincing. And he carefully cites his sources.

35j

4

sales by 25 percent for one manufacturer.[11] A Gloucester
fish packer increased his sales 33 percent simply by adding
color to his advertising circular.[12] Currently, the
emotional appeal of cartoon characters increases sales 10
to 20 percent when the characters are printed on products
or their packages. Some say the emotional appeal of cartoon
characters is hero worship; some say it is nostalgia.[13] But
the facts are clear that the appeal _is_ emotional and that
sales go up because of it.

Two of the classic advertising campaigns centered on
emotional appeals are Hathaway's and Marlboro's. After ads
for Hathaway shirts began to include a well-built, mysterious
man with a patch over one eye, sales of shirts tripled.[14]
The manufacturers of Marlboro cigarettes experienced an
even more dramatic increase in sales because of a change in
advertising. In 1954 Philip Morris decided to enter one of
its worst-selling cigarettes, Marlboro, in the new filter-
tip market.[15] To change the product's image as only a
woman's cigarette, the advertisers eliminated all women from
the ads and substituted virile men who were not professional
models. Each new ad emphasized a tattoo on the hand of the
man smoking a Marlboro. The tattoos were the symbol that
seemed to give the whole ad campaign an emotional unity.[16]
This change in emotional appeal improved Marlboro's sales
drastically: from near zero in 1954 to 6.4 billion in 1955,
14.3 billion in 1956, and 19.5 billion in 1957.[17]

But advertisers' success stories are not the last word.
An informal survey and more formal studies of advertising
show that appeals to emotion predominate and that consumers

19

20

21

22

35j

19. In his first draft Fuller described his examples of sales successes by using phrases such as "sales increased" and "sales improved" rather than actual figures, and his point lacked force. When he realized he needed to be more specific, he referred to his bibliography cards (showing the call numbers) and to his note cards (showing page numbers) and was able to collect the figures he wanted in a quick trip to the library.

20. Fuller is citing only two sources in notes 15, 16, and 17—the first and third from one source, the second from another (see p. 468). He finds it necessary to use three notes because he wants to insert the interpretation of the advertisement provided by one source between two factual items provided by another.

21. Fuller's blending of material from five different sources to make one point and his arrangement of the material in order of increasing drama indicate that he is not merely stringing together other people's ideas but is using research to express and support his own views.

22. This paragraph makes the transition between Part II and Part III of the outline and states the main idea of Part III. Fuller is moving from sales evidence that supports advertisers' claims about consumers to studies by nonadvertisers that are equally supportive.

5

seem to go out of their way to make choices for emotional
reasons.

My own informal survey of ads in an issue of <u>Newsweek</u>   23
revealed that most of the ads (thirty of forty-two) used a
predominantly emotional appeal (see Table 1, next page).   24
Only one-fifth of the ads (nine of forty-two) depended on
rational appeal as much as 50 percent. Some ads of
products for which rational appeal would be easy or likely--
products such as a newsletter, an economy car, and
insurance--barely used appeals to reason (under 20 percent
rational appeal). The conclusions of this limited (one-
reader, one-magazine) study were: (1) that most ads appeal
primarily to consumers' emotion; (2) that only a tiny
fraction of ads (one of forty-two) appeal primarily to
reason; and (3) that no ads use rational appeal 100 percent,
although many (twelve of forty-two) use emotional appeal
100 percent.

In an experimental study of advertising, Robert Settle
and Linda Golden found that admitting a product's inferiority
on one or two minor points of comparison was more effective
in advertising than claiming the product's superiority on
all counts. The researchers asked 120 business students to   25
evaluate a series of ads. (The products advertised were
fictitious.) Half the ads claimed that the fictitious
product was superior to the best-selling and well-known
actual product on five points of comparison. The other
half claimed the fictitious product was superior on only
three counts and inferior on two minor points. The students
found the latter ads, which admitted some inferiority, to be

35j

23. Because he is a consumer, Fuller feels that his subjective reactions to ads are legitimate responses to evaluate and use. Nevertheless, he wisely admits the limitations of his survey. Fuller's study of magazine ads is a primary source because it is direct, firsthand information. His other sources are secondary because they contain other people's reports and interpretations of primary or secondary sources.

24. Here Fuller refers specifically to the table that shows the complete results of his survey.

25. Fuller's descriptions of experiments here are detailed enough to let readers know how the experiments were conducted, yet not so detailed that readers will get bogged down in the experiments and lose track of his ideas. He might have enlivened his description by including more quotations from the studies as well as even more specific information (such as some of the products evaluated in the first study). Again, as in presenting the examples of successful advertising campaigns earlier, Fuller arranges material in order of increasing detail and drama.

35j

6

Table 1

Survey of Advertisements in <u>Newsweek</u>, 19 February 1979[a]

Advertisement	Percentages Emotional/ Rational	Advertisement	Percentages Emotional/ Rational
Tobacco Institute	100/0	Jameson Irish	
American Forest		Whiskey	100/0
Institute	50/50	Jack Daniels	90/10
Jeep	80/20	Ronrico Rum	90/10
Datsun	60/40	Canadian Club	100/0
Horizon TC3	90/10	Royal copier	60/40
MGB	80/20	Sharp copier	50/50
Ford Pinto	60/40	Mutual Life	
VW	100/0	Insurance	100/0
Winnebago	80/20	Sun Life Insurance	100/0
Exxon	50/50	GE TV	10/90
Lonestar Building		Vivitar lens	50/50
Supplier	80/20	Book ad	95/5
Alcoa aluminum	50/50	Famolare shoes	50/50
Tareyton	100/0	Trinity missions	100/0
L&M Lights	50/50	St. Elizabeth	
Marlboro	100/0	Hotel	90/10
Doral II	90/10	Newsletter on	
Merit	80/20	new products	80/20
Winston Lights	100/0	Anderson	50/50
Salem	100/0	Windowwalls	
Beechcraft Aviation	80/20	Anacin	50/50
Pan Am	50/50	Preparation H	50/50
Pakistan Airlines	80/20	United Cerebral	
Chivas Regal	90/10	Palsy	100/0

[a]My method for determining what percentage of an ad appealed to emotion and what percentage to reason involved (1) recording the overall impact of the ad as emotional or rational; (2) evaluating the proportions of space given to different purposes and the effects of layout, color, type, and artwork; (3) thinking of the possible ways to advertise the product without appealing to emotions and evaluating the ad against these; and (4) weighing my observations and assigning percentages to emotional and rational appeals. As an example, the Ronrico Rum ad contains an illustration occupying 80 percent of the space. It shows an upright bottle of rum (label facing out) and the shape of a bottle, tilted at 60°, containing a photograph of a couple kissing, palm trees, beautiful water--a scene whose greenness stands out against the mostly white ad and the pale bottle of rum. The angle of the bottle outline suggests it is about to fall and makes the viewer want to reach out and grab it. The ad's brief copy discusses the rum's "authentic" relation with Puerto Rico. Only the words "smooth, light taste" describe a rationally desirable quality of rum. I rated the ad (perhaps generously) 90 percent emotional, 10 percent rational.

35j

26. Fuller has put the table as close to the table reference (p. 5) as he can while placing it on a separate sheet of paper. He gives the table a title that tells readers what magazine the advertisements appeared in. His column headings clearly label the information beneath them.

27. Since the table contains Fuller's original material, no acknowledgment (source note) is needed. However, Fuller's explanatory note is needed to give background information on his method so that readers can judge the value of his survey. The note is keyed as a footnote, but a raised letter (ᵃ) is used instead of a raised number to prevent possible confusion of text notes with the table note.

7

more successful in persuading them to buy the new
(fictitious) product instead of the best-seller.[18] They
made an emotional choice in favor of ads that simply sounded
truthful without having evidence that the claims of truth
were in fact valid.

    In another study with experimental ads, Seymour
Lieberman had an advertising agency create two television
ads for each of six fictitious products. Each product had
one deceitful ad containing a false or made-up scientific
claim and one truthful ad that did not contain the scientific
claim. For instance, the deceitful ad for a fictitious
plant fertilizer stressed that the fertilizer contained
protein--though in fact protein does not help plants grow--
whereas the truthful ad did not mention protein. The
deceitful ad for a fictitious bunion remedy stated that the
remedy contained "four times as much methylglyoxal"--although
methylglyoxal does not help treat bunions--whereas the
truthful ad did not mention methylglyoxal. Both pairs of
ads used the same actors and the same language; the only
difference was the presence or absence of the scientific
claim. After being asked to say which products interested
them, one hundred middle-income consumers watched the
deceitful ads and another hundred middle-income consumers
watched the truthful ads. More consumers showed interest
in the deceitful fertilizer ad than showed interest in the
truthful ad. And four times as many consumers showed
interest in the deceitful four-times-as-much methylglyoxal
ad for a bunion remedy as showed interest in the truthful
ad. Similar results occurred with two of the other four

28

29

28. Fuller places footnote numbers after his descriptions of the experiments (here and below) but before the conclusions he draws to support the second part of his thesis (that consumers choose products irrationally). In fact, the experimenters may not have used their results for quite the same purposes as Fuller does. By separating the studies' results from his own conclusions about the results, Fuller demonstrates the amount of thought he has given his sources, and he hopes to avoid misrepresenting them (always a danger in reporting and interpreting the work of others). However, since Fuller's conclusions are not those of the researchers, he might have mentioned briefly the researchers' goals and conclusions so that his readers could evaluate his use of their results.

29. Fuller's use of well-chosen quotation from the study makes his description more concrete and simultaneously illustrates how successfully the researchers imitated real ads in their fictitious ones.

8

pairs of ads tested.[19] The consumers did not examine the
ads' claims rationally. Instead, they gravitated to what
sounded like fact, responding emotionally to claims of
scientific improvements without rationally evaluating the
claims.

    The critics of advertising accuse advertisers of using   30
emotional appeals deliberately and irresponsibly. They
imply that consumers would make rational decisions about
products if the ads for those products gave them facts
about performance and quality on which to base a rational
choice. Advertisers freely admit their emphasis on
emotional appeals but maintain that consumers make choices
irrationally. As proof, they offer the sales successes
brought about by purely emotional appeals. One informal
survey verifies advertisers' reliance on emotional appeals.
And formal experiments suggest that consumers do not require
hard information on which to base decisions but will accept
the appearance of truth or fact as a substitute for the real
thing. We may say we object to the overdone advertisement
with no informative content. That is certainly the kind of
ad we see the most of. But it also seems to be the kind of
ad we deserve.

35j

30. Fuller's conclusion might be faulted for lack of imagination, but it is satisfactory for his purpose. He shows that his thesis is valid by combining it with summaries of the evidence he has presented in the paper. In his last few sentences, he switches to *we* in a way that emphasizes the relevance of his conclusion for himself and his readers. His last sentence provides a final edge.

35j

Notes

[1] Herbert Marshall McLuhan, The Mechanical Bride: Folklore of Industrial Man (Boston: Beacon Press, 1951), p. v.

[2] Vance Packard, The Hidden Persuaders (New York: Pocket Books, 1958), p. 4.

[3] Quoted in Robert Glatzer, The New Advertising: The Great Campaigns (New York: Citadel Press, 1970), p. 85.

[4] David Bernstein, Creative Advertising (London: Longman, 1974), p. 295.

[5] Pierre Martineau, Motivation in Advertising: Motives That Make People Buy (New York: McGraw-Hill, 1957), pp. 139-40.

[6] Martineau, p. 121.

[7] George H. Smith, Motivation Research in Advertising and Marketing (1954; rpt. Westport, Conn.: Greenwood Press, 1971), p. 6.

[8] Martineau, p. 120.

[9] See, for example, James F. Engel, David T. Kollats, and Roger D. Blackwell, Consumer Behavior, 2nd ed. (New York: Holt, Rinehart and Winston, 1973), p. 58. There the same idea is stated in a complex diagram, the "Complete Model of Consumer Behavior Showing Purchasing Processes and Outcomes." Out of twenty-three boxes of factors only one box, "Evaluative Criteria," seems to represent rationality.

31. The word "Notes" is centered two inches from the top of the page and is followed by four lines of space. The notes are double-spaced. The first line of each entry is indented five spaces and preceded by a raised number corresponding to the number used in the text.

32. Note 1 shows a first reference to a book with a single author. The page number, *v*, refers to material (probably the preface or introduction) that occurs near the front of the book and is numbered with lowercase Roman numerals.

33. Note 3 shows how to indicate a direct quotation taken from secondary material. Since the original speaker is mentioned clearly in the text, Fuller does not need to identify him here.

34. Note 6 shows a second reference to a source already cited (in footnote 5).

35. Note 9 demonstrates the use of a note to provide additional relevant information or examples. Fuller could include this material in the text (in fact, he did so in the first draft), but it is more evidence than he needs at that point and could weigh down his discussion. This note also shows how to acknowledge an edition other than the first edition.

35j

10

[10] Howard Ketcham, <u>Color Planning: For Business and Industry</u> (New York: Harper & Bros., 1958), p. 7.

[11] Ketcham, p. 8.

[12] George Burton Hotchkiss, <u>An Outline of Advertising: Its Philosophy, Science, Art, and Strategy</u>, 3rd ed. (New York: Macmillan, 1950), p. 164.

[13] Sharon Johnson, "The Cartoon Creature as Salesman," <u>The New York Times</u>, 11 Feb. 1979, Sec. F, p. 3.

[14] Martineau, p. 148.

[15] Glatzer, pp. 122–23.

[16] Martineau, p. 147.

[17] Glatzer, p. 134.

[18] Gary Gregg, "To Sell Your Product, Admit It's Not Perfect," <u>Psychology Today</u>, Oct. 1974, p. 35. This article concerned an experiment published in <u>The Journal of Marketing Research</u>, 11 (May 1974).

[19] "Truth Doesn't Sell," <u>Time</u>, 14 May 1973, p. 96.

36

37

38

35j

36. Note 13 shows how to acknowledge a signed newspaper article.

37. Note 18 shows how to acknowledge a signed article in a magazine and also how to indicate a journal's volume number. Fuller explains that his description of the experiment was based on another writer's description, not on the primary source. However, he should have consulted the original report of the experiment, not only to be sure his description is accurate but also to check for additional useful information.

38. Note 19 shows how to acknowledge an unsigned article in a magazine. Again, Fuller is describing an experiment as described by a secondary source. If possible, he should have consulted the original report of the experiment.

35j

Bibliography   39

Bernstein, David. <u>Creative Advertising</u>. London: Longman,   40
    1974.

Engel, James F., David T. Kollats, and Roger D. Blackwell.   41
    <u>Consumer Behavior</u>. 2nd ed. New York: Holt, Rinehart
    and Winston, 1973.

Glatzer, Robert. <u>The New Advertising: The Great Campaigns</u>.
    New York: Citadel Press, 1970.

Gregg, Gary. "To Sell Your Product, Admit It's Not Perfect."   42
    <u>Psychology Today</u>, Oct. 1974, p. 35.

Hotchkiss, George Burton. <u>An Outline of Advertising: Its</u>
    <u>Philosophy, Science, Art, and Strategy</u>. 3rd ed. New
    York: Macmillan, 1950.

Johnson, Sharon. "The Cartoon Creature as Salesman." <u>The</u>   43
    <u>New York Times</u>, 11 Feb. 1979, Sec. F, p. 3.

Ketcham, Howard. <u>Color Planning: For Business and Industry</u>.
    New York: Harper & Bros., 1958.

McLuhan, Herbert Marshall. <u>The Mechanical Bride: Folklore</u>
    <u>of Industrial Man</u>. Boston: Beacon Press, 1951.

Martineau, Pierre. <u>Motivation in Advertising: Motives that</u>
    <u>Make People Buy</u>. New York: McGraw-Hill, 1957.

<u>Newsweek</u>, 19 Feb. 1979.

Packard, Vance. <u>The Hidden Persuaders</u>. New York: Pocket
    Books, 1958.

Smith, George H. <u>Motivation Research in Advertising and</u>
    <u>Marketing</u>. 1954; rpt. Westport, Conn.: Greenwood
    Press, 1971.

"Truth Doesn't Sell." <u>Time</u>, 14 May 1973, p. 96.   44

35j

39. The word "Bibliography" is centered two inches from the top of the page and followed by four lines of space. The entries are double-spaced. The first line of each entry begins at the left margin; subsequent lines of the same entry are indented five spaces. The entries are alphabetized. The page (and subsequent pages, if any) is not numbered.

40. Typical entry for a book with one author.

41. Entry for a book with three authors. The edition, because it is not the first, is also indicated.

42. Entry for a signed article in a magazine.

43. Entry for a signed article in a newspaper.

44. Entry for an unsigned article in a magazine.

35j

36

Practical Writing

Writing an essay examination and writing a business letter to request something or to apply for a job require the same attention to unity, coherence, and development that go into an essay or research paper (see Chapters 1 and 35). The special problems of writing essay examinations and business letters are the subject of this chapter.

36a

Answering essay questions

In writing an essay for an examination, you summarize or analyze a topic, usually in three or more paragraphs, usually within a time limit. An essay question not only tests your knowledge of a subject (which short-answer and objective questions also do), but also tests your control and synthesis of that knowledge and helps you see it in a new way (which other kinds of questions usually can't do).

1

Preparing for an essay examination

Taking lecture notes, thoughtfully reading the assigned texts or articles, and reviewing regularly can help you prepare for any kind of examination. (See Appendix C on study skills.) In addition, for an essay examination you can practice synthesizing what you know by creating summaries or outlines that reorganize the course material. For instance, in a business course you could evaluate the advantages and disadvantages of several approaches to management. In a short story course you could look for a theme running through all the stories you have read by a certain author or from a certain period. In a psychology course you could contrast the different theorists' views of what causes a disorder like schizophrenia. Any one of these is a likely topic for an essay question. Thinking of such categories not only can help you anticipate the kinds of questions you may be asked but also can increase your mastery of the material.

| 2
| Planning your time and your answer

When you first look at your examination, always read it all the way through before you start answering any questions. As you scan the examination, determine which questions seem most important, which ones are going to be most difficult for you, and approximately how much of the total time you'll need for each question. (Your instructor may help by assigning a point value to each question as a guide to its importance or by suggesting an amount of time for you to spend on each question.) You will want to give your best answer for every question, so this initial planning stage is important.

To avoid straying from an essay question or answering only part of it, read it at least twice. Examine the words and consider their implications. Look especially for words like *describe, define, explain, summarize, analyze, evaluate,* and *interpret,* each of which requires a different kind of response. For instance, the instruction *Define dyslexia and compare and contrast it with two other learning disabilities* contains important clues for how an essay should be written. *Define dyslexia* tells you to specify the meaning of the term. A description of how children with dyslexia feel about their disability, however well done, would be irrelevant. Instead, you should say what dyslexia is—a perceptual impairment causing a reader to reverse or scramble letters—and extend the definition by providing distinctive characteristics, how the impairment seems to work, examples of its effects, and so on. The words *compare and contrast it with two other learning disabilities* tell you to analyze not only its similarities with but also its differences from the other disabilities. Answering this part of the question thus involves thinking of categories for comparison, such as causes, treatments, frequency of occurrence, and severity of effect. An essay that described only similarities, or only differences, would not answer the question completely.

After you're sure you understand the question, make a brief outline of the main points you want to include in your essay. Use the back of the test sheet or exam booklet for scratch paper. Jot down a brief thesis for your essay that represents your view of the topic. Include key phrases that can be expanded into supporting evidence

36a

for your view. This stage in writing an essay for an exam is much like the planning of an essay or a research paper. Though you haven't got as much time to refine and rearrange your ideas, planning will help make your essay unified, coherent, well supported, and concise.

3
Starting the essay

A well-constructed thesis can contribute a great deal to an examination essay. Drawing on the brief thesis you devised during planning, you can begin an essay effectively by stating your thesis immediately and including in it an overview of the rest of your essay. Such a capsule version of your answer lets your reader (and grader) know generally how much command you have and also how you plan to develop your answer.

The opening statement should address the question directly and exactly. The following thesis, in response to the question below, does *not* meet these criteria.

QUESTION

Given humans' natural and historical curiosity about themselves, why did a scientific discipline of anthropology not arise until the twentieth century? Explain, citing specific details.

TENTATIVE THESIS

The discipline of anthropology—the study of humans—actually began in the early nineteenth century and was strengthened by the Darwinian revolution, but the discipline did not begin to take shape until people like Franz Boas and Alfred Kroeber began doing scientific research among nonindustrialized cultures.

This tentative thesis says nothing about *why* anthropology did not arise as a scientific discipline until the twentieth century. Instead, it supplies an unspecific (and unrequested) definition of anthropology, vaguely reasserts the truth implied by the question, and adds irrelevant details about the history of anthropology. The following thesis—revised to address the question directly, to state the writer's view, and to preview the essay—is a more effective beginning.

36a

REVISED THESIS

Anthropology did not emerge as a scientific discipline until the twentieth century because nineteenth-century Westerners' limited contact with remote peoples and the corresponding failure to see those other people as human combined to overcome natural curiosity and to prevent objective study of different cultures.

This thesis specifies the writer's view of the two main causes of the slow emergence of anthropology—limited contact with remote peoples and, related to that, a narrow definition of humanity—that she will analyze in her essay.

4
Developing the essay

You develop your essay by using sound generalizations to support your thesis, generalizations that are supported by details, examples, and reasons. Avoid filling out your essay by repetition. Avoid substituting purely subjective feelings about the topic for real analysis of it.

The student answering the anthropology question must show that contact was limited between Western and non-Western cultures and must specify how the limitations dulled curiosity, prevented objective study, and hampered the development of anthropology. She also needs to demonstrate how a related narrow definition of humanity had the same results. And she must support her assertions with examples. For instance, she might cite nineteenth-century writings that illustrate disinterest or feelings of superiority toward distant peoples.

The anthropology question leaves plenty of room for generalizations that cannot be supported, such as a blanket statement that all nineteenth-century Westerners were narrow-minded. It also leaves room for the substitution of the writer's subjective feelings for analysis of the problem. For instance, a paragraph condemning the narrow-mindedness of some nineteenth-century Westerners, no matter how earnest it was, would only pad the essay.

5
Rereading the essay

The time limit on an essay examination doesn't allow for the careful rethinking and revision you would give an essay or research paper. You need to write clearly and concisely the first time. If you do have a few minutes after you have finished the entire exam, reread the essay (or essays) to correct illegible passages, misspellings, grammatical mistakes, and accidental omissions. Verify that your thesis is accurate—that it is, in fact, what you ended up writing about. Check to be sure your generalizations are well supported. Cross out irrelevant ideas and details, and add any information that now seems important. (Use another page if necessary, keying the addition to where you want it to be read.)

36a

36b

Writing business letters

Whether you are requesting information, complaining about a product or a bill, or applying for a job, your letters to businesses will be written to busy people who want to see quickly why you are writing and what they can do for you. Be straightforward, clear, objective, and courteous, but don't avoid direct insistence if the context warrants it. Observe conventions of grammar and usage, for these not only make your writing clear but also impress a reader with your care.

1

Using a standard form

Business correspondence customarily adheres to one of several acceptable forms. Use either unlined white paper measuring at least 5½″ x 8½″ or what is called letterhead stationery with your address printed at the top of the sheet. Type the letter if possible, single-spaced, on only one side of a sheet. Follow a standard format for each of the letter's parts. (The form described below and illustrated in the sample letters on pp. 477 and 479 is one common form.)

The return address heading of the letter gives your address (but not your name) and the date. (If you're using letterhead stationery, only the date must be added.) Align the lines of the heading on the left, and place the whole heading on the right of the page, allowing enough space above it so that the entire letter will be centered vertically on the page.

The inside address shows the name, title, and complete address of the person you are writing to, just as this information will appear on the envelope. Begin the address a few lines below the heading at the left side of the page.

The salutation greets the addressee. Place it two lines below the address and two lines above the body of the letter. Always follow it with a colon, not a comma or dash. If you are not addressing a particular person, use a general salutation such as *Dear Sir or Madam* or *Dear Smythe Shoes* (the company name). Use *Ms.* as the title for a woman when she has no other title, when you don't know how she prefers to be addressed, or when you know that she prefers to be addressed as *Ms.* If you know a woman prefers to be addressed as *Mrs.* or *Miss*, use the appropriate title.

The body of the letter, containing its contents, begins at the left margin. Rather than indenting paragraphs, place an extra line of space between them so they are readily visible.

The letter's close, beginning two lines below the last line of the body, aligns at the left with the heading at the top of the page. Typi-

17A Revere St.
Boston, MA 02106   Return address heading
January 1, 1980

Ms. Ann Herzog
Circulation Supervisor   Inside address
Sporting Life
25 W. 43rd St.
New York, NY 10036

Dear Ms. Herzog: Salutation

Thank you for your letter of December 20, telling me that
Sporting Life would resume my subscription after stopping
it in error when I had received the July issue. Since I
missed at least five months' issues because of the magazine's error, I expected my subscription to be extended for
five months after it would have lapsed, that is, through
June 1980. Instead, you tell me that the magazine will
send me the back issues that it failed to send and that the
January issue (which I haven't received) will complete my
current subscription.

I have no interest in receiving the back issues of Sporting
Life because the magazine is not useful or interesting
unless it is current. Since Sporting Life erred in stopping
my subscription prematurely, I still expect it to make up
the difference on the other end of my subscription.   Body

Unless I hear otherwise from you, I will count on my subscription's extending at least through June 1980. If
Sporting Life can't make up for its error in this way, I
will cancel my subscription and request a refund.

Close ── Sincerely,

Signature ── *Janet M. Beatty*
              Janet M. Beatty

Janet M. Beatty
17A Revere St.
Boston, MA 02106

Envelope ──

Ms. Ann Herzog
Circulation Supervisor
Sporting Life
25 W. 43rd St.
New York, NY 10036

36b

cal closes include *Yours truly* and *Sincerely*. Only the first letter is capitalized, and the close is followed by a comma.

The signature of a business letter has two parts—a typed one, four lines below the close, and a handwritten one filling in the space. The signature should consist only of your name, as you sign checks and school documents.

Below the signature, at the left margin, you may want to include additional information such as *Enc.* (something is enclosed with the letter), *cc: Margaret Newton* (a carbon copy is being sent to the person named), or *CHC/enp* (the initials of the author/the initials of the typist).

The envelope for the letter (see p. 477) should show your name and address in the upper left corner and the addressee's name, title, and address to the right of the center. Use an envelope that is the same width as your stationery and about a third the height. Fold the letter horizontally, in thirds.

2
Writing requests, complaints, and applications

Letters requesting something—for instance, a pamphlet, information about a product, a T-shirt advertised in a magazine—must be specific and accurate about the item you are requesting. The letter should provide a complete description of the item and, if applicable, a copy or description of the advertisement or other source that prompted your request.

Letters complaining about a product or a service (such as a wrong billing from the telephone company) should be written in a reasonable but firm tone. (See the sample letter on p. 477.) The letter must contain a description of exactly what you see as the problem. It may contain relevant details from past correspondence (as the sample letter does). It should always contain your opinion of how the problem can be solved. Note that many companies are required by law to provide a specific procedure to cover complaints about products and services. If you know of such a procedure, be sure to follow it.

In writing to apply for a job or to request a job interview, you should announce at the outset what job you are interested in and how you heard about it. (See the sample letter on p. 479.) Then summarize your qualifications for the job, including facts about your education and employment history that prepare you for it. Include only the relevant facts, mentioning that additional information is contained in an accompanying résumé. Include any special reason you have for applying, such as a specific career goal. At the end of the letter, mention that you are available for an interview at the con-

36b

venience of the addressee, or specify when you will be available (for instance, when your job or classes leave you free).

The résumé that you enclose with your letter of application contains, in table form, your education and employment history as well as other interests and information about how to obtain your references. (See the sample résumé on p. 480.)

```
                                    3712 Swiss Ave.
                                    Dallas, TX  75204
                                    March 2, 1980

Personnel Manager
Dallas News
Communications Center
Dallas, TX  75222

Dear Sir or Madam:

In response to your announcement posted in the English
department of Southern Methodist University, I am applying
for the summer job of part-time editorial assistant for the
Dallas News.

I am now enrolled at Southern Methodist University as a
sophomore, with a dual major in English literature and
journalism.  As the enclosed résumé shows, I have worked on
the university newspaper for nearly two years, I have
published articles in my hometown newspaper, and I worked
a summer there as a copy-boy.  My goal is a career in
journalism.  I believe my educational background and my
work experience qualify me for the opening you have.

I am available for an interview at any time and would be
happy to send you samples of my newspaper work.  My tele-
phone number is 744-3816.

                         Sincerely,

                         Ian M. Irvine

Enc.
```

36b

RÉSUMÉ

Ian M. Irvine
3712 Swiss Ave.
Dallas, TX 75204

<u>Position desired</u>   Part-time editorial assistant

<u>Education</u>
1978 to present   Southern Methodist University.
Current standing: sophomore.
Major: English literature and journalism.

1974–1978   Abilene (TX) Senior High School.
Graduated with academic degree.

<u>Experience</u>
1978 to present   Reporter on the <u>Daily Campus</u>, student
newspaper of Southern Methodist University.
Responsibilities include writing feature
stories and sports coverage; proofreading;
some editing.

Summer 1979   House painter and free-lance writer.
Published two articles in the <u>Abilene</u> (TX)
<u>Reporter News</u>: "A Hundredth Birthday
Party" (7/1/79) and "A New Way to Develop
Photographs" (8/6/79).

Summer 1978   Copy-boy at <u>Abilene Reporter News</u>. Responsible for transmitting copy between writers,
editors, and typesetters. Watched over
teletype, ran errands, occasionally accompanied reporters and photographers on
assignments.

<u>Special interests</u>   Fiction writing, photography, reading,
squash

<u>References</u>   Academic references available from the
placement office at Southern Methodist
University, Dallas, TX 75275.

Employment   Ms. Joanne Hale
reference   <u>Abilene Reporter News</u>
Abilene, TX 79604

Personal   Ms. Sheryl Gipstein
reference   26 Overland Dr.
Abilene, TX 79604

36b

Appendixes

Appendix A
Avoiding Plagiarism

Plagiarism (from a Latin word for "kidnapper") is presenting someone else's ideas or words as your own. If you copy an article from an encyclopedia and make minor changes to pass it off as your writing, or if you buy someone else's term paper to hand in, you are plagiarizing deliberately. If you carelessly forget to include quotation marks or a footnote to show whose words or ideas you are using, you are plagiarizing accidentally. Whether deliberate or accidental, plagiarism is a serious offense.

It is not plagiarism, however, to use other writers' material when you acknowledge whose material it is. That procedure is a part of honest research writing (see Chapter 35). Nevertheless, because writing a research paper requires using other people's ideas in combination with your own, you may not always be sure what constitutes plagiarism. This appendix shows you how to avoid plagiarism by acknowledging sources when necessary and by using them accurately and fairly.

A1
Knowing what to acknowledge

When you write a research paper, you use information from three kinds of sources: (1) your independent thoughts and experiences; (2) common knowledge, the basic knowledge people share; and (3) other people's independent thoughts and experiences. Of the three, you must acknowledge only the third, the work of others.

Your independent material

You need not acknowledge your own independent material—your thoughts, compilations of facts, or experimental results, expressed in your words or format—to avoid plagiarism. Such material includes observations from your experience—for example, a conclusion you draw about crowd behavior by watching crowds at concerts or shopping centers—as well as tables or diagrams you construct from information you have gathered. However, someone else's ideas and facts are not yours; even when they are expressed entirely in your words and format, they require acknowledgment.

A1

Common knowledge

Common knowledge consists of the standard information of a field of study as well as folk literature and commonsense observations. Standard information includes, for instance, the major facts of history. The dates of Charlemagne's rule as emperor of Rome (800–814) and the fact that his reign was accompanied by a revival of learning—both facts available in many reference books—do not need to be acknowledged, even if you have to look up the information. However, an interpretation of facts (for instance, a theory of how writing began) or a specialist's observation (for instance, an Asian historian's opinion of the effects of Chinese wall posters) is considered independent, not common, knowledge and must be acknowledged.

Folk literature, which is popularly known and cannot be traced to particular writers, is considered common knowledge. Mother Goose nursery rhymes and fairy tales like "Snow White" are examples. However, all literature traceable to a particular writer should be acknowledged. Even a phrase from a poem, such as "miles to go before I sleep" (from Robert Frost's "Stopping by Woods on a Snowy Evening"), is literature—not folk literature—and requires acknowledgment.

Commonsense observations, such as the idea that weather affects people's spirits or that inflation is most troublesome for people with low and fixed incomes, are considered common knowledge and do not require acknowledgment, even when they also appear in someone else's writing. But a scientist's findings about the effects of high humidity on people with high blood pressure, or an economist's argument about the effects of inflation on immigrants from China, will require acknowledgment.

You may use common knowledge as your own, even if you have to look it up in a reference book. You may not know, for example, the dates of the French Revolution or the standard definition of *photosynthesis*, although these are considered common knowledge. If you look them up in a dictionary or reference book, you do not need to acknowledge the source.

Someone else's independent material

To avoid plagiarism you do not need to acknowledge your own material or common knowledge, but you do need to acknowledge other people's independent material. Facts found in reference books and many basic textbooks are often common knowledge. But otherwise any ideas or facts from signed or copyrighted sources require acknowledgment. The source may be a book, letter, magazine, newspaper, movie, speech, interview, television program, or microfilmed document. You must acknowledge not only ideas or facts themselves but also the language and format in which the ideas or facts are presented, if you use them. That is, the wording, sentence structures, arrangement of thoughts, and special graphic format (such as a table or diagram) created by another writer belong to that writer just as his or her ideas do.

You need to acknowledge another's material when you use it either directly by quotation or indirectly by **summarizing** or by **paraphrasing**, expressing the material in your own words. Neither the amount of material you use nor the frequency with which you use a source affects the need to cite the source. Whether you are paraphrasing a single sentence or quoting three paragraphs, and whether you are using the source only once or a dozen times, you must acknowledge the original author every time.

If you read someone else's material during your research but do not include any of that material in your final draft, you need not acknowledge the source with a footnote because you have not actually used the material.

See 35h for information on how to use footnotes to acknowledge sources.

A2
Quoting, summarizing, and paraphrasing

When writing a research paper, you can present the ideas of others either through direct quotation or through summary or paraphrase, depending on your purpose. For direct quotation, copy the material from the source carefully, and place it in quotation marks within your running text. (See 24c for the style to use with poetry and long quotations.) Use quotation marks for even a single word if the original author used it in a special or central way. Do not change any wording, spelling, capitalization, or punctuation. Be careful not to leave out or add any words or punctuation marks accidentally. Use an ellipsis mark (three spaced periods) to indicate the exact point at which you have deliberately left out part of a direct quotation (see 25e). Use brackets to surround any word, comment, or punctuation mark you add within the quotation (see 25d). Place the word *sic* (meaning "in this manner") in brackets immediately after any mistake in spelling, grammar, or common knowledge that your reader might otherwise believe to be a misquote.

When you summarize or paraphrase, you state in your own words and sentence structures the meaning of someone else's writing. Since the words and the sentence structures are yours, you do not use quotation marks, though, of course, you must acknowledge the author of the idea. If you use the original sentence pattern and substitute synonyms for key words or use the original words and change the sentence pattern, you are not paraphrasing but plagiarizing, even if the source is acknowledged, because both methods use someone else's expression without quotation marks. The following poor paraphrase is based on a quotation from Frederick C. Crews, *The Tragedy of Manners: Moral Drama in the Later*

Novels of Henry James (1957; rpt. Hamden, Conn.: Shoe String Press, 1971), p. 8.

A2

<table>
<tr><td>ORIGINAL</td><td>In each case I have tried to show that all the action in a "Jamesian novel" may be taken as a result of philosophical differences of opinion among the principal characters, and that these differences in turn are explainable by reference to the characters' differing social backgrounds.</td></tr>
<tr><td>POOR PARAPHRASE</td><td>The action in a "Jamesian novel" comes from philosophical differences of opinion between characters. These differences can be explained by examining the characters' differing social backgrounds.[5]</td></tr>
</table>

The paraphrase uses several expressions verbatim from the source, without change and without quotation marks: "action in a 'Jamesian novel' "; "philosophical differences of opinion"; "the characters' differing social backgrounds." Thus even though the writer acknowledges the use of the author's work (indicated by the footnote number 5), he plagiarizes because he does not also acknowledge the use of the author's words with quotation marks. The improved paraphrase below captures and acknowledges the author's meaning without resorting to his manner of expression.

<table>
<tr><td>IMPROVED PARAPHRASE</td><td>In Henry James's novels, the characters live out philosophies acquired from their upbringing and their place in society.[5]</td></tr>
</table>

In this revised paraphrase, although the writer retains Crews's essential meaning, he restates that meaning in a sentence that is clearly his own construction, designed to fit his larger purpose.

In paraphrasing it is crucial not only to use your own form of expression (or to place quotation marks around the author's expressions), but also to represent the author's meaning exactly without distorting it. In the following poor paraphrase, the writer has avoided plagiarism but has given a meaning exactly opposite to the original author's. The quotation, by the artist Henri Matisse, is from Jack D. Flam, *Matisse on Art* (London: Phaidon, 1973), p. 148.

<table>
<tr><td>ORIGINAL</td><td>Thus, for the artist creation begins with vision. To see is itself a creative operation, requiring an effort. Everything that we see in our daily life is more or less distorted by acquired habits, and this is perhaps more evident in an age like ours when cinema posters and magazines present us every day with a flood of ready-made images which are to the eye what prejudices are to the mind.</td></tr>
</table>

A2

<table>
<tr><td>**POOR**
PARAPHRASE</td><td>Matisse said that seeing is the first step of the artistic act and that we learn how to see by looking at posters and magazines.[7]</td></tr>
</table>

The revision below uses a combination of paraphrase and quotation to represent the author's meaning exactly.

<table>
<tr><td>**IMPROVED**
PARAPHRASE</td><td>Matisse said that seeing is the first step of the artistic act because we must overcome our visual "habits" and "prejudices," particularly those we develop in response to the popular images of our culture.[7]</td></tr>
</table>

To be sure you acknowledge sources fairly and do not plagiarize, review this checklist before beginning to write your paper and again after you have completed your first draft.

1. What type of source are you using: your own independent material, common knowledge, or someone else's independent material?

2. If you are quoting someone else's material, is the quotation exact? Have you used quotation marks for quotations run into the text? Are omissions shown with ellipses and additions with brackets?

3. If you are paraphrasing someone else's material, have you rewritten it in your own words and sentence structures? Does your paraphrase employ quotation marks when you resort to the author's exact language? Have you represented the author's meaning without distortion?

4. Is each use of someone else's material acknowledged with a footnote?

5. Do all footnotes contain complete and accurate information on the sources you have cited?

Appendix B
Preparing a Manuscript

Preparing a manuscript to make it legible, consistent, and attractive is an important part of writing a paper. This appendix discusses the materials necessary for manuscript preparation and some conventions of format. (Most of these guidelines are standard, but your instructor may request that you follow slightly different conventions in some matters.)

B1
Choosing the appropriate materials

Typewritten papers

For typewritten papers, use 8½″ x 11″ white bond paper of sixteen- or twenty-pound weight. Some instructors also accept the same size surface-coated bond paper (called "erasable" or "corrasable"). Onionskin sheets, paper torn from notebooks, colored paper, and paper smaller or larger than 8½″ x 11″ are unacceptable. Use the same type of paper throughout a project. Type on only one side of a sheet and double-space.

Use a black typewriter ribbon that is fresh enough to make a dark impression, and make sure the keys of the typewriter are clean. To avoid smudging the page when correcting mistakes, use a liquid correction fluid or a correction tape. Don't use hyphens or *x*'s to cross out mistakes and don't type corrections (strikeovers) on top of mistakes.

Handwritten papers

For handwritten papers, you can use regular white notebook paper, 8½″ x 11″, with horizontal lines spaced about a half inch apart. Don't use paper torn from a notebook, unlined paper, paper with narrow lines, colored paper, or paper other than 8½″ x 11″ (such as legal or stenographer's pads). Use the same type of paper throughout a project. Write on only one side of a sheet and write on every line, unless your instructor requests otherwise.

Use black or blue ink, not pencil. If possible, use an ink eraser or eradicator to correct mistakes rather than drawing a single line through them. Scribbling over or blacking out a mistake and writing corrections on top of mistakes are unacceptable.

B2

Following a standard format

A consistent physical format makes the script, margins, paging, title, and identification visually effective and avoids the illegibility and the confusion of inconsistencies. See the sample research paper in Chapter 35, pages 446–471, for examples of the items below.

Script

Handwritten script should be reasonably uniform and clear. Be sure letters are easily distinguishable. Cross all *t*'s; dot all *i*'s with dots, not circles; form the loops of letters carefully. Make capital letters and lowercase letters clearly different. Use consistent spacing between words and sentences. If your handwriting is very difficult to read, submit a typed paper if possible. If you don't have access to a typewriter and your handwriting is illegible or unusual in size, decoration, or slant, try to make it more legible or conventional when writing the final manuscript. Indent the first line of every paragraph about an inch.

In typewritten script, leave one space between words and after commas and semicolons. Leave two spaces after sentence periods, colons, question marks, and exclamation points. Use one space before and after as well as between the three periods of an ellipsis mark. To make a dash, use two consecutive hyphens with no space before or after. To make symbols that aren't on your typewriter, leave two spaces and insert the symbol by hand in ink. Indent the first line of every paragraph five spaces.

For both typewritten and handwritten script, try to avoid breaking words at the ends of lines. If you must break a word, follow the guidelines provided in Chapter 30. Don't start a line with any mark of punctuation other than an opening parenthesis or quotation marks when they are called for.

Set off quotations of more than four lines of prose or of two or more lines of poetry. (If you are quoting a great deal of poetry, you may want to set off only quotations of more than two lines.) In handwritten copy, indent all lines of the quotation an inch from the left margin. In typewritten copy, indent all lines ten spaces. Double-space above and below each quotation. The quotation itself may be single-spaced, though it should be double-spaced if you are preparing the manuscript for publication.

Margins

Leave about one and a half inches for the margins at the left and top of each page. Leave one-inch margins at the right and bottom of each page. (The right margin will be uneven but should not be narrower than an inch.)

Paging

Don't number or count in your numbering the title page of your paper. The outline pages at the front of a research paper may be numbered with lowercase Roman numerals (i, ii). The first text page in a paper is considered number 1 but is usually unnumbered. Number with Arabic numerals all pages after the first text page (2, 3, 4, etc.). There's no need for a period after the numeral or parentheses or hyphens around it. Place the numeral two spaces above the top line of text—or approximately half an inch from the top of the page—and align it with the right margin.

Title and identification

If you don't use a separate title page for an essay, center your title about two inches from the top of a typed page and on the top line of a handwritten page. Leave four lines of space or two ruled lines before starting the first paragraph. Capitalize the first and last words of the title, any word after a colon or semicolon, and all other words except articles and conjunctions and prepositions of less than five letters. Don't underline the title or place quotation marks around it. Place your name, the date, the course number, and any other information your instructor requests at the top right corner of the first page.

For research papers use a separate title page. Center the title about a third of the way down the page. If the title is long, break it into two lines so that the longer line is on top, and leave a line of space between lines of the title. Center the word *By* about an inch below the title. Two lines below that, center your name. Starting about an inch below your name, and double-spacing, provide the date, the course number, and any other information your instructor requests.

B3

Proofreading, correcting, and submitting the final manuscript

Proofread each page of your paper carefully. Concentrate on spelling, punctuation, mechanics, grammar, and manuscript preparation. If a page has several errors, retype or rewrite the page. If it has one or two errors and you can't eradicate them, correct them in ink. Draw a line through a word you want to delete. Don't try to correct a misspelled word without crossing out and rewriting the whole word. To replace a word or mark of punctuation, draw a line through the item, place a caret (∧) underneath it, and write the new word or mark in the space above the old one. To add words or marks of punctuation, place a caret underneath the line at the point where you wish to insert the word or mark; then center the word or mark over the caret in the space above the line.

> An ecosystem is a community of ~~organisms~~ interacting
> with each other and with the environment.

(with *organisms* written above the crossed-out *argonisms* and *the* inserted with a caret before *environment*.)

If you have to add more words than will fit between the lines of text, rewrite or retype the page.

When you submit your final paper, be sure the pages will stay together when the paper is shuffled in with others. Depending on the wishes of your instructor, you may fold the paper in half lengthwise, paperclip or staple the pages in the upper left corner, or place the paper in a special binder.

Appendix C
Improving Study Skills

Three basic qualities underlie effective study skills: organization, repetition, and motivation. This appendix will show briefly how to develop these skills in reading, taking notes, and preparing for tests.

It's possible to study anywhere and at any time, but you will benefit from a place that is moderately comfortable, well lighted, and undistracting. Have handy the materials you'll need while studying, such as paper, pencils, pens, and a highlighter. Keep your expectations realistic. Don't plan to accomplish more in an hour or a day than you ever have before. Concentrate on specific goals, such as answering a question about a textbook chapter or even passing a test, rather than on more general, longer-term goals, such as getting a certain grade-point average or graduating from college. And plan to take a break after every hour or so of studying to refresh yourself.

C1
Remembering

In memorizing, you use short-term storage, where information may stay a few seconds or a few minutes, and long-term storage, where information may stay indefinitely—or at least through the final examination. Most academic learning requires conscious effort to move material from short-term storage into long-term storage.

The more organized your learning is, the more it will penetrate your long-term memory. Read a book's introduction before you read the book; skim a whole chapter before you read the chapter. Organize information into small groups of ideas or facts that make sense to you. For instance, memorize French vocabulary words in related groups such as words for parts of the body or parts of a house. Keep the groups small: psychological research has shown that we can easily memorize about seven items at a time but have trouble with more.

As you pick up new information, make associations between it and what you already know. For instance, to remember a sequence of four dates in twentieth-century English history, link the occurrences in England with simultaneous, and more familiar, events in the United States.

C3

Or try using **mnemonic devices,** tricks for improving your memory. Say the history dates you want to remember are separated by five then four then nine years. By memorizing the first date and then 5 + 4 = 9, you'll have command of all four dates.

Reviewing the material you want to learn will improve not only how long but also how completely and accurately you remember it. Since you forget a great deal right after you read a chapter or listen to a lecture, try to spend five minutes going over the material immediately after you first encounter it. You will probably remember more from that brief review than you will from a much longer review several days later. In addition, try to spread subsequent study over half-hour sessions three or four days a week, rather than concentrating all study time in a single, long session.

C2
Scheduling

To organize your time effectively for studying, examine how you spend your days. For a week, keep track of your activities and the time they absorb. How many of the 168 hours in a week do you spend eating, sleeping, watching television, attending classes, studying, working at a job, commuting, doing laundry, socializing, and so forth? If you think it will help you organize your time, make a chart like a calendar that divides the week into seven vertical columns (one for each day) and one horizontal row for each hour you are awake. Block out on the chart your activities that occur regularly and at specific times, such as commuting, attending classes, and working at a job. Then fill in your other regular activities (such as exercise, eating, and studying) that do not necessarily occur at fixed times.

Set aside regular time for study each week. During any given week, you will want to adjust how you spend the studying time to allow for different assignments in different courses. For courses requiring extensive reading or creative work such as writing, try to include several large blocks of time per week. If you have been given a long-term assignment (such as a research paper), include time for it in your planning.

When devising a weekly schedule, don't overorganize so that you have no time left for relaxing. An unrealistic schedule that assigns all available time to studying will quickly become so difficult to live by that you'll be forced to abandon it and start over.

C3
Reading

The assigned reading you do for college courses—in textbooks, journal articles, and works of literature—requires a greater focus on comprehension, analysis, and retention than does reading for entertain-

C3

ment. For most course reading, especially textbook reading, you'll benefit from at least three separate examinations of the material—once skimming, once reading carefully, word by word, and once reviewing. Though these processes may seem detailed and time-consuming, with practice you will be able to perform some steps simultaneously and follow all the steps almost habitually.

The purpose of **skimming** is to give you an overview of the material that will aid your understanding of any part of it. Your goal is not to comprehend all the details or even the structure of the author's argument. Rather, you want to achieve a general sense of how a piece of writing is organized and what the major ideas are. The steps outlined below constitute a typical procedure for skimming a textbook chapter.

1. Examine the chapter title. What does it mean? What do you already know about this subject?
2. Read the first couple of paragraphs carefully to introduce yourself to the topic and to the author's writing style. The author often gives an overview of his or her ideas at the start.
3. Move through the chapter from heading to heading, reading each one as if it were a headline. Viewing the headings as the levels of an outline will give you a feeling for which ideas the author sees as central or as subordinate.
4. As you move from one heading to the next, scan the text and note any key words that are in color, **boldface**, or *italic* type.
5. Slow down for all pictures, diagrams, tables, graphs, and maps. These often contain concentrated information.
6. Read the last paragraph of the chapter or its summary carefully. These often give an overview of the main ideas of the chapter.
7. Take a moment to think over what you've skimmed. Try to recall the sequence of ideas. Ask yourself what the main idea or thesis is.

As soon as possible after you have skimmed a chapter, read it carefully for a thorough understanding of each idea or group of ideas. Here is a procedure you might follow for such word-by-word reading:

1. Distinguish the main ideas from the supporting ideas. Look for the chapter's thesis or central argument, for the central idea in each section or paragraph, and for terms the author takes pains to define and perhaps highlights with special type.
2. Read the chapter's structure as if it were a map of the author's ideas. Look for the introduction to the chapter, which outlines the ideas that follow; for the step-by-step explanations of main ideas found in the body of the chapter; for transitions between ideas that signal shifts in thought and highlight relationships; and for summaries or conclusions at the ends of sections or the end of the chapter that condense the text to its main concepts.
3. After reading a section or a group of ideas, test your comprehension by summarizing the material in your own words and then skimming it to check your understanding. Reread parts you have forgotten or misunderstood until you're sure of your comprehension.

C5

4. Once you feel you understand the entire chapter, go back to underline important points and to add marginal notes (or to make separate notes if you don't want to mark your book). Underline or take notes on only main ideas, key terms, and specific supporting evidence you've chosen to remember. Use marginal notes to add your own ideas or to summarize the author's.

When you review a chapter, reread headings, summaries, and key terms as well as the passages you have underlined or taken notes on. Concentrate on how the parts fit together. Stop to read carefully any passages that don't seem familiar or clear. Before a test skim the material a section at a time, and then recite or write out the main ideas before going on to the next section. If you have trouble remembering, read the section instead of skimming it.

C4
Taking notes

Your aim in taking notes from a class lecture or discussion is to record it as completely as possible while sorting out the main ideas from the secondary and supporting ones. By doing so, you not only provide yourself with complete material for study later, but also learn about the instructor's integration of the course material.

As you take notes, use your own words as much as possible to help you comprehend and retain the material, but resort to the speaker's words if necessary to catch everything. If you miss some material while making notes, leave a space to be filled in later. Don't count on going back to copy over and expand your notes. You may not be able to recall the missing information, and copying is little more than a time-wasting, mechanical activity. If you have already read the textbook chapter related to the lecture, you may be tempted to omit from your notes any lecture material you could find in the text. But you would be missing an important opportunity to integrate all the components of the course—the text material, your instructor's views, and your own thoughts. And you would risk forgetting exactly how your instructor made use of the text.

If, when you review your notes, you discover holes in them or confusing shifts in thought, consult a fellow student for his or her version of that part of the lecture. When you feel you understand the material, underline key words and important ideas in the notes and add comments (or cross-references to the text) in the margins.

C5
Preparing for examinations

No matter how much time you have, what material you are studying, or what kind of test you will be taking, studying for an examination involves three main steps, each requiring about a third of the total preparation time: (1) reviewing the material; (2) organizing summaries of the material; and (3) testing yourself. Your main goals are to strengthen your overall understanding of the subject, making its ideas and details more memorable, and to increase the flexibility of your new knowledge so that you can recognize it and apply it in new contexts.

C5

As you begin studying for a test, organize your class notes and reading assignments into manageable units. Reread the material, recite or write out the main ideas and selected supporting ideas and examples, and then skim for an overview. Proceed in this way through all the units, returning to earlier ones as necessary to refresh your memory or to relate ideas.

Allow time to reorganize the material in your own way so that your knowledge is applicable in a variety of situations. Create categories that will help you understand the information in different contexts. For instance, in studying for a biology examination, work to understand a process, such as how a plant develops or how photosynthesis occurs. Or in studying for an American government test, explain the structures of the local, state, and federal levels of government, or outline the differences between the levels. Other useful categories include advantages or disadvantages, causes or effects, and repeated ideas. Use categories that bring together as much of the material as possible, and think through each one as completely as you can. Such analytical thinking will enhance your mastery of the course material and may even prepare you directly for essay questions (see 36a).

Spend the last portion of your preparation time testing yourself. Convert to a question each heading in your lecture notes or textbook and each general category you have devised. Recite to yourself or write out the answers to the questions, going back to the course material to fill in missing information. Be sure you can define and explain all key terms. For subjects that require solving problems (such as mathematics, statistics, chemistry, and physics), work out a difficult problem for every type on which you will be tested. For history, test yourself on events and their causes or consequences. For a subject like psychology, be certain you understand the principal theories of behavior and their implications. For a literature course, test your knowledge of each work by thinking of the author's style and meaning, main characters, and plot developments.

ABOUT CRAMMING: Everything psychologists report about learning under stress suggests that cramming for an examination is about the least effective way of preparing for one. It takes longer to learn under stress, and the learning lasts for less time, is shallower, and is more difficult to apply. Information learned under stress is even harder to apply under conditions of stress, such as the stress of taking an examination. And the lack of sleep that usually accompanies cramming makes a good performance even more unlikely. If you must cram for a test, determine what is most important. Skim chapters and notes to select central ideas. Face the fact that you can't learn everything that will be on the test, and spend what time you have reviewing main concepts and facts.

Glossaries

Glossary of Usage
Glossary of Grammatical Terms

Glossary
of Usage

This glossary provides notes on the use of words or phrases that often cause problems for writers. The usage recommendations for standard, written English are based on current dictionaries and usage guides. Items labeled *nonstandard* should be avoided in both speech and writing. Those labeled *colloquial* occur commonly in speech and informal writing but are best avoided in the more formal writing usually expected in college and business. (Words and phrases labeled here as *colloquial* also include those labeled by many dictionaries with the equivalent term *informal*.) See 31a for further discussion of appropriate word choice, and see 32c–2 for a description of dictionary labels. Also see 34a–1 for a list of commonly confused words that are pronounced the same or similarly. The words and definitions provided there supplement this glossary.

The glossary is necessarily brief. Keep a dictionary handy for all your writing, and make a habit of referring to it whenever you doubt the appropriateness of a word or phrase.

a, an Use *a* before words beginning with consonant sounds, including those spelled with an initial *h* and those spelled with vowels that are sounded as consonants: *a historian, a one-o'clock class, a university*. Use *an* before words that begin with vowel sounds, including those spelled with an initial silent *h*: *an orgy, an L, an honor*.

When you use an abbreviation or acronym in writing (see 28b), which article to use depends on how the abbreviation is to be read: *She was once an HEW undersecretary.* (*HEW* is to be read as three letters, not as a word or as *Health, Education and Welfare*.) *Many Americans opposed a SALT treaty.* (*SALT* is to be read as one word, *salt*, not as four separate letters.)

accept, except *Accept* is a verb meaning "receive." *Except* is usually a preposition or conjunction meaning "but for" or "other than"; when it is used as a verb, it means "leave out." *I can accept all your suggestions except for the last one. I'm sorry you excepted my last suggestion from your list.*

advice, advise *Advice* is a noun, and *advise* is a verb: *Take my advice; do as I advise you.*

affect, effect Usually *affect* is a verb, meaning "to influence," and *effect* is a noun, meaning "result": *The drug did not affect his driving; in fact, it seemed to have no effect at all. Effect* occasionally is used as a verb meaning "to bring about": *Her efforts effected a change.*

aggravate *Aggravate* means "make worse"; in writing it should not be used in its colloquial meaning of "irritate" or "exasperate." *The president was irritated by the Senate's stubbornness, because he feared any delay might aggravate the unrest in the Middle East.*

agree to, agree with *Agree to* means "consent to," and *agree with* means "be in accord with": *How can they agree to a treaty when they don't agree with each other about the terms?*

ain't Nonstandard for *am not, isn't,* or *aren't.*

all, all of Usually *all* is sufficient to modify a noun: *All my loving, all the things you are.* Before a pronoun or proper noun, *all of* is usually appropriate: *all of me, in all of France.*

all ready, already *All ready* means "completely prepared," and *already* means "by now" or "before now": *We were all ready to go to the movie, but it had already started.*

all right *All right* is always two words. *Alright* is a common misspelling.

all together, altogether *All together* means "in unison," or "gathered in one place." *Altogether* means "entirely." *It's not altogether true that our family never spends vacations all together.*

allusion, illusion An *allusion* is a reference to something, and an *illusion* is a deceptive appearance: *Paul's constant allusions to Shakespeare created the illusion that he was an intellectual.*

almost, most *Almost* is an adverb meaning "nearly"; *most* is an adjective meaning "the greater number (or part) of." In formal writing, *most* should not be used as a substitute for *almost: We see each other almost* (not *most*) *every day.*

a lot *A lot* is always two words. *Alot* is a common misspelling.

among, between In general, *among* is used for relationships involving more than two people or things. *Between* is used for relationships involving only two, or for comparing one thing to a group to which it belongs. *The four of them agreed among themselves that the choice was between New York and Los Angeles.* It is becoming increasingly acceptable, though, to use *between* for relationships involving three or more comparable people or things, especially when *among* would be awkward or unclear: *Let's keep this just between the three of us, shall we?*

amount, number *Amount* refers to a quantity of something that cannot be counted. *Number* refers to countable items. *The amount of leftover ice we can save depends on the number of containers we have to put it in.*

and etc. *Et cetera* (*etc.*) means "and the rest"; *and etc.* therefore is redundant. See also *et al., etc.*

gl/us

and/or Many consider *and/or* awkward. It should be avoided in formal writing.

and which, and who When *which* or *who* is used to introduce a relative clause, *and* is superfluous: *WCAS is my favorite AM radio station, which* (not *and which*) *I listen to every morning.* And which or *and who* is correct only when used to introduce a second clause beginning with the same relative pronoun: *Jill is my cousin who goes to school here and who always calls me at seven in the morning.*

ante-, anti- The prefix *ante-* means "before" (*antedate, antebellum*); *anti-* means "against" (*antiwar, antinuclear*). Before a capital letter or *i, anti-* takes a hyphen: *anti-Freudian, anti-isolationist.*

anxious, eager *Anxious* means "nervous" or "worried" and is usually followed by *about. Eager* means "looking forward" and is usually followed by *to. I'm eager to get new running shoes. I've been anxious about getting blisters.*

anybody, any body; anyone, any one *Anybody* and *anyone* are indefinite pronouns; *any body* is a noun modified by an adjective; *any one* is a pronoun or adjective modified by *any. Can't anybody invent a shampoo that will give hair any body? Can anyone help Amy? She has more work than any one person can handle.*

any more, anymore *Any more* is used in negative constructions to mean "no more." *Anymore,* an adverb meaning "now," is also used in negative constructions. *He doesn't want any more. She doesn't live here anymore.*

anyplace Colloquial for *anywhere.*

anyways, anywheres Nonstandard for *anyway* and *anywhere.*

apt, liable, likely *Apt* and *likely* can be used interchangeably. Strictly speaking, though, *apt* means "having a tendency to": *Horace is apt to forget his lunch in the morning if Trudy doesn't remind him. Likely* means "probably going to": *Horace is leaving so early today that he's likely to catch the first bus.*

Liable is normally used to mean "in danger of" and should be confined to situations with undesirable consequences: *If Horace doesn't watch out, he is liable to trip over that lawn sprinkler.* In the strictest sense, *liable* means "responsible" or "exposed to": *If Horace trips over that lawn sprinkler, the owner will be liable for damages.*

as *As* is often used to mean *because, since, while, whether,* or *who.* It may be vague or ambiguous in these senses: *As we were stopping to rest, we decided to eat lunch.* (Does *as* mean "while" or "because"?) Usually a more precise word is preferable. See also 16c.

As never should be used as a substitute for *whether* or *who: I'm not sure whether* (not *as*) *we can make it. That's the man who* (not *as*) *gave me directions.*

as, like In formal speech and writing, *as* may be either a preposition or a conjunction; *like* functions as a preposition only. Thus, if the construction being introduced is a full clause rather than a phrase, the preferred choice is *as* or *as if* (see 16c): *This cigarette tastes good, <u>as</u>* (not <u>*like*</u>) *a cigarette should. This cigarette tastes <u>as if</u>* (not <u>*like*</u>) *it were made of oregano. This cigarette tastes <u>like</u> oregano.*

When *as* serves as a preposition, the distinction between *as* and *like* depends on meaning. *As* suggests that the subject is equivalent or identical to the description: *She was hired <u>as</u> an engineer. Like* suggests resemblance but not identity: *People <u>like</u> her do well in such jobs.* See also *like, such as.*

gl/us

assure, ensure, insure *Assure* means "to promise": *He <u>assured</u> us that if we left early, we would miss the traffic. Ensure* and *insure* often are used synonymously, meaning "make certain," but some reserve *insure* for matters of legal and financial protection and use *ensure* for more general meanings: *We left early to <u>ensure</u> that we would miss the traffic. It's expensive to <u>insure</u> yourself against floods.*

as, than In comparisons, *as* and *than* may be followed by either subjective or objective case pronouns: *You are as tall <u>as he</u>* (subjective). *They treated you better <u>than him</u>* (objective). The case depends on whether the things being compared are subjects or objects of verbs. To determine whether you are dealing with subjects or objects, you may have to supply an omitted verb: *I love you more <u>than he</u> (does)* (*he* is the subject of the missing verb *does*). *I love you more <u>than</u> (I love) <u>him</u>* (*him* is the object of the missing verb *love*). See also 6e.

as to A stuffy substitute for *about: The suspect was questioned <u>about</u>* (not <u>*as to*</u>) *her actions.*

at The use of *at* after *where* is wordy and should be avoided: <u>*Where* are *you meeting him?*</u> is preferable to <u>*Where* are you meeting him <u>at</u>?</u> Another reason to avoid the unnecessary *at* is that colloquially it has come to imply a state of mind rather than a geographic location: *When Judy heard Paul was refusing to see any of his friends, she asked if I knew <u>where he was at</u>.*

at this point in time Wordy for *now, at this point,* or *at this time.*

awful, awfully Strictly speaking, *awful* means "awe-inspiring." *Awful* and *awfully* are colloquial intensifiers meaning "very" or "extremely" (*He tried <u>awfully</u> hard*) and should not be used in formal speech or writing.

a while, awhile *Awhile* is an adverb; *a while* is an article and a noun. Thus *awhile* can modify a verb but cannot serve as the object of a preposition, and *a while* is just the opposite: *I will be gone <u>awhile</u>* (not <u>*a while*</u>). *I will be gone for <u>a while</u>* (not <u>*awhile*</u>).

bad, badly In formal speech and writing, *bad* should be used only as an adjective; the adverb is *badly. He felt <u>bad</u> because his tooth ached <u>badly</u>.* In *He felt <u>bad</u>,* the verb *felt* is a linking verb and the adjective *bad* is a subject complement. See also 9b.

being as, being that   Colloquial for *because,* the preferable word in formal speech or writing: *Because* (not *being as*) *the world is round, Columbus never did fall off the edge.*

beside, besides   *Beside* is a preposition meaning "next to." *Besides* is a preposition meaning "except" but also an adverb meaning "in addition." *Besides, several other people want to sit beside Dr. Christensen.*

between, among   See *among, between.*

bring, take   Use *bring* for movement from a farther place to a nearer one and *take* for movement from nearer to farther: *Take these books back to the library, please, and bring home some new ones.*

bunch   In formal speech and writing, *bunch* (as a noun) should be used only to refer to clusters of things growing or fastened together, such as *bananas* and *grapes.* Its use to mean a group of items or people is colloquial; *crowd* or *group* is preferable.

burst, bursted, bust, busted   *Burst* is a standard verb form meaning "to fly apart suddenly" (principal parts *burst, burst, burst*). The past tense form *bursted* is nonstandard. The verb *bust* (*busted*) is slang.

but, hardly, scarcely   These words are negative in their own right; using *not* with any of them to indicate negation is redundant. *We have only an hour* (not *We haven't got but an hour*) *before our plane leaves. I could hardly* (not *I couldn't hardly*) *make out her face in the dark.*

but however, but yet   These and similar expressions, in which *but* is combined with another conjunction, are redundant and should be avoided: *He said he had finished, yet* (not *but yet*) *he continued.*

but that, but what   These expressions are usually wordy substitutes for *that* and *what* and should be avoided: *I don't doubt that* (not *but that*) *you are right.*

calculate, figure, reckon   As substitutes for *expect* or *imagine* (*I figure I'll go*), these words are colloquial.

can, may   Strictly, *can* indicates capacity or ability, and *may* indicates permission: *If I may talk with you a moment, I believe I can solve your problem.* In most speech the distinction is not observed, *can* being used for both meanings.

can't help but   This idiom is common but redundant. Either *I can't help wishing* or the more formal *I cannot but wish* is preferable to *I can't help but wish.*

case, instance, line   Expressions such as *in the case of, in the instance of,* and *along the lines of* are usually unnecessary padding in a sentence and should be avoided.

censor, censure   To *censor* is to edit or remove from public view on moral or some other grounds; to *censure* is to give a formal scolding. *The lieutenant was censured by Major Taylor for censoring the letters his men wrote home from boot camp.*

center around   *Center on* is generally considered more logical than, and preferable to, *center around.*

climatic, climactic   *Climatic* comes from climate and refers to weather: *Last winter's low temperatures may indicate a climatic change. Climactic* comes from *climax* and refers to a dramatic high point: *During the climactic duel between Hamlet and Laertes, Gertrude drinks poisoned wine.*

complement, compliment   To *complement* something is to add to, complete, or reinforce it: *Her yellow blouse complemented her suntan.* To *compliment* something is to make a flattering remark about it: *He complimented her suntan. Complimentary* also can mean "free": *a complimentary sample of our new product; complimentary tickets.*

contact   Often used imprecisely as a verb when a more exact word such as *consult, talk with, telephone,* or *write to* would be appropriate.

continual, continuous   *Continual* means "constantly recurring": *Most movies on television are continually interrupted by commercials. Continuous* means "unceasing": *Cable television often presents movies continuously without commercials.*

convince, persuade   In the strictest sense, to *convince* someone means to change his or her opinion; to *persuade* someone means to move him or her to action. *Convince* thus is properly followed by *of* or *that,* whereas *persuade* is followed by *to*: *Once he convinced Othello of Desdemona's infidelity, Iago easily persuaded him to kill her.*

could of   See *have, of.*

couple of   Used colloquially to mean "a few" or "several."

credible, creditable, credulous   *Credible* means "believable": *It's a strange story, but it seems credible to me. Creditable* means "deserving of credit" or "worthy": *Asked to play "Red River Valley," Steve gave a creditable performance. Credulous* means "gullible": *The credulous Claire believed Tim's statement that he was quitting school.* See also *incredible, incredulous.*

criteria   The plural of *criterion* (meaning "standard for judgment"): *Of all our criteria for picking a roommate, the most important criterion is a sense of humor.*

data   The plural of *datum* (meaning "fact"): *Out of all the data generated by these experiments, not one datum supports our hypothesis.* Usually, a more common term like *fact, result,* or *figure* is preferred to *datum.* Though *data* is very often treated as a singular noun, it is still treated as plural in much formal speech and writing: *The data fail* (not *fails*) *to support the hypothesis.*

deduce, deduct   *Deduce* means "infer": *From your smile, I deduce that you drew the deuce. Deduct* means "take away": *I can't afford all these groceries; can you deduct the duck?* The noun form of both words is *deduction.*

device, devise   *Device* is the noun, and *devise* is the verb: *Can you devise some device for getting his attention?*

differ from, differ with   To *differ from* is to be unlike: *The twins differ from each other only in their hairstyles.* To *differ with* is to disagree with: *I have to differ with you on that point.*

different from, different than   *Different from* is preferred: *His purpose is different from mine.* But *different than* is widely accepted when a clause follows, particularly when a construction using *from* would be wordy: *I'm a different person now than I used to be* is preferable to *I'm a different person now from the person I used to be.*

discreet, discrete   *Discreet* (noun form *discretion*) means "tactful": *What's a discreet way of telling Maud to be quiet? Discrete* (noun form *discreteness*) means "separate and distinct": *Within a computer's memory are millions of discrete bits of information.*

disinterested, uninterested   *Disinterested* means "impartial": *We chose Pete, as a disinterested third party, to decide who was right. Uninterested* means "bored" or "lacking interest": *Unfortunately, Pete was completely uninterested in the question.*

don't   *Don't* is the contraction for *do not*, not for *does not*: *I don't care, you don't care*, but *he doesn't* (not *don't*) *care.*

due to   *Due to* is always acceptable when used as a subject complement: *His gray hairs were due to age.* Many object to using *due to* as a preposition meaning "because of": *Due to the holiday, there will be no class tomorrow.* A good rule of thumb is that *due to* is always correct after a form of the verb *be*, but questionable otherwise.

due to the fact that   Wordy for *because.*

each and every   Wordy for *each* or *every.* Write *each one of us* or *every one of us*, not *each and every one of us.*

eager, anxious   See *anxious, eager.*

effect   See *affect, effect.*

ensure   See *assure, ensure, insure.*

enthused   Used colloquially as an adjective meaning "showing enthusiasm." The preferred adjective is *enthusiastic*: *The coach was enthusiastic* (not *enthused*) *about the team's victory.*

especially, specially   *Especially* means "particularly" or "more than other things"; *specially* means "for a specific reason." *I especially treasure my boots. They were made specially for me.*

et al., etc.   *Et al.*, the Latin abbreviation for "and other people," is often used in source references for works with more than one author: *Jones et al.* (see 35c, 35h). *Etc.*, the Latin abbreviation for "and other things," should not be used to refer to people. See also *and etc.*

every body, everybody; every one, everyone   *Everybody* and *everyone* are indefinite pronouns: *Everybody (everyone) knows Tom steals. Every one* is a pronoun modified by *every, every body* a noun modified by *every*; both refer to each thing or person of a specific group and are typically followed by *of*: *The game commissioner has stocked every body of fresh water in the state with fish, and now every one of our rivers is a potential trout stream.*

everywheres   Nonstandard for *everywhere.*

except   See *accept, except.*

except for the fact that   Wordy for *except that.*

expect   In formal speech and writing, *expect* should not be used as a substitute for *suppose, imagine,* or *presume: The results have been confirmed, so I presume* (not *expect*) *we can trust Parsons's conclusion.*

explicit, implicit   *Explicit* means "stated outright": *I left explicit instructions. The movie contains explicit sex. Implicit* means "implied, unstated": *We had an implicit understanding. I trust Marcia implicitly.*

farther, further   Strictly speaking, *farther* refers to additional distance (*How much farther is it to the beach?*), and *further* refers to additional time, amount, or other abstract matters (*I don't want to discuss this any further*). The distinction often is blurred in current usage.

fewer, less   *Fewer* refers to individual countable items, *less* to general amounts: *Skim milk has fewer calories than whole milk. We have less milk left than I thought.*

field   The phrase *the field of* is wordy and generally unnecessary: *Margaret plans to specialize in* (not *in the field of*) *family medicine.*

figure   See *calculate, figure, reckon.*

flaunt, flout   *Flaunt* means "show off": *If you've got style, flaunt it. Flout* means "scorn" or "defy": *Hester Prynne flouted convention and paid the price.*

flunk   A colloquial substitute for *fail.*

former, latter   *Former* refers to the first named of two things, *latter* to the second named: *I like both skiing and swimming, the former in the winter and the latter all year round.* To refer to the first or last named of three or more things, say *first* or *last: I like jogging, swimming, and hang gliding, but the last is inconvenient in the city.*

further   See *farther, further.*

get   This common verb is used in many slang and colloquial expressions: *get lost, get with it, get your act together, that really gets me, getting on.* In general, *get* is easy to overuse; watch out for it in expressions like *it's getting better* (substitute *it's improving*) and *we got done* (substitute *we finished*).

good, well   *Good* is an adjective, and *well* is nearly always an adverb: *Larry's a good dancer. He and Linda dance well together. Well* is properly used as an adjective to refer to health: *You don't look* <u>*well*</u>*. Aren't you feeling* <u>*well*</u>*?* (*You look* <u>*good*</u>, on the other hand, means "Your appearance is pleasing.")

good and Colloquial for "very": *I was* <u>*very*</u> (not <u>*good and*</u>) *tired.*

had better A legitimate way of saying *ought to. Had better* is a verb modified by an adverb; the verb is necessary and should not be omitted: *you had better* or *you'd better*, not *you better.*

had ought The *had* is unnecessary and should be omitted: *He* <u>*ought*</u> (not <u>*had ought*</u>) *to listen to his mother.*

half Either *half a* or *a half* is appropriate usage, but *a half a* is redundant: <u>*Half a*</u> *loaf* (not <u>*A half a*</u> *loaf*) *is better than none. We'd like* <u>*a half*</u> *bottle* (not <u>*a half a*</u> *bottle*) *of the house wine, please.*

hanged, hung Though both are past tense forms of *hang*, *hanged* is used to refer to executions and *hung* is used for all other meanings: *Tom Dooley was* <u>*hanged*</u> (not <u>*hung*</u>) *from a white oak tree. I* <u>*hung*</u> (not <u>*hanged*</u>) *the picture you gave me.*

hardly See *but, hardly, scarcely.*

have, of Following verbs such as *could, should, may,* and *might,* use *have,* not *of: You* <u>*should have*</u> (not <u>*should of*</u>) *told me when you were coming.*

he, she Many people today object to the use of *he* to mean *he or she* because nearly all readers think of *he* as male, whether or not that is the writer's intention. A good rule is to avoid the usage whenever possible, by pluralizing, using *he or she,* or rephrasing. For instance, *After the infant learns to crawl,* <u>*he*</u> *progresses to creeping* might be rewritten as follows: *After infants learn to crawl,* <u>*they*</u> *progress to creeping. After the infant learns to crawl,* <u>*he or she*</u> *progresses to creeping. After learning to crawl,* <u>*the infant*</u> *progresses to creeping.*

herself, himself See *myself, herself, himself, yourself.*

hisself Nonstandard for *himself.*

hopefully Strictly speaking, *hopefully* means "with hope": *Freddy waited* <u>*hopefully*</u> *for a glimpse of Eliza.* The use of *hopefully* to mean "it is to be hoped," "I hope," or "let's hope" is now very common; but since many readers continue to object strongly to the usage, it is better to avoid this use. *I* <u>*hope*</u> (not <u>*Hopefully*</u>) *Eliza will be here soon.*

illusion See *allusion, illusion.*

implicit See *explicit, implicit.*

imply, infer *Imply* means "suggest"; *Jim's letter* <u>*implies*</u> *he's having too good a time to miss us. Infer* means "conclude": *From Jim's letter I* <u>*infer*</u> *he's having too good a time to miss us.*

in, into *In* indicates location or condition: *He was* <u>*in*</u> *the garage. She was* <u>*in*</u> *a coma. Into* indicates movement or a change in condition: *He* *went into the garage. She fell into a coma.* Colloquially, *into* has also come to mean "interested in" or "involved in": *I am into Zen.*

in . . . A number of phrases beginning with *in* are unnecessarily wordy and should be avoided: *in the event that* (for *if*); *in the neighborhood of* (for *approximately* or *about*); *in this day and age* (for *now* or *nowadays*); *in spite of the fact that* (for *although* or *even though*); and *in view of the fact that* (for *because* or *considering that*). Certain other *in* phrases are nothing but padding and can be omitted entirely: *in the case of, in nature, in number, in reality, in terms of,* and *in a very real sense.* See also 31c.

incredible, incredulous *Incredible* means "unbelievable"; *incredulous* means "unbelieving": *When Nancy heard Dennis's incredible story, she was frankly incredulous.* See also *credible, creditable, credulous.*

individual, person, party *Individual* should be used to refer to a single human being in contrast to a group, or when uniqueness is stressed: *The U.S. Constitution places strong emphasis on the rights of the individual.* For other meanings *person* is preferable: *What person* (not *individual*) *wouldn't want the security promised in that advertisement? Party* means "group" (*Can you seat a party of four for dinner?*) and should not be used to refer to an individual except in legal documents.

infer See *imply.*

in regards to Nonstandard for *in regard to* (or *as regards* or *regarding*). See also *regarding.*

inside of, outside of The *of* is unnecessary when *inside* and *outside* are used as prepositions: *Stay inside* (not *inside of*) *the house. The decision is outside* (not *outside of*) *my authority. Inside of* may refer colloquially to time, though in formal English *within* is preferred: *I'll meet you within* (not *inside of*) *an hour.*

instance See *case, instance, line.*

insure See *assure, ensure, insure.*

irregardless Nonstandard for *regardless.*

is because See *reason is because.*

is when, is where Mixed constructions (faulty predication; see 15b) in sentences that define: *Adolescence is a stage* (not *is when a person is*) *between childhood and adulthood. Socialism is a system in which* (not *is where*) *government owns the means of production.*

its, it's *Its* is a possessive pronoun: *That plant is losing its leaves. It's* is a contraction for *it is: It's likely to die if you don't water it.* Many people confuse *it's* and *its* because possessives are most often formed with *-'s*; but *its* in the possessive sense never takes an apostrophe.

-ize, -wise The suffix *-ize* is frequently used to change a noun or adjective into a verb: *revolutionize, immunize.* The suffix *-wise* commonly changes a noun or adjective into an adverb: *clockwise, otherwise, likewise.* But the two suffixes are used excessively and often unnecessarily, especially in bureaucratic writing. Avoid their use except in established words: *The two nations are ready to settle on* (not *finalize*) *an agreement. I'm highly sensitive* (not *sensitized*) *to that kind of criticism. From a financial standpoint* (not *Moneywise*), *it's a good time to buy real estate.*

kind of, sort of, type of   In formal speech and writing, avoid using *kind of* or *sort of* to mean "somewhat": *He was rather* (not *kind of*) *tall.*

Kind, *sort,* and *type* are singular and take singular modifiers and verbs: *This kind of dog is easily trained.* If you're referring to more than one breed, write: *These kinds* (not *kind*) *of dogs are easily trained. Kind, sort,* and *type* should be followed by *of* but not by *a: I don't know what type of* (not *type* or *type of a*) *dog that is.*

Use *kind of, sort of,* or *type of* only when the word *kind, sort,* or *type* is important: *That was a strange* (not *strange sort of*) *statement. He's a funny* (not *funny kind of*) *guy.*

later, latter   *Later* refers to time; *latter* refers to the second-named of two items. See *former, latter.*

lay, lie   *Lay* is a transitive verb (principle parts *lay, laid, laid*) that means "put" or "place"; it is nearly always followed by a direct object. *If we lay this tablecloth in the sun next to the shirt Sandy laid out there this morning, it should dry pretty quickly. Lie* is an intransitive verb (principal parts *lie, lay, lain*) that means "recline" or "be situated": *I lay awake all night last night, just as I had lain the night before. The town lies east of the river.* See also 7b.

leave, let   *Leave* and *let* are interchangeable only when followed by *alone; leave me alone* is the same as *let me alone.* Otherwise, *leave* means "depart" and *let* means "allow": *Julia would not let Susan leave.*

less   See *fewer, less.*

let   See *leave, let.*

liable   See *apt, liable, likely.*

lie, lay   See *lay, lie.*

like, as   See *as, like.*

like, such as   When you are giving an example of something, use *such as* to indicate that the example is a representative of the thing mentioned, and use *like* to compare the example to the thing mentioned: *Steve has recordings of many great saxophonists such as Ben Webster, Coleman Hawkins, and Lee Konitz. Steve wants to be a great jazz saxophonist like Ben Webster, Coleman Hawkins, and Lee Konitz.*

Most writers prefer to keep *such* and *as* together: *Steve admires saxophonists such as* . . ., rather than *Steve admires such saxophonists as* . . . .

likely   See *apt, liable, likely.*

line   See *case, line, instance.*

lose, loose *Lose* is a verb meaning "mislay": *Did you lose a brown glove? Loose* is an adjective meaning "unrestrained" or "not tight": *Don't open the door; Ann's canary got loose. Loose* also can function as a verb meaning "let loose": *They loose the dogs as soon as they spot the bear.*

lots, lots of Colloquial substitutes for *a great deal, a great many,* or *much.*

may, can See *can, may.*

may be, maybe *May be* is a verb, and *maybe* is an adverb meaning "perhaps": *Tuesday may be a legal holiday. Maybe we won't have classes.*

may of See *have, of.*

media *Media* is the plural of *medium: Of all the news media, television is the only medium with more visual than verbal content.*

might of See *have, of.*

moral, morale As a noun, *moral* means "ethical conclusion" or "lesson": *The moral of the story escapes me. Morale* means "spirit" or "state of mind": *Victory improved the team's morale.*

most, almost See *almost, most.*

must of See *have, of.*

myself, herself, himself, yourself The *-self* pronouns are reflexive or intensive, which means they refer back to or intensify an antecedent (see 5a–3): *Paul and I did it ourselves; Jill herself said so.* Though the *-self* pronouns often are used colloquially in place of personal pronouns, especially as objects of prepositions, they should be avoided in formal speech and writing unless the noun or pronoun they refer to is also present: *No one except me* (not *myself*) *saw the accident. Our delegates will be Susan and you* (not *yourself*).

nohow Nonstandard for *in no way* or *in any way.*

nothing like, nowhere near As colloquial substitutes for *not nearly,* these idioms are best avoided in formal speech and writing: *The human bones found in Europe are not nearly* (not *nowhere near*) *as old as those found in Africa.*

nowheres Nonstandard for *nowhere.*

number See *amount, number.*

of, have See *have, of.*

off of *Of* is unnecessary. Use *off* or *from* rather than *off of: He jumped off* (or *from,* not *off of*) *the roof.*

OK, O.K., okay All three spellings are acceptable, but avoid this term in formal speech and writing.

on, upon In modern English, *upon* is usually just a stuffy way of saying *on.* Unless you need a formal effect, use *on*: *We decided on* (not *upon*) *a location for our next meeting.*

on account of Wordy for *because of.*

outside of See *inside of, outside of.*

owing to the fact that Wordy for *because.*

party See *individual, person, party.*

people, persons In formal speech and writing, *people* refers to a general group: *We the people of the United States.* ... *Persons* refers to a collection of individuals: *Will the person or persons who saw the accident please notify.* ... Except when emphasis on individuals is desired, *people* is preferable to *persons.*

per Except in technical writing, an English equivalent is usually preferable to the Latin *per*: *$10 an* (not *per*) *hour*; *sent by* (not *per*) *parcel post*; *requested in* (not *per* or *as per*) *your letter.*

percent (per cent), percentage Both these terms refer to fractions of one hundred and should be avoided except when specifying actual statistics. Use an expression such as *part of, a number of,* or *a high* (or *small*) *proportion of* when you mean simply "part."

Percent always follows a number (*40 percent of the voters*), and the word should be used instead of the symbol (%) in formal writing. *Percentage* follows an adjective (*a high percentage*).

person See *individual, person, party.*

persons See *people, persons.*

persuade See *convince, persuade.*

phenomena The plural of *phenomenon* (meaning "perceivable fact" or "unusual occurrence"): *We phoned the Center for Short-Lived Phenomena to find out whether the phenomenon we had witnessed might be a flying saucer.*

plenty A colloquial substitute for *very*: *He was going very* (not *plenty*) *fast when he hit that tree.*

plus *Plus* is standard as a preposition meaning *in addition to*: *His income plus mine should be sufficient.* But *plus* is colloquial as a conjunctive adverb: *Our organization is larger than theirs; moreover* (not *plus*), *we have more money.*

practicable, practical *Practicable* means "capable of being put into practice"; *practical* means "useful" or "sensible." *We figured out a practical new design for our kitchen, but it was too expensive to be practicable.*

pretty Overworked as an adverb meaning "rather" or "somewhat": *He was somewhat* (not *pretty*) *irked at the suggestion.*

previous to, prior to Wordy for *before.*

principal, principle *Principal* is a noun meaning "chief official" or, in finance, "capital sum." As an adjective, *principal* means "foremost" or "major." *Principle* is a noun only, meaning "rule" or "axiom." *Her principal reasons for confessing were her principles of right and wrong.*

question of whether, question as to whether Wordy for *whether.*

raise, rise *Raise* is a transitive verb and takes a direct object, and *rise* is intransitive: *The Bennetts have to rise at dawn because they raise cows.*

real, really In formal speech and writing, *real* should not be used as an adverb; *really* is the adverb and *real* an adjective. *Popular reaction to the announcement was really (not real) enthusiastic.*

reason is because Mixed construction (faulty predication; see 15b). Although the expression is colloquially common, more formal speech and writing require a *that* clause after *reason is*: *The reason he is absent is that* (not *is because*) *he is sick.*

reckon See *calculate, figure, reckon.*

regarding, in regard to, with regard to, relating to, relative to, with respect to, respecting Stuffy substitutes for *on, about,* or *concerning*: *Mr. McGee spoke about (not with regard to) the plans for the merger.*

respectful, respective *Respectful* means "full of (or showing) respect": *If you want respect, be respectful of other people. Respective* means "separate": *After a joint Christmas celebration, the French and the Germans returned to their respective trenches.*

rise, raise See *raise, rise.*

scarcely See *but, hardly, scarcely.*

sensual, sensuous *Sensual* suggests sexuality; *sensuous* means "pleasing to the senses." *Stirred by the sensuous scent of meadow grass and flowers, Leslie and Paul found their thoughts growing increasingly sensual.*

set, sit *Set* is a transitive verb (principal parts *set, set, set*) that describes something a person does to an object: *Set the pitcher on the table. Sit* is an intransitive verb (principal parts *sit, sat, sat*) that describes something done by a person who is tired of standing: *Let's sit on the sofa.* See also 7b.

shall, will *Will,* originally reserved for the second and third persons, is now generally accepted as the future tense auxiliary for all three persons: *I will go, you will go, they will go.* The main use of *shall* is for first-person questions requesting an opinion or consent: *Shall I order a pizza? Shall we dance?* (Questions that merely inquire about the future use *will*: *When will I see you again?*) *Shall* can also be used for the first person when a formal effect is desired: *I shall expect you around three.*

should, would *Should* expresses obligation for first, second, and third persons: *I should fix dinner. You should set the table. Jack should wash the dishes. Would* expresses a wish or hypothetical condition for all three persons: *I would do it. Wouldn't you? Wouldn't anybody?* When the context is formal, however, *should* is sometimes used instead of *would* in the first person: *We should be delighted to accept your kind invitation.*

should of See *have, of.*

since *Since* is often used to mean "because": *Since you ask, I'll tell you.* Its primary meaning, however, relates to time: *I've been waiting since noon.* To avoid confusion some writers prefer to use *since* only in contexts involving time. If you do use *since* in both senses, watch out for ambiguous constructions, such as *Since you left, my life is empty,* where *since* could mean either "because" or "ever since."

sit, set See *set, sit.*

situation Often used unnecessarily, as in *The situation is that we have to get some help* (revise to *We have to get some help*) or *The team was faced with a punting situation* (revise to *The team was faced with punting* or *The team had to punt*).

some *Some* is colloquial as an adverb meaning "somewhat" or "to some extent" and as an adjective meaning "remarkable": *We'll have to hurry somewhat* (not *some*) *to get there in time. Those are remarkable* (not *some*) *photographs.*

somebody, some body, someone, some one *Somebody* and *someone* are indefinite pronouns; *some body* is a noun modified by an adjective; and *some one* is a pronoun or an adjective modified by *some. Somebody ought to invent a shampoo that will give hair some body. Someone told Janine she should choose some one plan and stick with it.*

someplace Informal for *somewhere.*

sometime, sometimes, some time *Sometime* means "at an indefinite time in the future": *Why don't you come up and see me sometime? Sometimes* means "now and then": *I still see my old friend Joe sometimes. Some time* means "span of time": *I need some time to make the payments.*

somewheres Nonstandard for *somewhere.*

sort of, sort of a See *kind of, sort of, type of.*

specially See *especially, specially.*

such Avoid using *such* as a vague intensifier: *It was such a cold winter. Such* should be followed by *that* and a clause that states a result: *It was such a cold winter that Napoleon's troops had to turn back.*

such as See *like, such as.*

supposed to, used to In both these expressions, the *-d* is essential: *I used to* (not *use to*) *think so. He's supposed to* (not *suppose to*) *meet us.*

sure Colloquial when used as an adverb meaning *surely: James Madison sure was right about the need for the Bill of Rights.* If you merely want to be emphatic, use *certainly: Madison certainly was right.* If your goal is to convince a possibly reluctant reader, use *surely: Madison surely was right. Surely Madison was right.*

sure and, sure to, try and, try to *Sure to* and *try to* are the preferred forms: *Be sure to* (not *sure and*) *buy milk. Try to* (not *Try and*) *find some decent tomatoes.*

take, bring See *bring, take.*

than, as See *as, than.*

than, then *Than* is a conjunction used in comparisons, *then* an adverb indicating time: *Holmes knew then that Moriarty was wilier than he had thought.*

that, which *That* always introduces restrictive clauses: *We should see the lettuce that Susan bought* (*that Susan bought* identifies the specific lettuce being referred to). *Which* can introduce both restrictive and nonrestrictive clauses, but in formal speech and writing many prefer to use *which* only for nonrestrictive clauses: *The leftover lettuce, which is in the refrigerator, would make a good salad* (*which is in the refrigerator* simply provides more information about the lettuce). See also 21c.

their, there, they're *Their* is the possessive form of *they*: *Give them their money. There* indicates place (*I saw her standing there*) or functions as an expletive (*There is a hole behind you*). *They're* is a contraction for *they are*: *Get them now—they're going fast.*

theirselves Nonstandard for *themselves.*

then, than See *than, then.*

these kind, these sort, these type, those kind See *kind of, sort of, type of.*

this here, these here, that there, them there Nonstandard for *this, these, that,* or *those.*

thusly A mistaken form of *thus.*

till, until, 'til *Till* and *until* have the same meaning; both are acceptable. *'Til,* a contraction of *until,* is an old form that has been replaced by *till.*

to, too *To* is a preposition, *too* an adverb meaning "also" or "excessively": *I too have been to Europe.*

toward, towards Both are acceptable, though *toward* is preferred. The main thing is to use one or the other consistently.

try and, try to See *sure and, sure to; try and, try to.*

type of See *kind of, sort of, type of.*

uninterested See *disinterested, uninterested.*

until See *till, until, 'til.*

usage, use *Usage* refers to conventions, most often those of a language: *Is "hadn't ought" proper usage? Usage* is often misused to mean *use: Wise use* (not *usage*) *of insulation can save fuel.*

use, utilize *Utilize* means "make use of": *We should utilize John's talent* *for mimicry in our play*. In most contexts, *use* is equally or more acceptable and much less stuffy.

used to See *supposed to, used to*.

wait for, wait on In formal speech and writing, *wait for* means "await" (*I'm waiting for Paul*), and *wait on* means "serve" (*The owner of the store herself waited on us*).

ways Colloquial as a substitute for *way*: *We have only a little way* (not *ways*) *to go*.

well See *good*.

which See *that, which*.

which, who *Which* never refers to people. Use *who* or *that* for a person or persons and *which* or *that* for a thing or things: *The baby, who was left behind, opened the door, which we had closed*. See also 12f.

will, shall See *shall, will*.

-wise See *-ize, -wise*.

with regard to, with respect to See *regarding*.

would See *should, would*.

yourself See *myself, herself, himself, yourself*.

Glossary of Grammatical Terms

absolute phrase A phrase that consists of a noun or pronoun and a participle, modifies a whole clause or sentence (rather than a single word), and is not joined to the rest of the sentence by a connector: *Our accommodations arranged, we set out on our trip. They will hire a local person, other things being equal.* When the participle in an absolute phrase is a form of the verb *be* (*being*, *been*), the participle is often omitted: *They will hire a local person, other things equal.* See also 5c-3.

abstract noun See *noun*.

acronym A word formed from the initial letter or letters of each word in an organization's title: NATO (North Atlantic Treaty Organization). See also 20b and 28b.

active voice See *verb*.

adjectival A term sometimes used to describe any word or word group, other than an adjective, that is used to modify a noun. Common adjectivals include nouns (*wagon train, railroad ties*), phrases (*fool on the hill*), and clauses (*the man I used to be*). See *clause* and *phrase*. See also 5c.

adjective A word used to modify a noun or a word or word group used as a noun.

> **Descriptive adjectives** name some quality of the noun: *beautiful morning; dark horse.*

> **Limiting adjectives** narrow the scope of a noun. They include **possessives** (*my, their*); words that show number (*eight, several*); **demonstrative adjectives** (*this train, these days*); and **interrogative adjectives** (*what time? whose body?*)

> **Proper adjectives** are derived from proper nouns: *French fries, Machiavellian scheme.*

Adjectives also can be classified according to position.

> **Attributive adjectives** appear next to the nouns they modify.

> **Predicate adjectives** are connected to their nouns by linking verbs: *The moon is full.* See also *complement*.

The **degree** of an adjective indicates comparison (*pretty, prettier, prettiest*). See *degree.*
> See also 5b–1 and Chapter 9.

adjective clause   See *clause.*

adjective phrase   See *phrase.*

adverb   A word used to modify a verb, an adjective, another adverb, or a whole sentence. Any one-word modifier that is not an adjective, a word used as an adjective, or an article is an adverb: *If you go south you'll hit a more heavily traveled road. South* modifies the verb *go; heavily* modifies the adjective *traveled;* and *more* modifies the adverb *heavily.*) See also 5b–1 and Chapter 9.

adverb clause   See *clause.*

adverbial   A term sometimes used to describe any word or word group, other than an adverb, that is used to modify a verb, adjective, other adverb, or whole sentence. Common adverbials include nouns (*This little piggy stayed home*), phrases (*This little piggy went to market*), and clauses (*This little piggy went wherever he wanted*). See *clause* and *phrase.* See also 5c.

adverbial conjunction   See *conjunctive adverb.*

adverb phrase   See *phrase.*

agreement   The correspondence of one word to another in person, number, or gender. A verb must agree with its subject, and a pronoun must agree with its antecedent: *Every week the commander orders egg salad sandwiches for his troops.* (The verb *orders* and the pronoun *his* both agree with the noun *commander.*) See also Chapter 8.

antecedent   The noun, or word or word group acting as a noun, to which a pronoun refers: *Jonah, who is not yet ten, has already chosen the college he will attend.* (*Jonah* is the antecedent of the pronouns *who* and *he.*) See also 8b.

appositive   A word or phrase appearing next to a noun, or to a word or word group acting as a noun, which explains or identifies it and is equivalent to it: *My brother Michael, the best horn player in town, won the state competition.* (*Michael* is a restrictive appositive that identifies which brother is being referred to. *The best horn player in town* is a nonrestrictive appositive that adds information about *My brother Michael.*) See also 5c–5.

article   The words *a* and *an* (**indefinite articles**) and the word *the* (**definite article**). Articles are usually treated as adjectives, but they are sometimes called determiners because they always signal that a noun will follow.

auxiliary verb   A verb (also called a **helping verb**) used with a main verb in a verb phrase: *will give, has been seeing, could depend.* Auxiliaries indicate tense and sometimes also indicate voice, person, number, or mood. **Modal auxiliaries** include *can, could, may, might, must, ought,* *shall, should, will,* and *would.* They indicate a necessity, possibility, capability, willingness, or the like: *He can lift 250 pounds. You should write to your grandmother.* See also 5a–2 and Chapter 7.

cardinal number   The type of number that shows amount: *two, sixty, ninety-seven.* Contrast *ordinal number* (such as *second, ninety-seventh*).

case   The form of a noun or pronoun that indicates its function in the sentence. Nouns have two cases: the **plain case** (*John, ambassador*), for all uses except to show possession; and the **possessive** (or **genitive**) **case** (*John's, ambassador's*). Pronouns have three cases: the **subjective** (or **nominative**) **case** (*I, she*), denoting the subject of a verb or a subject complement; the **possessive case**, for use as either an adjective (*my, her*) or a noun (*mine, hers*); and the **objective case** (*me, her*), denoting the object of a verb, verbal, or preposition. See *declension* for a complete list of the forms of personal and relative pronouns. See also Chapter 6.

gl/gr

clause   A group of related words containing a subject and predicate. Clauses are either **main** (**independent**) or **subordinate** (**dependent**). A main clause can stand by itself as a sentence; a subordinate clause cannot.

MAIN CLAUSE	*Let's go to the movies.*
SUBORDINATE CLAUSE	We can go *if Julie gets back on time.*

Subordinate clauses may function as adjectives, adverbs, or nouns.

Adjective clauses modify nouns or pronouns: *The car that hit Fred was running a red light* (clause modifies *car*).

Adverb clauses modify verbs, adjectives, other adverbs, or whole clauses or sentences: *The car hit Fred when it ran a red light* (clause modifies *hit*).

Noun clauses, like nouns, function as subjects, objects, or complements: *Whoever was driving should be arrested* (clause is sentence subject).

See also 5c–4.

collective noun   See *noun.*

comma splice   A sentence fault in which two main clauses are linked by a comma with no coordinating conjunction.

COMMA SPLICE	The book was long, it contained useful information.
REVISED	The book was long, *but* it contained useful information.

See 11a and 11b.

common noun   See *noun.*

comparative   See *degree.*

comparison   See *degree.*

complement   A word or word group that completes the sense of a subject, an object, or a verb.

Subject complements follow a linking verb and modify or refer to the subject. They may be adjectives, nouns, or words or word groups acting as adjectives or nouns: *I am a <u>lion tamer</u>, but I am not yet <u>experienced</u>.* (The noun *lion tamer* and the adjective *experienced* complement the subject *I.*) Adjective complements are also called **predicate adjectives**. Noun complements are also called **predicate nouns**.

Object complements follow and modify or refer to direct objects. The complement can be an adjective, a noun, or a word or word group acting as an adjective or noun: *If you elect me <u>president</u>, I'll keep the unions <u>satisfied</u>.* (The noun *president* complements the direct object *me*, and the adjective *satisfied* complements the direct object *unions.*)

Verb complements are direct and indirect objects of verbs. They may be nouns or words or word groups acting as nouns: *Don't give the <u>chimp</u> that <u>peanut</u>.* (*Chimp* is the indirect object and *peanut* is the direct object of the verb *give*. Both objects are verb complements.)

See also *object* and 5a–3.

complete predicate   See *predicate.*

complete subject   See *subject.*

complex sentence   See *sentence.*

compound   Consisting of two or more words that function as a unit. **Compound words** include **compound nouns** (*milestone, hotdog*); **compound adjectives** (*two-year-old, downtrodden*); and **compound prepositions** (*in addition to, on account of*). **Compound constructions** include **compound subjects** (<u>*Harriet and Peter*</u> *poled their barge down the river*) and **compound predicates** (*The scout <u>watched and waited</u>*), or parts of predicates (*He grew <u>tired and hungry</u>*). See also 5d.

compound-complex sentence   See *sentence.*

compound predicate   See *compound.*

compound sentence   See *sentence.*

compound subject   See *compound.*

concrete noun   See *noun.*

conjugation   A list of the forms of a verb showing tense, voice, mood, person, and number. The conjugation of the verb *know* in present tense, active voice, indicative mood is *I know, you know, he/she/it knows, we know, you know, they know.* See also Chapter 7.

conjunction   A word that links and relates two parts of a sentence. **Coordinating conjunctions** (*and, but, or, nor, for, so, yet*) connect words or word groups of equal grammatical rank: *The lights went out, but the doctors and nurses cared for their patients as if nothing were wrong.* See also 5d–1. **Correlative conjunctions** or **correlatives** (such as *either . . . or, not only . . . but also*) are pairs of coordinating conjunctions that work together: *He was certain that either his parents or his brother would help him.* See also 5d–1. **Subordinating conjunctions** (*after, although, as if, because, if, when, while,* and so on) begin a dependent clause and link it to an independent clause. *The seven dwarfs whistle while they work.* See also 5c–4.

conjunctive adverb (adverbial conjunction) An adverb (such as *also, besides, consequently, indeed,* and *therefore*) that links two main clauses in a sentence: *We had hoped to own a house by now; however, housing costs have risen too fast.* See also 5d–2.

connector (connective) Any word or phrase that links words, phrases, clauses, or sentences. Common connectors include coordinating, correlative, and subordinating conjunctions, conjunctive adverbs, and prepositions.

connotation An association called up by a word, beyond its dictionary definition. See 31b–1. Contrast *denotation.*

construction Any group of grammatically related words, such as a phrase, a clause, or a sentence.

contraction A condensation of an expression, with an apostrophe replacing the missing letters: for example, *doesn't* (for *does not*), *we'll* (for *we will*).

coordinating conjunction See *conjunction.*

coordination The use of grammatically equal constructions to indicate that parts of a sentence, compound units within a sentence, or successive sentences within a paragraph are of equal importance: *He laughed, and I winced.* See also 16a. Contrast *subordination.*

correlative conjunction (correlative) See *conjunction.*

dangling modifier A word or phrase modifying a term that has been omitted or to which it cannot easily be linked.

DANGLING	*Having arrived late,* the concert had already begun.
REVISED	Having arrived late, *we* found that the concert had already begun.
REVISED	*Because we arrived late,* we missed the beginning of the concert.

See also 14g.

declension A list of the forms of a noun or pronoun, showing person (for pronouns), number, and case. See Chapter 6. The following chart shows a complete declension of the personal and relative pronouns.

Personal pronouns	Subjective	Objective	Possessive
Singular			
First person	I	me	my, mine
Second person	you	you	your, yours
Third person			
Masculine	he	him	his
Feminine	she	her	her, hers
Neuter	it	it	its
Plural			
First person	we	us	our, ours
Second person	you	you	your, yours
Third person	they	them	their, theirs
Relative pronouns			
	who	whom	whose
	which	which	whose, of which
	that	that	—

degree   The aspect of an adverb or adjective that shows its relative intensity. The **positive degree** is the simple, uncompared form: *gross, clumsily*. The **comparative degree** compares the thing modified to at least one other thing: *grosser, more clumsily*. The **superlative degree** indicates that the thing modified exceeds all other things to which it is being compared: *grossest, most clumsily*. The comparative and superlative degrees are formed either by adding the endings *-er* and *-est* or by preceding the modifier with the words *more* and *most*. See also 5b–1 and 9e.

demonstrative adjective   See *adjective.*

demonstrative pronoun   See *pronoun.*

denotation   The main or dictionary definition of a word. See 31b–1. Contrast *connotation.*

dependent clause   See *clause.*

derivational suffix   See *suffix.*

descriptive adjective   See *adjective.*

determiner   A word such as *a, an, the, my,* and *your* which indicates that a noun follows.

diagramming   A visual method of identifying and showing the relations between various parts of a sentence.

direct address   A word or phrase indicating the person, group, or thing spoken to: *Have you finished, John? Farmers, unite.*

direct object   See *object.*

direct quotation (direct discourse)   See *quotation.*

double negative   A nonstandard form consisting of two negative words used in the same construction so that they effectively cancel each other: *I <u>don't</u> have <u>no</u> money.*

double possessive   A possessive using both the ending -*'s* and the preposition *of*: *That is a favorite expression <u>of Mark's.</u>*

ellipsis   The omission of a word or words from a quotation, indicated by the three spaced periods of an **ellipsis mark**: *"that all <u>. . .</u> are created equal."* See also 25e.

elliptical clause   A clause omitting a word or words whose meaning is understood from the rest of the clause: *David likes Minneapolis <u>better than</u> (he likes) <u>Chicago.</u>* See also 5c-4.

expletive   A sentence construction that postpones the subject by beginning with *there* or *it* followed by a form of the verb *be*: *<u>It is</u> impossible to get a ticket; I don't know why <u>there aren't</u> more seats available.* (*To get a ticket* is the subject of *is*; *seats* is the subject of *aren't*.) See also 5e-4.

finite verb   A term used to describe any verb that makes an assertion or expresses a state of being and can stand as the main verb of a sentence or clause: *The moose <u>eats</u> the leaves.* See also 5c-2. Contrast *gerund, participle,* and *infinitive*—all formed from finite verbs but unable to stand alone as the main verb of a sentence: *I saw the moose <u>eating</u> the leaves* (participle). Contrast also *verbal.*

fragment   See *sentence fragment.*

function word   A word, such as an article, conjunction, or preposition, that serves primarily to clarify the roles of and relations between other words in a sentence: *We chased the goat <u>for an</u> hour <u>but</u> finally caught it.* Contrast *lexical word.*

fused sentence   See *run-on sentence.*

future perfect tense   See *tense.*

future tense   See *tense.*

gender   The classification of nouns or pronouns as masculine (*he, boy, handyman*), feminine (*she, woman, actress*), or neuter (*it, typewriter, dog*).

genitive case   Another term for possessive case. See *case.*

gerund   A verbal that ends in -*ing* and functions as a noun. The form of the gerund is the same as that of the present participle. Gerunds may have subjects, objects, complements, and modifiers: *<u>Working</u> is all right for <u>killing</u> time.* (*Working* is the subject of the verb *is*; *killing* is the object of the preposition *for* and takes the object *time*.) See also 5c-2, *verbal,* and *participle.*

helping verb   See *auxiliary verb.*

idiom   An expression that is peculiar to a language and that may not make sense if taken literally: for example, *dark horse, bide your time,* *agree with them, agree to the contract.* See 31b–3 for a list of idioms involving prepositions.

imperative See *mood.*

indefinite pronoun See *pronoun.*

independent clause See *clause.*

indicative See *mood.*

indirect object See *object.*

indirect quotation (indirect discourse) See *quotation.*

infinitive The plain form of a verb, the form listed in the dictionary: *buy, sharpen, rinse.* Usually in combination with the **infinitive marker** *to,* infinitives form verbals and verbal phrases that function as nouns, adjectives, or adverbs. They may have objects, complements, or modifiers: *Alex's goals are to make money and to live well.* (*To make* and *to live* follow the linking verb *is* and are complements of the subject *goal. To make* takes the object *money* and *to live* is modified by the adverb *well.*) See also 5c–2.

infinitive marker See *infinitive.*

infinitive phrase See *phrase.*

inflection The variation in the form of a word that indicates its function in a particular context. The inflection of nouns and pronouns is called **declension**; the inflection of verbs is called **conjugation**; the inflection of adjectives and adverbs is called **comparison**.

inflectional suffix See *suffix.*

intensifier A modifier that adds emphasis to the word(s) it modifies: for example, *very, so, awfully.*

intensive pronoun See *pronoun.*

interjection A word standing by itself or inserted in a construction to exclaim or command attention: *Hey! Ouch! What the heck did you do that for?*

interrogative Functioning as or involving a question.

interrogative adjective See *adjective.*

interrogative pronoun See *pronoun.*

intransitive verb See *verb.*

inversion A reversal of usual word order in a sentence, as when a verb precedes its subject or an object precedes its verb: *Down swooped the hawk. Our aims we stated clearly.*

irregular verb A verb that forms its past tense and past participle in some other way than by the addition of *-d* or *-ed* to the plain form: for example, *go, went, gone; give, gave, given.* See also 5a; and see 7a for a list of irregular verbs. Contrast *regular verb.*

lexical word A word, such as a noun, verb, or modifier, that carries part of the meaning of language. Contrast *function word.*

linking verb A verb that relates a subject to its complement: *Julie is a Democrat. He looks harmless. Those flowers smell heavenly.* Common linking verbs are the forms of *be*; the verbs relating to the senses, such as *feel* and *smell*; and the verbs *become, appear,* and *seem.* See also 5a–2 and *verb.*

gl/gr

main clause See *clause.*

misplaced modifier A modifier so far from the term it modifies or so close to another term that its relation to the rest of the sentence is unclear.

MISPLACED	The boys played with firecrackers that they bought illegally *in the field.*
REVISED	The boys played *in the field* with firecrackers that they bought illegally.

A misplaced modifier that falls between two nouns and could modify either is called a **squinting modifier**.

SQUINTING	The plan we have considered *seriously* worries me.
REVISED	The plan we have *seriously* considered worries me.
REVISED	The plan we have considered worries me *seriously.*

See also 14a to 14f.

mixed construction A sentence containing two or more parts that do not fit together in grammar or in meaning.

MIXED	Of those who show up, they will not all be able to get in.
REVISED	Not all of those who show up will be able to get in.

See also 15a and 15b.

modal auxiliary See *auxiliary.*

modifier Any word or word group that limits or qualifies the meaning of another word or word group. Modifiers are adjectives and adverbs as well as words, phrases, and clauses that act as adjectives and adverbs.

mood The form of a verb that shows how the speaker views the action. The **indicative mood,** the most common, is used to make statements or ask questions: *The play will be performed Saturday. Did you get us tickets?* The **imperative mood** gives a command: *Please get good seats. Don't let them stick us in the top balcony.* The **subjunctive mood** expresses a wish, a condition contrary to fact, a recommendation, or a request: *I wish George were coming with us. Did you suggest that he join us?* See also 7f.

nominal A word or group of words used as a noun: *The rich owe a debt to the poor* (adjectives acting as subject and object). *Babysitting can be exhausting* (gerund acting as subject). *I like to play with children* (infinitive phrase acting as object).

nominative See *case.*

nonfinite verb See *verbal.*

nonrestrictive modifier A modifying phrase or clause that does not limit the term or construction it modifies and that is not essential to the meaning of the sentence's main clause. Nonrestrictive modifiers are usually set off by commas: *This electric mixer, on sale for one week only, can be plugged directly into your kitchen counter* (nonrestrictive adjective phrase). *Sleep, which we all need, occupies a third of our lives* (nonrestrictive adjective clause). See also 21c. Contrast *restrictive modifier.*

noun A word that names a person, place, thing, quality, or idea: *Maggie, Alabama, clarinet, satisfaction, socialism.* Nouns normally form the plural by adding *-s* or *-es* (*clarinets*) and the possessive case by adding *-'s* (*Maggie's*). There are several types of nouns, some of which overlap:

> **Common nouns** refer to general classes: *book, government, music.*
>
> **Proper nouns** name specific people or places: *Susan, Athens, Candlestick Park.*
>
> **Collective nouns** name groups: *team, class, jury, family.*
>
> **Count nouns** name things that can be counted: *ounce, camera, pencil.*
>
> **Mass nouns** name things that aren't normally counted: *jewelry, milk.*
>
> **Concrete nouns** name tangible things: *ink, porch, bird.*
>
> **Abstract nouns** name ideas or qualities: *equality, greed, capitalism.*

See also 5a-1.

noun clause See *clause.*

number The form of a noun, pronoun, demonstrative adjective, or verb that indicates whether it is singular or plural: *woman, women; I, we; this, these; runs, run.* See also Chapter 8.

object A noun or a word or word group acting as a noun that receives the action of or is influenced by a transitive verb, a verbal, or a preposition.

> **Direct objects** receive the action of verbs and frequently follow them in a sentence: *We sat watching the stars. Emily caught whatever it was you had.*
>
> **Indirect objects** tell for or to whom or what something is done: *I lent Stan my car. Reiner bought us all champagne.*
>
> **Objects of prepositions** usually follow prepositions and are linked by them to the rest of the sentence: *They are going to New Orleans for the jazz festival.*

See also 5a–3 and 5c–1.

object complement   See *complement.*

objective   See *case.*

ordinal number   The type of number that shows order: *first, eleventh, twenty-fifth.* Contrast *cardinal number* (such as *one, twenty-five*).

parenthetical element   A word or construction that interrupts a sentence and is not part of its main structure, called *parenthetical* because it could (or does) appear in parentheses: *We will continue, barring further interruptions, with the next paragraph. This book, incidentally, is terrible.*

gl/gr

participial phrase   See *phrase.*

participle   A verbal showing continuing or completed action, used as an adjective, adverb, noun, or part of a verb phrase but never as the main verb of a sentence or clause.

> **Present participles** end in *-ing: My heart is breaking* (participle as part of verb with auxiliary). *I like to watch the rolling waves* (participle as adjective). *He came running* (participle as adverb). *Talking is not allowed in class* (present participle as noun, called a gerund).

> **Past participles** most commonly end in *-d, -ed, -n,* or *-en* (*wished, shown, given*) but often change the spelling of the verb (*sung, done, slept*): *Jeff has broken his own record* (participle as part of verb with auxiliary). *The meeting occurred behind a closed door* (participle as adjective).

See also 5b–2, 5c–2.

parts of speech   The classes into which words are commonly grouped according to their form, function, and meaning: nouns, pronouns, verbs, adjectives, adverbs, conjunctions, prepositions, and interjections. See separate entries for each part of speech. See also 5a to 5d.

passive voice   See *voice.*

past participle   See *participle.*

past perfect tense   See *tense.*

past tense   See *tense.*

perfect tenses   See *tense.*

person   The form of a verb or pronoun that indicates whether the subject is speaking, spoken to, or spoken about. In English only personal pronouns and verbs change form to indicate difference in person. In the **first person**, the subject is speaking: *I am* (or *we are*) *planning to go to the party tonight.* In the **second person**, the subject is being spoken to: *Are you coming?* In the **third person**, the subject is being spoken about: *She was* (or *they were*) *going.*

personal pronoun   See *pronoun.*

phrase   A group of related words that lacks a subject or a predicate or both and that acts as a single part of speech. There are several common types of phrases:

> **Verb phrases** are verb forms of more than one word that serve as predicates of sentences or clauses: *He says the movie <u>has started</u>.*
>
> **Prepositional phrases** consist of a preposition and its object, plus any modifiers. They function as adjectives, as adverbs, and occasionally as nouns: *We could come back <u>for the second show</u>* (adverb).
>
> **Infinitive phrases** consist of an infinitive and its object, plus any modifiers, and sometimes also include a subject. They function as nouns, adjectives, and adverbs: *I'd hate <u>to go all the way home</u>* (noun).
>
> **Participial phrases** consist of a participle and its object, plus any modifiers. They function as adjectives and adverbs: *The man <u>collecting tickets</u> says we may not be too late* (adjective).
>
> **Gerund phrases** are participial phrases that function as nouns: *<u>Missing the beginning</u> is no good, though.*
>
> **Absolute phrases** consist of a noun or pronoun and usually a participle. They modify whole clauses or sentences: *<u>Our seats being reserved</u>, we probably should stay.* See also *absolute phrase.*

See also 5c–3.

plain case   See *case.*

plain form   The infinitive or dictionary form of a verb. See *infinitive.*

positive degree   See *degree.*

possessive   See *case.*

predicate   The part of a sentence other than the subject and its modifiers. A predicate must contain a finite verb and may contain modifiers and objects of the verb as well as object and subject complements. The **simple predicate** consists of the verb and its auxiliaries: *A wiser person <u>would have made</u> a different decision.* The **complete predicate** includes the simple predicate and any modifiers, objects, and complements: *A wiser person <u>would have made a different decision</u>.* See also 5a and 5b.

predicate adjective   See *complement.*

predicate noun   See *complement.*

prefix   A letter or group of letters (such as *sub-, in-, dis-, pre-*) that can be added at the beginning of a root or word to create a new word: *sub-* + *marine* = *submarine*; *dis-* + *grace* = *disgrace.* See also 33b–2. Contrast *suffix.*

preposition   A word that links a noun, a pronoun, or a word or word group acting as a noun (the object of the preposition) to the rest of a sentence: *If Tim doesn't hear <u>from</u> that plumber <u>by</u> four, he'll put <u>in</u> a call <u>before</u> dinner <u>to</u> someone else.* Common prepositions include *about, after,*

gl/gr

beside, between, for, in, and *to.* See 5c–1 for a more complete list. See also *object* and *phrase.*

prepositional phrase   See *phrase.*

present participle   See *participle.*

present perfect tense   See *tense.*

present tense   See *tense.*

principal clause   An independent or main clause. See *clause.*

principal parts   The three forms of a verb from which its various tenses are formed: the **plain form** or **infinitive** (*stop, go*); the **past tense** (*stopped, went*); and the **past participle** (*stopped, gone*). See *infinitive, participle,* and *tense.* See also 5a–2 and Chapter 7.

progressive tense   See *tense.*

pronoun   A word used in place of a noun or noun phrase (its antecedent). There are eight types of pronouns, many of which differ only in function, not in form:

> **Personal pronouns** (*I, you, he, she, it, we, they*): *They want you to come with us.*
>
> **Reflexive pronouns** (*myself, themselves*): *Can't you help yourselves?*
>
> **Intensive pronouns** (*myself, themselves*): *I myself saw it. She herself said so.*
>
> **Interrogative pronouns** (*who, which, what*): *What was that? Which is mine?*
>
> **Relative pronouns** (*who, which, that*): *The noise that scared you was made by the boy who lives next door.*
>
> **Demonstrative pronouns** (*this, that, these, those*): *These are fresher than those.*
>
> **Indefinite pronouns** (*each, one, anybody, all*): *One would think somebody must have seen it.*
>
> **Reciprocal pronouns** (*each other, one another*): *I hope we'll see each other again.*

See also 5a–3, Chapter 6, 8b, Chapter 12.

proper adjective   See *adjective.*

proper noun   See *noun.*

quotation   Repetition of what someone has written or spoken. In **direct quotation** (**direct discourse**), the person's words are duplicated exactly and enclosed in quotation marks: *Polonius told his son Laertes, "Neither a borrower nor a lender be."* An **indirect quotation** (**indirect discourse**) reports what someone said or wrote but not in the exact words and not in quotation marks: *Polonius advised his son Laertes not to borrow or lend.* See also 13d, Chapter 24.

reciprocal pronoun   See *pronoun.*

reflexive pronoun   See *pronoun.*

regular verb   A verb that forms its past tense and past participle by adding *-d* or *-ed* to the plain form: *dip, dipped, dipped; open, opened, opened.* See also 5a and Chapter 7. Contrast *irregular verb.*

relative pronoun   See *pronoun.*

restrictive modifier   A phrase or clause that is essential to the meaning of a sentence because it limits the thing modified. Restrictive modifiers are not set off by commas: *The keys* <u>to the car</u> *are on the table. That man* <u>who called about the apartment</u> *said he'd try to call you tonight.* See also 21c. Contrast *nonrestrictive modifier.*

rhetoric   The principles for finding and arranging ideas and for using language in speech or writing so as to achieve the writer's purpose in addressing his or her audience.

rhetorical question   A question asked for effect, with no answer expected. The person asking the question either intends to provide the answer or assumes it is obvious: *If we let one factory pollute the river, what does that say to other factories that want to dump wastes there?*

run-on sentence (fused sentence)   A sentence fault in which two main clauses are joined with no punctuation or connecting word between them.

Run-on	I heard his lecture it was dull.
Revised	I heard his lecture; it was dull.

See 11c.

sentence   A complete unit of thought, consisting of at least a subject and a predicate that are not introduced by a subordinating word. Sentences can be classed on the basis of their structure in one of four ways: *simple, compound, complex,* or *compound-complex.*

Simple sentences contain one main clause: *I'm leaving.*

Compound sentences contain at least two main clauses: *I'd like to stay, but I'm leaving.*

Complex sentences contain one main clause and at least one subordinate clause: *If you let me go now, you'll be sorry.*

Compound-complex sentences contain at least two main clauses and at least one subordinate clause: *I'm leaving because you want me to, but I'd rather stay.*

sentence fragment   A sentence fault in which a group of words is set off as a sentence even though it begins with a subordinating word or lacks either a subject or a predicate or both. See also Chapter 10.

Fragment	She wasn't in shape for the race. *Which she had hoped to win.* [*Which,* a relative pronoun, makes the italicized clause subordinate.]
Revised	She wasn't in shape for the race, which she had hoped to win.

FRAGMENT	He could not light a fire. *And thus could not warm the room.* [The italicized word group lacks a subject.]
REVISED	He could not light a fire. Thus he could not warm the room.

sentence modifier   An adverb or a word or word group acting as an adverb that modifies the idea of the whole sentence in which it appears rather than any specific word: *In fact, people will always complain.*

simple predicate   See *predicate.*

simple sentence   See *sentence.*

simple subject   See *subject.*

simple tenses   See *tense.*

split infinitive   The often awkward interruption of an infinitive and its marker *to* by an adverb: *The mission is to boldly go where no one has gone before.* See also *infinitive,* and see 14f.

squinting modifier   See *misplaced modifier.*

subject   The noun, or word or word group acting as a noun, that is the agent or topic of the action or state expressed in the predicate of a sentence or clause. The **simple subject** consists of the noun alone: *The quick brown fox jumped over the lazy dog.* The **complete subject** includes the simple subject and its modifiers: *The quick brown fox jumped over the lazy dog.* See also 5a and 5b.

subject complement   See *complement.*

subjective   See *case.*

subjunctive   See *mood.*

subordinate clause   See *clause.*

subordinating conjunction (subordinator)   See *conjunction.*

subordination   The use of grammatical constructions to make one element in a sentence dependent on rather than equal to another and thus convey the writer's sense that the dependent element is less important to the whole: *Although I left six messages for him, the doctor failed to call me back.* See also 16b. Contrast *coordination.*

substantive   A word or word group used as a noun.

suffix   A **derivational suffix** is a letter or group of letters that can be added to the end of a root word to make a new word, often a different part of speech: *child, childish; shrewd, shrewdly; visual, visualize.* See also 33b–3. **Inflectional suffixes** adapt words to different grammatical relations: *boy, boys; fast, faster; tack, tacked.* See also 5a and 5b.

superlative   See *degree.*

syntax   The division of grammar that is concerned with the relations among words and the means by which those relations are indicated.

tense   The form of a verb that expresses the time of its action, usually indicated by the verb's inflection and by its auxiliaries.

The **simple tenses** include the **present** (*I race, you go*); the **past** (*I raced, you went*); and the **future**, formed with the auxiliary *will* (*I will race, you will go*).

The **perfect tenses**, formed with the auxiliaries *have* and *had*, indicate completed action. They include the **present perfect** (*I have raced, you have gone*); the **past perfect** (*I had raced, you had gone*); and the **future perfect** (*I will have raced, you will have gone*).

The **progressive tense**, formed with the auxiliary *be* plus the present participle, indicates continuing action (*I am racing, you are going*).
See also Chapter 7.

transitive verb   See *verb*.

verb   A word or group of words indicating the action or state of being of a subject. A **transitive verb** conveys action that has an object: *He shot the sheriff*. An **intransitive verb** does not have an object: *The sheriff died*. A **linking verb** connects the subject and a complement that describes or renames the subject: *The sheriff was brave*. Often the same verb may be transitive, intransitive, or linking, depending on its use in the sentence: *The dog smelled the bone* (transitive). *The dog smelled* (intransitive). *The dog smelled bad* (linking).

Transitive verbs also may be either in the **active voice**, when the subject is the agent of the action, or in the **passive voice**, when the subject is the recipient of the action. Active: *We all made the decision together*. Passive: *The decision was made by all of us*.

The inflection of a verb and the use of auxiliaries with it indicate its tense, mood, number, and sometimes person: *shall go, were going, have gone*.
See 5b, 5e–3, and Chapter 7. See also *tense* and *mood*.

verbal (nonfinite verb)   A verb form used as a noun (*Swimming is good exercise*), an adjective (*Blocked passes don't make touchdowns*), or an adverb (*We were prepared to run*). A verbal can never function as the main verb in a sentence. Verbals may have subjects, objects, complements, and modifiers. See *participle, gerund, infinitive,* and *phrase*. Contrast *finite verb*. See also 5b–2.

verbal phrase   A phrase consisting of a participle, gerund, or infinitive and its related words, used as an adjective, adverb, or noun. See *phrase*. See also 5c–2.

verb phrase   See *phrase*.

voice   The active or passive aspect of a transitive verb. See *verb*. See also 5e–3.

word order   The arrangement of the words in a sentence, which plays a large part in determining the grammatical relation among words in English.

Index

Index

Plan of the book and guide to correction code and symbols